Coding Literacy

Software Studies

Matthew Fuller, Lev Manovich, and Noah Wardrip-Fruin, editors

Coding Literacy

How Computer Programming Is Changing Writing

Annette Vee

The MIT Press
Cambridge, Massachusetts
London, England

This book was set in ITC Stone Serif Std by Toppan Best-set Premedia Limited. Printed and bound in the United States of America.

Library of Congress Cataloging-in-Publication Data

Names: Vee, Annette, author.
Title: Coding literacy : how computer programming is changing writing / Annette Vee.
Description: Cambridge, MA : The MIT Press, [2017] | Series: Software studies | Includes bibliographical references and index.
Identifiers: LCCN 2016041368 | ISBN 9780262036245 (hardcover : alk. paper)
Subjects: LCSH: Computers and literacy. | Literacy--History. | Computer literacy. | Written communication--History. | Programming languages (Electronic computers)--History. | Rhetoric--Study and teaching. | Computer programming--Study and teaching.
Classification: LCC LC149.5 .L44 2017 | DDC 302.22440285--dc23 LC record available at https://lccn.loc.gov/2016041368

ISBN: 978-0-262-03624-5

10 9 8 7 6 5 4 3 2

Contents

Series Foreword

Software is deeply woven into contemporary life—economically, culturally, creatively, politically—in manners both obvious and nearly invisible. Yet while much is written about how software is used, and the activities that it supports and shapes, thinking about software itself has remained largely technical for much of its history. Increasingly, however, artists, scientists, engineers, hackers, designers, and scholars in the humanities and social sciences are finding that for the questions they face, and the things they need to build, an expanded understanding of software is necessary. For such understanding they can call upon a strand of texts in the history of computing and new media, they can take part in the rich implicit culture of software, and they also can take part in the development of an emerging, fundamentally transdisciplinary, computational literacy. These provide the foundation for Software Studies.

Software Studies uses and develops cultural, theoretical, and practice-oriented approaches to make critical, historical, and experimental accounts of (and interventions via) the objects and processes of software. The field engages and contributes to the research of computer scientists, the work of software designers and engineers, and the creations of software artists. It tracks how software is substantially integrated into the processes of contemporary culture and society, reformulating processes, ideas, institutions, and cultural objects around their closeness to algorithmic and formal description and action. Software Studies proposes histories of computational cultures and works with the intellectual resources of computing to develop reflexive thinking about its entanglements and possibilities. It does this both in the scholarly modes of the humanities and social sciences and in the software creation/research modes of computer science, the arts, and design.

The Software Studies book series, published by the MIT Press, aims to publish the best new work in a critical and experimental field that is at once culturally and technically literate, reflecting the reality of today's software culture.

Acknowledgments

Like all monographs, this book wasn't a solo project. I've been helped by many people and material grants during the decade in which it has taken shape. The book came out of my dissertation, which was guided expertly by Deborah Brandt at the University of Wisconsin–Madison. Through her care, humor, gentle but spot-on critique, and infallible support, Deb has been a model researcher, teacher, writer, and person to me (among many others). When considering any professional decision, I often ask myself: "What would Deb do?" And then I know the way. I learned about 90% of what I know about teaching writing from the University of Wisconsin–Madison Writing Center and Brad Hughes, who brings intellectual rigor and careful research to administration and teaching and has a superhuman ability to juggle a hundred commitments and thousands of students while making everyone around him feel smart and capable. David Fleming helped to show me I was in the right field and doing good work. Kurt Squire and Greg Downey introduced me to sources beyond my own field and treated me like a colleague even when I was a grad student. Mike Bernard-Donals bore with me, an outsider, in my first graduate class and saw me all the way through my dissertation defense. His helpful skepticism strengthened my work; when he said it was ready, I knew that it finally was.

My fellow students at Wisconsin were also essential to the substance and style of this work, in particular, Kate Vieira, Tim Laquintano, Scot Barnett, Rik Hunter, and Adam Koehler. Tim, Rik, Scot, and I worked together to learn digital literacy scholarship and technologies. Kate has been a great friend and guiding star for me since 2004; without her, I might not have entered the field of composition or finished my dissertation, and I certainly would have had a duller and dimmer graduate school experience. Corey Mead, Alice Robison (Daer), Stephanie Kerschbaum, Mira Shimabukuro, Eric Pritchard, Maria Bibbs, Chrissy Stephenson, and Mike Shapiro were all excellent fellow-travelers. Kate and Tim read countless early drafts of this book and my other work. They are everywhere in it. Mike Shapiro's tough love on a full draft of the book helped me clarify ideas and language. I wish that all grad students had a peer group such as I enjoyed at Wisconsin.

I've been lucky to have brilliant and generous colleagues at the University of Pittsburgh as well. Ryan McDermott helped me find additional sources and vet my claims about medieval literacy. Steve Carr offered useful comments on an article version of this book. Jean Ferguson Carr has been a generous, encouraging, and savvy mentor to me, clearing the way for the book to get done. Johnny Twyning and Don Bialostosky have been supportive chairs of my department and have gone over and above to boost me up. Alison Langmead has been a stunning collaborator and I've learned at least as much from her as our students have. Pitt graduate students are the best: I've been lucky to run seminars brimming with their creative ideas. I owe particular thanks to Kerry Banazek, who is not only a strong and brilliant human, and willing to take a chance on me as an advisor, but who also helped me to proofread this book. Lauren Rae Hall and Lauren Campbell, I've cited you both here, but I can't cite everything I've learned from you. I've benefitted from research leave at Pitt, and even more importantly, maternity leave for the birth of my two children. A heartfelt thanks to the administrators and other women who paved the way for me to enjoy the privilege of being with my babies while not sidelining my research or career, especially Jean Ferguson Carr, Phil Smith, and Jim Knapp. I wish that all parents, especially mothers, had this right.

Composition and rhetoric, what I consider my home field, is a lovely place to be. It includes people like Jim Brown, who has been a good friend and collaborator; Doug Eyman, who has been a guide in digital rhetoric and publishing and a helpful, humorous mentor; Cheryl Ball, who does it all; Gail Hawisher and Cindy Selfe, who paved the way; Brian Ballantine, Alanna Frost, and Suzanne Blum Malley, who make conferences way more fun; Christina Haas and Elizabeth Losh, who have both offered smart and critical comments on my work; Alexandria Lockett, who brilliantly calls it like it is and inspires me to do better; Chris Lindgren, who has put ideas about coding and literacy into practice and put me in contact with great people ... and many more besides. Thanks for making comp/rhet feel like home.

Thanks also to the people I've met outside my little academic corner, who helped to shape this work by being interviewed, by hiring me, or just by being awesome. Kenn Hoekstra took a chance on me at Raven Software and taught me enough IT to get me (re)started along a path I'd abandoned. Greg Barr also kindly held my hand through rough learning stages.

Roxanne Prichard was a fierce companion and helped ground me and employ me when I needed it. Ruth Benca always trusted me to do my work in her lab and showed me how to be a strong administrator and advocate for people. My brief collaboration with Libbey White and Why the Lucky Stiff made me feel my work was important. Digital media, my home away from home, includes wonderful people like Matthew Kirschenbaum, Jentery Sayers, Wendy Hui Kyong Chun, and Stephen Ramsay, who have all been kind promoters of my work. Mike Silbersack, quoted here, was one of a dozen programmers who generously gave their time to me in interviews as this project took shape. I thank all of them for their time and ideas, which are diffusely refracted here.

I'm grateful to Doug Sery and the Software Studies Series editors at MIT Press for placing this book where I had always hoped it would be. The anonymous reviewers helpfully gave me points to sharpen and cut. Susan Buckley and Katherine Almeida have shepherded the book with keen attention and alacrity, and Richard Evans expertly prepared the index, gently teaching me about the process. An earlier version of parts of this book, scattered throughout, was published in *Literacy in Composition Studies*, to whom I am grateful for their generous licensing and dissemination of my work. A summary version of my argument on programming as a literacy is published in "Programming as Literacy," in *The Routledge Companion to Media Studies and Digital Humanities*, ed. Jentery Sayers (forthcoming 2017). The Richard D. and Mary Jane Edwards Endowed Publication Fund at University of Pittsburgh sponsored the cost of figure reprints and indexing. Summer funding and research leave from Pitt has also helped me to complete this book.

Last, but foremost, I want to thank my family, including my many supportive parents who helped to fund my education—Joyce, Steve, Joy, Jeff, and Bill—and who patiently waited for me to find a career. I'm sure they're as surprised as I am, but they were kind enough to keep quiet about it. I am proud to add my small stone to the pile of my foremothers' educational achievements, the ones that my grandmother and mother always told me about, the ones I will tell my children about. Thanks to Eleanor and Willoughby, who delayed this book's appearance, but made it worthwhile. And finally, Nathan, whose companionship inspired the book in the first place, and who has stuck around to see it finished.

Introduction: Computer Programming as Literacy

The coding literacy movement is in full swing. Websites such as Codecademy.org and Code.org have made teaching computer programming to everyone their central mission. Code.org not only has the backing of Facebook founder Mark Zuckerberg and Microsoft founder Bill Gates; it also convinced then U.S. Representative Eric Cantor and U.S. President Barack Obama to record video spots promoting a "code for everyone" agenda. (President Obama was called the "Coder in Chief" while promoting Code.org's Hour of Code initiative.) New York Mayor Bill de Blasio argued that "Too many students are learning to type when they should be learning to code."[1] The merits of "everyone" learning to code are debated not only on Reddit.com's tech-focused forums but also on National Public Radio and in *Mother Jones* and the *New York Times*.[2] Google has given $50 million to the Made with Code initiative for the purpose of encouraging young women to code.[3] MIT's Scratch community and language, codeSpark's game The Foos, and the programmable robots Dot and Dash aim to teach kids to code.[4] Coding has even made it into the kindergarten curriculum before kids can read.[5] Raspberry Pi, LilyPad Arduinos, and other physical computing tools bring coding to wearable technologies and other physical applications.[6] To emphasize the universality and importance of computer programming, promotional materials for coding often invoke the concept of literacy and draw parallels that associate reading and writing code with reading and writing text. They point to the fact that although the technology of code is now everywhere, the ability to read and write it is not (figure 1).

What does it mean to call computer programming a *literacy*? Since the late nineteenth century, reading has been promoted as a moral good under the term *literacy*. This heritage of moral goodness persists in public debates about reading and writing, which is especially apparent in the periodic waves of moral panic observed in articles about education and illiteracy.[7] Typified by an infamous 1975 article in *Newsweek*, "Why Johnny Can't

"I'm afraid that kidney went to somebody who can write code."

Figure 1
According to this 2015 *New Yorker* cartoon, people who can code are more valuable than others. Mike Twohy, *New Yorker*, June 25, 2015. Reprinted with permission from Condé Nast.

Write," these fears of failing schools and of generations of illiterates signaling the downfall of society have been around since at least the late nineteenth century. However, literacy research indicates that literacy rates in the United States aren't falling; rather, what we consider literacy is changing.[8] There is little contemporary or historical consensus on what literacy *is* or what kinds of skills one needs to be literate.[9] Thus, as a morally good but undefined concept, literacy can serve as a cipher for the kind of knowledge a society values. The various types of skills that come to be popularly named *literacies* reflect the perception of necessary and good skills for a society: health literacy, financial literacy, cultural literacy, visual literacy, technological literacy, and so forth.

However, what's called a literacy reflects more than just popular perception. Because of literacy's heritage of moral goodness, calling something a literacy raises the stakes for acquiring that knowledge. To lack the knowledge of something popularly considered literacy is to be *illiterate*. Beyond the practical disadvantages associated with missing a critical kind of knowledge, one can be penalized for the immorality of illiteracy—for dragging society down. People with poor financial literacy might, in addition to not enjoying ready access to monetary resources, fail credit checks and thus be denied employment because of their stigmatized status. Because literacy is deemed to be important to the status and financial health of a nation, to be illiterate is to be a less productive citizen. Thus, to call programming—or anything else—a literacy is to draw attention and resources to it by mobilizing the long history of reading and writing's popular association with moral goodness and economic success, and thus connecting programming to the health of a nation and its citizens.

But there is something more than pragmatism in the rhetorical connection of literacy to computer programming. First, the idea that programming is connected to literacy is more than a fad. Educators and programming professionals have made the connection between writing and programming since at least 1961—almost as soon as computers became commercially and educationally viable. Computer programming also appears to have parallels to writing that go beyond its rhetorical framing: it is a socially situated, symbolic system that enables new kinds of expressions as well as the scaling up of preexisting forms of communication. Like writing, programming has become a fundamental tool and method to organize information. Throughout much of the world, computer code is infrastructural: layered over and under the technology of writing, computer code now structures much of our contemporary communications, including word processing, e-mail, the World Wide Web, social networking, digital video production, and mobile phone technology. Our employment, health records, and citizenship status, once recorded solely in text, are now cataloged in computer databases. The ubiquity of computation means that programming is emerging from the exclusive domain of computer science and penetrating professions such as journalism, biology, design—and, through library databases and the digital humanities, even the study of literature and history. Because every form of digital communication is ultimately built on a platform of computer code, programming appears to be more fundamental than other digital skills dubbed literacies, especially those associated only with computer usage. Other literacies and activities build on programming, and so we might think of programming as a *platform literacy*. Programming is a literacy we can build other activities and knowledge on, as we have done with reading and writing in human languages. Because of its affordances for information creation, organization, and dissemination, the practice of programming bears other significant similarities to reading and writing. Programming and writing are both socially inflected by the contexts in which they are learned and circulated and are materially shaped by the technologies that support and distribute them. Literacy is a weighty term, to be sure. But in the case of programming, it also appears to be apt.

In this book, I treat these persistent links between computer programming and literacy as an invitation to consider questions about the nature of both. How can we understand the ways that computer programming is changing our practices and means of communication? And how do we account for new modes and technologies in literacy? Pursuing these questions, as I do in the chapters that follow, shifts our understandings of both programming and literacy. Looking at programming from the perspective of literacy and literacy from the perspective of programming, I make two central arguments: (1) programming shows us what literacy looks like in a moment of profound change; (2) the history and practices of reading and writing human languages can provide useful comparative contexts for contemporary programming. I intend the title of this book—*Coding Literacy*—to reflect both of these central arguments. Coding (*noun*) is a type of literacy, and programming is re-coding (*verb*) literacy.[10] That is, computer programming is augmenting an already diverse array of communication skills important in everyday life, and because of the computer's primary role in all digital literacies, programming's augmentation of literacy fundamentally reconfigures it. Literacy becomes much larger, and as it grows, the relationships and practices it characterizes change. When literacy includes coding, the ways we experience, teach, and move with our individual skills, social paradigms, communication technologies, and information all shift.

Literacy is a theoretically rich way to understand the relationship between communication and technology, in part because those who study literacy have long grappled with what it means for humans to work with socially situated, technological systems of signs.[11] But when computer enthusiasts invoke literacy in their calls for the broader teaching of programming, they generally do so without conveying its historical or social valences. Seeing programming in light of the historical, social, and conceptual contexts of literacy helps us to understand computer programming as an important phenomenon of communication, not simply as another new skill or technology. It also helps us to make sense of the rhetoric about "coding as a new literacy." Sylvia Scribner argued that how we define literacy is not simply an academic problem. What falls under its rubric gets implemented in large-scale educational programs and popular perceptions about who is and isn't literate.[12] Schooling, in turn, shapes perceptions of how literacy gets defined and what social consequences are faced by those considered illiterate.[13]

As programming is following a trajectory similar to that taken by reading and writing in society, the theoretical tools of literacy help us to understand the history and future of identities and practices of programming. While reading was once done collectively such that whole families or communities could rely on the abilities of a few, we now believe everyone should be able to read. And while writing was once a specialized skill with a high technical bar for entry—one needed to know how to prepare parchment, make ink, maintain writing instruments, or bind pages—it is now an expected skill for all members of developed societies. As reading and writing became more generalized, the diversity of their uses proliferated beyond their clerical and religious origins. Writers don't have to be "good"—as defined in particular, narrow, disciplinary ways—to benefit from their literacy skills. Most of us write for mundane but ultimately powerful activities: grocery lists, blogs, diaries, workplace memos and reports, letters and text messages to family and friends, fan fiction, and wills. People put their literacy to all kinds of uses, many of which are never anticipated by the institutions and teachers they learn from.[14]

Similarly, the bar to programming was once much higher—access to expensive mainframes, training programs, or a background in math or engineering was needed. But now, with ubiquitous computational devices and free lessons online, access to learning programming is easier. At the same time, the uses for code have diversified. The ability to read, modify, and write code can be useful not just for high-profile creative or business applications but also for organizing personal information, analyzing literature, publishing creative projects, interfacing with government data, and even simply participating in society. Literacy research can, then, provide a new lens on the intertwined social and technological factors in programming. It also offers fresh approaches to teaching programming— programming not as a problem-solving tool, but as a species of writing. And thinking of programming as literacy may help us to prepare for a possible future where the ability to compose symbolic and communicative texts with computer code is widespread.

Thinking about programming as written communication also jolts us to confront the ways literacy is changing. The field of literacy studies has now embraced a proliferation of new digital literacies pertaining to video games, audio and video composition, Web writing, and many other domains and genres and practices. However, these multiple literacies are often presented as atomized—proliferating and bouncing against each other in an ever-expanding field of digital and global communication. Considered separately, their multitude overwhelms us. Which literacies are enduring and which are tied to specific technologies likely to become obsolete? How do we choose among these literacies for educational programs and our own edification? A closer look indicates they are not separate at all: digital literacies operate as a complex ecology. Considered comprehensively, what digital literacies all have in common is computer programming. As a fundamental condition of contemporary writing, programming is the substrate in which these reactions occur; it's the platform on which they're constructed. Focusing on programming allows us to see this ecology of digital literacies more fully. We can, without attaching long-term significance to ephemeral technologies, take into account the computational, programmable devices that are now joining a panoply of other read-write tools. As programming now reveals a new assortment of social practices and technologies that constitute contemporary literacy, it can show us what a complex ecology of literacy looks like in a moment of profound change.

To suggest the ways that programming is becoming part of literacy, I often use the colloquial term *coding* in this book. The differences between *programming* and *coding* are hotly debated, but no clear boundaries exist between the terms, and they can be synonymous. Each term implicates different stakeholders—and diverse stakes—in the conversations about programming's contemporary uses and relevance. *Coding* echoes the popular rhetoric of the "learn to code" movement and signals a move away from programming as a profession. *Programmer* is the more standard term in job titles, but *coding* is associated with young companies trying to make the practice hipper (e.g., job ads for a "ninja coder"). The crispness of *code* lends itself well to publicity—or shorter URLs, as in the case of Code.org.[15] *Scripting*, a third term that is sometimes in this mix, can refer to simpler programming that doesn't need to be compiled, or that is specific to just one software suite, or that glues together more extensive code libraries and functions. But with the further development of so-called scripting languages such as JavaScript or ActionScript or TypeScript, the term has shed its technical specificity and gathered a rhetorical resonance instead. Scripting now can refer to simpler code or library combining or can be directed derogatorily at those who don't seem to know much about programming; for instance, at "script kiddies" who write malicious or faulty code and spread it indiscriminately on the Internet. Of the three terms commonly referring to the practice of writing code for computers, *coding* fits best with the focus of this book because it opens programming up to a wider population. I generally use the term *programming* when I am referring to the basic act and concept and *coding* when I'm discussing the more political and social aspects of writing code for computers. There is, inevitably, some overlap.

As this debate about terms suggests, language matters when we talk about computer programming. What we understand about programming changes with the words and lenses we choose to use for it. And when people use *literacy* in reference to programming, it generally indicates that they want to encourage or highlight the phenomenon of programming becoming a more widely held and generally applicable skill. That the words we use can indicate cultural ideas was central to Raymond Williams's keywords project, which sought not to define terms or pin them down, but instead to map them out rhetorically: to trace their histories, their stakeholders, and their dynamic cultural and social geographies. By mapping literacy as a heavily circulated term in programming, as I do in chapter 1, we can see programming's historical and cultural implications in a new light.[16] We can ask questions about programming invoked by literacy: Who programs, and who can call themselves a programmer? How is programming learned and sponsored? How is programming used? How do technologies and social factors intersect in programming? Similarly, Janet Abbate argues that how the computer is "cast"—for instance, as an adding machine or typewriter or piece of precision engineering—can influence whom we think of as its ideal users.[17] For example, metaphors of computing as akin to math made it more accessible to women than metaphors of engineering, Abbate observes: women were well represented in math majors and had a history of calculating, whereas they were largely shut out of engineering fields. Seeing literacy as a "keyword" not only indexes the users and uses of computing; it also reveals the contradictions between broad programming education programs as literacy and the narrower disciplinary concerns of computer science. My approach suggests that because programming is so infrastructural to everything we say and do now, leaving it to computer science is like leaving writing to English or other language departments.

Seeing coding through literacy mobilizes the insights we've gained from decades of research on social factors involved in learning literacy, helping us to explain who programs, how they do it, and why they learn. Although early literacy research credited reading and writing for organized government, the best of Western culture, and dramatic leaps in human intelligence, research since the 1980s has been much more cautious and has put the technological and cognitive achievements of literacy in social contexts. The result is a much more complicated picture of how writing systems are learned, circulated, and used by individuals, cultures, and nations. Scholars of New Literacy Studies, a sociocultural approach to literacy that emerged in the 1980s, found that social factors are critical to our understanding of what literacy is, who can access it, and what counts as effective literacy.[18] In Brian Street's "ideological model" of literacy, someone who has acquired literacy in one context may not be functionally literate in another context because literacy cannot be extricated from its ideology.[19] As James Paul Gee points out, even a task as basic as reading an aspirin bottle is an interpretive act that draws on knowledge acquired in specific social contexts.[20] Shirley Brice Heath's canonical ethnographic study of literacy shows that the people whom literacy-learners see using and valuing literacy can affect how they take it up.[21] Victoria Purcell-Gates demonstrates in her work on cycles of low literacy that children growing up in environments where text is absent and literacy is marginalized have few ways to assimilate literacy into their lives.[22] As Elspeth Stuckey has argued, literacy can even be a performance of violence in the way that it perpetuates systematic oppression.[23] If we think of coding in terms of literacy rather than profession, these insights from literacy studies show how we must think critically to expand access to coding.

Through such insights on social context, the concept of coding literacy helps to expand this access, or to support "transformative access" to programming in the words of rhetorician Adam Banks.[24] For Banks, transformative access allows people *to both* change the interfaces of that system *and* fundamentally change the codes that determine how the system works."[25] Changing the "interface" of programming might entail more widespread education on programming. But changing "how the system works" would move beyond material access to education and into a critical examination of the values and ideologies embedded in that education. Programming as defined by computer science or software engineering is bound to echo the values of those contexts. But a concept of coding literacy suggests programming is a literacy practice with many applications beyond a profession defined by a limited set of values. The webmaster, game maker, tinkerer, scientist, and citizen activist can benefit from coding as a means to achieve their goals. As I argue in this book, we *must* think of programming more broadly—as coding literacy—if the ability to program is to become distributed more broadly. Thinking this way can help change "how the system works."

I am certainly not the first to claim that the ability to program should be more equitably distributed. I join many others in popular discourse as well as other scholars in media studies and education—a lineage I outline in chapter 1. Equity in computer programming, especially along gender lines, has been the goal of countless studies and grants in computer science education.[26] And my concept of coding literacy is related to what some have called "procedural literacy,"[27] "computational literacy,"[28] "computational thinking,"[29] or what I have in the past called "proceduracy,"[30] and it is roughly compatible with most of them. Jeannette Wing's concept of "computational thinking," perhaps the most influential of these terms, relies on principles of computer science (CS) to describe its spectrum of abilities.[31] "Procedural literacy," for Ian Bogost, "entails the ability to reconfigure concepts and rules to understand processes, not just on the computer, but in general."[32] In this definition, Bogost equates literacy more with reading than writing—the understanding of processes rather than the representation of them. He ascribes the "authoring [of] arguments through processes" to the concept of "procedural rhetoric."[33] For Bogost, understanding the procedures of digital video games or recombining blocks of meaning in games can be procedural literacy, too.[34] While I agree that games can be a window into understanding the processes that underwrite software, I believe this turn away from programming sidesteps the powerful social and historical dynamics of composing code. Michael Mateas attends to code more specifically, and his approach to procedural literacy[35] most closely resembles mine. Although he focused on new media practitioners in his discussion of procedural literacy, he noted "one can argue that procedural literacy is a fundamental competence for everyone, required [for] full participation in contemporary society."[36] I embrace and extend this wide vision of procedural literacy from Mateas.

Andrea diSessa[37] shares my concern with programming per se, and his model of the social, cognitive, and material "pillars" that support literacy is compatible with my approach to coding literacy. His term and concept of computational literacy, which was intended to break with the limited and skills-based term computer literacy, emphasizes the action of computation over the artifact of the computer. Mark Guzdial, who also uses the term computational literacy, has been a longtime advocate of the fact that anyone can—and *should*—learn computer programming and, like diSessa, thinks that programming is an essential part of computational literacy.[38] Guzdial argues that programming provides the ideal "language for describing the notional machine" through which we can learn computing.[39] We learn arithmetic with numbers and poetry with written language, Guzdial points out; similarly, we should learn computing through the notation that best represents the computer's processes and potential.[40]

My approach is generally compatible with all of these other approaches; ultimately, I think we are all talking about roughly the same thing with slight differences in language and emphasis. Guzdial's and diSessa's computational literacy are illustrative: I agree with almost every detail of their description of what this literacy is and should be—except that I think fields outside of CS should be able to shape it and teach it as well. Like computational literacy, coding literacy points to the underlying mechanisms of the literacy of computer programming rather than the instrument on which one performs it. As computing becomes more deeply embedded in digital devices, the tools of coding literacy are beyond what we might traditionally consider a "computer"; consequently, we need a concept of literacy that abstracts it away from its specific tools. I often use the term computational literacy alongside coding literacy in this book. I don't use "computational thinking" here because Wing strongly emphasizes the link to CS and doesn't use the term literacy. I believe it's about more than thinking; it's also about reading and building and writing. Although the language of literacy matters to my argument here, the term it's paired with matters far less.

To this discussion of procedural/computational/coding literacy, I bring expertise on the literacy side, rather than the computer programming or computer science side. For this reason, I am also less concerned about defining the precise skills that make up coding or computational literacy than I am about their social history, framing, and circulation. As we will see below, lessons from literacy teach us that prescriptions for literacy are always contingent, so I do not attempt to pin one down for coding literacy. At any rate, hammering out the details of what coding literacy or computational thinking looks like in a curriculum or classroom is not the focus for this book.

A number of good models have been presented by computer science educators, however, which may serve as a general heuristic for my argument. Here is one I like from Ed Lazowska and David Patterson that provides a bit more specifics than most:

> "Computational thinking"—problem analysis and decomposition, algorithmic thinking, algorithmic expression, abstraction, modeling, stepwise fault isolation—is central to an increasingly broad array of fields. Programming is not just an incredibly valuable skill (although it certainly is that)—it is the hands-on inquiry-based way that we teach computational thinking.[41]

Wing's description of computational thinking is too long to quote here, but she covers everything from error detection, preparing for future use, describing systems succinctly and accurately, knowing what part of complex systems can be black-boxed, and searching Web pages for solutions.[42] Both of these prescriptions for computational thinking rely on fundamental concepts taught in CS classes, suggesting that the sole responsibility for teaching this literacy or form of thinking should be in CS. Aside from that, their descriptions work fine for our purposes here.[43]

Other specifications that I sidestep in this book include which languages might be best for coding literacy and what a hierarchy of literacy skills might be. Caitlin Kelleher and Randy Pausch's taxonomy of programming languages for novices is an excellent resource for specific languages.[44] More generally, Yasmin Kafai and Quinn Burke describe the need for languages to have low floors, high ceilings, wide walls, and open windows. That is, a language should have a low barrier to entry (low floors), allow a lot of room for growing in proficiency (high ceilings), make room for a diversity of applications (wide walls), and enable people to share what they write (open windows).[45] While most descriptions of computational literacy avoid specific discussion of how one might progress toward such goals, the UK Department for Education issued statutory guidance that nicely outlines goals for the four key stages of their program in computing: key stage 1 addresses writing simple programs and understanding what algorithms are; key stage 2 moves into variables and error detection; key stage 3 asks students to "design, use and evaluate computational abstractions that model the state and behaviour of real-world problems and physical systems"; and key stage 4 is focused on independent and creative development in computing. Although outlining or advocating for specific programs of coding literacy is out of scope for this book, these sites and others provide helpful guidelines.

My approach to coding literacy in this book builds on these models of computing by providing a socially and historically informed perspective on it as a literacy practice. A vision of coding with diverse applications has implications not only for what identities and contexts may be associated with computer programming but also for the ways we conceive of literacy more generally. Put another way, just as coding literacy reshapes computer programming, it also reshapes literacy.

Making Room for Computer Programming Outside of Computer Science

The relationship between programming as a practice and computer science as a discipline is a central tension in the contemporary programming campaigns that invoke literacy, so their history calls for a little unpacking. Although programming is usually framed from the perspective of CS, it predates CS. Donald Knuth traces the field of CS back to 1959, when the Association for Computer Machinery (ACM) claimed "'If computer programming is to become an important part of computer research and development, a transition of programming from an art to a disciplined science must be effected.'"[46] Programming was the dirty, practical, hands-on work with computers, and academic computer scientists often wanted a cleaner, theoretical identification with mathematics. As programming become more central than math in computing curriculum in the 1970s, Matti Tedre argues that "many serious academics cringed at the idea of equating academic computing with programming, which, since the 1950s, had gained a reputation as an artistic, thoroughly unscientific practice."[47] Knuth notes that since the late 1950s, the ACM has been continually working toward framing computing as a science rather than an art. Along with this effort to move computing toward science, a 1968 conference tried to apply the concept of engineering to software and came up with "software engineering," which Mary Shaw argues is still an aspirational term.[48]

As businesses and professionals have attempted to wrestle the difficult problems of code into predicable and workable components—as well as elevate the status of programming from its origins with women computers in World War II—they've tried to professionalize it.[49] Programming only emerged as a dominant term in the early 1950s, and then consolidated as a profession in the 1960s.[50] Even then, the profession was porous because places like IBM recruited untrained potential programmers through aptitude tests; most programming training was on the job.[51] There have been numerous attempts to certify and professionalize computer programming, as Nathan Ensmenger's, Janet Abbate's, and Michael Mahoney's historical work on software engineering attests. But programming has always resisted neat containment within CS, and this has become more apparent as languages and technologies become more accessible to those outside of universities and corporations in the computer-related industry.

Attempts to make computer programming a domain solely for professionals have failed, I would argue, because programming is too useful to too many professions. University physicists and biologists continued to write their own code after the birth of computer programming as a profession, and still do now. Once the financial barrier to computer use was lowered in the 1970s, we saw the rise of hobbyists who found computers useful and fun. The existence and practices of end-user programming has been a live topic in business and computer science for decades.[52] Many university science departments offer applied programming classes. And outside of formal schooling, with the advent of the World Wide Web and more accessible languages such as HTML, CSS, Javascript, Ruby, Scratch, and Python, as well as thousands of online resources to help people teach themselves programming, it appears that more and more people are doing just that. The learn-to-code websites Codecademy.org and Code.org boast 25 million and 260 million learners, respectively.[53] Organizations such as #YesWe-Code, Black Girls Code, Girl Develop It, and Google's Made with Code are targeted to groups underrepresented in programming as a profession.[54] Coding boot camps run by for-profit and nonprofit institutions, who often promise to help people get jobs, may soon be eligible for federal grants in the United States.[55] While some of these coding resources are directed at helping people to become professional programmers, they appeal far more broadly.

In these materials and many discussions of teaching programming more broadly, the discipline of computer science and programming are often collapsed. The rhetoric often goes like this: since we need more programmers than we have now, computer science must be recruited to professionally train them. An example of this conflation of terms is in the mission statement of Code.org, a prominent promoter of widespread programming education as discussed in chapter 1. Their mission statement's many revisions from 2013 to 2015 reveal some of the tension between computer science and programming in these efforts.[56] From August to September 2013, for example, Code.org changed its mission from "growing *computer programming* education" to "growing *computer science* education" (emphasis added).[57]

In a December 2013 blog post, I drew attention to this rhetorical collapsing of code and computer science in Code.org's mission statement at the time (emphasis added):

> Code.org is a non-profit dedicated to expanding participation in *computer science* education by making it available in more schools, and increasing participation by women and underrepresented students of color. Our vision is that every student in every school should have the opportunity to learn *computer programming*. We believe *computer science* should be part of the core curriculum in education, alongside other science, technology, engineering, and mathematics (STEM) courses, such as biology, physics, chemistry and algebra.[58]

I wondered why they said they wanted to promote computer programming, when the statement and the rest of the site seemed focused on computer science. I argued that: "Its rhetoric about STEM education, the wealth of jobs in software engineering, and the timing of the Hour of Code initiative with Computer Science Education Week all reflect the ways that Code.org—along with many other supporters and initiatives—conflate programming with computer science."[59]

In a comment on my post, Hadi Partovi, a cofounder of Code.org, clarified that this conflation was deliberate, but not meant to deceive:

> We intentionally conflate 'code' and 'computer science', not to trick people, but because for most people the difference is irrelevant. Our organizational brand name is "code.org," because that was a short URL, but our polls show that people feel more comfortable with the word "computer science," and so we use both, almost interchangeably. Again, not because we want to trick people from one to the other, but because when you know nothing about programming or CS, they are practically equal and indistinguishable.

As the most expedient approach to its objective, Partovi notes that Code.org was simply mobilizing a popular conception of coding as equivalent to CS.[60] When Guzdial, Wing, and others argue for CS-for-everyone, they don't necessarily conflate CS with programming; however, they do subordinate programming to CS, which opens the door for this conflation in popular treatments of coding literacy.

In a critique of coding literacy efforts, we can see a similarly problematic conflation between professional software engineering and a more generalized skill of programming. Jeff Atwood, the cofounder of the popular online programming forum Stack Overflow, claimed we do not need a new crop of people who think they can code professional software—people such as then New York City Mayor Michael Bloomberg, who in 2012 pledged his participation in Codecademy's weekly learn-to-code e-mails. Atwood writes: "To those who argue programming is an essential skill we should be teaching our children, right up there with reading, writing, and arithmetic: can you explain to me how Michael Bloomberg would be better at his day to day job of leading the largest city in the USA if he woke up one morning as a crack Java coder?"[61] As several of Atwood's commenters pointed out, his argument presents programming as a tool only for professionals and discounts the potential benefits of programming in other professions or activities. Could Bloomberg learn something from programming even if he didn't end up being good enough at Java to get a job writing it? Mark Guzdial responded to Atwood, homing in on the language of "programmer" and "code" that Atwood used: "Not everyone who 'programs' wants to be known as a 'programmer.'"[62] For Guzdial, Atwood's notion of programming as a profession-only endeavor discounted the many end-user programmers and other non-software engineers folk who might find programming useful in their lives. "There's a lot of code being produced, and almost none of it becomes a 'product,'" Guzdial points out.

As programming becomes more relevant to fields outside of computer science and software engineering, a tension is unfolding between the values for code written in those traditional contexts and values for code written outside of them. In the sciences, where code and algorithms have enabled researchers to process massive and complex data sets, the issue of what qualifies as "proper code" is quite marked. For example, *Scientific American* reported that code is not being released along with the rest of the methods used in scientific experiments, in part because scientists may be "embarrassed by the 'ugly' code they write for their own research."[63] A discussion of the article on *Hacker News*, a popular online forum for programmers, outlined some of the key tensions in applying software engineering values to scientific code. As one commenter argued, the context for which code is written matters: "There's a huge difference between the disposable one-off code produced by a scientist trying to test a hypothesis, and production code produced by an engineer to serve in a commercial capacity."[64] Code that might be fine for a one-off experiment—that contains, say, overly long functions, duplication, or other kinds of so-called code smells[65]—might not be appropriate for commercial software that is, say, composed by a large team of programmers or maintained for decades across multiple operating systems. Mary Shaw, an influential Carnegie Mellon University computer science professor and software engineer, points out that it's important to distinguish software that facilitates online mashups and baseball statistics from software that governs vehicle acceleration: the former could be done by anyone without much harm, whereas the latter calls for more systematic approaches and oversight.[66] If the values governing the mission-critical uses of code are applied more generally, they can discount casual, low stakes, or experimental uses of code.

Computer science values theoretical principles of design and abstraction, and software engineering emphasizes modularity, reusability, and clarity in code, as well as strategies such as test-driven development, to support codebases over long terms. Programming is often (though not always) taught in CS with abstract problem sets concerning the Fibonacci sequence and the Tower of Hanoi, which can make programming seem quite distant from art and science and language. While CS often emphasizes the technical and abstract over the social aspects of programming, CS education researchers have noted that singular and dominating approaches to CS can turn people away. Jane Margolis and Allan Fisher found that approaches to CS disconnected from real-world concerns tended to deter women from majoring in CS at Carnegie Mellon University in the 1990s.[67] In 1990, Sherry Turkle and Seymour Papert pointed out the problem of dominating values in programming education and argued that the field must make more room for epistemological pluralism. In particular, they noted that the abstract and formal thinking so valued in academics needed to be augmented by applied and concrete approaches to programming, especially if it were to appeal to more women. They describe the value of Claude Levi-Strauss's *bricolage* approach: recombining code blocks, trial and error, and knowledge through concrete experimentation.[68] There may be an important role for abstract problems and systematic approaches to software in CS training and for the production of code in manufacturing, engineering, and banking contexts, but the abstract approach tends to appeal to the kinds of people who are already well represented in CS departments and software engineering positions. Although these CS education researchers offer insight into new ways to configure CS, few of them consider extending programming education out from the CS curriculum.

But my objective here is not to critique CS curriculum. Instead, I want to draw attention to the problem of overextending CS and software engineering values into other domains where programming can be useful. The conflation of computer programming with CS or software engineering precludes many other potential values and possibilities for computer programming. We might agree that applying the principles of bridge engineering to home landscaping is overkill and would be cost and time prohibitive. Or that requiring all writing to follow the model of academic literary analysis might limit the utility and joy of other kinds of writing. Siphoning the production of code solely through the field of CS is like requiring everyone to become English majors to learn how to write. Moreover, letting the needs of CS or software engineering determine the way we value coding more generally can crowd out other uses of code, such as live-coded DJ performances, prototyping, one-time use scripting for data processing, and video-game coding. Allowing approaches to coding from the arts and humanities can make more room for these uses. These approaches might include (among many others): Noah Wardrip-Fruin's concept of "expressive processing," which uncovers the layers of programmatic, literary, and visual creative affordances of software in electronic literature and games; Michael Mateas's procedural literacy for new media scholars; N. Katherine Hayles's electronic literature analysis that allows computation to be "a powerful way to reveal to us the implications of our contemporary situation"; Fox Harrell's computational narrative; or Stephen Ramsay's "algorithmic criticism," which uses coding to reveal interpretive possibilities in literary texts.[69] Nick Montfort's *Exploratory Programming for the Arts and Humanities* offers an introduction to creative programming in Python and Processing that is compatible with these approaches.[70] This book is already being adopted in some humanities and arts courses, and creative computing courses are occasionally offered in CS departments, but these courses are still the exception.

Beyond precluding alternative values, this collapse of programming with CS or software engineering can shut entire populations out. In paradigms such as Atwood's, programming is limited to the types of people already welcome in its established professional context. This is clearly a problem for any hopes of programming abilities being distributed more widely. CS as a discipline and programming as a profession have struggled to accommodate certain groups, especially women and people of color. In other words, historically disadvantaged groups in the domain of literacy are also finding themselves disadvantaged in programming. Programming was welcoming to women when the division of labor was between male engineers and designers and female programmers and debuggers, but now it is heavily male-dominated.[71] As a profession, programming has resisted a more general trend of increased participation rates of women evidenced in previously male-dominated fields such as law and medicine.[72] The U.S. Bureau of Labor Statistics reported that only 23.0% of computer programmers in 2013 were women.[73] The numbers of Hispanic and black technical employees at major tech companies such as Google, Microsoft, Twitter, and Facebook are very low, and even lower than the potential employee pool would suggest.[74] High-profile sexism exhibited at tech conferences and fast-paced start-ups now appears to be compounding the problem.[75]

Nathan Ensmenger has shown that personality profiling was used for hiring and training programmers in the 1960s; businesses selected for "antisocial men."[76] Although it is no longer practiced explicitly, Ensmenger argues that this personality profiling still influences the perception of programmers as stereotypically white, male, and socially awkward. This is now sometimes called the "geek gene" mindset—the belief that people are born wired to program or they're not. Guzdial explains how this mindset can be a problem for introducing people to computing:

> The most dangerous part of the "Geek Gene" hypothesis is that it gives us a reason to stop working at broadening participation in computing. If people are wired to program, then those who are programming have that wiring, and those who don't program must not have that wiring. Belief in the "Geek Gene" makes it easy to ignore female students and those from under-represented minority groups as simply having the wrong genes.[77]

Margolis and Fisher note that the obsessive and stereotypical behavior of the CS student who stays up all night programming actually applies to very few CS students, and these few students are more likely to be men. Women and men alike distance themselves from this image to carve out an alternative model for themselves, but the "geek" stereotype hurts women more than men.[78] A quick Google image search of "geek" illustrates one reason why: I see glasses and button-up shirts on awkward-looking people who are almost exclusively white men, or occasionally Asian men, or young white women provocatively dressed in tight shirts that say "I ♥ geeks" and glasses and microskirts. Hundreds of results down in a recent search, I finally saw one African-American male: the character Steve Urkel, played by Jaleel White in the 1990s sitcom *Family Matters*. (I finally gave up scrolling without hitting results for anyone visibly Latino/a or a nonwhite/non-Asian female). Rhetorician Alexandria Lockett recalled this gendered, racialized, and problematic rhetoric of who is and isn't a "programmer" in a provocative talk about code switching in language and technologies titled "I am not a computer programmer."[79] The recent rise of the "brogrammer," associated with start-up culture only partially in jest, suggests a new kind of identity for programmers—as "bros," or young, male, highly social and risk-taking fratboys.[80] Although the so-called rise of the brogrammer suggests that programming *can* accommodate people beyond the socially awkward white male, it also means that these featured identities are still narrow and inadequate.[81]

For all of these reasons, I find it surprising that computer science and programming are persistently paired in the promotional materials and arguments for coding literacy. Hadi Partovi suggests that the two are indistinguishable to someone who doesn't know much about either, and I think he's right. But when the stereotypes for professional programmers and computer scientists are weighted so heavily toward white male "geeks," why emphasize that link? Programming can be useful to many professions and activities and can accommodate a much wider range of interests and of identities than those of most people currently associated with computer science. But even Guzdial, who argues in his book-length treatment of teaching programming that computer science methods for teaching programming are too narrow and overemphasize "geek culture," fails to imagine a way for programming to be taught outside of computer science.[82]

Programming is already taught outside of CS, however—in libraries, digital humanities classrooms, information science schools, and literature classrooms.[83] As John Kemeny (the coinventor of BASIC) wrote about the undergraduate curriculum, there are benefits to extricating programming from computer science: "If computer assignments are routinely given in a wide variety of courses—and faculty members expect students to write good programs—then computer literacy will be achieved without having a disproportionate number of computer science courses in the curriculum."[84] As programming moves beyond a specialized skill and into a more common and literacy-like practice, we must broaden the language and concepts we use to describe it. As Kemeny notes, there are benefits to teaching coding across the curriculum, and CS certainly has a place in more wide-reaching programming initiatives. A major argument of this book is that literacy studies does, too.

Programming as Writing

Programming is indeed part of computer science. We can also come at it another way—through writing. As this book shows, seeing programming through writing and literacy allows us to put it in a longer historical and cultural context of information management and expression. But we must keep in mind the particular technical limitations and affordances that distinguish programming from writing in human languages.

Programming is the act and practice of writing code that tells a computer what to do. In most modern programming languages, the code that a programmer writes is different from the code that a computer reads. What the programmer types is generally referred to as *source code* and is legible to readers who understand the programming language. This code often contains words that might be recognizable to speakers of English: jump, define, print, end, for, else, and so forth.[85] The source code a programmer writes usually gets compiled or interpreted by an intermediary program that translates the human-readable language to language the computer can parse. This translating program (called an assembler, compiler, or interpreter depending on how it translates the code) is specific to each programming language and each machine.[86] The compiler's translation of the source code is generally called *object code*, and with the object code translation, the computer can follow the directions the programmer has written. The computer parses object code, but it is often not readable by humans. For this reason, much commercial software is distributed in object code format to keep specific techniques from competitors. This is, of course, only a simplified explanation of code; in truth, the layers between source code and machine code are multiple and variable—even more so as machines and programming languages grow more complex.[87] And much of contemporary programming is done as bricolage: adding functions or variables or updating interfaces, combining libraries and chunks of code into bigger programs.

Although I use this basic explanation to introduce programming, programming in the wild rarely looks this clean and simple.

Programming has a complex relationship with writing; it *is* writing, but its connection to the technology of code and computational devices also distinguishes it from writing in human languages. Programming is writing because it is symbols inscribed on a surface and designed to be read. But programming is also *not* writing, or rather, it is something more than writing. The symbols that constitute computer code are designed not only to be read but also to be executed, or *run*, by the computer. So, in addition to being a type of writing, programming is the authoring of processes to be carried out by the computer. As Ian Bogost describes, "one authors code that enforces rules to generate some kind of representation, rather than authoring the representation itself."[88] The programmer writes code, which directs the computer to perform certain operations. Because it represents procedures to be executed by a computer, programming is a type of *action* as well as a type of writing. When "$x = 4$" is written in a program, the statement tells the programmer that x equals 4, but it also makes that statement true—it sets x as equal to 4. In other words, computer code is simultaneously a description of an action and the action itself. The fidelity between code's description of action and the action itself is a matter much debated. Alexander Galloway has written that "code is the only language that is executable,"[89] a popular but not quite accurate conception. Wendy Hui Kyong Chun breaks this conception down by pointing out, via Matthew Kirschenbaum, the materiality of memory involved in a computer's execution of language. Source code isn't logically equivalent to machine code, and the distance between these forms of programming was recognized even by Alan Turing, Chun asserts.[90] While the relationship between code language and execution is slippery, code's status as simultaneously description and action means it is both text and machine, a product of writing as well as engineering.[91]

Programming became a kind of writing when it moved from physical wiring and direct representation of electromechanics to a system of symbolic representation. The earliest mechanical and electrical computers relied on wiring rather than writing to program them. To name one example: the ENIAC, completed in 1946 at the University of Pennsylvania, was programmed by switching circuits or physically plugging cables into vacuum tubes. Each new calculation required rewiring the machine, essentially making the computer a special-purpose machine for each new situation.[92] With the development in 1945 of the stored program concept,[93] the computer could become a general-purpose machine. The computer's program could be stored in memory, along with its data. This revelatory design, which was put into practice with the ENIAC's successor, the EDVAC, moved the concept of programming from physical engineering in wiring to symbolic representation in written code. At this moment, computers became the alchemical combination of writing and engineering, controlled by both electrical impulses and writing systems. The term *programming* itself reveals this lineage in electrical engineering: *programming*, which contains the Greek root *gram* meaning "writing," was first borrowed by John Mauchly from the context of electrical signal control in his description of ENIAC in 1942.[94]

In subsequent years, control of the computer through code has continued to trend away from the materiality of the device and toward the abstraction of writing systems.[95] To illustrate: each new revision of Digital Equipment Corporation's popular PDP computer in the 1960s required a new programming language because the hardware had changed, but by the 1990s, the Java programming language's "virtual machine" offered an effectively platform-independent programming environment. Over the past 60 years, many designers of programming languages have attempted to make more writer-friendly languages that increase the semantic value of code and release writers from needing to know details about the computer's hardware. Some important changes along this path in programming language design include the use of words rather than numbers, language libraries, code comments, automatic memory management, structured program organization, and the development of programming environments to enhance the legibility of code. Because these specifics change, Hal Abelson argues that thinking about programming as tied only to the technology of the computer is like thinking about geometry as tied only to surveying instruments.[96] As the syntax of computer code has grown to resemble human language (especially English), the requirements for precise expression in programming have indeed changed—but have not been eliminated.[97]

David Nofre, Mark Priestley, and Gerard Alberts argue that this abstraction of programming away from the specificities of a machine is the reason we now think of controlling a computer through the metaphor of language and writing; that is, we *write* in a *language* computers can *understand*. In the 1950s and 1960s, universities, industry, and the U.S. military collectively tackled the critical problem of getting various incompatible computers to coordinate and to share code, which eventually led to the development of ALGOL. Nofre, Priestley, and Alberts claim that thinking of programming as *communication* with and across computers led to the ability to think of programs and programming languages as objects of knowledge in and of themselves. When computational procedures could be abstracted and distilled into formal algorithms—a combination of mathematics and writing—computer science as a field of study could develop.[98] While the dream of a universal language for computers hasn't played out as computer scientists in the 1950s and the developers of ALGOL imagined, the abstraction of computer control, the movement from engineering to math and writing, is essential for the conceptual approach to programming that I take here.

I see programming as the constellation of abilities to break a complex process down into small procedures and then express—or "write"—those procedures using the technology of code that may be "read" by a nonhuman entity such as a computer. To write code, a person must be able to express a process in hyper-explicit terms and procedures that can be evaluated by recourse to explicit logic rules. To read code, a person must be able to translate those hyper-explicit directions into a working model of what the computer is doing. Programming builds on textual literacy skills because it entails textual writing and reading, but it also entails process design and modeling that echo the practices of engineering. Although the computer is now the exemplar "reader" for this kind of procedural writing, a focus on the computer per se is shortsighted and misleading as the processes of computing make their way into more and more technologies.

Developments in programming languages and computer hardware have led many to believe that the knowledge needed to program will soon be obsolete; that is, once the computer can respond to natural human language, there will be no need to write code. As early as 1961, Peter Elias claimed that training in programming languages would soon cease because "undergraduates will face the console with such a natural keyboard and such a natural language that there will be little left, if anything, to the teaching of programming. [At this point, we] should hope that it would have disappeared from the curricula of all but a moderate group of specialists."[99] At first glance, Elias's claim appears to be supported by modern touchscreen interfaces such as that of the iPad. Thousands of apps, menus, and interfaces promise to deliver the power of programming to those who do not know how to write code. Collectively, they suggest that we can drag and drop our way to problem solving in software.

Elias's argument that computer interfaces and languages will evolve to be so sophisticated that very few people will need to know how to compose or read code is perhaps the most persuasive against the idea that programming is a growing part of literacy, and that it will someday become as necessary as reading and writing in human languages. Inevitably, programming will change as computing and computers change—just as literacy has changed along with its underlying technologies. But the historical trajectory of programming language development I've outlined here suggests that it is unlikely to become equivalent to human language or shed its requirements of precision—as well as the benefits that come with that (more on this in chapter 2). This was the dream of "automatic programming" in the 1950s, which Grace Hopper insisted was a dream of sales departments—never of programmers: "We still had to tell the compiler what to compile. It wasn't automatic. The way the sales department saw it was we had the computer writing the programs; they thought it was automatic."[100] Then, as now, any kind of programming still requires logical thinking and attention to explicit expressions of procedures. The central importance of programming is unlikely to dwindle with the increasing sophistication of computer languages.

In fact, if the history of literacy is any model—and in this book I argue it is—then the development of more accessible programming languages, libraries, techniques, and technologies will *increase* rather than decrease pressures on this new form of literacy. For writing, more sophisticated and more widely distributed technologies seem to have put *more* rather than *less* pressure on individual literacy, ratcheting up the level of skill needed for one to be considered "literate."[101] Indeed, as computers have become more accessible and languages easier to learn and use, programming appears to be moving further *away* from the domain of specialists—contrary to Elias's hope. As programming has become (at least in some ways) easier to master and as computational devices grow more common, it has become more important to the workplace and more integrated into everyday life—emulating and sometimes taking over the functions assigned to writing. Bombastically, Silicon Valley venture capitalist Marc Andreessen says that "software is eating the world"—taking over industries from hiring to shopping to driving.[102] What Andreessen doesn't mention, however, is that many of these industries were once organized through written communication.

Computation Intertwines with Writing

The world wasn't always organized by written communication either, of course. Writing became a substitute for certain functions of personal, face-to-face relationships during different historical eras. But despite the fact that contracts could stand in for personal agreements and written letters could stand in for oral conversations, people did not stop talking to each other. In other words, writing has never unseated orality altogether. As Walter Ong noted, "Writing does not take over immediately when it first comes in. It creates various kinds of interdependence and interaction between itself and underlying modalities."[103] In the same way, code and computation is not replacing writing. Instead, it has layered itself over and under our infrastructure of writing and literacy. The databases that governments and employers now require programmers to maintain often make themselves visible to us in the form of written records: paystubs, immunization records, search results, Social Security cards. Much of our textual writing is done on computers, through software programs: word processing, e-mail, texting on smartphones. Code is writing, but it also underwrites writing. As we have become increasingly surrounded by computation, we have, in many ways, become even more embedded in writing.[104]

So, writing is still with us. But code is taking on many of the jobs we previously assigned to writing and documentation. To name a big (brother) example, the surveillance project of government, which could scale up with the help of writing and records, can scale up again. A U.S. National Security Administration data center that opened in 2013 in Utah can store perhaps a yottabyte of data such as phone numbers, e-mails, and contacts on its servers.[105] We don't actually know how the data are being processed, but we can assume it is a combination of computation and human reading: search strings, speech-to-text conversion, and human intuition and hypotheses. The fact that the stock market and banking are now relying heavily on computational processes sometimes leads to strange glitches like the flash crash of May 6, 2010. Amid high volatility and worries about the Greek economy, a firm executed a large trade with a computer-implemented trading algorithm, which used variable inputs to determine what to buy and sell. This kind of trade just months earlier would have taken 5 hours to execute, but the algorithm sped it up to just 20 minutes. The other algorithms of high-frequency trading firms then kicked in and traded huge volumes of stock back and forth rapidly, leading to a spiral in prices that plummeted the New York Stock Exchange in just minutes.[106] Humans on the periphery of these algorithms took much longer to figure out what had happened to crash the market so quickly.

The use of code can allow us to accelerate aspects of surveillance, law, finance, information, and bureaucracy, but, perhaps less frighteningly, it can also facilitate greater accountability in governance. Applications designed to monitor spending and political donations can lead to more transparent governance, in the same way that text can serve not only to keep records on citizens but also as paper trails for government officials. For example, the Sunlight Foundation is committed "to improving access to government information by making it available online, indeed redefining 'public' information as meaning 'online,'"[107] They offer programs and apps that allow people to track state bills (Open States), view the many golf outings, breakfasts and concerts that comprise the political fundraising circuit (Party Time), and access the deleted Tweets of politicians (Politwhoops).[108] Local governments such as the City of Pittsburgh's have implemented open data initiatives and hired analytics experts focused on making government and community information more accessible.[109] The Western Pennsylvania Regional Data Center provides Pittsburghers easy access to maps of vehicle crashes, permit violations, and vacant lots available for adoption.[110] As Michele Simmons and Jeff Grabill explain, openly accessible information can also allow people to monitor potential polluters in their neighborhoods. Critical to this monitoring is the accessibility of the information; an online database is more accessible than boxes of files tucked away in a municipal office. To be accessible, Simmons and Grabill insist that these "democratized data," even if digital and online, also need to be organized in a way that allows people to retrieve the data they want and understand its context—which involves attention to the design and programming of the database.[111] Literally democratizing data was "MyBO," Barack Obama's social network website that helped him win the U.S. presidential election in 2008.[112]

In smaller ways, we have outsourced many of our personal tasks to computers that serve, process, and store writing. We get recommendations for where to eat from online Yelp databases where people write and share reviews. We make dinners by searching terms such as "chicken fennel roast" on sites like Allrecipes.com, where cooks upload recipes and review them—all in writing, of course. You can broadcast your inspiration for home remodeling projects in images and words on Pinterest, move money around bank accounts online, and keep track of your calendar with your phone, which is really a pocket computer. It is, of course, still possible to retrieve recipes from the dusty box in your kitchen or physically visit the bank or keep a written agenda. But many of those written or personal transactions *still* have computation lurking underneath: digital print layout, bank databases and records, and so forth.

Just as writing now circulates over a layer of computation, the circulation of computation has depended on an infrastructure of writing—in particular, print. Prior to the Internet, handbooks documented programming languages. In the 1970s and 1980s, when home computers were becoming popular, computer programs circulated through print magazines such as *Compute* or *Dr. Dobb's*. Tracing the ways BASIC programs were swapped in the 1980s, Nick Montfort et al. explain that books and magazines printed short programs that allowed people to do fun things with their new home computers.[113] Print infrastructure and a culture of sharing spread the knowledge of programming as well as a more general awareness of the existence and function of computation. Montfort et al. write, "The transmission of BASIC programs in print wasn't a flawless, smooth system, but it did encourage engagement with code, an awareness of how code functioned, and a realization that code could be revised and reworked, the raw material of a programmer's vision."[114] And underneath that structure of print was another familiar tool of storage and transmission: human memory. Many BASIC programs were simple enough for people to remember them and then recite them to demonstrate their cleverness to others, passing them on in the process.[115]

While writing substituted for certain functions of personal relationships during different historical eras, it did more than that: it facilitated new modes of interaction between individuals and between citizens and their governments. Authority ascribed to literary texts, letters written to family members far away (aiding in immigration[116]), and complex modes of surveillance were all not simply replacements for earlier oral interactions. No one knew at first what computers were meant for—they were universal machines, technologies upon which we could inscribe all sorts of things: educational value, home uses, play, and so forth. It wasn't clear what aspects of our routines and lives they would replace or augment. Now we can see that they eclipse certain face-to-face interactions and forms of documentation. But, like writing, computation also creates new relations and new possibilities for communication and information. These new possibilities include everything from the "virtual migration" of technology employees in India who work for American companies[117] to direct written contact that people have with celebrities through the medium of Twitter or to the extended network of friends and acquaintances that people can maintain through Facebook—which can jarringly connect one's high school friends, officemates, and ex-boyfriends from around the world through comments on a photo of a roasted chicken and fennel dinner.[118] Many of these new modes of communication haven't replaced writing but have instead augmented the systems that convey writing, changing writing's audience, access, storage, and distribution in the process.

Sociomaterialities of Literacy

As the contexts for communication are perpetually in flux, literacy is as well, which makes it very difficult to define. Literacy researchers generally agree that it is socially shaped and circulated, that it relies on and travels in material forms, and that the ways it is performed or taken up by individuals is ineluctably influenced by these social and material factors. But beyond those central principles are the dragons that always lurk in the spaces between abstractions and realities. Sylvia Scribner notes that people have been trying to pin down the concept of literacy for almost as long as the word has been in circulation.[119] Like others before her, she could offer no fixed definition, but instead she proposed thinking of literacy in metaphors that frame some of the functions the concept of literacy serves in a society. These metaphors function similarly to Raymond Williams's keywords in that they indicate what a society values enough to name *literacy*. Scribner's metaphors point to the role literacy plays in helping individuals function in society, to the ways literacy is attached to power, and to ideas framing literacy as morally good. While these indices are all valid in the concept of literacy used in this book, more useful is her concept of the metaphor itself. Literacy is a lot of things. Its metaphors never tell the whole story, but by allowing us to take a particular angle into literacy, they show us glimpses of the ways communications happen in a society.[120] So, in forwarding *coding literacy*, I don't mean to suggest that we can't think of literacy (or coding) in any other way. But I do want to provide a particularly fruitful way of considering how both literacy and programming are working now.

Given that any definition of literacy is one motivated by what it can illuminate, here's the one I use in this book: *Literacy is a widely held, socially useful and valued set of practices with infrastructural communication technologies.* This definition takes into account the current consensus in literacy studies that literacy is a combination of individual communication skills, a material system, and the social situation in which it is inevitably embedded. It also assumes that literacy refers to something like *mass* literacy; that is, a skill can do all of the things literacy does, but if it's not being practiced by a wider variety of people, I don't think of it as literacy. Literacy according to this book has both functional and rhetorical components—what makes it both "socially useful and valued." Literacy reflects *real* knowledge requirements (its functional component) as well as the *perception* of what kind of knowledge is required to get around in society (its rhetorical component). These components are entangled: what people perceive as literacy affects not only its social value but also its social utility. In other words, if a skill is believed to be more useful, it *is* more useful, in part because of the social cachet accorded to it.

A focus on an "infrastructural communication technology" is meant to draw attention to literacies connected to power and to differentiate them from other useful skills. Susan Leigh Star describes "infrastructure" as a comprehensive, societally embedded, structural standard that is largely transparent to insiders.[121] She writes, "We see and name things differently under different infrastructural regimes. Technological developments move from either independent or dependent variables, to processes and relations braided in with thought and work."[122] When infrastructure shifts, the technologies and practices built on it shift as well. A concept of infrastructure thus allows us to focus on the central processes of daily life. To become more widely held and useful and valued, the practices of writing and programming both had to be done with technologies that were infrastructural and thus suited for more people to use: not too expensive, unwieldy, or prone to break down. Imagine mass textual literacy with stone tablets or mass programming literacy with 1950s mainframes. No, we needed a technology more capable of becoming infrastructure on which to circulate and practice writing and programming. Writing and programming both look quite different depending on the technologies they're enacted in—quills, Fortran, laptops. This book tries to trace the practices that stay consistent across these technologies. But note that when these specific technologies become widely available and easy to use, they can facilitate more widespread literacy.

Finally, I often use the word *literacy* rather than *literacies*. In each society, literacy looks different, and most societies have some concept of literacy.[123] Moreover, literacy practices depend on technologies that are constantly changing and evolving. Desktop image-editing software puts new emphasis on visual design literacy, online social media platforms generate combined textual/social/visual literacies, and digital audio-mixing programs give new life and possibilities to sound literacies. Thus, current practice in literacy research is to talk about literacies rather than a monolithic literacy, which often presumes a static, elite literacy to be the norm. As these so-called new literacies multiply, it has become increasingly difficult to sort out which literacies matter most, and how any of them are related to the paradigmatic core of literacy: reading and writing human symbols. The zeal to name many socially contingent literacies as equally excellent or important has dampened the power dynamics embedded in different technologies. As Anne Wysocki and Johndan Johnson-Eilola have argued, when we call everything a literacy, we empty the term of its explanatory power.[124] While attention to each of these new literacies may be necessary, we need a way to understand the intertwined phenomena of literacies and technologies more comprehensively. Therefore, I will sometimes refer to a singular *literacy* here—not to deny the cultural, material, and historical diversity of literacies, but to focus attention on the skills and technologies (such as writing and programming) that are fundamental to the circulation and communication of information in any society. Earlier I referred to both programming and writing as *platform literacies*, and that's what I mean: together they provide the foundation on which the ecology of contemporary communication is built.

Lots of practices rely on human skills with technologies, and many of them help us to do and think new things. While some would call these literacies, Andrea diSessa stops short and calls them "material intelligences," or "intelligence[s] achieved cooperatively with external materials."[125] According to diSessa, several things need to happen for a material intelligence to graduate into a literacy. Its material component or technology must first become infrastructural to a society's communication practices; in other words, the stuff to practice it must be widely available and reasonably easy to use.[126] The possibilities of composition with that representational form must then become widespread and diverse.[127] And finally, so many people must become versed in this ability as to make the ability itself infrastructural. That is, society can begin to assume that most people have this ability and proceed to build institutions on that assumption. Today in the United States, for instance, advertisements, education, governance, grocery stores, and even yard sale and lost cat signs assume that most people will be able to read them. This makes literacy social in a way that material intelligences are not: individuals can benefit from material intelligences, but a literacy gains its value in circulation.[128]

According to diSessa, then, programming is a material intelligence but not yet a literacy. However, the fact that computers and software are already part of our societal infrastructure and everyday lives means that programming *could* become a literacy. Optimistically, diSessa believes it will, and that "A computational literacy will allow civilization to think and do things that will be new to us in the same way that the modern literate society would be almost incomprehensible to preliterate cultures."[129] Toward this goal, diSessa outlined an educational project by which this literacy might be achieved. My objective is different: whereas he concretized the premise of programming as literacy, I use the premise to step back and provide a historical and theoretical panorama of literacy and programming. I wonder: what *would* this computational or coding literacy look like? And I dig into what we know about textual literacy in order to answer that question.

We know a lot about literacy, although what we know and where researchers have directed their attention have shifted since literacy became a topic of study. My own approach to literacy as a sociomaterial phenomenon begs that we look at earlier work in literacy to focus our attention on new materialities. Materialities of literacy were once the sole focus of literacy research: books and alphabets purportedly carried out "revolutions" in thinking. Jack Goody and Ian Watt famously argued that many of the developments of Western society could be attributed to alphabetic literacy.[130] Marshall McLuhan hyperbolically drew bright lines between eras on the basis of their literate activities: the invention of the alphabet, the printing press, and the telegraph marked critical ruptures in who and what humans were.[131] The "cognitive revolution" in psychology led theories about literacy (education, in particular) to the individual. Rather than some technological innovation, the individual was the location in which to study literacy. B. F. Skinner's work was influential, and studies by Janet Emig and Linda Flower and John Hayes examined the individual writing process.[132] Responding to the perceived technological determinism of theorists like McLuhan, Goody, and Watt and the seemingly isolationist cognitive movement, "New Literacy Studies" (NLS) emerged in the 1980s and 1990s to emphasize social factors in the learning and valuing and practicing of literacy. NLS scholars insisted that the implications of literacy cannot be reduced to "consequences" of the adoption of writing, as Goody and Watt had famously argued in 1963.

Brian Street accused Goody and Watt of presenting a detached, skills-based model of literacy, erecting a "great divide" between oral and literate cultures, and holding the Western essayistic tradition up as the apotheosis of literacy. Opposing what he calls Goody's "autonomous model" of literacy, Street proposed an "ideological model" of literacy, which demonstrates a reciprocal rather than teleological relationship between orality and writing. His model recovers the cultural aspects of literacy, positing *literacies* as multidimensional, heavily inflected by orality, and acquired along with value systems.[133] He was influenced by Shirley Brice Heath's extensive ethnological study of Carolina Piedmont communities in the 1970s, which revealed that oral and literate discourse were impossible to separate. Her concept of "literacy events" captured the rich and diverse sets of activities that accompanied any act of reading or writing.[134] When Street and Heath looked closely at literacy in action, they each saw activity that could not be limited to individual cognition nor represent a complete break with earlier forms of discourse. Literacy gathered meaning in oral, traditional, and social interactions. James Paul Gee writes, "The NLS are based on the view that reading and writing only make sense when viewed in the context of social and cultural (and we can add historical, political, and economic) practices of which they are but a part."[135] Jenny Cook-Gumperz notes that this "ideological perspective" on literacy reveals it as "both a set of practices for understanding the world around us, in which written and spoken language form a continuum, and a set of statements about the value or necessity of these activities," echoing my assertion that literacy is both real and rhetorical.[136]

On another flank of NLS, Harvey Graff's historical research contradicted the popular notion of literacy as progress. Graff claims that the narrative of progress leading to the success of the alphabetic West, as told by Elizabeth Eisenstein and Marshall McLuhan, implies that underdeveloped areas should recapitulate the development model of the West.[137] He demonstrates through empirical historical research that literacy on its own does not "lift up" individuals or societies, and the idea that it might do so Graff calls the "literacy myth."[138] Together, Graff, Street, and other scholars in NLS demonstrated that the ways writing is learned, culturally framed, and individually performed shapes what might be written and what that writing means. By highlighting the sociocultural contingencies of literacy, NLS rescued literacy from the dominant frame of a technical continuum of skills that culminated in a narrowly Western tradition.

As I noted earlier, literacy researchers since NLS have been largely focused on the valuing and circulation of *literacies*, describing the diversity of literacies across materialities, cultures, and eras. David Barton and Mary Hamilton provide a snapshot of this concept of literacies:

> Literacy is not the same in all contexts; rather there are different *literacies*. The notion of different literacies has several senses: for example, practices which involve different media or symbolic systems, such as film or a computer, can be regarded as different literacies, as in *film literacy* and *computer literacy*. Another sense is that practices in different cultures and languages can be regarded as different literacies. While accepting these senses of the term, the main way in which we use the notion here is to say that literacies are coherent configurations of literacy practices; often these sets of practices are identifiable and named, as in *academic literacy* or *work-place literacy* and they are associated with particular aspects of cultural life.[139]

This approach clearly takes into account the diversity of media in which literacies might be enacted, including the computer. And although here it may appear that they place all symbolic systems on the same plane, they later clarify that "Literacy practices are patterned by social institutions and power relationships, and some literacies are more dominant, visible and influential than others."[140] This articulation of literacy bears the seeds of my own approach to coding literacy as literacy both based in computers and more powerful than many other literacies.

While NLS focused on the social aspects of literacy as partly a correction of an earlier course of literacy studies, researchers also attended to technological concerns of literacy. NLS scholars understood writing as a technology whose particular affordances depended on—yet were not determined by—its material manifestations. For example, Street posits literacy as a complex social *and* technological phenomenon: "Literacy, of course, is more than just the 'technology' in which it is manifest. No one material feature serves to define literacy itself. It is a social process, in which particular socially constructed technologies are used within particular institutional frameworks for specific social purposes."[141] Graff similarly admits that literacy technologies factor into literacy's social uses. For Graff, literature, religious material, and scholarship were "all amplified in important new, innovative ways with the addition of printing's technology,"[142] and with that technology, "literacy, though not actually causing politicization or collective action, did prove a valued, useful vehicle for presenting, airing and gaining larger audiences for grievances."[143] In their extensive sociological study of different script uses among the Vai people of Liberia, Sylvia Scribner and Michael Cole provide a practice-based account of literacy that accounts for technology: "We approach literacy as a set of socially organized practices which make use of a symbol system and a technology for producing and disseminating it. Literacy is not simply knowing how to read and write a particular script but applying this knowledge for specific purposes in specific contexts of use. The nature of these practices, including, of course, their technological aspects, will determine the kinds of skills ('consequences') associated with literacy."[144] The "New London Group," a meeting of prominent literacy scholars who produced several influential works in the late 1990s, argued that literacy pedagogy should be based on a concept of "multiliteracies." Multiliteracies encompasses both the changing nature of communication technologies and the diversification and globalization of language, particularly English.[145] For these and other NLS researchers, *literacies* are plural, multidimensional, heavily inflected by orality, acquired along with value systems, *and* intertwined with the technologies in which they are enacted.

Although these researchers point to materialities, a focus on social and cultural concerns of literacy tend to swamp those material aspects. Barton and Hamilton nod to the fact that literacies look different depending on their materiality, but their primary focus is on "situated literacies" in social contexts. Gee's description of NLS from 2000 mentions nothing about technologies of literacy (ironically, since his current line of research is about video-game literacy).[146] Scribner and Cole were primarily concerned with demonstrating that literacy made only modest psychological differences in individuals, and that the meanings of literacy among the Vai were social. The New London Group acknowledged that "new communications media are shaping the way we use language" and designed their pedagogical program to encompass continual change; yet they emphasize literacy's social situatedness and provide little in the way of guidelines for new technologies to be integrated into their pedagogical framework.[147] Thus, in their emphasis on the sociocultural aspects of literacy, NLS researchers often downplayed the material or technological aspects of literacy. Sometimes they even misrepresented the technological determinism of earlier work; for example, in Graff's lumping together of Eisenstein and McLuhan or Street's outright dismissal of Goody. So even though NLS never denied literacy's materiality, its focus on the social downplayed those concerns.[148]

While much of NLS was concentrated on the social aspects of literacies in the 1980s and 1990s, there were some who led the path of literacies toward new technologies and the proliferation of literacies they spawned. Cynthia Selfe and Gail Hawisher began asking questions about how computers were changing the practices and pedagogies of writing.[149] Christina Haas's 1996 study of the affordances of computer screens and software for reading made an argument for specificity in research on literacy technologies. Because "writing is language made material," she wrote "the materiality of literacy is both the central fact of literacy and also its central puzzle."[150] Technologies of literacy exist in time and space and each shapes literacy in its own way, Haas pointed out. In their influential article "Limits of the Local," Deborah Brandt and Katie Clinton look at the specificities of writing technologies in context, but encourage us to see broader influences on these specific contexts. Drawing on Bruno Latour's work in materiality and objects, they argue against myopic approaches to highly localized literacies and for greater attention to global and material forces that affect each of these literacies. For Brandt and Clinton, materiality is the thread that ties together the human and the nonhuman as well as the local and global. Literacy "participates in social practices in the form of objects and technologies," and attending to literacy's materiality allows us to see how it can "travel, integrate, and endure."[151] Literacies circulate in specific technologies such as pens, papers, and dictionaries, in symbolic systems such as alphabets and genres, and in social spaces like workplaces and families and schools. Within scenes of writing, the objects, the people, and their complex relations shape literacy. This line of literacy research that focuses on materiality—without denying the social—leads directly to my work in coding literacy.

The social turn of NLS led to key insights: literacy is shaped by social structures; it isn't bound by its technologies nor does it mark a fundamentally different kind of cognition from orality. But just as attention to the social erased important global and material threads of literacy,[152] focusing on the details of individual literacies has obscured a longer history of literacy shifts. Daniel Resnick and Lauren Resnick demonstrate that what a society considers literacy has varied historically, particularly in terms of who should be literate and what degree and type of reading and writing constitutes literacy. Historical conceptions of literacy have included reading aloud without comprehension, responding in writing to bureaucratic requests, or producing original analytical essays in academic contexts. The many different forms literacy has taken are shaped not only by the technologies through which language is made material, as Brandt, Clinton, and Haas all assert, but also by religious ideologies, education systems, and gender dynamics, among other social forces. When we can see a longer historical trajectory of literacy, including its social and material factors, we are better prepared to respond to "literacy crises." Yes, literacy is changing, as it always has, and technologies are helping to bring about those changes, as they always have.

Literacy and Power

A key point about literacy technologies made by Brandt and Clinton brings us back to coding literacy as I present it in this book: "Literate practices depend on powerful and consolidating technologies—technologies that are themselves susceptible to sometimes abrupt transformations that can destabilize the functions, uses, values, and meanings of literacy anywhere."[153] Programming is infrastructural; it undergirds *all* of our digital communications. It also lassos them all together, as the computer is an instrument on which we often both read and write texts in overlapping modes. Even when we're not reading or writing on a computer, we deal with texts that have passed through the computer at some point. Computer programming is, then, one of these "powerful and consolidating technologies" that is fundamentally changing the meanings of "literacy anywhere." Put another way, programming is not simply another of many literacies; it is, as I called it earlier, a platform literacy. Critically, its power is not limited to technologically advanced societies. The world is now networked, and computation, programming, and code compose those networks. While these networks are not uniform across the globe, it is no longer possible for any society to live completely "off the grid." Everyone is caught up in global climate policies, undersea cables, mineral harvesting, satellites, and labor.[154] So whether a society embraces coding literacy or not, it is built on a foundation of computation.

With this bigger picture, we can see the power dynamics in literacy more clearly. Literacy has real consequences—not necessarily for individual cognition or a society's store of information, but for the movement and voices of people in the world. Writing about Jack Goody's work, Charles Bazerman notes, "Though written words move minds, minds move people, and people move in the social and material worlds. Changes in our communicative lives have consequences for our lives in these worlds."[155] Nowhere is this more apparent than with people who struggle to obtain literacy, people who are disproportionately poor, women, or people of color. For this reason, Kate Vieira admits having "sympathy for the bold, and currently unpopular, question that anthropologist Jack Goody and literary critic Ian Watt posed in 1963: What are the consequences of literacy?"[156] Her attention to the material forms of literacy that circulate with citizenship, employment, and educational documents for twenty-first-century Brazilian immigrants to the United States provides evidence for literacy as a material thing, a thing with social origins but with material effects on people in the world.[157] These real and perceived "consequences" of literacy are not a historically unique phenomenon. Literacy historian David Vincent insists, "People learned to read and write because they wanted to … People made arrangements for the education of their children at great expense, and knew more the costs of illiteracy than the people who were exhorting for its demise."[158] Although Graff's research shows we cannot credit literacy for social uplift, people still value it—especially people who have needed to make the most sacrifices to obtain it.

One potential reason people seek literacy is for the materially instantiated but socially built and maintained networks of knowledge that it allows people to access. William Gilmore describes how this works:

> Differential access to the basic vehicles of print and written communications was one of the most important distinctions among people in early America. Wide inequality of opportunity in this respect existed throughout the early national period; information reached people in widely varying amounts and kinds. In a time of considerable stability in material and cultural life this might have been a

small matter, but as the pace of change accelerated, access to print offered people a means of ensuring they would not be left behind in the economic, social and cultural transformation.[159]

As Gilmore suggests, literacy allows people to connect to powerful and central information networks. These networks are not everywhere and always the same; they depend on which technologies carry communications in that society and how those communications socially circulate.

The computational networks conveying our communications demand that we account for programming in any contemporary discussion of literacy's power dynamics. The calls for teaching programming show that some educators and computer enthusiasts have recognized this fact for decades. Stripped-down interfaces such as that of the iPad and Web templates such as those offered by Dreamweaver or Weebly can accommodate only limited design choices. They are built for the consumption rather than production of software. This means the programmers and software designers (or the companies they work for) still call the shots. Daniel Kohanski warns that ceding too much power to programmers—fallible humans who control perfect machines—can be dangerous. The abstractions that digital computers afford us are powerful; if we don't know how programmers and computers arrive at those abstractions, we give up significant control of our understandings of the world. Kohanski writes, "To the extent that we accept computer-digested data instead of seeking it on our own, our ideas about the world are based on incomplete approximations filtered through some programmer's judgment calls and the limitations of the machine."[160] Researchers examining the role of code, computation, and algorithms in our daily lives trace the significant degree to which most of us now implicitly cede control of our communications, social relations, media choices, employment, and information-gathering habits to the programs that govern these digital arenas.[161]

A recent controversy about Facebook's adjustment of their opaque "news feed" algorithm for (perhaps dubious) research purposes is only one of many moments when the control that algorithms exert over our lives has risen to the surface. Wryly commenting on this incident, comic artist Randall Munroe points out that regardless of the ethical merits of this "research," Facebook's algorithm has always been controlling (see figure 2).

Scrolling over the comic reveals another layer to Munroe's sarcastic commentary: "I mean, it's not like we could just demand to see the code that's governing our lives. What right do we have to poke around in Facebook's private affairs like that?"[162] While our primary experience of a social networking site such as Facebook or Tumblr or Instagram is text and

Figure 2
In light of a controversial adjustment in Facebook's algorithms for research, popular comic xkcd questions whether Facebook's algorithms were ever ethical. Randall Munroe, "Research Ethics," xkcd [comic], July 4, 2014, http://xkcd.com/1390/.

audiovisual material, behind our personalized "feed" are black-boxed, proprietary algorithms. These algorithms are constantly tweaked by the companies in charge of them, sometimes amid loud protests from users.[163] Their results are rarely fully automatic; they are adjusted by human readers, apparently to account for human bias or for political reasons. As Safiya Umoja Noble has pointed out, the reification of racial and gender bias in search results can be naturalized by algorithms, ostensibly absolving humans from blame because the "computer did it." Hypersexualized images of black women are simply a reflection of society's racism, not their own algorithms, Google may claim. And yet, subjects depicted in negative ways still have very little control over their portrayal.[164] Aneesh Aneesh describes how workplace surveillance programs can intervene between employees and supervisors, cataloging errors or forbidden behavior and otherwise "shaping an environment in which there are no alternatives to performing the work as desired."[165]

What does it mean that our relationships are now at least partially embedded in proprietary algorithms? What's the line between private and public or between human and algorithmic bias when we trust much of our private affairs to programs run by companies like Facebook? An EU law scheduled to go into effect in 2018 gives people a "right to explanation" for an algorithmic decision that was made about them.[166] Code's entanglement with our social lives is complicated legally, socially, and ethically. These entanglements are the concern of scholars in software studies, information science, and new media. At a similar nexus between code and society, work in "procedural rhetoric" examines the ways that computational procedures make arguments.[167] One of the aims of rhetorical education is to help students understand the ways arguments are constructed. If a similar goal were broadly taken up with coding literacy, could it do the same for our understanding of algorithms? If everyone really did learn to program, would this help to shift the balance of power to control ideas and information more toward users, *all* users?

The parallels I draw in this book between programming and writing tell us about a potential future for coding literacy, and they suggest responsibilities educators and communication specialists might have in shaping that future. As with the dispersal of textual literacy, coding literacy is not poised to be dispersed evenly across populations along lines of race, age, class, or gender. When literacy became widespread and when institutions began to be built on the assumption that many citizens were literate, some people began to be marked as *illiterate*. Although individuals could draw on literacy resources in their community, eventually "illiterates" suffered social and economic consequences from this label and from their inability to access certain aspects of culture and society directly. With this historical precedent, educators in particular must begin to think about how programming knowledge might be distributed more equitably. Individuals already economically and educationally disadvantaged are becoming more so by their relative dearth of computational literacy. Those who cannot program or do not understand what programming can do cannot see its potential applications to their communities' concerns. Therefore, disadvantaged communities are less likely to have software suited to their needs. Paying attention to who learns to program and how computational knowledge is filtering through the population is, then, a social justice issue. *Who* is designing the software that is so central to our lives, why are they designing it, and what concerns are they addressing? Should we be designing it ourselves? The historical precedence of literacy distribution and power that I provide in this book sheds light on those questions.

About This Book

In this book, I argue that programming is augmenting what we think of as literacy and is thus shifting the balance of skills we consider to be under the rubric of *literacy*—paradigmatically, the reading and writing of text. We can see that programming is entering literacy through the way that it is being framed in popular discourse, its expansion of our ability to represent knowledge, and its accelerating role in communication. Chapter 1 looks at the ways programming is being rhetorically coupled with literacy and writing in coding literacy campaigns. Comparisons with mass textual literacy campaigns allows me to highlight some of the ideologies that accompany this coupling, ideologies that shape the ways that coding is taught, learned, and circulated. Chapter 2 considers the ways that both writing and programming encode and distribute information, thereby influencing how we think about information and create knowledge. In chapters 3 and 4, historical parallels between writing and programming shed light on our contemporary moment with programming, when code is infrastructural but the ability to read and write it is not—*yet*. Together, these chapters indicate the ways that programming is becoming part of a more expansive literacy, built on new configurations of technologies and new social and cultural arrangements.

We begin in chapter 1 with the calls to teach programming broadly—arguments that "everyone should learn to code." Many of these calls evoke concepts and terms of literacy and use them to justify this educational vision. Recent calls from Code.org and President Obama provide some of the exigence for this book, but these calls actually began in the 1960s. I tell a history of national literacy campaigns to shed light on the ideologies and methods that have been used in calls for universal programming. From the development of BASIC at Dartmouth in 1964 to the Berkeley-based People's Computer Company in the 1970s to the Cold War–fueled STEM initiatives that brought Apple computers into the classroom in the 1980s, programming has been promoted for the general U.S. population for as long as computers have been programmed. Although the promotion of programming didn't die out in the 1990s, it has experienced a recent resurgence with the technical boost and popularity of Web languages such as Ruby, Javascript, and Python and the availability of online learning opportunities. Through this exploration of calls for programming to be more widely practiced, this chapter provides a portrait of programming as it has grown more central in the popular imagination of what constitutes literacy.

The analogy to literacy has been rhetorically expeditious for computer enthusiasts seeking to promote programming, but it is also apt. Chapter 2 explains how programming works as a "material intelligence"—like writing does—to construct knowledge. Using Andrea diSessa's theory of material intelligences, the chapter connects a brief history of how programming became writing with work that speaks to the relationship between writing and programming from J. L. Austin, N. Katherine Hayles, and Bernard Stiegler. I trace the ways that writing and programming have materially aided people in thinking, but steer around the technological determinism of McLuhan and others by weaving in the sociomaterial perspectives of literacy studies. The structural overlaps and commonalities between programming and writing help to demonstrate that they are increasingly intertwined practices under the larger rubric of literacy.

In chapter 3, I establish a historical framework for coding literacy by tracing the movements of computation and writing into society's communication and information infrastructure. This chapter works in conjunction with the next, as both address historical parallels key to our understanding of computational literacy: the transition of writing into the infrastructure of English society in the eleventh to thirteenth centuries and the transition to mass textual literacy in the eighteenth to twentieth centuries. During the first transition, covered in this chapter, writing became central to people's lives because it helped developing institutions such as government bureaucracy and the law to scale up and accommodate population and information growth. I use this historical lens to help us understand the trajectory of code from military and government infrastructure in the 1940s and 1950s to large-scale businesses such as airlines and, finally, to personal uses through home computers and mobile phones.

Building on the account in chapter 3, chapter 4 looks at histories of writing and computation from their institutionalization to their domestication and then their establishment as a basis for literacy. For writing, this transition meant that institutions such as the postal service, the legal system, public signage, and mass education could be built on the assumption that a majority of citizens were literate. Surrounded and defined by writing, societies began to demonstrate a "literate mentality," regardless of the literate status of individuals. In a similar way, I argue that we now have a "computational mentality," although the ability to program computers is still a specialized skill. The comparative history in this chapter provides insight into programming's trajectory from specialized to diversely applicable. Increasing demands for technical skills in communication and workplaces suggest that code is following the pattern of text, and that we are moving from programming being a specialized profession to programming as a more general skill.

I conclude by discussing the implications of the historical, technical, and cultural parallels I have drawn between writing and programming in the book. What does this perspective from literacy offer to those who seek to promote coding for everyone? If programming is indeed augmenting our conception of literacy, what does it mean that a lot of the code that governs our lives is hidden and inaccessible? How might we approach the problem that coding literacy is unequally distributed? What possibilities exist for new infrastructures if code is used to adjudicate disputes or commercial transactions? The precedents set by writing and literacy again offer insights into this brave new world.

The methods I use in this book are necessarily hybrid. Despite the perennial framing of programming as a "new literacy" in the popular media, there is a dearth of analytical work on programming from the perspective of literacy. Some approaches to programming that draw from theories of language include Donald Knuth's "literate programming," Mark Marino's literary-based "critical code studies," J. L. Austin's speech act theory, and Terry Winograd and Fernando Flores's linguistic and cognitive perspective on computer languages. Literacy is a core concept to help draw these contemporary concerns together, because writing is promiscuous and because literacy studies is necessarily interdisciplinary. I draw inspiration from David Olson, who notes that because the study of literacy applies to multiple fields, he can take on "trespassing as scientific technique."[168] In addition to studies of literacy and programming, I borrow from literary theory, technology studies, history, and philosophy.

When we consider programming a mode of written communication, it is no longer bounded by the field of computer science. Its roots are no longer solely in math, engineering, and science; they include written communication as well. Decoupling programming from CS not only helps us understand programming as communication but also frees CS from being overly identified with just one of their practices. Computer scientist Peter Denning argues that the field of CS is much more than programming at any level, including not only programming paradigms and language design but also artificial intelligence, information architecture, user interfaces, network security, and countless other things that are minimally connected to programming.[169] If Denning claims that thinking of CS as just programming is limiting, it is equally limiting to think of programming as *just* computer science. Thus, neither programming nor CS is well served by the idea that they map perfectly onto each other. It should be clear, then, that I do not intend to contribute directly to the discipline of CS—although I hope computer scientists find my approach to programming useful. Instead, I situate this book in current conversations about computer programming that are happening outside of CS, especially in interdisciplinary fields such as digital humanities, comparative media studies, new media studies, composition and rhetoric, and software studies.[170] Computation doesn't respect national, material, or academic boundaries. Like writing, coding is promiscuous.

Because this conversation about programming spills over emerging and fluctuating disciplinary boundaries, I hope to have made this text accessible to anyone interested in how programming and literacy interact. In this way, I intend for it to join a larger contemporary effort seeking to bridge a conceptual gap between the sciences and the humanities, between numbers and language, between engineering and English. At the university level, these areas of inquiry have been historically split, from the inherited trivium versus quadrivium model, to the "two cultures" famously named by C. P. Snow, to the segregated architecture of modern college campuses. Approaching software with the theoretical tools of the humanities and social sciences is a central project of the new field of software studies, and one to which I hope this book contributes. Scholars working in the interdisciplinary fields I mentioned earlier often aim to assuage these stubborn tensions between the two cultures; I think it is no accident that computer programming is a medium and focus of inquiry they all share. Programming is a way of structuring and communicating information not easily bounded by any one discipline. Its mercuric status positions it across and between both cultures of the university, and it is thus more available to fields that transcend those historical divisions. This book's focus on the intersecting interests of these two ends of campus will, I hope, help to show that their interests do indeed intersect, and that closer collaboration might be a productive path forward in literacy education at every level. Beyond the university and education more generally, the ubiquity and power of software demands that we use diverse theoretical tools to unravel what it means to live in an algorithmic culture. Through a historical, rhetorical, and literacy-based approach to programming, *Coding Literacy* seeks to contribute to this understanding.

1 Coding for Everyone and the Legacy of Mass Literacy

> Literacy was not a neutral technology. As a tool for individual and social transformation it was always governed by purpose.
> —Edward Stevens[1]

Since the 1960s, computer enthusiasts have employed the concept of *literacy* to underscore the importance, flexibility, and power of writing for and with computers. Computer scientist Alan Perlis argued in 1961 that all undergraduates should be taught programming, just as they are taught writing in first-year composition courses. At Dartmouth College in the 1960s, mathematicians John Kemeny and Thomas Kurtz designed and promoted the BASIC programming language for students and nonspecialists to program computers. Later, Kemeny wrote: "Someday computer literacy will be a condition for employment, possibly for survival, because the computer illiterate will be cut off from most sources of information."[2] In his 1999 U.S. Defense Advanced Research Projects Agency (DARPA) grant application, Guido van Rossum, the creator of the Python programming language,[3] tapped into the positive cultural associations of literacy in order to secure funding for his project of broad programming education. He wrote:

> We compare mass ability to read and write software with mass literacy, and predict equally pervasive changes to society. Hardware is now sufficiently fast and cheap to make mass computer education possible: the next big change will happen when most computer users have the knowledge and power to create and modify software.[4]

In 2015, Mark Guzdial echoed Van Rossum's allusion to literacy history in his argument that everyone should learn to code: "The printing press was a huge leap in human history, but that leap didn't happen until many more people became literate."[5] Programming has long been touted for its intellectual, creative, and communicative possibilities as well as its utility for workers, businesses, and government applications—and this rhetoric often involves connecting it with the advantages of writing and literacy.

The parallel between programming and literacy has also made its way into popular commentary: Douglas Rushkoff says that learning programming gives people "access to the control panel of civilization,"[6] and Marc Prensky argues that "as programming becomes more important, it will leave the back room and become a key skill and attribute of our top intellectual and social classes, just as reading and writing did in the past."[7] Code.org, a nonprofit started in 2013 and supported by Mark Zuckerberg and Bill Gates, showcases on its website a litany of quotes from educators, technologists, and public figures claiming that learning to code is an issue of "civil rights," the "4th literacy," and a way to "control your destiny, help your family, your community, and your country." One of Code.org's promotional videos is titled, "Code: The New Literacy."[8] The connection between programming and literacy is often invoked in order to support educational initiatives. In support of a major educational initiative that included a "Computer Science for All" program in New York City public schools in September 2015, Mayor Bill de Blasio stated, "A computer science education is literacy for the twenty-first century. Just like reading, writing and arithmetic, computer science is an essential skill."[9] John Naughton recently argued in the *Guardian* that "Starting in primary school, children from all backgrounds and every part of the UK should have the opportunity to: learn some of the key ideas of computer science; understand computational thinking; learn to program; and have the opportunity to progress to the next level of excellence in these activities."[10] Like many others, Naughton and de Blasio connect computer science to coding and to literacy.[11] Estonia has actually implemented a program similar to what Naughton describes: programming is now taught at the primary and secondary levels in schools, thanks to the Tiger Leap initiative supported by President Toomas Hendrik Ilves.[12] Like New York City schools, many K–12 schools in the United States are implementing smaller-scale initiatives through programs that teach coding through algebra (Bootstrap), colorful blocks on a screen (Scratch, from MIT), games (CodeCombat), or cute robots, like Dash and Dot, whose promotional video opens up with the statement, "Our children are growing up in a world where computer literacy is as essential as reading, writing and arithmetic."[13] These programs often invoke analogies to reading and writing in order to justify their educational approaches and agenda.

Arguments about education are always ideological: they reflect the values of a particular society and moment. Arguments about literacy education may serve as uniquely effective ciphers of their time because of literacy's perceived central role in nation-building and individual success. In her exploration of the metaphors for literacy, Sylvia Scribner notes that we can learn much about a society by looking at "the functions that the society in question has invented for literacy and their distribution throughout the populace."[14] Jenny Cook-Gumperz insists that every definition of literacy has prescriptive elements embedded in it: the way that we define literacy suggests how we should teach it and why.[15] Because it is always used for some purpose, the term and concept of *literacy* index cultural interests and anxieties. *Literacy* functions as an epistemological "keyword" in the Raymond Williams sense, "particularly useful for thinking about how history is summoned by the present and circumscribed by the language we use in the summoning."[16] To call a skill a literacy is to anchor that skill with the moral weight and importance of reading and writing.

This chapter focuses on the purposes to which literacy has been put, from historical campaigns for reading and writing to the current push for "coding for everyone." Rather than evaluate the merits or the success of these campaigns, I focus here on their rhetoric: how writing and reading have been promoted as literacy, and what that means—or could mean—for the push for programming literacy in the twenty-first century. I outline some of the dominant ideologies evident in the rhetoric of programming promotion from the 1960s to the present and connect them to the values that have historically been associated with literacy promotion. The rhetorical couplings of literacy can reflect larger ideological trends, especially as campaigns begin to make the case for programming to be a standard part of educational curricula.

Morality has been the ideological lynchpin for literacy since at least the Reformation, but in the mid twentieth century, technology surpassed morality as literacy's dominant ideological force. Literacy now is more about efficiency, production, and information manipulation than moral connections to God or the nation. In this chapter, I trace literacy's shift from a moral quality to a technological "good" in Western society and its rhetorical connection to national economic development and personal success. Computation, which emerged as a technology of literacy after World War II, is intimately tied up in literacy's shift from morality to technology and economics.

I highlight the rhetoric of Code.org's 2013–2014 "Hour of Code" campaign both because it has been a popular recent campaign and because it weaves together four dominant arguments for coding literacy: individual empowerment; learning new ways to think; citizenship and collective progress; and employability and economic concerns. Like many of the other campaigns, it presents its argument in both reactionary and proactive ways: "everyone should learn to code" because otherwise they will be left behind (reactionary) and because programming is fun and powerful and can help you get a job (proactive). Code.org's rhetoric serves as a lens on other programming initiatives from the United States and Europe, the two places where the rhetoric appears to be most pronounced, and also, not coincidentally, where computation has been very influential in society. (Although out of scope for this book, a study of how this rhetoric is taken up or developed elsewhere would be illuminative for global literacy conversations.) I put this contemporary rhetoric in perspective with other campaigns, including the push for the BASIC programming language among Dartmouth undergraduates in the 1960s and the installation of the Logo language on Apple IIs in elementary school classrooms in the 1980s, along with more focused contemporary campaigns such as Black Girls Code. In all of these promotional campaigns and statements, we see echoes of the historical arguments for literacy programs: both literacy and coding are portrayed as good for education, intellectual development, defense, civic participation, individual success, and national economic productivity, although the balance of these motivations are different in each campaign.

That these campaigns often link coding to literacy is reflective of the importance they accord to coding and their interest in seeing the ability to program distributed more widely. Looking at the various ways *literacy* has been rhetorically recruited to describe the function and value of programming in society, we can not only uncover values embedded in the "learn to code" movement, but also point to which technologies and skills and ideas are now included under literacy's rubric. Attention to literacy's value in a longer course of history[17] helps to explain programming's shifting value and role in society in the twentieth and twenty-first centuries. If literacy has been ideologically linked to morality and the health of a society, what social goods are now being attributed to programming under the rubric of literacy? What are the ideologies of this new so-called literacy, and what do they mean for programming or for our larger concept of literacy? These new ideologies signal a massive shift in what literacy and communication have become, whom they benefit, and to what ends they might be put.

What Do We Mean by Literacy?

The growth of the term *literacy* reveals the ways that literacy is a rhetorically malleable, socially contextual concept ripe for repurposing. *Illiteracy* preceded *literacy* by at least a century: David Barton observes that the word *literacy* is absent in dictionaries before World War I, although *illiterate* appeared in Samuel Johnson's 1755 dictionary. *Literacy* as connected to the ability to read and write doesn't manifest itself until the late nineteenth century, and until the twentieth century *illiterate* meant something more like "uneducated" than "unable to read."[18] After World War II, the idea of "functional literacy" began, perhaps spurred by the United Nations Educational, Scientific, and Cultural Organization's (UNESCO's) uses of the term coupled with its initiatives to promote functional literacy as a "human right" across the globe. But UNESCO's functional literacy is not a strictly technical definition—as Cook-Gumperz notes, no definition of literacy can avoid ideology. As a global organization, UNESCO forwarded a socially contingent approach to functional literacy, specific to each nation and culture.[19] After World War II, we begin to see other applications of literacy, such as sexual literacy, film literacy, economic literacy, and so forth, suggesting that the term literacy referred more to "access to information" than reading and writing per se.[20] This history of the term suggests that the paradigmatic association of literacy with just reading and writing text was only operative for a brief period of literacy's short lifespan. Even during that brief period, the degree of reading and writing necessary for one to be literate changed. The rest of the time, and in every place in which the term has had purchase, *literacy* has served many different purposes. In this section, we look at the metaphors behind these shifts in literacy and how they connect with historical trends in our expectations of literacy skills.

Metaphors for Literacy

Literacy's rhetorical malleability—the fact that it can be effectively pinned to any number of skills and practices, and the fact that people are motivated to do so—stems partly from its rich metaphorical resources. In addition to his etymological history described above, David Barton charts the social uses to which *literacy* and *illiteracy* have been put. Illiteracy is a disease, a link to criminality, a drain on the economy, and a cause for joblessness and individuals being held back from reaching their potential.[21] Literacy is a proxy for education, and it means access to information, for instance, in the idea of "computer literacy." While the ways that people talk about literacy might have real connections to the functions of literacy in the world,[22] the rhetoric of literacy has a life of its own and can make its own effects on people's lives, especially through education. Which metaphor we choose for literacy affects the ways we respond to it—as a problem to be solved, for instance, or an opportunity for educational initiatives.[23]

Sylvia Scribner names three major metaphors that drive literacy promotion: literacy as adaptation, as power, or as a state of grace.[24] The first refers to functional literacy, or the minimum literacy deemed necessary for successful social and economic integration in a society. This idea may seem relatively uncontroversial, but functional literacy is no less fraught than literacy. To determine what minimum amount of literacy is necessary to function, we must ask: which activities are essential, and which are expendable, and for whom? Functional literacy also implies a look ahead: what programs should we implement now to plan for the future?[25] In Scribner's second metaphor, literacy is power—but power in two opposing ways: "Historically, literacy has been a potent tool in maintaining the hegemony of elites and dominant classes in certain societies, while laying the basis for increased social and political participation in others."[26] We may see the latter form of power more explicitly invoked in literacy promotion; however, the hegemonic power of literacy is present in the ways that schooling is designed and in the ways that literacy campaigns tend to promote the kinds of literacy possessed by higher echelons of society. A campaign might lament: isn't it a shame that those people can't do something that we know how to do? Finally, literacy as a state of grace: here is literacy's virtue as a tool for self-enhancement, from its religious connection to its role in autodidacticism. All of these metaphors can contribute to literacy's positive valences, and Scribner proposes that they could help us to determine what ideal literacy might be: "simultaneously adaptive, socially empowering, and self-enhancing."[27] I return to these metaphors for "ideal literacy" in my analysis of programming initiatives later.

Shifting Expectations

One phenomenon suggested by changes in literacy as a term is its tendency to expand. Standards for so-called functional literacy have been rising for a long time, as the kinds of reading and writing one needs for success in jobs and school has grown significantly more complex over the past hundred years. Horizontal shifts in genres and modes have accompanied vertical elevations in the expectations of literacy. Once sufficient to get by in most jobs, letter writing, simple reading comprehension, and writing summaries of texts are now skills expected to be mastered by middle school. By college, we want students to combine sources, make original arguments, and express themselves clearly with "standard" grammatical language. Literacy no longer implies just reading for comprehension, but also reading for critical thought as well as writing with complex structures and ideas. As Deborah Brandt has pointed out, real changes in workplace literacy expectations can affect people's abilities to meet the requirements of their jobs.[28] Individuals may not necessarily lose their literacy, but literacy moves on without them. In the past century, this dramatic expansion of what literacy entails is also tied up with the technologies through which literacies are learned and practiced, from the expansion of the postal system to the written job application to the computer. In this way, popular notions of what literacy is have changed as more complex communication tasks and means become commonplace. We might use the same word or concept of literacy in each of these cases, but it means something different.

The increasing complexity of required literacy skills has accompanied expectations for broader distribution of these skills. Sophisticated literacy skills such as analysis and argument have always been necessary at the highest educational echelons, but we now expect *all* students to achieve this level of skill under the rubric of literacy. The popular concern about "why Johnny can't write"[29] that periodically seizes media attention, for example, only begins when we expect that every "Johnny" should be able to write. This expectation is unique in history, argue Daniel Resnick and Lauren Resnick. In the past, literate societies have supported either broad, low-level literacy skills or specialized, high-level literacy skills. But developed nations such as the United States now expect—and demand—their entire population to possess high-level literacy skills.[30] Jobs that might not have required literacy skills in the past now do. Construction contractors must negotiate federal regulations, compose invoices, and send e-mailed estimates for work. Restaurant servers must write order tickets, record them in a computer, and report their tips for federal taxes. A thickening web of government regulations, business practices, and client expectations drives demand for high school degrees and higher literacy skills. Now an American—male or female, Latinx, white, African American, Native American, or non-native English speaker—who struggles to produce an organized, argumentative essay in English with a word processing program on a computer might raise the red flags of illiteracy in the popular press. We expect more literate activities from more people than ever before.

The expansion of literacy into activities beyond reading and writing also signals a rise in expectations for literacy. Literacy is used to describe a wide variety of activities now, including computer programming. That programming is increasingly coupled with literacy in popular discourse means it is increasingly seen as one critical form of access to information. This may reflect realities of diversifying forms of information in contemporary society—and in later chapters, I argue it does—but programming's *rhetorical* linking with literacy is also interesting as a window into both the role of computational technology in everyday life and the role of literacy and education in society. It is one way in which programming is changing what literacy is, or is *re-coding* literacy.

Thus, three major factors affect a shifting perception of literacy: changes in the types of "writing" that literates are supposed to read and produce; the increased complexity of this writing; and the widened scope of who is expected to be able to be literate. Underneath all of those changes in literacy are often broader changes in politics, economics, technology, and culture. In this way, how literacy is perceived—and perhaps more important, how *illiteracy* is perceived—can reflect social trends and also shape them. We can see the mobilization of *illiteracy* in perennial cries of a "literacy crisis," or claims that "kids today can't write," where new modes of writing or new modes of thought are blamed for a supposed decline in general reading and writing abilities. John Trimbur describes several historical literacy "crises" and demonstrates that they often indicate anxieties about class erosion.[31] Literacy crises aren't about real declines in test scores or performance, he says; they are instead a response to threats to the middle class that get played out on the stage of education and language. Trimbur writes, "Middle-class anxieties about loss of status and downward mobility have repeatedly been displaced and refigured in the realm of language practices and literacy education. For the middle class, literacy appears to go into crisis precisely because of the faith they have invested in schooled literacy as the surest means of upward mobility and individual success, a form of cultural capital that separates their children from those of the working class and the poor."[32] Anxieties about schools and their ability to foster literacy skills are echoed in some of the contemporary coding campaigns as well. We will revisit literacy's relationship to schooling and its role in maintaining hegemonic power later.

Because a society deeply values what it considers literacy, a perceived gap or lack in literacy is cause for alarm and often a call to reform education. Rather than naming a real decline in a population's writing ability, however, these alarms generally reflect shifts in what literacy is perceived to be. Literacy refers to skills that a society values and finds essential to successful communication in a society, but it is a moving target. The term's rhetorical malleability allows it to be recruited for new ends when necessary. There are real changes in the skills people have needed to function in workplaces and everyday life, and when these real changes are tacitly absorbed into literacy, it can appear as though literacy is decreasing. The continually changing expectations of literacy lead to perpetual "literacy crises," which can then serve to support educational agendas.

What We Call *Literacy* Is Literacy

These proliferating kinds of writing, rising standards, diversifying technologies, and the expanded population expected to be functionally literate change what we think of as literacy, but they are not only rhetorical. These changes also reflect societies' increasing reliance on reading and writing skills in a wide variety of professions and in everyday life. Put another way, the popular use of the term *literacy* reveals a rough consensus about the importance of a skill for everyday life.[33] If enough people call something *literacy*, it *becomes* literacy. This relationship between literacy's rhetoric and reality helps to demonstrate the complexity of both the term and the concept. What skills a society includes under the rubric of literacy can point to real changes in skills required of students, workers, and citizens, as well as changes in *perceptions* of what it means to be a productive citizen or worker. The change in these perceptions can have real effects on educational programs, and the treatment of people who do or do not have what is considered literacy. If a skill considered a literacy is a skill a person lacks, that person's perceived illiteracy can have real effects on her or his employment prospects and social class—separate from any consequences of the lack in skill. The rhetoric of literacy—at least in part—makes people's realities.[34]

The recent upsurge in the rhetoric of literacy surrounding programming suggests that it is becoming part of what we consider literacy. When we call something a literacy, we mean that it is important and that it should be taught widely, perhaps even included in formal, public education. As useful as skills such as car maintenance, carpentry, and interior decorating are, we don't have specific words for people who are not skilled in them, and people rarely claim to be "car illiterate." But people feeling left behind by the ongoing integration of computers into their lives often claim to be "computer illiterate." Terms such as *non-coder* or *non-programmer* have begun to emerge in conversations about software and business and in tutorials on "coding for the non-coder" or "installation help for the non-coder" or "What non-coders need to know about SEO markup."[35] As many of the coding campaigns argue, non-coders are beginning to find themselves disadvantaged in areas as diverse as social communication, employment, and personal information management.

Literacy's rhetorical malleability allows it to get repurposed for many different agendas, anxieties, and societies. In the following section, we look at some historical ways the term and concept of literacy has been mobilized.

The Origins of Mass Programming Ideologies in Literacy

Literacy began as a religious virtue, a way for individuals to connect directly with God. Then, as governments sponsored mass education in the nineteenth century, literacy became a civic rather than religious virtue. In the twentieth century, national literacy campaigns could literally "count" on literacy rates as indicators of national progress. Around the time of World War II, when computers were initially being developed and the information demands on soldiers, nations, and citizens were ramped up, the technologies through which literacy circulated began to figure heavily in literacy's valuation. It is at this point that the literacy of reading and writing and the literacy of programming begin to merge.

Literacy as a Moral Good

Literacy first gained its status as a moral good through its connection to religious devotion and salvation. The Protestant belief in the necessity of reading the Bible for salvation drove the connection between reading and morality. As French literacy historians François Furet and Jacques Ozouf memorably put it, by "turn[ing] a technological invention into a spiritual obligation" and proliferating the demand for the written word, "Luther made necessary what Gutenberg made possible."[36] Furet and Ozouf argue that once the Reformation had established literacy as a moral good, the Catholic Church was compelled to adapt. In seventeenth and eighteenth century Catholic France, for example, the parish priest was responsible for literacy education, and school was intended to instill both Christian and "practical morality."[37] Beginning in the sixteenth century, German states and Scotland conducted literacy campaigns inspired by Martin Luther. Sweden began its first religious campaigns for reading in the seventeenth century; France, Britain, Spain, and others followed beginning in the eighteenth century.[38] The battle for souls between the Catholic and Protestant churches was waged, in part, on the grounds of literacy.[39]

In North America, Britain, and much of Western Europe, the meaning of literacy shifted in the nineteenth century: it was still a moral good, but for civic rather than religious reasons. Without the religious consensus available in many European countries, America promoted mass literacy through public schooling, where civic literacy retained the moral weight it had gained in its religious context. Schooling in the nineteenth century rehearsed "a new catechism based on patriotic devotion and civic duty," according to Resnick and Resnick.[40] In the United States, Lee Soltow and Edward Stevens link the ideology of literacy as a moral good with the spread of schools and an increase in literacy rates after 1830. By the latter half of the nineteenth century, literacy's connection with morality was multivalenced: literacy had come to be associated with the progress not only of souls but also of the modern state.[41] In his 1897 inaugural address, U.S. President William McKinley declared that the United States should "with the zeal of our forefathers encourage the spread of knowledge and free education. Illiteracy must be banished from the land if we shall attain that high destiny as the foremost of the enlightened nations of the world which, under Providence, we ought to achieve."[42] Broadly held literacy was necessary to propel the nation forward. The replacement of the religious model of literacy with the civic model coincided with the establishment of nonreligious public schools and the transition to an industrial economy. Thus, for the church, literacy was connected to the spiritual state of devotees; for the state, literacy indicated the moral contributions of citizens to the nation. Once literacy accrued this collective national value in the middle of the nineteenth century, illiteracy became a social problem, not just a spiritual one.

The educational expense of public schools in North America was justified through perceived societal benefits: lower crime rates, better hygiene, and obedience were touted as results of literacy and schooling. Education reformers Egerton Ryerson in Canada and Horace Mann in America were both vociferous advocates of literacy to quell crime and the baser elements of human nature.[43] Indeed, illiteracy rates among prisoners were (and remain) higher than in the general population. Causation between literacy and criminality was never firmly established, although it may have been partly a self-fulfilling prophecy: in England, for instance, a criminal penalty was more lenient if the defendant could read.[44] But even with a lack of proof, literacy was credited across North America and Europe as a bastion of morality that held much worse outcomes at bay.[45]

Early arguments about compulsory schooling had indicated that it could be dangerous for the lower classes because it could make them unhappy with their lot[46]; however, it became clear to elites that the social structure could be enforced through mass schooling.[47] Schooling promoted literacy, but, perhaps more important, it instilled in young people a panoply of skills useful for industrial contexts, including time management, obedience, and perseverance in repetitive tasks. Through schools and factories, the Industrial Revolution in nineteenth-century Europe and America bolted economic order onto social order. Work was stratified by class, with lower classes carrying out semiautomatic tasks, and higher classes making decisions about those tasks.

In the twentieth century as well, Americanization and adult literacy education efforts supported industry. In part because it increased efficiency, Ford Motor Company and U.S. Steel both partnered with the YMCA to offer classes to both immigrant and native-born American workers. Their motivation was primarily pragmatic: posted signs directing proper equipment usage and safety protocols were more effective if workers were literate in English.[48] A typical lesson in the program the YMCA developed in 1913 for U.S. Steel looked like this:

Start work	I go to the Mill to start work.
Clock House	First I go to the Clock House.
Card rack	I take my number card from the CARD RACK.
Go	I go to the CLOCK.
Put	I put my CARD in the CLOCK.
Ring	I RING the CLOCK.
Shows	The clock shows the TIME I START WORK.
Sign	I see A SIGN ON THE CLOCK HOUSE.
Safety rules	It reads I MUST KNOW THE SAFETY RULES.[49]

Ideologically, as long as schooling was infused with morality and respect for social hierarchies, it could impress the importance of keeping this established social and economic order.

In Europe and America, popular literacy had existed prior to publicly supported schools: people learned informally from clerks, mothers, clergymen, and itinerant tutors.[50] Popular literacy in the eighteenth century and earlier fueled working-class politics and religious dissent, but mass education standardized literacy. Cook-Gumperz argues that "the shift from the eighteenth century onwards has not been from total illiteracy to literacy, but from a hard-to-estimate multiplicity of literacies, a *pluralistic* idea about literacy as a composite of different skills related to reading and writing for many different purposes, and sections of society's population, to a notion of a single, standardized *schooled literacy.*"[51] The benefit of schools was not in promoting literacy per se, but in the way that schools could standardize and control it.[52] This control was a huge economic and national benefit attached to schooling, which added another layer to literacy's perceived "goodness."

Militaries as well as factories recognized the benefits of nineteenth century mass education in "training in being trained."[53] A soldier who was educated and literate could follow orders more reliably than one who was not. Consequently, militaries began to share the burden of literacy education. In mid-nineteenth-century France, for instance, the military established adult literacy classes in the army and navy. Literacy was deemed good for officers, but the education of the lower ranks also promised to "spread the 'beneficial contagion into the home.'"[54] There was also perhaps a sense of obligation to veterans, at least in the United States around the time of World War I. During the hearings on a bill for World War I veterans, the commissioner of education asserted "we owe these people something" for their defense of democracy.[55]

In these examples, we can see how early mass education fostered patriotism and respect for authority rather than critical or original thought. Harvey Graff argues that the differences in timing of mass education in the United States and England explain why the transition to the factory model of work was violent in England, but not in the United States: in England, industrialization preceded mass schooling, whereas in the United States it came afterward.[56] From their compulsory schooling, American factory workers were already accustomed to following orders, schedules, and social hierarchies. Connecting literacy to industry and capital, Richard Ohmann writes that "once the lower orders came to be seen as masses and classes, the term 'literacy' offered a handy way to conceptualize an attribute of theirs, which might be manipulated in one direction or the other for the stability of the social order and the prosperity and security of the people who counted."[57]

Given the utility of literacy for the activities of industry, it should not be surprising that literacy recapitulated class divisions in the era of compulsory schooling. In fact, schooling made finer-grained class distinctions and also served to justify these distinctions. Thomas Laqueur notes that literacy served to unite the working class in eighteenth century Britain: it was a source of collective political power and a defense against oppression. But after mass education, "the new cultural meaning of literacy marked a discontinuity. It drove a wedge through the working class. It came, for the first time, to be a mark distinguishing the respectable from the non-respectable poor, the washed from the unwashed."[58] Schooled literacy made someone respectable, in part, because of the cultural values of obedience and morality that were delivered along with schooling.

In the twentieth century, the availability of education to the masses served to justify class distinctions. If everyone had access to schooling, failures to achieve literacy could be seen as individual failures, and indicative of other weaknesses as well. As literacy became something upon which the rest of schooling rests, "a non-literate person counts as an *uneducable* person, not merely an uneducated one," Cook-Gumperz points out.[59] Illiteracy is no longer a situational phenomenon but a personal vice, a deep and pervasive fault that can be used to justify one's place at the bottom of a meritocratic ordering of individuals.[60] The promotion of literacy and schooling was not always done with the goals of reifying class divisions and reinforcing ideas about meritocracy and individual worth. Nevertheless, the concept of literacy began to mean *schooled* literacy, which provided a standard concept of literacy that could sort people more effectively and rigidly. We might notice the correlation between the birth of standardized literacy and the birth of the term *literacy*. When reading and writing were pluralistic, perhaps one term could not encompass it.

In these ways, beginning with developments of the Industrial Revolution in the nineteenth century and continuing into the twentieth century, literacy has been valued as a collective good for its benefits of efficiency and national economic growth.

Measuring Literacy

When literacy became an asset to ruling powers, they began to measure it.[61] The first records of literacy rates come from Sweden in the seventeenth century. As Egil Johansson describes, church laws stipulated that both men and women must be able to read and recite certain religious passages in order to get married—a powerful incentive for many citizens. The connection of literacy to marriage meant that women's rates of literacy were comparable to men's in Sweden. Yearly public exams were conducted in parishes and results were recorded, although not consolidated across the country. Public shaming for failing literacy tests helped Sweden achieve near-universal reading ability ahead of the rest of Western Europe, even in rural areas, which elsewhere generally lagged behind urban areas.[62]

Literacy was not comprehensively measured in the rest of Europe until the nineteenth century, when it was seen as a benefit not only to the church but also to the state.[63] The first study of signatures as a reflection of historical and contemporary literacy rates was conducted in France in 1854. In the late nineteenth century, French school administrator Maggiolo conducted a retrospective school survey study to determine which French government administration could take credit for widespread French literacy.[64] As literacy historians Furet and Ozouf point out, this debate was interesting not so much for the answer it might reveal but for what it signified: both the church and the state valued literacy in the general population.

The first study of illiteracy in the United States was conducted in 1870 in conjunction with educational policy, when literacy became valuable as a civic virtue. In the United States around the time of World War I, the measuring of literacy became much more systematic[65] with the use of standardized tests for recruits—tests that were influenced by French psychologist Alfred Binet's intelligence tests. Prior to these tests, illiteracy in America was thought to be primarily a problem of isolated groups: immigrants, African Americans, Appalachian whites. According to Samantha NeCamp, the poor performance of recruits on these tests "nationalized illiteracy," which galvanized adult literacy education efforts beyond Appalachia.[66]

In World War II, it was still important for soldiers to follow orders, but they had to do much more. The U.S. military adopted a different perspective toward literacy, which took into account the increased information-processing demands on individual soldiers. As Deborah Brandt describes, the literacy skills of soldiers were a kind of matériel, and illiteracy became grounds for rejection.[67] The U.S. Department of Education has since produced many reports on the reading skills of young people in schools. Its 1983 report *Nation at Risk* invokes the rhetoric of war in its opening lines, echoing the military interest in literacy and encapsulating some of the anxiety of the Cold War—"If an unfriendly foreign power had attempted to impose on America the mediocre educational performance that exists today, we might well have viewed it as an act of war." Echoing McKinley in 1897, the reports cites competition from Japan, Korea, and Germany as threatening "America's position in the world." At the heart of this risk are low literacy levels.[68] Responding to such anxieties about low literacy levels, the American National Adult Literacy Surveys in 1992 and 2003 provided comprehensive data on adults.

What these and other literacy measurements tell us is more than statistics: the state began to quite literally count on individual literacy as a collective economic and social resource. Because the contributions of citizens to the state were difficult to measure directly, literacy rates, which were easier to calculate, could stand in for progress.[69] By the mid-nineteenth century, literacy had become interesting to chart because so much was ascribed to literacy—too much, as later theorists indicate. In this way, literacy was "transformed from an attribute of a 'good' individual into an individual 'good.'"[70] The ability to read and write became suggestive not only of individual skills, but also of the individual's worth—literally, how much the person was worth for the state's calculations of its own value. This societal "good" of literacy is evidenced in the "takeoff theory" of literacy—that a literacy rate of at least 40% is necessary for economic modernization and development—a baseless claim that has often been repeated as well as critiqued.[71] Because low literacy rates reflect wasted personal potential as well as a drag on national resources, being illiterate becomes not just a personal issue but instead a public one for which individuals bear some responsibility.[72] Cook-Gumperz argues, "Over the past hundred years or so of universal schooling, literacy rates have served as a barometer of society such that illiteracy takes on symbolic significance, reflecting any disappointment not only with the workings of the educational system, but with the society itself."[73] The social stigma of illiteracy is, in this way, compounded by its collective economic and social implications. Because programming is part of literacy's post–World War II ideological heritage of productivity, efficiency, and technology, this wasted national potential is reflected in contemporary programming campaigns as well.

Ideologies Enacted in Literacy Campaigns

The measuring and marking of illiteracy in individuals historically correlates with efforts to eradicate it.[74] Indeed, beginning in the nineteenth century, large-scale literacy campaigns proliferated along with national measures of literacy. These large-scale campaigns mobilized multiple meanings and uses of literacy to achieve ideological ends. Robert Arnove and Harvey Graff go so far as to say that it might not be possible for a literacy campaign to get off the ground *without* an ideological purpose driving it. In most of these campaigns, "literacy is almost never itself an isolated or absolute goal. It is rather one part of a larger process *and* a vehicle for that process"; for example, mass religious conversion or political change.[75] As Soltow and Stevens write, "literacy and the act of becoming literate are an expression of a system of values."[76] This isn't necessarily a bad thing. Maria Bibbs provides a specific example of this ideological influence on individual literacy-learning in her historical research: while literacy may not have elevated the status of blacks, the *idea* that it could elevate them operated independently among blacks in the Progressive Era and inspired many to learn to read.[77] What kind of ideology is packaged along with literacy can affect who learns it and how literacy gets used.

Literacy campaigns often happen in response to major political shifts—revolutions, for instance, in Russia, Cuba, and China.[78] Campaigns can signal significant shifts not only in political structures but also in social and belief systems: they call for a new kind of political or moral individual to participate in a new society.[79] In the nineteenth century United States, a need for educated citizens in a republican government was part of the drive for mass schooling and literacy efforts. As Sarah Robbins details, the work of creating new American citizens through literacy was intertwined with Christian-influenced morality and the social order. To give one example, through women's literacy narratives and other literary tropes and trends, middle-class white women were tasked with molding their children—especially their sons—to participate in the nation as moral, upstanding citizens. Like the mass literacy produced in schools, this informal literacy teaching supported the existing social order: mothers' literacy work was facilitated by lower classes of servants who took care of domestic duties, and their own learning was directed not toward themselves but the future of others, especially men.[80]

Postrevolutionary Russia offers another useful illustration of literacy campaigns' sociopolitical dimensions. Like Britain and the United States, Russia consolidated and centralized informal schools in the nineteenth century, yoking a previously decentralized system to the new "modern" state.[81] Literacy found new impetus in the Revolution of 1917, where "the new socialist man" needed to be literate to understand and carry out the ideals of the USSR. In 1919, a "Decree of Illiteracy" adopted war-siege rhetoric to combat illiteracy and to criminalize those who would not teach or study.[82] Literacy was supposed to enable new Soviet citizens to grapple with their past exploitation by the Czarist regime and participate in the new societal organization under Communism.[83] Lenin was a great champion of literacy for these reasons and sought a nonauthoritarian approach to schooling that would tap into learners' interests and overthrow the existing social order.[84] In contrast, Stalin tightened censorship and surveillance at the time of the education ramp-up in the 1930s. Just as Martin Luther had warned about in the sixteenth century, elites in the USSR feared unchecked literacy—literacy decoupled from proper values. Literacy must be linked with Soviet ideology to benefit the nation.[85] The standard Soviet literacy text began with the proclamation, "We are not slaves, slaves we are not."[86] Arnove and Graff note that this pattern of socialist ideology in education is roughly repeated in China after 1949, although the literacy campaign there was largely unsuccessful.[87]

Revolutionary zeal mobilized and provided a metaphor for the successful literacy campaigns in Nicaragua and Cuba: literacy workers were uniformed "brigadistas" waging a war on illiteracy. The Cuban campaign emphasized the patriotic role of both teacher and student in such rhetoric as: "if you were literate you could teach; if you were illiterate you could study." Launched by an address Fidel Castro gave to the United Nations in 1960 that promised Cuba would banish illiteracy within a year, the campaign was designed to excite the entire population into literacy with a patriotic edge. Upon completion of the literacy program, new literates wrote a letter to Castro; thousands of the letters, which typically thank the Socialist Revolution for their newfound literacy, are on display at the Literacy Museum in Cuba that commemorates the successful campaign.[88]

Influential in these campaigns was Paolo Freire's philosophy, which focused on inductive learning strategies to help students articulate their own goals and challenges, especially in the context of revolution. Freire's "consciousness-raising" approach also influenced many other global literacy campaigns of the twentieth century after the 1960s, when there was a greater emphasis on empowerment in education.[89] The influential 1975 International Symposium for Literacy, which met in Persepolis, is indicative of this focus on empowerment. It declared: "Literacy ... [is] not just the process of learning the skills of reading, writing, and arithmetic, but a contribution to the liberation of man and to his full development."[90]

Julie Nelson Christoph's study of ProLiteracy, an influential adult literacy organization in the United States, suggests that the ideological legacy of evangelical Christianity is still embedded in large-scale adult literacy programs. Frank Laubach, the founder of ProLiteracy's precursor, recognized the power of controlling literacy and reading materials in areas like the Philippines in the 1930s. He sought to make moral Christians out of illiterates and developed materials to teach reading and Christianity together. While ProLiteracy, partially funded by the public, no longer has any explicitly Christian content, its materials continue to emphasize avoiding conflict and maintaining social order, thus, Christoph argues, echoing those conservative Christian values. Laubach had also recognized the way literacy teaching could be used to combat communism: he saw that poor, illiterate people would attach themselves to any ideology that alleviated their situation. While communism (through the Soviet campaign) was ahead of the literacy game, capitalism could also be furthered through literacy education. Laubach also agreed with Luther in the need to couple religion with knowledge. In 1964 he wrote, "They need Christ in their hearts to make knowledge safe in their heads and power safe in their hands."[91]

The American government passed several education acts in the twentieth century that reflect and emphasize the connection between literacy and productivity. The Economic Opportunity Act of 1964 and the Adult Education Act of 1966, which split off the literacy component from the 1964 act, were focused on the individual economic disadvantages of illiteracy. They sought specifically to widen opportunities for disadvantaged American adults, in concordance with the civil rights movement and President Lyndon B. Johnson's War on Poverty. But the disadvantages of illiteracy were national as well, which is more directly noted in the National Literacy Act of 1991. A U.S. Census Bureau survey in 1986 revealed that 1 out of 8 Americans couldn't pass a basic literacy test, and an additional 1 out of 5 refused to take the test—primarily to avoid revealing their lack of literacy, it is supposed. Most of those surveyed were under 50, and many had high school diplomas.[92] Coupled with the *Nation at Risk* report, these statistics were alarming and prompted action. In 1990, President George H.W. Bush included adult education for the first time in the National Goals, which optimistically declared, "By the year 2000, every adult in America will be literate and will possess the knowledge and skills necessary to compete in a global economy and exercise the rights and responsibilities of citizenship."[93] Established in 1991 with the National Literacy Act (and closed in 2010), the National Institute for Literacy in its mission statement connects the expanding terrain of literacy to its development as "a national asset":

> Since its creation in 1991, the National Institute for Literacy has served as a catalyst for improving opportunities for adults, youth, and children to thrive in a progressively literate world. At the Institute, literacy is broadly viewed as more than just an individual's ability to read. Literacy is an individual's ability to read, write, speak in English, compute, and solve problems at levels of proficiency necessary to function on the job, in the family, and in society. ... The mission of the National Institute for Literacy is to develop literacy as a national asset.[94]

These statements indicate a greater emphasis in the United States on literacy for national strength, although the acts also sought to improve the conditions for individuals and families by encouraging education and literacy.

In these examples, we see how the inevitable attachment of ideology to literacy can serve both conservative and revolutionary ends. We can also see the inherent tension between the goals of literacy for individuals and for a collective entity such as a nation or church. In Scotland's sixteenth and seventeenth century literacy campaigns, for example, Rab Houston argues that "the individual [had] no right to learning for its own sake. The overall aim was societal advancement."[95] The Soviet drive for literacy, which criminalized noncompliant individuals, and the Nicaraguan campaign, which compelled young urban literates to enter rural areas to teach (where they were occasionally killed for teaching), forced citizens to participate in literacy campaigns for the good of the state.[96] And yet possession of literacy could also benefit individuals and give them increased access to information of all kinds, beyond the materials and ideologies associated with the campaigns.

Most literacy campaigns have relied on voluntary participation and investment of time and resources into learning. Schools could be established by the state, but, as Furet and Ozouf point out in the French context, they could not achieve success without the support of society.[97] When the

French state took up the project of mass schooling in the nineteenth century, schooling had been in the domain of the church but also of independent tutors and schools that had been responding to a demand for literacy for centuries.[98] This was also the case in Russia, Scotland, Britain, and the United States. Cora Wilson Stewart's Moonlight Schools, which began in Kentucky in 1911 and enjoyed some state and federal funding, relied on volunteer teachers and participation from a wide variety of illiterate adults and were largely supported by Kentucky clubwomen.[99] In other words, literacy campaigns are driven by citizens as well as states, and they can serve both. To whom, then, does literacy belong? The fact that it can be both conservative and revolutionary, and beneficial to both nations and citizens, makes literacy powerful in both rhetoric and reality. We will observe later that the same can be said for programming.

Literacy campaigns are generally focused on reading rather than writing.[100] Reading was intimately connected to salvation in Protestantism and enabled people to receive information, including dogma and propaganda. For these reasons, reading accrued most of the moral weight associated with literacy. Writing, however, opened up possibilities for sedition and heresy, and so it was less likely to be promoted. As Furet and Ozouf suggest, "If all one wants is to make good Christians, then reading will do."[101] People's memories of learning to read and write can reflect their differential valuing, Brandt observes. Memories of reading include sitting on a mother's lap and exploring new and exciting worlds in safe and domestic spaces. In contrast, memories of writing often include punishment for writing in unauthorized spaces or making controversial arguments.[102] An emphasis on writing abilities for the collective good of society is more recent and associated with increased interest in production in a knowledge economy. Writing became a good to be traded on for individual and national productivity. As we see in the next section, this shift to writing over reading is tied to another shift: the way technology begins to organize literacy.

Technology Organizes Literacy

Something interesting happens to literacy during World War II. As it became a national resource to be mined from citizens, and as the military made efforts to increase the literate skills of soldiers, what counted as literacy also changed. Brandt argues that at this time, "technology, not morality, began to organize the meanings of literacy."[103] As literacy became important for national economic and military strategies, especially during World War II, it was increasingly tied to the rhetoric of productivity, and productivity was tied to technology. The speed and progress of technologies shaped how literacy was measured and taught. In the United States for example, literacy was required for soldiers because they needed to use rapidly developing technologies of communication for the war effort. The manpower needs of the state became the yardstick for literacy, so what was considered "literacy" took the shape of those needs. Literacy became a moving target. Brandt explains, "Whereas at one time literacy might have been best achieved by attending to traditional knowledge and tight locuses of meaning, literacy in an advanced literate period requires an ability to work the borders between tradition and change, and ability to adapt and improvise and amalgamate."[104] What gets included under the rubric of this dynamic literacy expands rapidly with postwar technologies. This is when we see a proliferation of "other" literacies, including "computer literacy." Literacy efforts now often focus on the delivery of text through computational devices, and it's common to hear of information literacy coupled with traditional textual literacy.

In the United States, the increased demand for information processing for war strategies drove literacy initiatives, but it also drove research in computation. Computer technology and programming were developed in World War II and added to the strategic communication and information resources in the United States and Britain. Shortly thereafter—not coincidentally, I argue—the rhetoric of programming as literacy began. When literacies proliferated with new technologies, then literacy could be rhetorically recruited to refer to communication with technologies other than pen, paper, and print—technologies like computer programming. The technologies of programming and writing, then, began to be linked in their connections to literacy as national strategies of defense and productivity. In this way, programming inherits the World War II–era ideologies of literacy associated with productivity, citizenship, and employment rather than those of earlier campaigns with roots in religion and morality. Mass programming campaigns have tapped into the rhetoric of literacy that reflects the individual's economic and productive contributions to the state. Put another way, in the shift from reading to writing as a focus of literacy, programming slipped in, too. Programming is a good; it produces information. Thus, it is more tightly connected to the heritage of literacy that focuses on writing rather than reading.

The first broad campaign to teach programming, John Kemeny and Thomas Kurtz's National Science Foundation–funded drive to teach programming to all Dartmouth undergrads in the early 1960s, argued that citizens and future leaders needed programming to understand modern systems of communication.[105] The rhetoric of individual empowerment through programming comes later, with the microcomputers that came home to middle-class families in the late 1970s and early 1980s. The Cold War in the 1980s, which produced such demonstrations of anxiety about traditional literacy as the 1983 *Nation at Risk* report, also produced widespread programming education. Funding was available for American public schools to teach programming in part because this high-tech knowledge was in the service of the state. Many recent programming campaigns are driven by Silicon Valley leaders, sometimes in conjunction with government. These campaigns stress the ways programming can get people jobs, as well as the ways these jobs can strengthen the place of these nations in the world. Global economic factors are reflected in campaigns that export these values, such as the One Laptop Per Child project, which makes computers and programming accessible to kids in underdeveloped countries.[106] Other contemporary advocates of programming-for-everybody, such as Mitchel Resnick at MIT and Mark Guzdial at Georgia Tech, express concern over the mercenary focus of some campaigns and instead emphasize the kinds of thinking and building possible with computer programming.[107] Thinking carefully about what programming appears to be *for* can help us to better understand what these initiatives are doing—and perhaps help them to succeed.

What Is Programming For?

The calls for programming as a form of literacy came long before the personal computer revolution made them seem feasible, and now they are accelerating. What these calls claim programming is good for has shifted as computer technology has rapidly advanced and as code has increasingly embedded itself into our work, homes, and governance. Initially, programming campaigns focused on benefits to citizenship and child development, but now many of them emphasize employability. The role of programming for national defense strategies and its purported cognitive benefits and personal empowerment have consistently featured in the rhetoric of mass programming since the 1960s. Given the history and ideological impetus of literacy campaigns that we explored earlier, we'll now look at the campaigns for mass programming. As we saw, religious, political, and economic ideologies form the rhetorical glue that connects reading and writing to a concept of literacy. Literacy campaigns are driven by ideologies; these ideologies reflect particular worldviews and serve as justifications in order to encourage donors, institutions, and individuals to participate or sponsor them. Just as arguments supporting reading and writing literacy campaigns tell us something about the changing perceptions of literacy, so, too, do the arguments supporting programming literacy campaigns.

Mass Programming Campaigns Since the 1960s

In 1959, George E. Forsythe of the Stanford University Mathematics Department argued that all students should be exposed to coding an automatic computer. While ostensibly making an argument for math majors to use computers, Forsythe ultimately favors a computing course for all undergraduates so that they might "learn that [computers] are no substitute for creative thought, and yet that they can do a good deal of what passes for thought in this world."[108] He writes

> we think every undergraduate mathematics student should know how to code some machine fairly well. (I would also include all undergraduate students, for I feel that the computer revolution will have such a great impact on all our lives that every college graduate should understand it intimately. Possibly it will eventually be taught in the ninth grade for the same reason.) Since coding presupposes no mathematics beyond arithmetic, it can be taught to freshmen. I recommend a two-hour-per-week semester course in coding, to be taken as early as possible.[109]

This was, as far as I know, the first public argument for what we might consider coding literacy.

Alan Perlis, who directed the computation center at Carnegie Tech, was another early and influential advocate for what he called a Freshman Computer Appreciation Course. At a 1960 conference on "The Use of Computers in Engineering Classroom Instruction" at the University of Michigan, he argued that computers were tools of formal reasoning and should be available to freshmen upon entering the university. Richard W. Hamming from Bell Laboratories elaborated that this course would not rely on engineering knowledge and could teach students about computer music, languages, and symbol manipulation rather than arithmetic. Hamming argued, "This is a liberal arts course that ought to be basic to everyone in order that the student can better understand the civilization into which he will emerge."[110]

Perlis reiterated this vision at a 1961 conference at MIT called "Computers and the World of the Future," the conference attendee list for which reads like a who's-who in the history of computing: Vannevar Bush, John Kemeny, J. C. R. Licklider, Norbert Weiner, and more. In front of this audience, Perlis proposed a computing course that resembles the first-year undergraduate composition courses still standard at American universities:[111]

> The first student contact with the computer should be at the earliest time possible: in the student's freshman year. This contact should be analytical and not

purely descriptive, and each student during this first course should program and run or have run for him a large number of problems on the computer. ... This course should share with mathematics and English the responsibility of developing an operational literacy. ..., In a liberal arts program the course could be delayed until the sophomore year, but certainly deserves inclusion in such a program because of the universal relevance of the computer to our times.[112]

Perlis's vision to teach programming to all undergraduates, including those in the liberal arts, is particularly striking given the state of computers at the time. In 1961, only a few college campuses had mainframe computers (MIT, the conference host, was one). But computers were increasingly important to large-scale business and government, including defense. The broad emphasis on programming in undergraduate education suggested that future leaders of America should know something about these "universally relevant" machines.

Perlis's proposal was at least partially realized with the BASIC programming language and Dartmouth Time-Sharing System, designed at Dartmouth College in the early 1960s by John Kemeny and Thomas Kurtz. Kemeny may have been inspired by hearing Perlis's speech at the 1961 MIT conference. However, Kemeny writes that the possibility of widespread access to computing first occurred to him in 1953, when he saw an early version of FORTRAN (now Fortran) while working as a consultant at Remington Rand and thought "all of a sudden access to computers by thousands of users became not only possible but reasonable."[113] Through its relatively straightforward mathematical syntax, Fortran was a programming language that made the computer's processing power more readily available to scientists and mathematicians—in other words, people who weren't engineers or computer specialists.[114] Kemeny wanted to make the computer even more accessible to nonspecialists by designing a language that had more intuitive syntax and a system that allowed the mainframe hardware to serve multiple users at once. Like Perlis, Kemeny and Kurtz saw the computer as universally relevant and designed BASIC to be accessible to *all* undergraduates— not just those in engineering or physics.

The syntax of BASIC was designed to be "simple enough to allow the complete novice to program and run problems after only several hours of lessons."[115] Paired with the Dartmouth Time-Sharing System (DTSS), BASIC opened up programming to a huge percentage of Dartmouth undergrads and faculty in the 1960s. It was taught to Dartmouth freshmen in a popular introductory math course beginning in the 1964 fall term, and by 1968, 80% of Dartmouth students plus several hundred faculty had learned to write computer programs.[116] Telephone terminals hooked faculty and

students up to the mainframe, and DTSS managed requests so that computing resources could be effectively used and shared in what appeared to users
as "real time" rather than the slow feedback loop of batch processing.
Kemeny and Kurtz's generous licensing terms allowed DTSS and BASIC to
spread to New York University and many other universities in the 1960s. It
is impossible to overestimate the impact of the BASIC programming language in the movement for programming literacy, and it becomes particularly important again in the 1980s, when it came installed on many home
computers.

Efforts to teach programming broadly were focused on undergraduates
in the 1960s, in part because computers could be found only in government offices, large corporate centers, and some campuses. But as the technology and culture of computing spread, the movement branched out from
college campuses in the 1970s. In his book *Hackers,* Steven Levy traces the
epicenter of programming innovation from the East Coast to the West
Coast around this time,[117] and at least some of the impetus to promote programming to the masses seems to have followed the same trajectory. West
Coast programming initiatives were imbued with post-1960s San Francisco–
area politics: hobbyists and hackers thrived, typified by the San Francisco
area's The Homebrew Computer Club and People's Computer Company. In
this context, mass programming took on a vibe of liberation and individual
empowerment.

The People's Computer Company (PCC) was founded in Menlo Park,
California, and launched with a 1972 publication that proclaimed: "Computers are mostly used against people instead of for people, used to control
people instead of to free them. Time to change all that. We need a PEOPLE'S
COMPUTER COMPANY" (figure 1.1). Like Kemeny and Kurtz, PCC founders Bob Albrecht and George Firedrake wanted code to be freely shareable
and adaptable. They aligned themselves with 1960s counterculture in
opposition to corporate computing, as symbolized by "Big Blue"—IBM. Ted
Nelson, who influentially described a file structure he named "hypertext"
in 1965, was part of this computer counterculture movement. His 1974 self-
published *Computer Lib/Dream Machines* envisioned a world where "technoids" would no longer hold a monopoly on computers and computation,
and people would be liberated from the "cybercrud" of giants like IBM,
which he dubbed a "concentration camp for information" (figure 1.2).

His bombastic rhetoric and jargon are typified in this introductory state-
ment to the book: "THIS BOOK IS FOR PERSONAL FREEDOM, AND
AGAINST RESTRICTION AND COERCION … COMPUTER POWER TO THE
PEOPLE. DOWN WITH CYBERCRUD!"[118] People should rise up and demand

Figure 1.1
The cover of the first *People's Computer Company Newsletter* in 1972 declared computers to be for the people. "The People's Computer Company Newsletter." Source ID: M1141_B9_1:1. Collection: People's Computer Company. Courtesy of Department of Special Collections and University Archives, Stanford University Libraries.

that the computers and computer people don't control them, Nelson insisted. Computers should belong to everybody. BASIC figures into this era of computing, too. The PCC founders wanted to promote computers for everyday users, and BASIC was their flagship language (figure 1.3). Their version of Kemeny and Kurtz's language, TinyBASIC, was provided with instructions within PCC publications,[119] and also in a popular book that humanized computers, *My Computer Likes Me When I Speak BASIC*. BASIC was also part of an experimental high school math curriculum from Columbia University Teachers College that was taught in the New York

Figure 1.2
The People's Computer Company supported BASIC as an accessible programming language. "The People's Computer Company Newsletter." Source ID: M1141_B9_1:1. Collection: People's Computer Company. Courtesy of Department of Special Collections and University Archives, Stanford University Libraries.

metropolitan area in the late 1960s and expanded to more than 25,000 enrolled students across the country in 1974.[120]

The first barrier to mass programming outside the context of the college campus was the inaccessibility of hardware. Kemeny and Kurtz had solved this problem through time-sharing on a mainframe; however, in the 1970s there was a push for personal computers. In 1971, Seymour Papert and Cynthia Solomon at the MIT Artificial Intelligence Lab focused on children as computer users and claimed, "If every child were to be given access to a computer, computers would be cheap enough for every child to be given access to a computer." They wrote about "twenty things to do with a computer" using the Logo programming language, including drawing men, bird turds, and playing Spacewar.[121] In 1972, Alan Kay imagined a "Dynabook" personal computer for "children of all ages" that would be portable and connect them with libraries, schools, and stores. He, too, addressed the issue of cost and dismissed it optimistically.[122] Both of these visionary memos about computers for children assumed that programming was part of the package. In the mid-1970s, we start to see computers emerge at prices that made them affordable to middle-class Americans, at which point the entanglement between software and hardware accessibility becomes especially apparent. The January 1975 *Popular Electronics* issue famously declared

Figure 1.3
Ted Nelson's 1974 *Computer Lib/Dream Machines* insisted that people take power back from the technoids. Reprinted with permission from Ted Nelson (author and copyright holder) and Alison Langmead (book owner). Scanned image courtesy of University of Pittsburgh Libraries.

"THE HOME COMPUTER IS HERE" when introducing the MITS Altair 8800.[123] A version of BASIC later circulated with the Altair 8800, written by Paul Allen and Bill Gates, who bucked the tradition of giving BASIC away for free and launched Microsoft in the process. The Altair 8800 was the first popular hobbyist computer and represents that side of the popular programming movement in the 1970s. It was difficult to run and program, and it didn't do much, but it was the first affordable computer for individual enthusiasts. In 1976, *Popular Science* claimed that "the home computer is here because the price of a central processing unit … has gone down by 99%," noting that thousands of Americans had bought hobbyist kits such as the Altair, and computer clubs (such as the Southern California Computer Society founded by Ted Nelson) had exploded in membership over the past year.[124] The September 1977 issue of *Scientific American* contained articles about personal computers and the changes in computer science based on miniaturization of components, as well as ads for a dozen different kinds of computers aimed at businessmen, families, and hobbyists—including an ad introducing the Apple II.[125]

From educational experiments and the liberation rhetoric and hobbyist movement in the 1970s, the mass programming movement went mainstream in the 1980s as the hardware hurdle lowered. Computers became easier to use. The Commodore 64, Apple II, and other commercially available machines didn't require assembly language programming like cheaper hobbyist computer systems. Many adults saw their workplaces restructured to accommodate computers, computer science enjoyed its height as an undergraduate major, and movies like *War Games* and *Tron* showcased the strategic and entertainment possibilities of the computer.[126] By the early 1980s, personal computers had become common in middle-class households. In 1982, *Time* magazine named the computer "Machine of the Year." Because machines at this time often required some knowledge of BASIC to use them, simple computer programming was a relatively accessible and sometimes necessary hobby. Built-in programming was marketed as a feature in ads for home computers,[127] and BASIC became the "lingua franca of home computing."[128] Lines between computer usage and computer programming were blurry in these early years of home computing. When home computers went mainstream, they shed much of the hobbyist vibe, and the rhetoric of political empowerment gave way to educational opportunity, commercial competition, and workplace efficiency.

Cheap computers brought programming into homes and classrooms in the 1980s, but they also brought commodity software (see also chapter 3 for how computers made their way into American homes in the 1980s). Prior to the 1980s, software was generally free and bundled with hardware. Hardware was expensive and specialized, and software was not considered sellable. But as the computer market expanded and as several important legal decisions were made in the 1980s about the copyrightability of software, software became a commodity separate from hardware.[129] In defiance of this commodification and its accompanying restrictions on the sharing of code, Richard Stallman at MIT launched the Free Software Movement in 1985.[130] Free and open-source software—which was the rule rather than exception before the 1980s—has contributed significantly to the material infrastructure that mass programming initiatives draw upon. Open-source software, programming languages, and libraries gained popularity with distribution on the Web, but in the 1980s they were decidedly counterculture.

Affordable and easy-to-use home computers in the 1980s meant that, for the first time, computers became accessible to kids. K–12 education was the

focus of mass programming initiatives at this time. Ads for home computers often focused on their educational value. The idea of computers as tools
for kids owes much to pioneering educational research done in the 1970s,
especially by Seymour Papert, Cynthia Solomon, and Alan Kay. With Wal-
lace Feurzeig at Bolt, Beranek and Newman in 1967, Papert developed the
Logo programming language, a sophisticated LISP (now Lisp) language vari-
ant. Papert began piloting it in classrooms with Cynthia Solomon and others in the late 1960s.[131] At Xerox PARC in California in the 1970s, Alan Kay
and Adele Goldberg led a team of researchers to prototype the Dynabook
laptop as well as the programming language Smalltalk, both of which were
designed to make computing and programming more accessible to children.[132] Increasingly affordable classroom computers, available through
grants from Apple and from Cold War funding for math, science, and technology initiatives, could—at least theoretically—scale up these early efforts
by Papert and others. The association of programming education with the
term *literacy* becomes more common at this point, perhaps because literacy
is often thought of as a primary goal of elementary education and, since the
nineteenth century mass education movement, children have often been
the site where literacy is measured. Literacy and technology initiatives in
the 1980s (as well as the 1986 Grammy won by Whitney Houston) indicated that children were our future.

By the 1980s, some colleges had implemented Perlis, Kemeny, and
Kurtz's vision of computer literacy at the undergraduate level. Echoing Perlis's argument from the 1960s, John Kemeny draws an analogy to freshman
writing in 1983:

> Many colleges now offer an elementary introduction to computers. A question
> frequently asked is whether such an elementary introduction suffices, and if not,
> how room for further computer courses in an already overcrowded curriculum
> can be made. We can answer this question by comparing the achievement of
> computer literacy to that of writing skills. Although freshman English is very im-
> portant, it cannot carry the total responsibility for the teaching of writing. Unless
> there are courses throughout the curriculum that assign a substantial amount of
> writing—and in which professors are willing to hold students responsible for do-
> ing it well—the majority of graduates will write poorly. Similarly, if computer as-
> signments are routinely given in a wide variety of courses—and faculty members
> expect students to write good programs—then computer literacy will be achieved
> without having a disproportionate number of computer science courses in the
> curriculum.[133]

What Kemeny describes here is now commonly referred to as "computing
across the curriculum" (CAC). Begun in the 1980s, CAC is informed by

what is called "writing across the curriculum" (WAC), which is a popular educational strategy to spread the responsibility of teaching writing across multiple disciplines.[134] Contrary to the "kids today can't write" argument that assumes a singular concept of "writing," WAC approaches writing as situated within disciplines. If the practices and forms of writing or computing look different across multiple disciplines, it follows that each one should teach its own kind of writing or computing. Kemeny's argument implies that programming education would need to be decoupled from computer science in the same way that WAC decouples writing from departments of English or other languages.[135] Although Kemeny made this case in 1983, CAC is still relatively uncommon.

In the 1990s, the mass programming movement's focus moved to the new World Wide Web, which widened access to programming. The architect of the Web, Tim Berners-Lee, insisted on technical and organizational protocols that would make it accessible to and programmable by everyone.[136] For their introduction to programming, many young people today credit HTML, the simple markup language on which the Web is built. HTML does not have the technical capabilities of Logo or BASIC; it doesn't enact procedures like those and other Turing-complete languages. However, HTML was inspired by BASIC, and it shares BASIC's accessibility and ubiquity. As the authors of *10 PRINT*, a collaborative book based on a BASIC maze program widely circulated in the 1980s, write:

> Though HTML is a markup language used for formatting, not a programming language used for data processing and flow control, it copied BASIC's template of simplicity, similarity to natural language, device independence, and transparency to become many users' first introduction to manipulating code.[137]

The easy-entry possibilities of HTML, plus the fact that it can lead users to other more extensive languages like Javascript, Perl, and PHP, enacts that gentle novice-to-expert climb that Kemeny and Kurtz sought for BASIC. However, even with most Web browsers' capability to show the source code for any webpage, people aren't automatically exposed to code now in the same way that they were on their Commodore 64 in the 1980s. Coding literacy advocates have pointed to this as a problem.[138]

Software consumerism took the spotlight from mass programming campaigns in 1990s, although coding in HTML and the Web took off. Java, a language that emphasized good software engineering, became dominant in computer science classrooms, in part because of its integration with the burgeoning Web. In contrast to BASIC, Java was a proprietary language and controlled by Sun Microsystems.[139] The numbers of computer science majors sagged in the mid-1990s.[140] Low reading skills were a greater national concern, as we saw earlier with the National Literacy Act. Public attention about technology in the 1990s was focused on the digital divide of access to the hardware of computers rather than programming them. Adam Banks signals this moment in his book *Race, Rhetoric, and Technology* when he breaks down the concept of *access* at work in the 1990s, particularly for poor and minority groups. In reports such as the U.S. government's "Falling through the Net" series, access was imagined as strictly material and focused on the *use* of computers rather than any transformative activities such as programming. After the initial enthusiasm that accompanied Logo in elementary schools in the early 1980s, we see a shift from the rich concept of literacy from Kemeny, Papert, and Kay to a surface notion of computer literacy, which focused on computer user tasks such as saving files and searching for resources on the Web.[141]

After the decline in programming sponsorship at universities and through the government in the 1990s, the early 2000s saw a rise again in computer science majors—a delayed response to the late 1990s dot.com boom, which dropped again after the bust.[142] In the 2000s, resources for informally learning programming had never been greater, and many people also sought out diverse online communities with little connection to formal computer science and institutions. The growth of the Web allowed for ready circulation of open-source programming languages that offer more features and computational possibilities than HTML, such as Javascript, Python, Perl, PHP, and Ruby. Today, all of these languages have robust libraries, frameworks, and Web communities supporting and promoting them. People can learn programming by downloading copies of language compilers and development environments, asking questions on forums, contributing to open-source projects and getting feedback, taking free massively open online courses (MOOCs) made available by universities and education companies, and watching help videos and reading blog posts by thousands of individuals throughout the globe.

Along with this decentralized culture of how-to videos and forums online, we see countless large- and small-scale commercial and nonprofit initiatives supporting programming education. One initiative focusing on developing countries is the One Laptop Per Child (OLPC) project. OLPC is part of the mass programming tradition, as it emphasizes production as well as consumption of computational technology through open-source software and language tools. The OLPC project includes the Python programming language, among several others, and its open-source operating system (Sugar, a version of Linux) makes it possible for users to install many others.[143] Organizations that promote mass programming in more developed countries, such as Code.org, Khan Academy, and Codecademy.org, offer free educational resources online. They feature video lessons, e-books, interactive online code-checking, and a wealth of other resources helpful to anyone wanting to learn programming. These groups are typically funded by overflow Silicon Valley capital, and they echo interest in mass online education, typified by Lynda.com, free lectures from MIT and UC Berkeley, TED Talks, plus MOOCs. Together, these privately funded online education initiatives often signify an increasing emphasis on large-scale, technology-based educational structures to replace traditional publicly funded classroom education. (Notably, Code.org has been working extensively with K–12 teachers and school districts and seeks to get computer science in schools rather than supplant classroom education.) Vocational training outfits in the United States promise a kind of "boot camp" for programming (e.g., devbootcamp, CodeFellows, Code School).[144] Noncommercial meetup groups also provide space to support people learning to program (e.g., Code & Supply, FreeCodeCamp, GirlDevelopIt). Others are aimed specifically at young people (CoderDojo, Assemble in Pittsburgh). The philosophies of these various groups, as reflected in mission statements and promotional videos, consolidate many different motivational strands of the mass programming movement since the 1960s, including the focus on empowerment, social justice, and citizenship, but many also put greater emphasis on the market for programming and programmers. Knowing how to program means empowerment and liberation in addition to—and often in tension with—access to employment.

Throughout the decades' waxing and waning of popular attention to teaching coding to all, there have been core groups of educators consistently focused on the effort, including (at different times) John Kemeny, Thomas Kurtz, Alan Kay, Seymour Papert, Cynthia Solomon, Idit Harel Caperton, Yasmin Kafai, Randy Pausch, Jane Margolis, Maria Klawe, Mitchel Resnick, and Mark Guzdial. While their arguments supporting programming vary, they tend to advocate for the intellectual challenge of the activity.

What Drives Mass Programming Movements?
As with literacy campaigns, there are inevitably motivations and ideologies behind mass coding campaigns. Several specific ideologies carry over from the movement for mass literacy into mass programming campaigns. Just as these ideologies provided the reason and resources for mass literacy campaigns, they can fuel coding literacy campaigns. Rhetorically, they manifest

as arguments, implied or explicit, in the promotional materials for why everyone should learn to code. They reflect inherent beliefs about what programming does, who does it and why, and how a broader computational or coding literacy might benefit individuals, groups, or nations.

There are, as I see it, four dominant arguments at work in calls for mass programming,[145] and any one call may draw on several of them at once:

- Individual empowerment
- Learning new ways to think
- Citizenship and collective progress
- Employability and economic concerns

In February 2013, Code.org launched a high-profile campaign promoting widespread computer programming education that consolidated these motivational strands. Code.org was founded by identical twin brothers—Hadi and Ali Partovi—who grew up in Iran, majored in computer science at Harvard, and sold their start-ups for millions each to Microsoft. The brothers recruited Microsoft founder Bill Gates, Facebook founder Mark Zuckerberg, NBA star Chris Bosh, and many others to appear in a promotional video that got 5 million views in just two days.[146] In December 2013, Code.org launched the "Hour of Code" campaign to encourage people to spend just one hour learning code. This campaign included videos by President Barack Obama and House Majority Leader Eric Cantor. On December 9, 2013, Google's homepage displayed a "doodle" to celebrate Grace Hopper's 107th birthday, and underneath was a tagline and link that read "Be a maker, a creator, an innovator. Get started now with an Hour of Code." Code.org declared the September 2015 Hour of Code the "largest learning event in the world," with almost 200,000 registered events and 50 million students participating in just one week.[147] As of July 2016, more than 260 million people had participated in the Hour of Code.[148]

Code.org has expanded greatly since launching the Hour of Code campaign in 2013 and now offers self-paced learning resources in more than 30 languages, professional development courses for K–12 teachers both online and in person, and has partnerships with more than 70 school districts and many leading figures in computer science education, such as Mark Guzdial and Barbara Ericson.[149] Although many of its resources are directed at teaching programming, its mission focuses on promoting computer science as an offering in American public schools. (See the introduction for a discussion of how this mission changed from promoting computer programming to promoting computer science.) With its international reach, its influence on American curriculum, and its long list of educational advisors and corporate sponsors, Code.org is undoubtedly the highest profile contemporary campaign for programming in the world right now. Because of Code.org's high profile and influence on other campaigns, and also because its widely viewed February 2013 video "What Most Schools Don't Teach" serves as a rhetorical clearinghouse for the arguments I outline above, I use this video in the four subsections that follow to discuss each strand of argument in turn.[150] I also include contemporary and historical examples of other calls for coding literacy.

Individual Empowerment Perhaps the most dominant current motivation for coding literacy is that of individual empowerment. Programming is, indeed, a powerful technology for personal expression and information generation. And as computers become ubiquitous, the ability to program them gives a person access to more avenues of control and creativity. This strand generally appears in the mass programming calls made after computers and computation became common, although a few visionaries who sought to make computers more accessible, such as Ted Nelson, the People's Computer Company, and Alan Kay, referred to individual empowerment early on.

Discussing what he calls "Universal Programming Literacy," computer scientist Ken Perlin invokes a popular trope for this motivational strand, that of the computer as "servant": "Those of us who program know that our skill provides us with an enormous increase in our ability to take advantage of the power of computers—the computer becomes a fantastically powerful and extremely protean servant."[151] Code.org's promotional video echoes this rhetoric of empowerment:

Hadi Partovi (Code.org cofounder): Whether you're trying to make a lot of money or whether you want to just change the world, computer programming is an incredibly empowering skill to learn.

Drew Houston (Dropbox founder): To be able to come up with an idea, and then see it in your hands, and then be able to press a button and be in millions of people's hands … I mean, I think we're the first generation in the world that's been able to have that kind of experience.

Gabe Newell (Valve Software cofounder): The programmers of tomorrow are the wizards of the future. You know, you're going to look like you have magic powers compared to everybody else.

Many of the themes in this video recur in other arguments about programming and empowerment, especially the fact that programming allows ideas to reach a massive scale quickly and the association of programming with wizardry. Code.org's 2015 Hour of Code video features HoloLens Engineer Dona Sakar telling an audience, "By learning to code today, you guys are already getting a head start on taking over the world."[152] As we saw at the beginning of this chapter, the pop technology theorist Douglas Rushkoff invokes individual empowerment from a defensive perspective, arguing, provocatively, "Program or be programmed. Choose the former and you gain access to the control panel of civilization. Choose the latter and it could be the last real choice you get to make."[153]

For literacy ideologies, the rhetoric of individual empowerment is a relatively recent addition. It emerged in the twentieth century along with socialist movements, the educational philosophy of Paolo Freire, and global literacy campaigns. It was especially connected to larger social justice movements in the 1960s. Edward Stevens quotes the executive director of the U.S. Adult Education Association arguing that helping someone achieve literacy helps that person to exercise his constitutional right to "life, liberty, and the pursuit of happiness."[154] Literacy initiatives for women and other globally disadvantaged groups often focus on the idea of individual empowerment, and, indeed, there is significant evidence that literacy classes help women achieve greater financial, social, and familial autonomy.[155] Given Code.org's goal of attracting more women and minorities to programming, the focus on empowerment is unsurprising. Ali Partovi writes, "Computer programming gives girls a sense of confidence and empowerment unlike any other study I can think of. Moms and dads who want their daughters to grow up feeling empowered to play an active role in the world around them ought to get them exposed to coding young."[156]

More directly focused on attracting and empowering underrepresented groups to programming are initiatives such as Black Girls Code. Several literacy-based arguments are wrapped up in its promotion of programming, including empowerment:

> Black Girls Code has set out to prove to the world that girls of every color have the skills to become the programmers of tomorrow. By promoting classes and programs we hope to grow the number of women of color working in technology and give underprivileged girls a chance to become the masters of their technological worlds. ... By teaching the girls programming and game design, we hope to have started the lifelong process of developing in them a true love for technology and the self-confidence that comes from understanding the greatest tools of the 21st century.[157]

Programming gives these girls self-confidence, tools for lifelong learning, and access to employment. Most distinctively in this call, young women in

Black Girls Code can "become *masters* of their technological worlds." Black Girls Code redirects the masculine and racialized resonances of "wizards" and "masters" toward young black women. As with #YesWeCode, which is geared toward both men and women in groups underrepresented in the tech industry, there's a sense of flipping a dominant script about coding. Van Jones founded #YesWeCode after a conversation with pop star Prince, who pointed out after the tragic shooting of Trayvon Martin in 2012 that the stereotype of white men in hoodies was Mark Zuckerbergs, but the stereotype of black men in hoodies was thugs. "More black Mark Zuckerbergs" to combat that stereotype is one goal of the group.[158] Through programming, participants in Black Girls Code and #YesWeCan can seize power that has historically been wielded against them.

Learning New Ways to Think   Forsythe argued in 1959 that the way the automatic computer taught precise thinking was a reason to introduce it to all undergraduates.[159] In their 1968 article "The Computer as Communication Device," J. C. R. Licklider and Robert Taylor, both early computer visionaries, argued that the computer was "intelligence amplification" and should therefore be widely accessible to people.[160] The designer of Logo, Seymour Papert, called computers "objects to think with"[161] and encouraged children to engage with programming to learn math. His 1980 *Mindstorms* is still one of the most important books on programming and learning.[162] Along with BASIC, Logo was the language learned by schoolchildren in the 1980s in the United States, an essential part of the Cold War educational strategy. Papert's focus was never on defense or nationalism, however, and Logo got traction in K–12 education because of its graphics and accessible syntax. As a student of Jean Piaget, Papert was far more interested in cognitive development, and his theory of "constructionism," which proposed that learning was best achieved through tangible examples and building, prefigures the "maker movement" aspects of computer programming.[163] Papert's legacy is everywhere in mass programming promotion, especially for young children. Alan Kay cites him as a strong influence in his design of the Dynabook, for instance.[164]

John Kemeny was also interested in how computer programming could revolutionize thinking. In 1971 he said, "We can expect that in the next generation college graduates will have routinely learned how to make use of a high-speed computer. This is likely to have a revolutionary effect on the way human beings attack intellectual tasks."[165] In 1983, in his "case for computer literacy," he again described programming as a tool for changing how people think:

We have a unique opportunity to improve human thinking. If we recognize the areas of human knowledge where ordinary languages are inappropriate, and if computer literacy is routinely achieved in our schools, we can aspire to human thought of a clarity and precision rare today. This development would be of immense value for science, for the organization and retrieval of information, and for all forms of decision-making. Forcing humans to develop such thought processes may be the major fringe benefit of the coming of computers.[166]

Reflecting on his visionary work on laptops and programming languages in the 1970s at Xerox PARC, Alan Kay wrote, "If the personal computer is truly a new medium then the very use of it would actually change thought patterns of an entire civilization."[167] Code.org begins its video by invoking Steve Jobs in a statement that echoes this motivation: "Everybody in this country should learn how to program a computer ... because it teaches you how to think."[168]

For literacy, the evidence that it is connected to the development of new ways of thinking has been hard to come by. In an exhaustive study, Sylvia Scribner and Michael Cole demonstrated that much of what we attribute to literacy is actually attributable to schooling: categorization, higher-order thinking skills, and so forth.[169] The difficulty of extricating the influence of schooling from literacy and vice versa means that we don't know much about whether literacy actually expands cognitive capability. However, the claim that literacy shapes intelligence is a tacit force and sometimes explicitly stated in many promotions of universal literacy.

Perhaps because it is less fashionable now in education to claim broad cognitive benefits for learning or because it is impossible to measure such benefits, this motivational strand is less prominent in contemporary calls for mass programming than it was in the 1960s and 1970s. Stephen Ramsay, a digital humanist at the University of Nebraska who promotes coding literacy, writes, "Learn to code because it's fun and because it will change the way you look at the world. Then notice that we could substitute any other subject for 'learn to code' in that sentence."[170] In this clever turn, Ramsay captures the unease many advocates now feel with making broad claims about coding literacy's specific benefits for intellectual development.

Today, we can see a milder version of the idea that coding teaches you to think in the rhetoric surrounding Scratch, developed by the Lifelong Kindergarten team at MIT. Mitchel Resnick et al. write, "Since programming involves the creation of external representations of your problem solving processes, programming provides you with opportunities to reflect on your own thinking, even to think about thinking itself."[171] Inspired by Logo and the tinkering possibilities of Lego blocks, Scratch inherits the enthusiasm of Papert and Kay as well as their focus on fostering children's imagination and development. The Scratch team aims not to produce programmers or future employees but rather wants kids to learn programming in order to express themselves and understand computational principles.[172] In their discussion of "connected code" and "computational participation" with Scratch, Yasmin Kafai and Quinn Burke extend an emphasis on individual cognition into the social realm. In this way, they reflect more recent developments in literacy research as well: literacy is not simply an isolated cognitive skill but instead gains its meaning and power in social interactions.[173]

Citizenship and Collective Progress   The rhetoric of citizenship figured prominently in drives for mass education and literacy, particularly in the nineteenth century. A democracy—at least ideally—demands an informed citizenry, and when information circulates in text, being informed means being able to read. However, this idealistic democratic rhetoric came at some cost: pluralistic, unschooled literacies from the eighteenth century, especially those that supported workers' rights in Britain, were homogenized into a more standardized and hierarchized schooled literacy.[174] Stevens argues that as the voting qualifications of property, race, and sex were eventually abolished in the United States, education came to bear more weight in the definition of rational citizenship.[175] Literacy thus became a qualification for voting as states implemented tests to exclude illiterates—an exclusion that, not coincidentally, fell disproportionately on people who were poor, African American, or foreign-born.[176] Thus, literacy became tied up with idealistic notions of collective citizenship and exclusionary concepts of nationhood.

The rhetoric of citizenship is central to mass programming campaigns, too, although the exclusionary rhetoric has dropped away in mainstream discourse. The analogy to reading and writing literacy is often explicit when groups seek funding from government sources, as programming promoters point out that our communication and information is now structured in code in addition to text. Promoters argue that just as the mass education movement deemed it essential for citizens to manipulate and understand text, they now need to do the same with code.

John Kemeny and Thomas Kurtz make this case strongly to describe the motivation for their National Science Foundation–funded project at Dartmouth in the 1960s: "We felt exposure to computing and its practice, its powers and limitations must also be extended to nonscience students, many of whom will later be in decision-making roles in business, industry and government."[177] Reflecting on the success of the Dartmouth initiative in 1971, Kemeny said,

> Until we can bring up a new generation of human beings who are thoroughly acquainted with the power and limitations of computers, who know what questions have to be asked and answered, and who are not intimidated by computer experts in a debate, we cannot hope for fundamental change. I see great promise in the reactions of recent Dartmouth students. Now that most of them have first-hand experience with computers, they approach computer applications without fear or superstition and with considerable understanding of how computers can serve mankind.[178]

Still making the case for computer literacy in 1983, Kemeny referenced the powerful printing press as one of the ways society has progressed and asked, "What capabilities will mankind develop once it fully masters the use of computers and intelligent machines?"[179]

In the 1970s, Ted Nelson referenced democracy and power in his *Computer Lib/Dream Machines* manifesto: "If you are interested in democracy and its future, you'd better understand computers. And if you are concerned about power and the way it is used, and aren't we all now, the same thing goes."[180] We can also recall Guido van Rossum's argument for collective progress through coding literacy: "We compare mass ability to read and write software with mass literacy, and predict equally pervasive changes to society."

The investment of local and national governments in coding initiatives means that this line of argument is more than just window dressing. The nonprofit Code for America program and its affiliated grassroots Code Brigades connect the democratic process to programming by facilitating collaboration between programmers and participating city governments. The *New York Times* reported in 2014 that the governments of Estonia, Singapore, and the United Kingdom have invested in bringing programming to K–12 education in the form of computer science.[181] The implementation in Estonia is due, in part, to initiatives related to Kemeny and Kurtz's early drive. In New Jersey in 1968, Toomas Hendrik Ilves learned to program with BASIC in the experimental Columbia Teachers College math curriculum I mentioned earlier. He later became President of Estonia, and led Estonia's Internet connectivity initiative in the late 1990s; he credits this math program for inspiring him to launch a curriculum to teach programming beginning in the first grade.[182]

In Code.org's "What Most Schools Don't Teach" video, the citizenship idea is invoked by pop musician Will.i.am, who here and elsewhere has been a vocal advocate for mass programming:

Will.i.am: Here we are, 2013. We all depend on technology to communicate. To bank. Information. And none of us know how to read and write code! … It's important for these kids. It should be *mandatory* to be a citizen on this planet to read and write code.

Will.i.am's idea of global citizenship elevates the rhetoric above the national level, underscoring programming's universal applications to daily life and activity. Hadi Partovi connects Code.org's mission to the American dream, which invokes the rights an American citizen has to education: "It is a fundamental American ideal—and an ideal people worldwide aspire to—that access to education and opportunity should be equal for all. It seems un-American to accept that computer science classes are only available to the privileged few, in only 10 percent of schools. That is the problem we're trying to solve."[183]

The argument about coding literacy for citizenship often merges with concerns about social justice, as a small segment of the population is designing the software on which America and other nations now run. #YesWeCode's founder Van Jones says that coding literacy campaigns must focus on underrepresentation of minorities and women in coding because

> First, coding is the new literacy. It's the key to the future. Second, and I think even more important, the future is not being written in laws in Washington, DC—it is being written in code in Silicon Valley. That's where change is happening—and that's what's driving humanity forward. It is very dangerous to have a tiny, tiny demographic control all the technology to build the future. Democratizing the tools to create the future is a civil rights issue, a human rights issue, and a commonsense issue.[184]

Here, Jones echoes Lawrence Lessig's characterization of East Coast Code (laws on the books) versus West Coast Code (law in code).[185] He also ties it to demographics and civil rights, tapping into notions of citizenship and empowerment.

The argument for mass programming for democracy and social justice is perhaps the most idealistic ideologically, as it suggests that mass programming literacy will transform society in wholly positive ways by leveling out access to government and jobs and helping us to govern better.

Employability and Economic Concerns   Software production was in crisis in the 1960s. At that time, software was becoming necessary for large-scale commercial enterprise, defense, and banking, and there weren't enough programmers to write and manage the code needed to run these systems.[186] The software crisis is alive and well today in the United States: major software corporations like Electronic Arts and Google partner with universities to train potential future employees, H1B visas are used to import trained software workers, and there is constant media coverage about the employment possibilities for programmers.

Although the software crisis was a U.S. national concern in the 1960s, the energy it generated went toward professional training rather than toward broad coding literacy initiatives. The situation today is different in two significant ways. First, recruitment strategies are not focused, as they were in the 1960s, exclusively on the types of people traditionally thought to be good programmers. Companies are looking for a more diverse workforce, and they claim to be interested in hiring women and people of color. This claim has not been well supported by evidence, however, at least in Silicon Valley, where the vast majority of employees at big tech companies are male and white or Asian.[187] Broad programming initiatives can deepen the potential pool of workers. This is an explicit goal of #YesWeCode: in addition to its citizenship goals above, founder Van Jones notes that computer programmers are in demand and proposes "high-end vocational training" in programming to "target African Americans, Latinos, single moms, Native Americans, women of all colors" to help them get these jobs.[188] Made with Code, which is funded by Google, has a similar goal: it is focused on getting women into the pipeline of hirable programming talent.[189]

The second major difference from the 1960s software crisis is our more globalized economy, which means that the employment and economic concerns for individuals, companies, and nations intersect in more complex ways. Educated citizens can collectively increase the economic stability of a nation, but they can also emigrate. Companies can also rely on "virtual migration" by employing people in India to work in real-time in the United States.[190] U.S. tech companies in particular are focused on attracting skilled workers from all over the world. Having more American workers makes the employment situation of powerful American tech companies more stable, but having more international workers can help companies keep salary costs down.

This employment/economic strand is perhaps the dominant one in Code.org's 2013 promotional video, as it showcases the modern-day software crisis at the same time it features employability as a benefit of learning programming. Here's an example of both:

Drew Houston (Dropbox founder):   There is a much greater need in the world for engineers and people who can write code than there will ever be supply. And so, we all live these very charmed lives. [video of young men skateboarding through a bright, spacious office] To get the very best people, we try to make the office as awesome as possible.

Because the primary audience for Code.org's video is individuals who might potentially learn programming, especially young people, it emphasizes some of the perks of employment as a programmer. Infographics, videos, and statistics on Code.org's website also underscore the imminent employability of people who can program. Code.org's February 2013 video "Code Stars" notes that there will be 1.4 million jobs in computer science and a shortage of 1 million people to fill these jobs.[191] An infographic featured on the site claims, "Computer science is a top paying college degree and computer programming jobs are growing at 2X the national average" (figure 1.4).[192] This infographic shows intertwining national and individual interest in boosting programming education. While the statement at the bottom of the figure seems directed at individuals who might want a good job after college, the graph speaks to national interests: the "$500 billion opportunity." Individuals can get a piece of that $500 billion opportunity, but the United States has an interest in meeting that demand for economic growth and stability.

A March 2014 report in the *New York Times* on widespread programming education efforts encapsulates this complex relationship between individual workers, the technology industry, and national economic stability:

> From Singapore to Tallinn, governments, educators and advocates from the tech industry argue that it has become crucial to hold at least a basic understanding of how the devices that play such a large role in modern life actually work. Such knowledge, the advocates say, is important not only to individual students' future career prospects, but also for their countries' economic competitiveness and the technology industry's ability to find qualified workers.[193]

Here we see the benefits of adding coding to the curriculum in three ways: individual employment, national economies, and the (global) tech industry's human resources concerns. Ali Partovi, a cofounder of Code.org, puts an interesting twist on this amalgamation of interests: "We felt that coding is the new 'American Dream' and should be available to everybody, not just the lucky few." In this short statement, he ties together a trope of American national identity, individual success, and the idealistic democratizing strand of programming promotion. This trope is also echoed in the "Computer Science for All" initiative for New York City schools, announced in September 2015. Positing New York City schoolkids as future workers for the city, Mayor de Blasio stated, "We're calling this program Computer

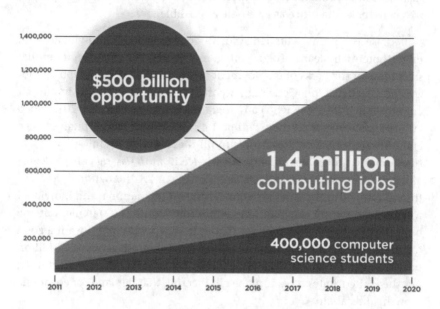

1,000,000 more jobs than students by 2020

Computer science is a
top-paying college degree
and computer programming
**jobs are growing at 2X the
national average.**

Figure 1.4
Using data from the U.S. Bureau of Labor Statistics, Code.org emphasizes that computer programming skills are highly employable. "Code.org Stats: What's Wrong with This Picture?" Code.org, n.d., accessed June 23, 2015, https://code.org/stats/. Source data are from the U.S. Bureau of Labor Statistics and linked from the infographic. Reprinted with permission from Code.org.

Science for All: Fundamentals for Our Future because it speaks to the reality of the world we live in now. From Silicon Alley to Wall Street to the fashion runways, industries all across our city are increasingly relying on new technologies—and are in need of workers with the experience to help them achieve success."[194] Similarly, President Obama's Computer Science for All initiative, announced in his final State of the Union Address in January, 2016, aims to "empower all American students from kindergarten through high school to learn computer science and be equipped with the computational thinking skills they need to be creators in the digital economy, not just consumers, and to be active citizens in our technology-driven world."[195] He uses the word *empower*, but this empowerment is primarily directed toward a collective "digital economy." Supporting this national "CS for all" initiative are arguments for greater diversity in technology careers and firms as well as statistics about unfilled jobs in comp1uter science-related fields. The White House blog describing the initiative showcases footage from President Obama's participation in Code.org's Hour of Code initiative in 2014, demonstrating a connection between these initiatives.[196]

Like the current campaigns for mass programming, earlier literacy campaigns often presented literacy as important to individual employment and national economies. Literacy does appear to boost national productivity, but its symbolic value outstrips this economic value. National literacy campaigns, if successful, can heighten the international status of a developing country, thus attracting more aid and investment.[197] Estonia's mass programming campaign, ProgeTiiger, seems to echo this motivation, at least as reflected in English-language media.[198] Individual programming skills can contribute to national progress—although no survey of programming skills in the general population has yet been conducted in any nation, to my knowledge. (The closest we get are estimates of end-user programmers.[199]) Thus, we see in mass programming campaigns a similar tension as between individual versus collective uses of literacy observed by Arnove and Graff in national literacy campaigns.[200] This tension, I argue, is connected to global economic trends.

Programming Campaigns and Larger Trends in Education and Work

While current programming campaigns such as Code.org's emphasize empowerment, the ideologies expressed in their videos, charts, and arguments for mass programming suggests a more confining role for computational literacy than earlier campaigns such as Kemeny and Kurtz's and Kay's. This shift has been noted disappointingly by computer science educators such as Mitch Resnick, Mark Guzdial, Matti Tedre, and Peter

Denning.[201] In addition to empowering individuals, mass coding campaigns want to help steer a more diverse workforce into American software corporations, some of which also sponsor these campaigns. Of course, the goal to create workers for the information giants such as Facebook and Google is not necessarily incompatible with the goal to educate people to wield this powerful communication technology for their own ends, and the homogeneity of the software industry is a widely recognized problem. But the tension between these goals is at the heart of what makes contemporary programming campaigns different from those in the past. As Kevin Brooks and Chris Lindgren observe, "The coding crisis narrative over-emphasizes global economic competitiveness at the expense of computational literacy's ability to empower users' expressive, aesthetic, and rhetorical abilities." Brooks and Lindgren also admit to finding this "crisis narrative" seductive, as they used it to secure Google Rise funding for their own coding initiative.[202]

In his 1985 "Literacy, Technology, and Monopoly Capital," Richard Ohmann offered a critique of "computer literacy." Paralleling it to textual literacy campaigns, he recognized it as "literacy from above," which tends to reify existing structures of monopoly capital.[203] He admits that computer literacy has the potential to be more liberatory, but he could not see it in its configuration at the time, which was, incidentally, the turn of the Papert constructionism approach into a more instrumental and user-focused approach to computer literacy. While there is considerable demand from people to learn programming to boost their résumés and challenge themselves intellectually, the campaigns themselves echo this hierarchical arrangement. They might empower people, but several of them also align with the concerns of capital. In this way, the campaigns share a tension with mass education more generally, which provides "literacy from above"—along with opportunities for students.

This tension in coding literacy campaigns is exacerbated by the fact that there is a lot of money in software. Software engineering presents a unique opportunity for capital: the software labor force is non-unionized and doesn't require credentials from conservative institutions such as universities; it is globalized both in its workers and the distribution of its products; and it can provide profits at scales impossible in manufacturing, where physical materials must be purchased, processed, and shipped. Aneesh Aneesh goes so far as to note "both money and code are 'global' in that they both provide liquidity to labor and merchandise through symbolization."[204] Code's ability to traverse networks allows for its globalized flow along with global capital, or practically, it allows workers in India to write software with and for Americans. This capital component of code doesn't mean that the software companies that sponsor code initiatives or their education advisors obviously subscribe to a global market–focused worldview. But these economic realities provide the backdrop when these initiatives purport to be training youth to be future software workers—many of whom may, indeed, want to get a piece of that pie.

A September 2013 op-ed arguing for teaching programming in the Pittsburgh public schools reflects some of this rhetoric directly: the writer seeks to match a New York City teacher's boast that "his students graduated 'Google ready'—with skills enough to join a software firm." To pay for the program, Pittsburgh can look to "local businesses and universities[, which] have a real interest in well-trained students."[205] The New York City teacher the writer refers to, Michael Zamansky, is sensitive to the ways that training students for software jobs might conflict with instilling higher-order thinking skills through programming. A director for New York City's program, which was inspired by Zamansky but diverged from his vision of it, explains: "We're interested in giving students marketable skills so that when they're done, they can take industry certifications and get jobs." This instrumental focus upsets Zamansky, who argues, "But what's important is what you're doing with the language. I'm trying to teach deeper concepts of thinking."[206] While Zamansky and the city's Academy for Software Engineering teach many of the same programming languages and concepts, they differ in what they think programming education is for: training for employment or intellectual development. Zamansky seems to be attuned to the argument I am making here with the history of literacy—that the ideas driving the promotion of literacy matter. His approach shares the rhetoric of the Logo and Scratch lineage. In this lineage, Kafai and Burke write, "The point of teaching young people to use introductory programming languages is not to help them become computer scientists or secure a spot at Google or Apple but rather to help them become more effective creators and discerning consumers of digital media."[207]

Many contemporary campaigns and educational curricula for programming rely on public-private partnerships such as the one the Pittsburgh editorialist suggested. Half of the funding for an $81 million project announced by New York City Mayor Bill de Blasio in 2015 will come from private and corporate foundations. A representative for AT&T, one of the corporate sponsors, stated, "For companies like AT&T, the skills gap is real and likely to grow as our core technologies become more sophisticated. ... We see this as a smart investment in our company's future."[208] These partnerships can heighten the contradictions in the ideologies they associate with programming. They should also give educators pause: who or what is determining the purpose of education? As public funding for education is cut, educational institutions seeking ways to support learning at low costs are turning to "free" services that come with political costs. Apple's iTunes U distributes lectures and Google handles official university e-mail communication at no direct cost to universities. Through his $170 million push for Common Core standards,[209] Bill Gates has more influence on public education in the United States than perhaps any other individual. Local knowledge, security, and educational design are often sacrificed for these cost-sharing measures that outsource education to corporations.

This outsourcing of education is happening with programming as well. The United Kingdom will be using Codecademy's lessons in its new national curriculum, which includes programming. This arrangement benefits the UK because Codecademy can help UK teachers learn programming prior to teaching it, and the ready-made lessons mean they can implement curriculum without the delay of designing it from scratch. The benefits to Codecademy for providing this "free" service is summed up in this explanation from its CEO: "CEO Zach Sims hopes that countries across the globe will follow Britain's lead, and that just might happen. Codecademy's lessons are completely free. 'The more people who are learning,' he says, 'the better it is for the company.'"[210] Codecademy appears to be working closely with UK educators. But as Sims reveals in this statement, UK schoolchildren are also a test market for Codecademy's products. Such an arrangement reflects the shift from thinking of education as a process to thinking of it as a product, a shift that is common in public-private educational partnerships—perhaps leading to, Elizabeth Losh argues, a "war on learning" itself.[211] Indeed, these programming initiatives often invest more in technology than in human resources, with the idea that technology can support learning at scale. Automated, online lessons can carry the bulk of the weight of teaching, with support from local advisors and key partners in education. Whether or not market logics are overtaking educational motivations in the contemporary push for mass programming, the money for these initiatives is now coming from software corporations rather than government grants.

Contemporary programming initiatives reflect our current trends toward flexible work environments where individuals are expected to integrate multiple skills and domains but learn how to do this on their own time. They can achieve this with sponsorship from Silicon Valley, the new leaders in economic productivity and a major source of America's global prestige. But the market for these workers is not only local or national. Just as online resources are by default globally distributed, we see here a blurring of national boundaries and national pride as U.S. companies recruit the best tech workers from all over the world and employ them either in the United States or abroad. The simultaneous emphasis on homegrown tech workers can undermine worker autonomy and drive salaries down. As we saw earlier, literacy initiatives of the nineteenth century reinforced the strict hierarchies of the military and factory, the dominant economic and productivity arrangement of the nineteenth century. Despite their stated good intentions to make coding available to all, as part of the "American Dream," these contemporary programming initiatives at times appear to be reinforcing the dominant global-market economic system in the same way that nineteenth century literacy initiatives did. If programming is being subsumed into market logics along with other educational projects, as Losh argues, what powerful aspects of programming might be lost? What happens if coding literacy campaigns shift their rhetoric from individual empowerment to programming as a practice that can build one's marketability? I am not arguing that Code.org or any other campaign has a "secret agenda" or that the people who are learning to code are misguided if they're doing it to enhance their employability. My hope is that by uncovering the ideologies and motivations behind these coding literacy campaigns, we can at least begin to consider these difficult questions.

Conclusion

Like literacy, programming is all of the things these campaigns suggest: it is useful for employment, powerful, intellectually enriching, and inherent in contemporary power structures. But the evidence from historical literacy campaigns suggests that we should consider carefully the impact these ideological frames have on the way we think about programming, as well as the way we think about contemporary literacy. As literacy historian David Vincent argues, the meaning of literacy is not just the technical act of interpreting aspects of a text, but the meaning imbued to the process itself— what people think literacy is for: "What [young children] think literacy is for, what kind of event they envisage it as being, will have greater influence on their journey towards a competence in written communication than the particular methods by which they are taught."[212] Is literacy liberatory or hegemonic? It depends, in part, on what motivations structure literacy education.

Because the values embedded in literacy campaigns reflect contemporary concerns, it is no accident that the promotion of reading in mass literacy campaigns invoked ideas of citizenship, morality, hierarchy, and homogeneity during times when factories and democratic structures were being built and when heterogeneous populations and industrial technologies threatened traditional order. Mass programming campaigns also reflect the concerns of their time periods: the recognition that future leaders needed to understand the computer in the 1960s, the liberatory rhetoric of the 1970s hackers and hippies, the minicomputer revolution and free software movement of the 1980s, the 1990s promise of the World Wide Web and technological consumerism, and now, the massive scale of online courses and mobile apps and venture capital that wants to change the world. As with mass literacy campaigns, the contemporary push for programming appears to signal a new economic and political order. It is, I think, no accident that many programming initiatives are now emerging from Silicon Valley. A lot of code gets written and released in Silicon Valley, but the area and its software are also focused on "disruption" of established corporate and governmental structures.

To add programming to our general concept of literacy means to enfold computational technology with print and other technologies of communication. What will this mean for people who are "noncoders?" Paul Ford writes, "If coders don't run the world, they run the things that run the world."[213] Will coding as a literacy solidify class divisions by reinforcing the idea that programmers run the world? Or do coders already run the world, and our best bet for social equity is to diversify the kinds of people who code? We will not soon retreat from a world saturated with code and computers. And, as I argue in this book, thinking of coding as a literacy gives us access to new ways of teaching programming and thinking about its role in our lives. But—despite the fact that literacy appears to be an uncontroversial and apolitical topic[214]—calling something a *literacy* can exacerbate the hierarchies a skill creates. If enough people say that coding is a literacy, and that noncoders are left behind, then they will be pushed behind not only by their lack of skills but also by that rhetoric.

Because education cannot escape ideology, my point here has been to simply uncover some of those motivations for programming campaigns and relate them to the motivations we've seen in literacy campaigns. While I worry about the ways that contemporary campaigns often reflect the incentives of technology companies and the economics of efficiency rather than the more aspirational approaches of earlier campaigns, I still applaud these efforts. If programming is indeed part of an enlarged literacy, then wider appeal and access to the means to learn it are critical. As a *New York Times* editorial recently warned, "If coding is the new lingua franca, literacy rates for girls are dropping."[215] Will framing programming as a literacy and promoting it as part of the standard educational curriculum address these disparities? Perhaps. While Harvey Graff famously busted the "literacy myth" that literacy automatically led to progress, he still wonders whether retaining literacy myths might be useful for collective progress.[216] For all their faults, mass literacy campaigns and formal schooling have helped women and other oppressed groups gain access to literacy, and we also need this for programming.

While this chapter has focused on the inclusion of programming under the rhetorical rubric of literacy, the next chapter takes on the functional aspects of coding literacy, how programming functions like writing. We will look at the characteristics of the technological systems of programming and writing to see how they both operate as ways of building knowledge and what programming adds to our larger arsenal of communication.

2   Sociomaterialities of Programming and Writing

As ambiguously as that first apple, programming and writing help to create and reveal knowledge. Jack Goody called writing a "technology of the intellect," Walter Ong considered it a "technology that restructures thought," and Marshall McLuhan considered writing a form of media that was an "extension of man."[1] While these concepts of writing are deliberately imprecise, even horoscopic, they suggest the differences between a technology that works with knowledge and one that works with materials. Goody, Ong, and McLuhan don't tell the whole story, but writing—and programming—are fundamentally different from other technologies that make our lives easier or help us fight or eat or stay healthy. They help us to think; they build knowledge.

While Goody, Ong, and McLuhan asked important questions about what it means for people and societies to write, they answered those questions by putting too much pressure on the technologies themselves, in isolation from the complex social worlds in which technologies are created and used. More recent approaches to writing as a technology avoid their tendencies toward technological determinism by accounting for social and material factors that complicate the use of writing. This chapter draws on those sociomaterial approaches in order to explore the shared characteristics of programming and writing, what makes them both technologies that build, create, and communicate knowledge. Programming and writing are not the same thing, but they have a lot in common and can even merge into each other. Because of their complex and multiple intersections, I want to suggest that programming and writing both deserve a central place in our thinking about human relationships with communication technologies; they should both be part of our concept of contemporary literacy. If the previous chapter examined the ways this claim was justified rhetorically, the current chapter does so theoretically, examining the productive overlaps between theories of writing and programming as social and material technologies.

I rely on Andrea diSessa's concept of "material intelligences" as a frame because I find it productive for exploring the possibilities—as well as the limits—of how programming builds knowledge, particularly in terms of procedures. According to diSessa, a "material intelligence" combines a material component—a book, a piece of paper, an alphabet—with an ability to interpret that material. He writes, "We can install some aspects of our thinking in stable, reproducible, manipulable, and transportable physical form. These external forms become in a very real sense part of our thinking, remembering, and communicating."[2] A material intelligence becomes a literacy when the ability to interpret its material component becomes widespread—as has been true with writing, but not yet with programming.[3] Because material intelligences can be precursors to literacy, I sometimes refer to programming and writing as literacy technologies here.

According to diSessa, any material intelligence or literacy is supported by three "pillars": technological, social, and cognitive. The cognitive pillar concerns human intelligence; people need certain cognitive skills in order to learn to read and write, for instance. The technological intersects with the social and cognitive in the ways that the material form of literacy affects its circulation. diSessa uses the example of calculus to illustrate this point: we use Leibniz's notation rather than Newton's because it is more transparent and easier to understand. Calculus would never have become so widely taught if its notation were as arcane as Newton's, diSessa argues.[4] Thus, a specific notation technology made the kinds of knowledge that calculus fosters more available to a broader group of people. Of course, social factors can also mean that the easier or more transparent technology does not always win out, as demonstrated by the QWERTY keyboard's persistence. A concept of material intelligences can explain how specific technologies affect the kinds of cognitive abilities fostered and the circulation of those abilities in a society. I focus here on the social and the technological (what I sometimes call material) pillars of literacy rather than the cognitive pillar. Although I don't disagree with diSessa's assertion that there are individual cognitive factors in the learning and practicing of literacy, I find the humanistic and historical tools at my disposal inadequate for attending to them.

Below, I begin by distinguishing my claim that programming and writing are literacy technologies from claims about overly deterministic "consequences" of technologies on societies and cognition. Much work was done in the 1950s and 1960s on the relationships between orality and literacy and speech and writing—including work by Goody, Ong, and

McLuhan—and was then subsequently dismissed as technologically deterministic. Particularly in the case of McLuhan, too much emphasis was placed on the technology of writing as a sole cause of change in human society and individual consciousness. Contemporary work in rhetoric, media, and literacy studies has revived this attention to material technologies, however, with the language of "affordances" rather than "consequences." As diSessa argues, we can think of writing and programming as technologies that make certain kinds of thinking easier, and thus more probable.

To understand the kinds of affordances programming provides, it is helpful to go into detail on what programming is and how it relates to writing and speech. To do this, I outline a historical trajectory of programming: how it moved from being a feat of machine engineering to being a complex symbolic system that could be deployed across multiple computers and global networks. As a symbolic system embodied in text, computer programming becomes similar to writing. But as a time-based performance, something that "runs," programming bears similarities to speech. Theories of writing and speech provide ways to think about programming as a symbolic system used to encode, communicate, and enact information. Speech act theory has taught us that differences between writing and speech are best measured by degree rather than kind, and I contend that this is also the case for speech, writing, and programming. All three are symbolic systems that can effect changes in the world, but their differences in audience and context of use mean they function quite differently.

The complex ways that code affects and effects things in the world can be attributed, in part, to the fact that the computer calls for explicit definitions of concepts. To see how this relates to human language and writing, I use Wittgenstein's theories of language-in-use and Bernard Stiegler's theories of *grammatization*—or, the discretizing of information. Discretization—for example, any move from analog to digital—always throws out some information. That code reduces information is a common source of critique for its ability to represent processes. But discreteness gives programming certain affordances of replication, distribution, and scale. Writing, of course, is also discrete, which allows it to travel in ways that speech cannot, albeit stripped of the nuances of tone and gesture that speech performances can have. Constraints in form such as those that discretization provides can foster creativity, even poetry, in both programming and writing. In programming, these poetic forms often highlight the dual audience for code: computers and humans. Different programming languages and paradigms offer different trade-offs between the expression of processes for the computer and the legibility of these processes for the programmers. All of these constraints and trade-offs contribute to the ways that programming and writing help to build knowledge, or function as material intelligences.

The arguments presented in this chapter hinge on the idea that programming, like writing, is a symbolic system operating through an inscribed language. As such, programming follows a particular grammar, encodes and conveys information, and is socially shaped and circulated. Programming as a symbolic system distinguishes it from physical technologies. It is a "media machine," such as Mark Poster describes. Media machines (such as programming and writing) "process texts, images, and sound" and are different from other forms of technology that act on natural objects such as wood and iron.[5] Unlike media that have predetermined physical capacities for recording events and ideas—such as the phonograph—programming and writing are both subject to constant interpretive acts that unfold as humans produce them, although they are clearly always subject to certain physical limitations as well. And unlike media that primarily record events and ideas—such as the phonograph—programming and writing are both interpretive; they can be used to construct new ideas.

This view of programming as a symbolic, sociomaterial system similar to writing cannot fully encompass it or describe it; no approach could do that alone. However, it is a productive lens on programming, one that fills a gap left by approaches through math, logic, cognitive science, and engineering, and which gives us ways of thinking about writing and programming as related and inextricable forms of composition. Considering programming and writing together also points to ways that people can, as individuals and societies, create knowledge and structure information. Although I intend the chapter to provide justification for some of the rhetoric that connects programming to writing, I also use it to extend the argument for coding literacy that sees programming expanding the mind and human capability. As I observed in chapter 1, this humanistic argument has been subsumed by connections between programming and economic advantage. I am reviving it here—idealistically, perhaps, but alloyed with the knowledge that ideologies of literacy, even if necessary, are not necessarily good. This chapter lays the theoretical groundwork for subsequent chapters on the historical and contemporary explorations of the ways writing and programming have shaped society.

Thinking with Technologies

Vannevar Bush's visionary 1945 article in the *Atlantic*, "As We May Think," outlined some of the ways that computers could help us organize information and lead to new ways of thinking. Noting that Gottfried Leibniz and Charles Babbage were both stymied by manufacturing constraints in their efforts to create calculating machines, Bush writes: "The world has arrived at an age of cheap complex devices of great reliability; and something is bound to come of it."[6] That "something" he imagines through a technology he calls a "Memex," which he proposes as an extension of human thinking. Through better organization and access to the world's trove of knowledge, the Memex would allow people to create new "trails" through information, thus building new knowledge through those new connections. Reflecting on the piece in 1964, Martin Greenberger writes, "By 2000 AD man should have a much better comprehension of himself and his system, not because he will be innately any smarter than he is today, but because he will have learned to use imaginatively the most powerful amplifier of intelligence yet devised."[7] Bush revisits his argument in 1967, reminding readers that he had proposed a *personal* device, rather than the mainframes then in use. This personal device was to have "serve[d] a man's daily thoughts directly, fitting in with his normal thought processes, rather than just do chores for him."[8] J. C. R. Licklider envisioned a similar "symbiosis" in 1960, when he hoped that "in not too many years, human brains and computing machines will be coupled together very tightly, and that the resulting partnership will think as no human brain has ever thought and process data in a way not approached by the information-handling machines we know today."[9]

Although it took some time for this process to happen, we now appear to have arrived at the moment when our personal computational devices "fit in" with our thought processes; I argue that computers are augmenting our intellect. Programming, now that it is relatively accessible and broadly applicable, is the critical link between these cheap, ubiquitous devices and their function as extensions to our minds. To examine the intelligence amplification that Bush and Licklider and Greenberger imagined, we should move beyond a discussion of specific devices and look instead toward computation and the functions of programming.

What Makes Something an "Intelligence"?

In "The Question Concerning Technology," originally given as a lecture in 1949, Heidegger says that we tend to think of technology as a tool for greater efficiency, a better way to get things done. But this is wrong, he argues. To push beyond thinking of technology in only instrumental ways, Heidegger claims we must see that "the essence of technology is by no means anything technological."[10] Instead, the essence of technology is in its "way of revealing." Thinking of writing and programming as material intelligences, we can see that they reveal knowledge that might be more difficult to access through other means. Much of what is done in programming could also be done in writing or speech or engineering, but programming unlocks properties of knowledge that might be obscured through those other methods.

The kind of knowledge revealed by programming concerns procedures. Programmers and computer scientists have often insisted that the programmed computer reveals ways of understanding and encoding procedural knowledge. Of course, procedural knowledge has always been present in human reasoning, but programming highlights it as a central way to understand and represent the world. In a discussion among technological luminaries at MIT in 1961, for example, John McCarthy described how programming reveals a knowledge process previously concealed: "Programming is the art of stating procedures. Prior to the development of digital computers, one did not have to state procedures precisely. Now we have a tool that will carry out any procedure, provided we can state this procedure sufficiently well."[11] Licklider responded to McCarthy to suggest that while programming was novel, what it reveals is something more fundamental: "computer programming [is] a way into the structure of ideas and into the understanding of intellectual processes that is just a new thing in this world."[12] More recently, Ian Bogost points out that although procedural representations can be found elsewhere, "the computer magnifies the ability to create representations of processes."[13] That programming highlights knowledge about procedures has prompted Bogost and others to claim that it contributes to "procedural literacy."

Some go so far as to altogether remove the computer in their characterization of programming as the human ability to express processes. In their seminal programming textbook, *Structure and Interpretation of Computer Programs*, Hal Abelson, Gerald Sussman, and Julie Sussman write:

> Underlying our approach to this subject is our conviction that "computer science" is not a science and that its significance has little to do with computers. The computer revolution is a revolution in the way we think and in the way we express what we think. The essence of this change is the emergence of what might best be called *procedural epistemology*—the study of the structure of knowledge from an imperative point of view, as opposed to the more declarative point of view taken by classical mathematical subjects. Mathematics provides a framework for dealing precisely with notions of "what is." Computation provides a framework for dealing precisely with notions of "how to."[14]

Abelson imagines future historians looking back at our current age with some amusement at our shortsightedness concerning computers, as we fetishize the specific tool of the computer. He notes that just as geographers' work was once identified solely through their surveying equipment, the technological and material presence of the computer has overshadowed its ability to encapsulate how-to knowledge.[15] And, of course, this knowledge was present in the concept of programming before computers existed: Ada Lovelace's description of how one would program Charles Babbage's Analytical Engine walks carefully through the procedures to make the machine function.[16] Because we are forced to make the procedural, or how-to, knowledge highly explicit through code in order to communicate with the computer, this knowledge, which was present but tacit in many human activities prior to the computer, is laid bare in programming.

We can connect this procedural knowledge in programming to the claims that programming enables certain kinds of thinking, which were introduced in chapter 1. For example, Seymour Papert calls programming an "object to think with," likening it to the gears he played with as a child and which later allowed him to have a feel for engineering and physics.[17] A student of Jean Piaget, Papert argued that programming is a kind of "scaffold" for knowledge, a way to boost thinking. Programming is a technological version of teachers who help kids understand concepts just beyond their reach—concepts within their Piagetian "zone of proximal development." Through exercises where children "programmed" each other to navigate paths, Papert taught them more sophisticated spatial and logical reasoning than they were capable of on their own. Similarly, Papert designed his Logo programming language to be an "object to think with." Beginning with pilot projects in a handful of British schools in the 1970s, the Logo programming language expanded its reach into American classrooms through defense-related education spending in the 1980s. Scaled up and distributed across thousands of classrooms and teachers, Logo was less effective at teaching students the concepts that Papert was able to teach them in his pilots. As this educational experiment seems to suggest, the Logo programming language—by itself—was not an object to think with. Like any technology, it could not act independently to alter cognition. Among other things, Logo needed to be combined with good teachers and support to help kids think about procedures and problem solving.[18]

Programming fosters procedural knowledge, but as the example of Logo demonstrates, programming does not and cannot do this on its own. The social milieu and the notation in which code circulates affect the kinds of thinking it fosters, who does this thinking, and how widespread it can become. Programming languages matter. Teaching matters. These points were forcefully made by Roy Pea and Midian Kurland in their 1984 critique of the contemporary hype about teaching Logo in elementary school class-rooms.[19] Pea and Kurland note that the cognitive benefits of programming are the same as those that were once attributed to math, Latin, writing, and logic. Yet the claim that "spontaneous experience with a powerful symbolic system will have beneficial cognitive consequences" is merely "technoro-manticism" and cannot be empirically verified.[20] The main problem, they say, is that these claims treat programming as a "unitary skill." However,

> Like reading, [programming] is comprised of a large number of abilities that inter-relate with the organization of the learner's knowledge base, memory and pro-cessing capacities, repertoire of comprehension strategies, and general problem-solving abilities. ... As reading is often equated with skill in decoding, "learning to program" in schools is often equated with learning the vocabulary and syntax of a programming language. But skilled programming, like reading, is complex and context-dependent.[21]

In other words, programming—like reading or writing—inextricably inter-twines the technological, the social, and the cognitive. Following up on his work with Papert, diSessa appears to have taken some of Pea and Kurland's points into consideration in his concept of material intelligences.

A Sociomaterial Approach to Writing Technologies

Pea and Kurland's critique of the claims for Logo, as well as diSessa's (indi-rect) response, emerge from a broader context of debates about the effects of technologies on individual cognition and society. This has been tricky territory for anyone wanting to make claims for literacy and writing, as evidenced by the controversy around Goody, Ong, and McLuhan's claims. Although popular discourse still might accept those claims uncritically, it is very difficult to prove the effects of writing on thinking. My argument about the sociomateriality of programming and writing differs from these now passé and technologically deterministic theories about writing (and programming) because of its attention to social factors and its silence on cognitive "consequences." It is useful to review where these ideas came from, however, and how we got sociomaterial theories of literacy as a corrective.

Harold Innis argued in the 1950s that governments whose laws were written on paper had different characteristics than those whose laws were etched in stone tablets. There appeared to be different "biases" for these media. For example, tablets were more difficult to carry long distances than paper, and so paper governments had a larger geographic range.[22] His stu-dent, Marshall McLuhan, took the idea of "bias" in communication further, asserting that materiality was everything, that "the medium is the message."[23] Walter Ong zeroed in on writing specifically, arguing that it is "a technology that restructures thought."[24] Jack Goody and Ian Watt published an (infamously) influential paper in 1963 on "The Consequences of Literacy," which credited literacy, specifically the ability to read and write the alphabet, with the development of Western civilization.[25] Although Goody and Watt had implicitly intended to counter the arguments that certain societies were racially superior to others by locating successes in their writing technologies rather than the inherent characteristics of their people, their argument about the superiority of alphabets has largely been discounted as ethnocentric, and Goody went back to revise these claims significantly.

These early claims for writing and literacy were decimated by the social turn in writing studies. Influenced by larger movements of postmodernism and poststructuralism, social theories of writing pointed out that communication is not fully determined by its technologies. The way writing is learned, culturally framed, and individually performed also shapes what might be written. Brian Street helped to knock down the so-called theoretical "great divide" between oral and literate societies with his "ideological model" of literacy, which posited literacies as multidimensional, continuous, and inflected with value systems.[26] In an extensive study of the Vai people in Liberia, Sylvia Scribner and Michael Cole demonstrated that only modest changes in thought could be attributed to literacy.[27] The work by "New Literacy Studies" (NLS) researchers such as Street, Scribner, and Cole moves literacy from the value-neutral, technical continuum of skills that culminates in a narrowly Western tradition—as depicted in Goody and Watt's account—and recovers the sociocultural aspects of literacy. Thus, after the work in NLS, we can no longer go so far as to mark the "literate man" as fundamentally different from "oral man," as McLuhan claimed. McLuhan and Ong and Goody emphasized technologies at the expense of attending to the ways that they were adopted and circulated in societies.

Yet, surely it makes a difference if we type on our cheap laptops with QWERTY keyboards instead of painstakingly handwrite with quills that need constant sharpening and expensive ink? There are bound to be differences in what we say in 140-character messages on smartphones and letters written longhand and mailed. These questions prompted by new technologies of reading and writing have led scholars to revisit Ong, McLuhan, and others.[28] As part of a larger "material turn" in the social sciences and humanities, studies of writing and communication are attending to the materials of composition: the codex format, the history of paper, the surfaces of physical computer memory, the platform of the e-book.[29] But instead of resuscitating McLuhan's "electronic man" they ask: What might it mean for people to use digital modes to communicate? Deterministic histories of technologies such as McLuhan's are no longer tenable, but, as Bruno Latour has convincingly argued, neither are purely social histories.[30] In place of "the social" or "the consequences" of technology, we have *social* histories of technology, "new materialism," and "media archaeology."

However, a closer look at the work in NLS reveals that this material focus was there all along.[31] In other words, those interested in the nature of writing have long understood writing as a technology whose social effects depend on its material manifestations. The problem with determinist or "great divide" theories was not that they were wrong to attend to the technologies of literacy, but that they were not specific enough to be useful.[32] David Olson, whose early work was accused of reproducing the "great divide" between oral and literate cultures, later retracted his boldest claims and wrote, "The excitement of McLuhan's writing springs from its sheer scope; the particulars of his hypothesis regarding oral man, literate man, electronic man, and so on continue to be apt metaphors but have limited theoretical use. They fail, I believe, not because they are false, but because they do not indicate precisely how writing or printing could actually have produced those effects."[33] In Olson's revisions, we can see echoes of Pea and Kurland's argument that treating programming as a "unitary skill" dismisses so much of its complexity as to dismiss any claims for its benefits.

New Literacy Studies offers a nuanced and careful look at the ways writing intersects in complex ways with social situations. Work in NLS that attends more specifically to the technological as well as the social includes Deborah Brandt demonstrating the palimpsest of twentieth century literacy technologies in contemporary American lives; Niko Besnier charting the global circulation of English literacy as manifested in such material objects of capitalism as T-shirts worn by people on the island of Nukulaelae; Christina Haas describing differences in navigating texts on computer screens versus paper; Kate Vieira exploring the ways document technologies impinge on literacy practices in immigrant communities; and Timothy Laquintano revealing the strategies of e-book authors to restrict and expand the circulation of their work.[34] For these researchers, literacies circulate in technologies such as pens, papers, and dictionaries; in symbolic systems such as English, alphabets, and genres; and in networks such as workplaces, families, schools, and the global post. Literacies are plural, multidimensional, heavily inflected by orality, acquired along with value systems, *as well as* intertwined with the technologies in which they are enacted.

This sociomaterial perspective on literacy resonates with what social history of technology scholar Thomas Misa calls a "softer" approach to the influence of technologies on society. Rather than the "hard" determinism of McLuhan and rather than "consequences" of technologies, this "softer" approach uses the concept of technological affordances. It is represented by technology theorists such as Ruth Schwartz Cowan, who claim that technologies have certain politics and uses embedded in their design—what Innis might have called "biases."[35] Misa writes, "Accounts such as these are not content merely to explain the 'social' by the 'technical' (technology as a social force), or the 'technical' by the 'social' (technology as a social product). These accounts shift to an interpretive framework presenting technology at once as socially constructed and society-shaping. They view technology as a social process."[36] It is this approach that I see present in sociomaterial perspectives on literacy such as diSessa offers with his three-pillar model of material intelligences.

So, when I say that programming builds new knowledge, I do not mean that the technology of programming inevitably leads to certain cognitive or societal effects. As a technologically mediated symbolic system, programming makes some kinds of thinking more available than did previous technologies of communication. Through the ways it enables people to structure and express information, it uncovers certain kinds of tacit knowledge. Here, I follow Heidegger in his assertion that technologies can *reveal* certain things latent in their design and implementation. By looking simultaneously at the social and the technological aspects of programming, I draw on sociomaterial theories of literacy and attempt to avoid the determinism of McLuhan and the Toronto School. Programming and writing are both socially shaped and shaping technologies that have "become in a very real sense part of our thinking, remembering, and communicating."[37]

Programming Is/and Written Language

Some shared characteristics contribute to the ways that programming and writing both help us build knowledge. Below, I outline some of these shared characteristics and overlaps, beginning with the historical and technological process that turned programming into writing. (With the caveat, of course, that Lovelace and Turing both programmed in writing ahead of the machines that could run their code.) This transformation meant that programming could merge writing's capabilities of scale, replication, and distribution with engineering's capabilities to control machines. I then trace the evolution of programming languages further into the ways they balance human and computer time and legibility. As programming languages that more closely resemble human language emerge, can we maintain our theoretical distinctions between programming, writing, and speech? Yes and no. Speech act theory helps to explain and complicate those boundaries.

A Brief and Incomplete History of Programming Languages

The earliest mechanical and electrical computers were not controlled by code at all: they relied on physical engineering rather than writing to program them. They were more closely related to ship navigation instruments or machines of industrial production such as the Jacquard loom. Then, intermediary systems were developed that allowed people to write something that resembled English yet still communicate to the computer in binary numbers. As programming languages and these intermediary translating systems grew more sophisticated, programming code became more abstract, more symbolic—less about the constraints of the machine, and more about the processes the programmer wanted to enact. This evolution allowed nonspecialists to harness the computational power of the digital computer. It also brought programming into a closer relationship with writing.

Computers in World War II such as the Mark I at Harvard, the ENIAC at the University of Pennsylvania, and the Colossus at Bletchley Park carried out their calculations on relays, wires, or vacuum tubes. These computers were used for massive mathematical calculations, such as breaking code or weapons ballistics, and for each new calculation, the machines had to be reconfigured. Complicated calculations had to be worked out using basic functions such as adding and subtracting, and these operations would be assigned specific sequences by a circuit designer. When working on the ENIAC, John von Neumann's team developed a concept of a "stored program," which would allow the computer to store its instructions along with its data.[38] This design meant that computers did not need to be rewired for each new calculation. Computers could then be general-purpose machines; that is, they could be used for many different calculations without being physically manipulated. The implications of this development were huge: "von Neumann architecture" (as it is now called) moved the concept of programming from physical engineering to symbolic representation. Media theorist Friedrich Kittler locates this transition earlier; he argues that when Konrad Zuse designed the first programmable computer in 1938, "the world of the symbolic really turned into the world of the machine."[39] With these developments, programming became the manipulation of code, a symbolic text that was part of a writing system. Computers became technologies of writing as well as engineering.

Although many of the fundamental concepts of programming were in place at this time, there was no difference between source code and machine code. Computers then and now really only understand two commands: off and on, which are usually represented by 0 and 1. The concept of binary programming has roots in nineteenth-century mathematical logic by George Boole and Claude Shannon's 1937 adaptation of those theories to communications. Represented in ones and zeros, binary operation looks like this:

11000000 0110010111001010 1101001101100100

where "11000000" is the operation ADD and the next two numbers (represented in binary format) are what the computer adds together.[40] Binary code was a direct representation of the on/off states of the vacuum tubes translated into ones and zeroes. With the introduction of octal and hexadecimal numerical representations, programs became slightly more legible to programmers, but were still fairly arcane.[41]

Then, in 1948, a group at Cambridge figured out that the computer could be made to understand letters as well as numbers. Letters could be made into numbers: human-readable source code could be translated into computer-readable machine code through an intermediary program they called an "assembler."[42] Following is a more contemporary assembly language procedure to determine whether a number is higher or lower than average[43]:

```
cmp edx,32h
jle wmain+32h
push offset string "Higher than average\n"
jmp wmain+37h
push offset string "Lower than average\n"
call dword ptr [__imp__printf]
```

Assembly programs are specific to the architecture of a particular machine. Although they are more readable than binary or hexadecimal code, they still require programmers to assign specific, physical memory locations to data (e.g., "wmain+32h") and are therefore determined by hardware architecture.

In the 1950s, compilers, a new generation of translation programs, allowed source code to be imbued with more semantic value by making the computer a more sophisticated reader—and writer—of code. They were part of an effort then called "automatic programming," which strove to eliminate programmers by shifting more of the burden of the program to the computer. As Grace Hopper articulated in 1952, "It is the current aim to replace, as far as possible, the human brain by an electronic digital computer." (She later softened this stance, and instead outlined various roles and hierarchies for programmers.)[44] The legacy of automatic programming includes government funding from DARPA in the 1970s and 1980s and some design aspects of the Java programming language in the 1990s.[45]

Working on the UNIVAC computer, Hopper wrote the first compiler in 1951, A-0. She credited ENIAC programmer Betty Snyder (Holbertson), who wrote a sort-merge generator—the first program that wrote a program—as inspiration for her compiler.[46] Janet Abbate notes that women were disproportionately well-represented in these early efforts to streamline programming, perhaps because they were often the operators of computers in this era. The first successful higher-level language to work with a compiler—FORTRAN (now Fortran)—was released in 1957 by John Backus at IBM.[47] The language was quickly adopted by IBM programmers as it allowed them to write code much more quickly and concisely than assembly language did, and it had a significant influence on other programming language development. Here is a snippet of Fortran code:

```
A = (x * 2) / Y
```

Anyone familiar with mathematical notation can read this as A equals x times 2, divided by Y.[48] In Fortran, like most programming languages, the equal sign (=) refers to assignment rather than equation; therefore, this statement *assigns* the value of $(x * 2) / Y$ to the variable A. In assembly language, the loading, storing, and dividing of the numbers would have been separate instructions, but Fortran allows the steps to be combined in a more familiar and legible notation. Fortran, which stands for "formula translation," points to the primary use of computers at the time, to calculate complex formulas, but it also gestures forward to an idea of programming less tied to the field of engineering or mathematics. Fortran's more legible notation meant that programming could be done by nonprofessionals; physicists, chemists, and other scientists could and did use the computer without learning specific assembly languages. In other words, Fortran allowed programming to move outside of the exclusive domain of computer specialists.

LISP (now Lisp) was developed shortly afterward by John McCarthy at MIT and has been the vehicle for many language developments, such as dynamic typing and conditional statements. On the heels of Lisp and Fortran was COBOL (Common Business Oriented Language), which was based

on Hopper's B-0 compiler and designed in 1959 by a committee of representatives from government and computer manufacturers to read with English-
like syntax. The COBOL equivalent of the above Fortran statement is:

```
MULTIPLY X by 2 giving TEMP
DIVIDE TEMP by Y giving A
```

COBOL was friendlier to report layouts and large data structures and
used more English words to represent orders, so it was more accessible to
managers and businesses.[49] COBOL was also designed to be platform
independent—that is, to work across a number of different manufacturers'
machines—in order to streamline the local and idiosyncratic practices of
programming that had cropped up around shared machines. COBOL
pointed toward increasing standardization in programming but also suggested that the computer had become a more useful and versatile tool for
many different fields, including business. COBOL became an industry standard not only because of its committee-based design but also because the
U.S. Department of Defense announced in 1960 that it would not lease or
purchase a computer without a COBOL compiler.[50] The standardization for
COBOL process emphasized corporate and management interests over the
interests of academics and individual programmers.[51] Registering their dis-
satisfaction with business-biased COBOL and IBM-controlled Fortran, the
Association for Computer Machinery developed the more "elegant" language ALGOL in 1962.[52] ALGOL never achieved the popularity of its rivals,
in part because of the Department of Defense order and other social pressures that encouraged adoption of COBOL.

In the 1960s, the social influence on the design of programming languages is visible in the ways that COBOL and ALGOL accommodated the
increasingly collaborative work of programming. COBOL did this through
its widespread adoption by Department of Defense fiat, and ALGOL fostered collaboration through its structured design. "Structured programming," pioneered in ALGOL, is a design that allows programmers to trace
the path of a program's execution. For any given line of code, the programmer can tell where the program came from and where it flows next, making
programs easier to follow and debug. Structured programming also lends
itself well to modularity, so that programmers can divide a program into
different sections of code on which they can work individually before
reassembling them. Languages with standards and structure, such as
COBOL and ALGOL, helped increasingly large programming teams to collaborate. Structured style was key to the professionalization of programmers in business.[53] However, this structure enforced rigidity around styles

of programming, which seemed to attract or enforce certain kinds of people working as programmers. Sherry Turkle argues that structured programming, especially in the 1970s and 1980s, emphasized "a male-dominated computer culture that took one style as the right and only way to program."[54]

Another important development in programming languages emerged from academic artificial intelligence research in the late 1950s, represented by Lisp. Lisp's innovation is that it is unusually flexible. Using logical principles from Alonzo Church's lambda calculus, it does not draw distinctions between data and procedures—roughly, the nouns and verbs of computer programming languages. Lisp, which stands for "list processor," uses linked lists to structure both data and processes.[55] The ways that Lisp handles data and procedures highlights the recursive and symbolic aspects of programming—which are also features of human language, of course. Lisp's features made it challenging to implement with the hardware at the time, but many of its ideas have been absorbed in subsequent languages. Versions of Lisp continue to be popular in education, artificial intelligence, and for scripting languages, and it can boast high-profile acolytes such as Paul Graham and Richard Gabriel, who writes: "Lisp is the language of loveliness. With it a great programmer can make a beautiful, operating thing, a thing organically created and formed through the interaction of a programmer/artist and a medium of expression that happens to execute on a computer."[56] Abelson, Sussman, and Sussman's popular *Structure and Interpretation of Computer Programs,* designed for the MIT introductory computer science course, uses a version of Lisp called Scheme.

As computers became cheaper to own and to run in the middle decades of the twentieth century, programmer time became more valuable than computer time, and languages were increasingly biased toward human comprehension over computational efficiency. This emphasis on human comprehension meant that programming language design has trended away from the materiality of the device and toward the abstraction of the processes that control it.[57] Defined more by its social achievements than its technical ones, the BASIC programming language developed in the 1960s by Dartmouth professors John Kemeny and Thomas Kurtz (discussed in chapter 1) represented this move toward greater human comprehension. BASIC represents the beginning of a lineage of programming languages geared toward novices, including languages such as Logo, Etoys, Alice, and Scratch. Using many different approaches—combinable text blocks, English language syntax, graphics—novice languages have aimed to make concepts of programming easy initially, although most of them are not meant to be used professionally or long term.[58] Other visual programming languages such as Blockly, Node-RED, Max/MSP, and Modkit make specific tasks easier, such as creating apps for mobile phones, programming the so-called Internet of Things, Arduino control, and music generation.[59]

A focus on human-friendly abstraction is illustrated in object-oriented languages such as Simula from the Norwegian Computing Center in the 1960s or Alan Kay's Smalltalk developed at Xerox PARC in the 1970s. Object-oriented languages "black-box" some of the details of programs in order to allow programmers to plug in "objects"—encapsulated packages of functions and data—to build even more complex programs.[60] In the 1990s, increasingly robust language libraries in object-oriented languages such as Java allowed individual programmers to string together long series of functions written by other programmers, creating complex programs that could run on almost any machine. This practice of writing with language libraries complied with the need for programming modularity in businesses of the era, but also has allowed less experienced programmers to write programs that build on the work of other, more specialized programmers.

The 2000s saw an upswing in the social circulation of languages such as Python, Javascript, and Ruby, with accompanying frameworks such as Ruby on Rails or Django that allow programmers to do specific tasks in extremely streamlined ways. Continuing the trend of valuing programmer time above computer time, these languages allow programmers to write and run code very quickly, although they tend to run less efficiently. These languages have grown in popularity because they are well suited for Web applications, where time for network or database access rather than code-running efficiency is the limiting factor.[61] These languages thrive in the communication bazaar of the Web, collecting communities and code libraries that enrich them. They also interact with the markup language of the Web, HTML (Hypertext Markup Language). Their ease of use and implementation in addition to their applicability to the Web and interaction with HTML means they are often learned by nonprofessional programmers in more casual contexts.

Programming languages make different trade-offs between freedom and constraint and offer different affordances for creativity, safety, standard means of expression, and reliability to programmers working in various contexts. These trade-offs are often related to the legibility of code for its dual audiences: the computer and the programmer. For example, the legibility and ease of learning for novices are reasons for the BASIC programming language's popularity, although it is not a particularly fast or efficient language for the computer to execute. These trade-offs are visible in the evolution of programming languages I discussed earlier, but these trade-offs also apply across the thousands of languages currently available. Software running in Ruby might be easier to write, but it tends to run more slowly than software in the C programming language, in part because C offers fewer "safety nets" for programmers. The C and C++ programming languages offer features such as direct memory manipulation, operator overloading, and the ability to redefine key words in a preprocessor that can help optimize programs for specific contexts, but these features can make it difficult to check errors and can decrease legibility if a programmer isn't careful. Some of these useful but "dangerous" features are not available in languages like Java. The software environment in which a person programs—often called integrated development environments, or IDEs—also makes a huge difference in what is possible to say or even for a programmer to learn what is possible to say in a language. Some IDEs highlight syntax and automatically tab and organize code in ways that are easier for programmers to read. Thousands of code languages, frameworks, libraries, and support software have features tailored to specific programming contexts and are shaped by unique technical factors. Specificities of tools matter for programming, just as they do for writing.

The technical affordances of programming languages intersect in complicated ways with the communities that use the languages and the composition spaces in which they circulate. As their trade-offs with memory manipulation and safety might suggest, C and C++ are used in memory and graphics-heavy contexts such as game programming, where efficiency is critical and programmers are highly specialized. In contrast, Ruby is useful for development of Web and mobile software applications. Java has an organizational structure that can mimic a top-down bureaucracy, similar to some of its commercial contexts for use. Niche languages such as Objective C for the iPhone and Processing for art and design circulate among specialized communities and are imprinted by the communication and composition practices of those communities. Another social factor shaping programming languages is their popularity: texts written in more common computer languages have a larger pool in which to circulate, just as texts written in more common human languages do. If a software program needs to circulate widely on the Web, it will need to be written in a language such as Javascript, PHP, or Ruby, but if a person is writing a small program for their personal use or if a development team doesn't need to circulate their code widely, they can implement their program in a less common language such as Scala or Lua or Haskell.

Any linear history of programming languages tells only part of the story. Programming languages have evolved along many paths, which alternately merge, run parallel to each other, or diverge. And popular programming languages never go away: COBOL and Fortran still have millions of lines of code running in legacy business and manufacturing software. We can still, however, make a few generalities about this evolution: over the past 60 years, designers of programming languages have attempted to make more writer-friendly languages that increase the semantic value of source code and release writers from needing to know details about the computer's hardware. Some important changes along this path in programming language design include the use of words rather than numbers, automatic memory management, structured program organization, code libraries, code comments, and the development of programming environments to enhance the legibility of code. The historically persistent trade-offs between the roles of hardware and the many layers of software point to the difficulties of drawing lines between the physical engineering of computational machines and the many different languages we use to control them. Moreover, the rise and fall and rise again of languages such as Lisp suggest that language specifications inevitably intersect with social and technical factors. Lisp was an academic language impractical for production software until computer processors could run it more efficiently. I've concentrated here on the evolution of programming languages rather than computer hardware, but as the popularity of Lisp demonstrates, the two threads are inseparable.

While programming languages have continued to evolve toward greater abstraction, they still have a long way to go to be "natural language." As the syntax of computer code has grown to resemble human language (especially English[62]), the requirements for precise expression in programming have shifted but not disappeared. Highly readable languages such as Python, Ruby, and Javascript still require logical thinking and attention to explicit expressions of procedures. This persistent requirement of precision is key to our exploration of programming as a tool for thought and to our next discussion about the relationship between programming and human language.

Language in Action

Programming became a kind of writing when it moved from physical wiring and electromechanics to a system of symbolic representation. But there are significant differences between writing and programming as symbolic systems. Programming *is* writing because it is symbols inscribed on a

surface and designed to be read, but programming is also designed to executed by the computer. Because it represents procedures to be executed by
a computer, programming is a type of *action* as well as a type of writing.

The capability of code to make things happen through language has led
some to present it as fundamentally different from writing and speech, as
when Alexander Galloway claims, "Code is the only language that does
what it says."[63] However, this distinction is as false as the "great divide"
scholars have tried to make between writing and speech. Contrary to Galloway's claim, theories of language as symbolic action in rhetoric from Kenneth Burke and theories of speech acts from J. L. Austin suggest that we
cannot definitively distinguish between code and traditional writing
through their abilities to perform actions in language.[64] This is most clearly
seen in the written language of the law and the language of verbal promises. But, as Burke argued, "All acts of language materialize a certain reality."[65] Programmer and essayist Richard Gabriel would agree: "Artists who
create by writing or producing other representations of what the world is or
could be are also laying out a map for how the world could become."[66] Textual writing and code represent as well as construct the world.

However, the ways that code can enact things in the world are quite different from the ways that text or human language can. Speech act theory
can help us characterize those differences: code and text both have audiences, intent, and effects, which play out very differently between the
two symbolic writing systems. In contrast to prior theories that focused on
language as description, Austin noted that statements such as "I bet you
a dollar that he makes the next shot" or "I now pronounce you married"
or "Bring me my shoes" are not descriptive, nor are they true or false;
instead, they *enact* something in the world. Or, rather, they are *attempting*
to enact something in the world. Many factors can intervene to sabotage
their actions; if someone does not accept the bet, if the speaker lacks the
authority to marry a couple, or if the intended audience fails to hear that
the speaker wants her shoes, then the implied action does not happen.
Austin calls these failed statements "infelicitous." To be "felicitous," statements like these must be uttered in the right context and according to
the conventional procedure they invoke, they must be stated by a person
with the right authority, and they must be heard by the person to whom
they are directed. Austin begins his lectures in *How to Do Things with Words*
by naming such statements "performative," but he ultimately fails to find a
basis to separate performative statements from descriptive statements. By
the end of the lecture series, he proposes that *all* language implies a kind
of action.[67]

Instead of thinking of code or human language as purely performative or descriptive, then, we can think of them as being performative and descriptive to different degrees.[68] To characterize the degrees to which language is performative and descriptive, Austin introduces three forces: locutionary, illocutionary, and perlocutionary. An act with locutionary force describes something. Illocutionary force refers to the speaker's intention in uttering the act. Perlocutionary force "is *the achieving* of certain *effects* by saying something," such as persuading or warning someone.[69] All speech is both locutionary and illocutionary, although the achievement of effects—the perlocutionary force—depends on social context.[70] Extending Austin, John Searle argued that we must consider language rules in social context in order to understand speech acts.[71] Searle draws an analogy: although baseball is governed by rules, a study limited to its formal rules would not tell us much about the game. To study the speech act is to study the whole game of baseball—not just its formal rules, but its context, culture, and participants.[72] For baseball as well as speech, context shapes what it means to perform within a rule system.

In the same way, we must look at programming as more than just formal rules. As the history of programming language use and development above suggested, programming is also a sociolinguistic system. This is, in part, because human programmers inevitably operate in social contexts. Yasmin Kafai and Quinn Burke argue that programming draws its power and worth from its circulation in social networks and communities.[73] Computers are also socially contextualized; they are objects that are both controlled by language and can be used to manipulate linguistic symbols. Exploring the connections between computer and human language, Terry Winograd and Fernando Flores argue that "computers do not exist ... outside of language."[74] Their power as well as their social context is derived from the human language on which programming builds. For Winograd and Flores, the computer is controlled by code language in social contexts and can be used to produce socially embedded text. These linguistic objects are speech acts, they claim: code language makes commitments and changes in the world just as human speech does. And just as human speech has both locutionary and illocutionary forces, so does computer code.[75]

Yet computer code does not collapse completely into human language. Code has separate audiences for its descriptive and performative functions: programmers must imagine the procedure's performance to read and write the description of a procedure, but the computer actually performs it. While writers can and do describe procedures to human readers in documents such as operation manuals, procedures are one of several "relatively nonverbal representations [that are] difficult, but sometime necessary, to capture in words," according to writing researchers Linda Flower and John Hayes.[76] Part of the difficulty in capturing procedures in prose lies in the author's need to assume what the audience already knows and what they must learn to enact the procedure. If the reader does not have enough information or does not want to be persuaded, the perlocutionary effects of speech or text, as Austin reminds us, can be infelicitous. The social properties of language can cause infelicitous interactions, but they also facilitate literature and human communication as we know it. However, in programming, the computer only "knows" what it is told; it has a predictable perlocutionary force. As Ada Lovelace wrote in her notes to Charles Babbage's protocomputer, "The Analytical Engine has no pretensions whatever to *originate* anything. It can do whatever we *know how to order it* to perform."[77] With a perfect explanation of procedures, a program is automatically felicitous—nebulous social factors cannot sabotage it.

While this can eliminate some of the confusion about what the computer needs to be told to enact procedures, it presents a different challenge to writers: describing a procedure perfectly. Describing procedures perfectly is nontrivial, and as programs grow in complexity, the capacity for a person or team to envision the whole system and scenario for software becomes impossible. Invoking Ada Lovelace's statement about the computer's predictability, Alan Turing winked at this complexity and declared that computers did not infallibly do what programmers tell them to do; on the contrary, he wrote, "Machines take me by surprise with great frequency."[78] Code's perfect *technical* perlocutionary affordance is no guarantee of results in software.

This perlocutionary affordance of programming is both an advantage and a disadvantage of code relative to writing. In the next section, we'll explore more of these trade-offs and interactions between code and human language as forms of communication.

Affordances of Form in Code

As Wittgenstein observed, human language works not through explicit definitions or explanation, but through use and exchange. Human language, in other words, works in a bottom-up and social fashion: it gathers meaning gradually as it circulates among its users.[79] Walter Ong contrasts this property of human language with programming:

> Computer "languages," ... resemble human languages ... in some ways but are forever totally unlike human languages in that they do not grow out of the un-

conscious but directly out of consciousness. Computer language rules ("grammar") are stated first and thereafter used. The "rules" of grammar in natural human languages are used first and can be abstracted from usage and stated explicitly in words only with difficulty and never completely.[80]

Programming works in a formal and top-down fashion: it gathers meaning only as terms and procedures are explicitly defined by its writers. Code must adhere strictly to set formats to be understood by computers, whereas human language can convey a "gist" of an idea even if the details are fuzzy. Along these lines, Jay David Bolter draws on Charles Peirce to claim that computer programming is an "exercise in applied semiotics," a sign system in which everything is defined in relation to another sign—a closed system.[81]

The fact that code relies on explicit definitions and form is sometimes a source of critique. Programming is misrepresented as strictly technical practice, a right-or-wrong activity with little creative potential. For example, composition scholar Joel Haefner argues that code cannot capture the nuances, double meanings, and richness of human language and experience. After translating Hamlet's "To be or not to be" statement into a yes/no Boolean statement in the C programming language, he laments that "the simultaneous dichotomy Shakespeare demands—to consider being and nonbeing—cannot exist in the text of code."[82] Although Haefner admits his translation is "contrived," it is worse than that; it is misleading. In fact, a computer program is capable of offering far more complex representations than Haefner proposes. Defending the computer against accusations of inflexibility such as the one Haefner wages, Ian Bogost writes, "We think of computers as frustrating, limiting and simplistic not because they execute processes, but because they are frequently programmed to execute simplistic processes."[83] A more inventive way to translate the speech would be to use complex fuzzy logic common in artificial intelligence programming. But even better would be to leave poor Hamlet alone, with the understanding that neither programming nor writing can serve as a direct translation of the other. We might say that critiques of computers chopping up the world too cleanly or not responding thoughtfully to their users are modern versions of Socrates's complaint about writing as being a dull child who travels too far from its parent, the author. While it is true that Socrates's dull child cannot directly engage in meaningful discourse, Walter Ong points out that the only way we know about Socrates is through Plato's writing.[84] It might be nice to have seen Socrates in live discourse, but Socrates in writing is the Socrates that was able to survive for centuries.

Neither speech nor writing perfectly represents the other; they have different possibilities of scale, audience, and duration. Similarly, code allows for a form of representation different from writing. To measure programming by the standards of writing is to call it mechanistic and unnuanced. To measure writing by the standards of programming is to call it sloppy and unclear. From a rhetorical standpoint, we might think of the ways speech, writing, and code represent and convey information as their Aristotelian "available means." From a design standpoint, we can think of their various affordances. Although the arguments above indicate that it is difficult to distinguish between speech, writing, and programming at their borders, we still must attempt to take code on its own terms, rather than as a poor substitute for speech or writing. Below, I point to some of the affordances of code's form for representing and scaling up as well as for creative purposes.

Discreteness and Abstraction, Fidelity and Scale

Although it may not serve well to represent the nuances of Hamlet's indecision, the discrete nature of code gives it power to represent a different form of complexity. Code can be used to build complex, chained, and multilayered procedures because of its discreteness. In working code, each process is represented unambiguously from the perspective of the computer, and has a concrete location and description. The computer will interpret procedures as precisely as one writes them (not, as Turing pointed out, as one *means* them).[85] Because of their discreteness and precision, processes can be piled on each other, making complex and interconnected systems. Through loops, a program can perform the same operation millions of times in a row; through recursion, a process can call itself, nesting those loops. The discrete representation of code also enables one to copy a procedure from one program and paste an exact copy into another program or to use code libraries. The exact same results of the code are not guaranteed in this new context, but this perfect transfer of process is something to which written instruction manuals can only aspire. This perfect transfer is even more difficult in speech, as the game of "Telephone" attests. Code can convey and transfer information about procedures across space and time on a larger scale than speech or writing.

Of course, writing is also discrete. In written English, 26 letters plus punctuation are routinely used to convey complex ideas on a large scale. Attending a performance of *Hamlet*'s original staging is no longer possible, but we know about *Hamlet*'s text because its text can travel across space and time. To travel in this way, the written text of *Hamlet* necessarily eliminates the gestural, vocal, nuanced complexity of *Hamlet*'s staging. And, as any letter writer or Emily Dickinson scholar will attest, the translation of handwritten text to print also sacrifices meaning. With this sacrifice, print enables multiple and *identical* copies of a text to circulate beyond a writer's immediate contexts.[86] The availability of photocopiers in the 1960s meant that handwritten text could also circulate in facsimile editions, although it may say something about written language that few print publications call for this fidelity.[87]

The trade-offs between fidelity and scale in continuous and discrete representations of processes go beyond just speech and writing and have been central to philosophical discourse about industrial processes since Karl Marx. Max Weber, drawing on Marx and commenting on industrial capitalism's reduction of information and action in order to scale up production, feared that this "rationalization" of practice would result in a dampening of human spirit. Marx frames this separation of worker from knowledge about processes as political and material; Weber pinned it to the faceless grind of industry. While machines discretize human gesture, writing does the same for *logos*, philosopher Bernard Stiegler claims.[88] Stiegler's concept of *grammatization* takes the concept of rationalization from theories of industrial processes to symbolic representations such as programming and writing. He draws on Jacques Derrida's concept of grammatology, Sylvan Auroux's "grammatisation," and Heidegger's theories of technics to claim that grammatization "concerns all processes of discretization of the continuous."[89] He describes the grammatization of industrial machines—machines that discretized the gestures of human factory workers—alongside the grammatization of writing. Writing, like these machines, discretizes language and thought, breaks it up into words and sentences. In this way, writing throws out gesture, nuance, and tone of speech. But in exchange for this fidelity, it can scale; writing can be perfectly replicated in other contexts.[90]

Stiegler draws this grammatization process forward from writing to digital technologies and points out its benefits and drawbacks. To explore the trajectory and implications of digital grammatization, he takes a cue from Weber and traces rationalization back to the Enlightenment. He observes that the regularization of science led to repeatable experiments and an explosion of knowledge. But there was another side to this rationalization. As Adorno and Horkheimer argued, the Holocaust was another result of "the rationalization of the world," with radically different implications than the Enlightenment.[91] The Holocaust parsed humanity into "rational" and discrete categories and allowed for a devastating othering of certain human categories. Just as Weber feared a loss of humanity through industrialization, Stiegler argues that digital technologies threaten our mind and memory through the way they externalize it, discretize it, and displace "the infinities" that make human life possible or worth living.[92] His connection to Plato's anxiety about writing is obvious and intentional. And, indeed, by way of Derrida's explication of Plato, Stiegler calls the rationalization of information through digital technology a *pharmakon*,[93] something that is both poison and medicine. Recalling Marx, Stiegler argues that the relentless and blind forces of capitalism drive rationalization toward poison.

But to focus only on the information lost in the process of rationalization is to tell only the poison side of the *pharmakon* story. While digital technologies "rationalize" certain information and knowledge, they also reveal and enable the creation of new kinds of knowledge. In a broad, historical analysis of the Industrial Revolution, James Beniger argues that crises of control drove the rationalization of human action, which then led to new ways of organizing information. Rationalizing technologies such as the clock, factory, and train—the technologies that Weber feared were stealing our souls—allowed Western society to scale up governance of an increasing population and respond to increasingly complex demands on organization. In Beniger's terms, the "control revolution" led to the "information society." To put a finer point on these historical arguments: saying that rationalizing technologies have *affordances* is altogether different from saying they lead to either genocide or progress. Rationalizing technologies make certain things possible that were not possible before, at least not in the same way.

Like machine manufacture over individual craftsmanship, there are complicated trade-offs between the symbolic representation systems of writing over speech or programming over writing. Although analog, continuous representations such as speech or handwriting allow for infinite variation, their information does not scale well. Both writing and programming cut out some of the contextual information of their lower-order representations—they rationalize or grammatize it—in order to scale up. Programming and writing both sacrifice richer context and nuance for precision, scalability, interactivity, and widespread dissemination. These trade-offs are key to understanding their affordances. Even technologies that circulate analog representations—the photocopier, the telephone, or the tape recorder, for instance—carry only some of the nuances of their originals. But digital information scales and can travel: Daniel Kohanski notes, "Digital technology trades perfect representation of the original data for a perfect preservation of the representation."[94] This is the difference between the bootleg concert tape, which is muddied after too many copies, and the digital MP3. Although it can never fully represent nuanced experiences of live performances, the discreteness of the digital is where the power of modern computing lies.

But code and writing do more than just *reduce* information from writing and speech; they transform it. They spatialize temporal information. In a transcribed speech, Stiegler argues,

> The grammatisation of a type of behaviour consists in a spatialisation of time, given that behaviour is above all a form of time (a meaningful sequence of words, an operational sequence of gestures, a perceptual flow of sensations, and so on). Spatialising time means, for example, transforming the *temporal flow* of a speech such as the one I am delivering to you here and now into a *textual space*, a de-temporalised form of this speech: it is thus to make a spatial object. And this is what is going on from alphabetic writing to digital technology, as shown by Walter Ong: "Writing ... initiated what print and computers only continue, the reduction of dynamic sound to quiescent space."[95]

Ong uses the word *reduction* in the sentence that Stiegler highlights here, although space is not simply a reduction of time. It is something different altogether. Code, as a digital technology, follows this same process of grammatization that Stiegler describes for speech's transformation to text. But, additionally, code can *retemporalize* information. When code is written, it translates processes into text. When it runs, it turns text into process, albeit a process that is digitized, rationalized, grammatized. This transubstantiation of code is captured in its multifaceted manifestations in the law, as text *and* machine, or, as description *and* process.[96]

Jacques Derrida provides a rich way of looking at this translation of information across modes. For Derrida, writing does not reduce speech; it exceeds it. Exploding Saussure's differentiation of the word as *signifier* from the concept of being *signified*, Derrida argued that, without writing, we would not have organizing concepts at all. Derrida's surprising move in *Of Grammatology* was to posit that writing rather than speech was primary.[97] N. Katherine Hayles takes this argument one step further by arguing that code exceeds rather than reduces writing. The way that code represents processes makes us look at the world in a new way, a worldview she calls "The Regime of Computation." This new worldview sees processes as potentially discrete in the same way that the worldview we got from writing sees concepts as discrete.[98] Like Derrida and Stiegler, Hayles sees a complicated and reciprocal relationship across modes. Even if we aren't writing with the computer, and even if we cannot program, she observes that we are always working in *language plus code*: code has forever changed writing in the same way that writing has forever changed speech.[99] The existence of multiple modes changes our rhetorical choices and how we think about them.

Derrida, Hayles, and Stiegler all posit a hierarchy of abstraction from speech to writing, with vectors of influence pointing both directions; Hayles and Stiegler take the hierarchy already established between speech and writing and elevate it to programming. If writing is a second-order semiotic system that builds on speech, programming is a third-order semiotic system that builds on writing. This hierarchy of abstraction does not imply a hierarchy of value, however. Because of the complicated relationship between these modes, we cannot convey equivalent information across them. Through the grammatization of sound, writing can excise tonal nuance and dialogism from speech, and through the grammatization of processes, programming can excise ambiguity and affect from writing or other source ideas. Both can attempt to account for this loss—through punctuation, typography, or style in writing or through fuzzy logic or human input in programming, for example. But, as this section has argued, grammatization is a transformation that provides certain affordances. We might choose to write rather than speak if we are making a complicated argument that we'd like to reach a large audience at different times, as I am doing in this book. We might choose to program if we want to simulate a complicated system that we would like for many others to engage with, as computer game makers do. The way that code grammatizes processes means that it facilitates procedural ways of thinking and allows new kinds of information to circulate in new ways. The availability of speech, writing, and code for composition makes for complex rhetorical choices: none is now a default, and all offer different, intermediated affordances. Complex literacies—which include the ability to engage with speech, writing, and code—may now be necessary to make these rhetorical choices.

Creativity with Code

Although code is often written primarily for its functional value (as read by the computer) rather than its aesthetic value (as read by other programmers), its dual audience introduces creative possibilities. Creative exploits in code, including what is sometimes called "codework," esoteric languages, and "pseudocode" poetry-code hybrids, demonstrate that it can accomplish some of the imaginative work of writing and speech. However, code's dual human and machine audience and its unique affordances of form allow for different kinds of creativity than these other modes. Significant work in critical code studies and software studies has been dedicated to these practices, in part because the creative affordances of code vis-à-vis writing can be most clearly illustrated through these literary-leaning examples. Creative code plays with the textual form of code and the machine interpretations of its processes, highlighting the tension between code's form and function as well as its audiences.

While these creative software and coding practices are only small slices of the landscape of contemporary composition in code, everyday coding is also a creative endeavor, a process by which people learn to think in new ways—although it's not always framed that way. Richard Gabriel complains, "Writing and programming are creative acts, yet we've tried to label programming as engineering (as if engineering weren't creative)."[100] As an example of creativity possible in coding style, Crista Videira Lopes's *Exercises in Programming Style,* inspired by Raymond Queneau's *Exercises in Style,* presents one common programming problem with 33 different constraints, each generating a different solution in code.[101] Creative code thus points to a much broader phenomenon about the affordances of code, the value of different constraints, and programming's complicated relation to human and machine audiences. As Mateas and Montfort argued, the play inherent in obfuscated and weird languages "refutes the idea that the programmer's task is automatic, value-neutral, and disconnected from the meanings of words in the world."[102] This connection of code to "words in the world" reminds us that programming of all kinds is imbricated in the social world where programmers learn and practice their craft.

As Videira Lopes suggests, code, like poetry, gains some of its expressive capabilities from the fact that its form is restricted.[103] For human readers of poetry and code, the structure helps them to interpret and appreciate the writer's creativity within the form. Referring to the parallels between the restricted forms of code and art, former IBM programmer and manager Frederick Brooks argues that "form is liberating."[104] Constraints engender creative solutions, and programs and poetry both offer flexible tools with which to work creatively within those forms. In an often-quoted passage, Brooks writes, "There is a delight in working in such a tractable medium. The programmer, like the poet, works only slightly removed from pure thought-stuff. ... Few media of creation are so flexible, so easy to polish and rework, so readily capable of realizing grand conceptual structures."[105] Brooks echoes the concept of programming as knowledge-building in his vision of it building grand conceptual structures. He goes on to distinguish the programmer from the poet in that the programmer can create tangible things: "The program construct, unlike the poet's words, is real in the sense that it moves and works, producing visible outputs separate from the construct itself."[106] But as we saw in our exploration of speech act theory and poststructuralist theories of language, we cannot draw lines between programming and writing so cleanly.

For standard programming environments, the objective is generally to produce code that is clear and consistent for both the computer and the human reader, to omit unnecessary processes for the computer and make active processes transparent to human readers. But even standard code can be poetic—"elegant"—when meaning and form merge in aesthetically pleasing ways, as Brooks suggests. Emphasizing the aesthetic value of code for human audiences, the influential computer scientist Donald Knuth famously conceived of "literate programming," arguing "Literature of the program genre is performable by machines, but that is not its main purpose. The computer programs that are truly beautiful, useful and profitable must be readable by people."[107] Through the idea of literate programming, Knuth has focused on human readers of code, promoting the idea of programming as an aesthetic as well as functional activity.

In their article on "obfuscation, weird languages and code aesthetics," Michael Mateas and Nick Montfort focus on these trade-offs between human and computer legibility in order to highlight some of the potentials of code as a form of creative expression. Mateas and Montfort argue that traditional values in programming—elegance and clarity—must be expanded to include the alternative aesthetic values and rhetorical purposes of playful code exemplified in "weird languages." Weird languages are not generally useful for business or production, though the ways they communicate different messages to computers and humans highlight some of programming's affordances. Pulling from theories of aesthetics and communication, Mateas and Montfort argue that "All coding inevitably involves double-coding. 'Good' code simultaneously specifies a mechanical process and talks about this mechanical process to a human reader."[108] They draw parallels from computational double-coding to words that have meanings in more than one language (e.g., *dire* in both French and English); we could extend their parallel to slang words and puns, which can push on double meanings to index different audiences.

The Shakespeare Programming Language (SPL) draws particular attention to the double-coding of programs for humans and computers. Here is a program, or "scene," from the language[109]:

```
Act II: Determining divisibility.
Scene I: A private conversation.
Juliet: Art thou more cunning than the Ghost?
Romeo: If so, let us proceed to scene V.
```

```
[Exit Romeo]
[Enter Hamlet]
Juliet: You are as villainous as the square root of Romeo!
Hamlet: You are as lovely as a red rose.
```

This function, or "scene," in SPL may not be any more poetic than Haefner's "To be or not to be" Boolean speech in C, but it is more inventive. In
SPL, variable names are Shakespearean characters—in this case, Romeo,
Juliet, and Hamlet—and constants are nouns such as "rose" and "codpiece."
SPL's compiler is built with a list of nouns designated 1 or –1. Nouns with a
negative connotation are assigned the value of –1 and prefixing them with
adjectives doubles the number; "sorry little codpiece" then has the value of
–4.[110] The SPL language allows for conditional jumps and value comparisons, as we can see in this example; scene V is a specific place elsewhere in
the program, and "art thou more cunning ..." is a value comparison. The
Chef programming language is another example of double-coding: Chef
programs are simultaneously recipes and machine instructions. The point
of SPL, Chef, and other weird languages is not to provide ways to solve
problems effectively in code, but to play with the borders between human
and computational interpretations of code. As Geoff Cox and Alex McLean
argue, these languages show that "rendering speech or code as mere written
words fails to articulate the richness of human-machine expression."[111]

Like weird languages, so-called obfuscating or esoteric code languages
are another creative play with the form of code. Rather than resembling
human genres like plays or recipes, they double-code by being very difficult
for programmers yet perfectly interpretable by the computer. Languages
such as Brainfuck remove the niceties of human legibility, such as meaningful variable and function names and white space, to produce code that is
nearly impossible for people to read. A Brainfuck "hello world" program—a
program that simply prints "hello world" on the screen—looks like this[112]:

```
++++++++++[>+++++++>++++++++++>+++>+<<<<>++.>+.++
+++++..+++.>++.<<++++++++++++++++.>.+++.------.---
-----.>+.>.
```

Malbolge, another obfuscating language, plays with the convention that
source code is a static text. It is self-modifying, which means that not just
the data is manipulated through the course of the program, but the code
also changes on the basis of its own instructions.[113] Here is a Malbolge
"HELLO WORld" [sic] program[114]:

```
(=<`$9]7<5YXz7wT.3,+O/o'K%$H"'~D|#z@b=`{^Lx8%$Xmr
kpohm-kNi;gsedcba`_^]\[ZYXWVUTSRQPONMLKJIHGFEDCBA
@?>=<;:9876543s+O<oLm
```

Although the language was specified in 1998, it took two years and complex cryptography and artificial intelligence techniques to write a program in it.[115]

Software performances like algoraves and the demoscene also speak simultaneously to the human and machine audiences for code. In algoraves, people perform by coding live on stage, generating visuals and sound.[116] The audience may not understand the code that drives the music, but the code—projected onto screens on the stage—is part of the performance. Sometimes even the live-coders don't understand why the algorithms generate particular audiovisual output, but the glitch and the bugs are part of the aesthetic.[117] Demoscene code is also performative at the nexus of code, visuals, and sound, but its code is honed and revised. Demoscene programs have highly compacted source code—often only a few kilobytes of data—that result in very sophisticated audiovisual "demonstrations." Demosceners show their skills by pushing archaic computer processors such as that of the Commodore 64 to their limit with graphical demos, usually in complex animations and audio. The aesthetic values of the demoscene are dependent not only on the resulting visual and audio display but also on the cleverness of the code tricks and processor used to create the display. Algorave and demoscene performances demand that audiences acknowledge both the human-accessible output and the computational processes that drive it. The code isn't just driving the art; it is inseparable from the art.

Attention to form is essential to working with any creative object, but this attention is especially critical for reading or analyzing code-based creative objects. Without this attention, Mateas and Wardrip-Fruin both argue, we cannot fully account for the interactive aspects of a piece of creative software.[118] Espen Aarseth's early work with electronic literature provides one analytical framework that accounts for a text's code as well as its output; he named the two different writings that result in dynamic, digital compositions "scriptons" and "textons." Scriptons are essentially the code that runs the creative works, and textons are the visible, human-accessible outputs of the scriptons. Aarseth calls the combination of these writings "ergotic literature."[119] Similarly, in the field of composition, David Rieder argues that we need an approach that "recognizes interplay and upholds the distinction between the two species [of code and text]."[120] N. Katherine

Hayles calls phenomena like this interplay of code and text a "creolization" of new media and offers "media specific analysis" as a way to analyze the objects that result from this interplay.[121]

Because writing and critiquing these kinds of works—ergotic literature, weird languages, games, demos, algorave coding, and so forth—requires some understanding of both the code and its output, Mateas argues that "procedural literacy" is essential for any new media practitioner or critic. Mateas goes further to say that procedural literacy is important for people beyond just those associated with creative new media projects—it's an essential skill for everyone.[122] Echoing the arguments for coding literacy that we saw in the past chapter, Mateas brings us full circle, connecting creative coding with the code that we see structuring so much of our world now. Although they circulate in different spheres, "everyday code" can be inflected by the same creative play that literary code highlights. And both operate among the combined social and technical audiences of humans and machines. What's more, these examples show that coding and writing can no longer be fully separated from each other—further proof that they are intertwining in a new iteration of literacy.

Social Coding

In his extended description of code in *Bloomberg Business*, Paul Ford lucidly explains many of the technical aspects of programming, but he also attends to who writes it, how they think, and what it means for the type of software that gets written. Understanding how code works, according to Ford, includes understanding some of its social aspects. Programming is often projected as a pure meritocracy—if the code runs, you're good; if you contribute good patches to open-source software, you're good.[123] While programmers will sometimes talk about the power they accrue from working alone and communicating directly with their machine, this asocial vision of code is a myth. Networks of mentorships, work habits, and word of mouth about techniques and opportunities are just some of the social structures that surround and support programming. The machines that run software are not social in the same way that humans are, but the ways that software gets written and circulated and taken up are still shaped by social factors.[124]

In this section, I use contemporary literacy studies to think through some of the social processes that impinge on programming as a form of writing. The intersecting social and material forces in programming are different from those in writing, but theories of literacy can help us understand how they work and how they shape the practices of programming, as well as the populations who do it.

Collaborative Coding

Ultimately, all programming is collaborative—although it is often asynchronously so. Even if they aren't working alongside other programmers physically or online, programmers work with languages, machines, and programming environments designed by others. They work with libraries of procedures or codebases or frameworks programmed by teams of other programmers. Social influences in programming are particularly apparent for a programmer entering a new coding community and learning to communicate effectively within that space. She is often faced with *legacy code*—code that constitutes an ongoing software project. This is a common situation in workplaces where software is used and written—the project may be 5 or 20 or even 50 years old or it must interact with preexisting software or hardware. Even with perfect knowledge of a particular language, a programmer must learn to work within the existing system that has been established by previous teams of programmers. Nathan Ensmenger explains how social and historical forces are at work in legacy code maintenance:

> When charged with maintaining a so-called legacy system, the programmer is working not with a blank slate but a palimpsest. Computer code is indeed a kind of writing, and software development a form of literary production. But the ease with which computer code can be written, modified, and deleted belies the durability of the underlying document. Because software is a tangible record, not only of the intentions of the original designer but of the social, technological, and organization context in which it was developed, it cannot be easily modified.[125]

Entering into a preexisting software project, a programmer must work within the history of the legacy code and the "palimpsest" of human influences on the code in order to successfully update it. Frederick Brooks likens this kind of programming to the building of cathedrals: they are built over many generations, and to maintain their structural integrity, subsequent generations of builders must bow to the original designer's grand vision.[126] The writing of code is shaped by previous practices of organization, and for this reason, large commercial codebases often change slowly.

These code palimpsests and communities recall both James Paul Gee's concept of "Discourse" and Mikhail Bakhtin's theory of speech genres, both of which have been foundational to social theories of literacy. Bakhtin argued that all speech occurs in socially shaped genres and that all "utterances" are refractions of words from previous speakers. In the same way that Bakhtin portrays every act of communication as building on previous ones, code is always written by refracting previous code, or "utterances" from other programmers, either in the form of palimpsistic codebases or programming languages. No speaker is "after all, the first speaker, the one who disturbs the entire silence of the universe," Bakhtin writes.[127] No programmer codes as if she were the first programmer.

Even before joining a team of programmers or an established software project, programmers learn to code by following examples from others who have come before them. Programmers shape their coding styles on the basis of what they see in particular language communities or in workplaces where they first learned to work with a large body of code. Every coding community has conventions of style, and a programmer joining a new community must learn how to communicate successfully not only with the computer, but also within that community. We might think of this learning process for programming through Gee's description of learning secondary "Discourses." For Gee, people travel within and among different Discourse communities, each of which is loosely marked by common sets of practices. These practices are constantly shifting and layered with established conventions.[128] Discourses are not formally defined, but instead live within their communities, specifically within the people who inhabit these communities: "The individual instantiates, gives body to a Discourse every time he or she acts or speaks, and thus carries it, and ultimately changes it, through time."[129] Our home languages and cultures, the ones we acquire effortlessly, make up our primary Discourse communities. The Discourses we explicitly learn—such as any form of literacy—are secondary.[130]

We can see each new programmer as adding her discourse performance to the palimpsest of code and coding practices. Programmers may prefer to rewrite code in order to enact their own style and because reading other people's code can sometimes be more challenging than writing it from scratch. But because code is written in communities and programmers must collaborate across time and space to maintain it, a fresh programmer coming to a project is often constrained by the local discourse of the project. As programmers learn and work in different project discourses, they are shaped by these discourses in turn. In this way, individual programmers are also palimpsests—layered with coding practices learned in school, on the Web, and from a history of workplaces. This is also, of course, true of individual literates: we are affected by our personal history of education and reading and writing. As Web-based applications and communities that organize themselves through the Web grow to dominate the contexts in which people learn to code, this social impact on learning may even be accentuated.[131]

A look at a couple of specific collaborative practices will help to illustrate some of the ways code and programmers are shaped by discourse and the code "utterances" that precede their work. We look here at "code review" and "pair programming," both of which are central to the software development style called "agile." Agile development has been a popular response to "waterfall" development, which is top-down software design that outlines an entire project, parses it out into separately coded subsections, and then assembles the project once these subsections are completed. The complexities of software can foil waterfall's trickle-down process, whereas agile development acknowledges the inevitability of these complexities with frequent testing and code review. Agile methodologies attempt to work *with* social factors in coding.[132]

Code review, which follows some of the same patterns as peer review in writing, is a common practice on larger software projects. Programmers put their code out to be reviewed by their coworkers, some of whom may even work in different countries. Rather than testing whether the code works, they read its text, asking questions similar to those asked by peer reviewers of writing, but with an eye toward the collaborative model of software writing. A reviewer of code, then, acts as an authentic human reader, evaluating not whether the code can be executed by the computer, but whether the code works for its intended purposes and whether other programmers will be able to read and understand how the code works.

For instance, the Mozilla Development Center notes that one of the issues a code reviewer should consider is maintainability: "Code which is unreadable is impossible to maintain. If the reviewer has to ask questions about the purpose of a piece of code, then it is probably not documented well enough. Does the code follow the coding style guide?"[133] Mozilla outlines its style explicitly in a "coding style guide" in part because it follows an open-source development paradigm, but the conventions of style are implicit in many other workplaces and coding communities, just as they are in discourse communities.[134] Here is an excerpt of the Mozilla Style Guide that enforces the community-based standards of code review and introduces it to newcomers:

> This document attempts to explain the basic styles and patterns that are used in the Mozilla codebase. New code should try to conform to these standards so that it is as easy to maintain as existing code. Of course every rule has an exception, but it's important to know the rules nonetheless!

This is particularly directed at people new to the Mozilla codebase, who are in the process of getting their code reviewed. Before getting a review, please read over this document and make sure your code conforms to the recommendations here.[135]

Through enforcing style rules and good coding practices, code review helps to keep the code written within development communities intelligible to all participants in the community. It enforces the discourse of the community. But code review also influences the programmers who participate in the project. Programmers cite feedback from the open-source community as a primary motivator for their participation because it helps them improve their skills.[136]

In pair programming, another common social design practice in agile development, the time between code writing and reviewing is collapsed: pairs of programmers write code together. This practice not only helps programmers anticipate bugs but also helps programmers share knowledge of the particular codebase, local programming style, and general knowledge about programming. Pair-programming code is then collectively rather than individually owned, like the coauthorship common in many professional writing contexts. The pair has to understand the code together, which forces them to communicate.[137] Because of its social aspects, pair programming and its enforcement of social rules of programming can be stifling for some programmers.[138] However, many people learn efficient or good programming practices through pair programming. In a debate about the benefits of pair programming on Jeff Atwood's popular programming blog, Bryan Arendt writes, "Although it feels like running with weighted shoes at times I have been able to quickly pick up some quick tips, shortcut keys and other little tricks that I would have never known about. Also when I am back to programming all by myself it feels like I have removed the weights from my shoes. I can run that much faster after practicing with the weights."[139]

Both code review and pair programming highlight the fact that code is *simultaneously* technical and social. The computer's interpretation of code is only one factor in good programming. The legibility of code and its processes for other human readers is also critical, and the values for code reading are socially shaped.

Social Organization of Code in an Online Coding Community

Open-source software communities, in particular, demonstrate the ways that coding is influenced by social as well as technological factors. Large open-source software projects such as the Linux operating system and the

Firefox browser (developed by Mozilla, discussed earlier) have thousands of active contributors who program on their own time, on their companies' time (both sanctioned and in secret), and for school projects.[140] These communities have an array of formal and informal requirements for membership that are enforced in both the code-based permission structure and the socially situated discourse of the project. As Karim Lakhani and Robert Wolf report from a study of 684 software developers in 287 free or open-source software projects, community identity is very strong and cohesive in these projects and structures the participation of members of the community.[141] Anthropologist Gabriella Coleman describes the open-source community of Debian as being held together not only by their shared coding project but also by "a set of moral precepts—transparency, openness, accountability, and non-discrimination—that are used to establish correct procedures for technological production, licensing, and social organization."[142]

To see this in practice, we can look at the community surrounding the FreeBSD operating system, an open-source programming project that has been actively maintained for more than 20 years. FreeBSD is a UNIX-based operating system focused on security and stability, so it is often used for mission-critical servers and embedded computing in commercial devices. NASA and other areas of the U.S. government as well as corporations such as Apple take advantage of the fact that FreeBSD's lenient license does not require them to give back to the community as the more common open-source GNU General Public License (GPL) does. In the FreeBSD community and many other open-source development communities, the membership and boundaries of the community are as much about social protocol as about writing code.

In a personal interview, Mike Silbersack, a FreeBSD developer who has been part of the community for more than fifteen years, offers advice to programmers looking to join an open-source project: "The important thing is finding something you're interested in and a community you feel comfortable with. And, just like with any group, you've got to join their mailing lists, and just absorb it. Don't try to join in the conversation for the first month. You've got to, you know, you've got to understand what's going on around you before you jump in."[143] In other words, membership in open-source communities such as FreeBSD depends not simply on the quality of code written but also on how fully someone masters the discourse of the particular community. The FreeBSD project has an elaborate structure for participation involving several hundred "committers," a nine-person core team that loosely oversees the project, and the FreeBSD Foundation, whose goal is to support the project.[144] Committers can mentor new members interested in working on FreeBSD and joining their ranks. As Mike describes it, the mentorship process requires a significant commitment from both parties but ultimately results in tighter social ties, a stronger community, and a better codebase.

The process of membership in FreeBSD and other open-source programming communities evokes Jean Lave and Etienne Wenger's theory of "communities of practice." A "community of practice" is shaped by discourse and contains masters, apprentices, and people along a whole continuum of participation levels.[145] Open-source projects often rely on a handful of strong personalities to keep them going, but successful communities have socially enforced structures that ensure new members can join as others lose interest.[146] In this way, as Lave and Wenger write, the "mastery resides not in the master, but in the organization of the community of practice of which the master is a part."[147] Mike explains, "There's no person who's in charge of FreeBSD." He goes on to describe the decentralized organization of the FreeBSD project: "Basically, once you—if you—go through the process and become a FreeBSD committer, you can go work on whatever you want, as long as people aren't objecting to it. So of course, usually you would want to build a consensus among other people in your subject area." A good community member, then, is highly cognizant of his audience—the other programmers working on FreeBSD and the end users of the software.

Being aware of both audiences involves a sophisticated understanding of the codebase as well as the use cases for it. In response to my question about what makes a good contributor to FreeBSD, Mike replied:

> First of all, if they're adding something to the system, they have to make sure—well, if it's going to be disruptive, it has to be useful to a large number of people. Socially, I think, of course they have to be aware of whoever else cares about that area they want to work on, and try to be preemptive talking to them about the changes they're going to make. And on the other hand, if they put the change in, and they get some sort of flak back from it, they have to be prepared to back the change out, which early on seems like a big deal to you. … And learn who's giving you a reasonable response, and what the consensus is, because you can't always make everybody happy.

Successful contribution of code depends on the committer's understanding of how significant a change will be, and that understanding is based on a deep awareness of the range of users for FreeBSD. In other words, a rhetorical awareness of the community's range of responses is critical to successful participation in it. Coleman notes a similar phenomenon in another open-source community, where the "technical rhetoric" that accompanies a commit can affect its status: technical rhetoric "includes a presentation of the code, a corollary written statement, or a justification as to why no change should be made."[148]

For Mike, success in the FreeBSD project has translated into a sophisticated social and procedural awareness of audience: "Certainly it's taught me how to work with a large piece of code with lots of different developers interacting. And made me aware of how changes I make interact with other people." When he fails to fully account for one of these audiences, the community will police the infraction in writing on the collective listserv. Enforcement of shared procedural discourse norms can contribute to the sense of community. Mike explains, "I never got my hand slapped too badly. Occasionally, I did. You know I really felt like I was part of a community." In this statement, we can see how Mike connects the enforcement of community norms to the identity of the community itself.

This feeling of being part of a community is central to programmers' enjoyment of free or open-source software (F/OSS) participation, according to Lakhani and Wolf. Models of extrinsic motivation, in terms of cost-benefit calculations, have been unable to fully account for the intense participation patterns of F/OSS; Lakhani and Wolf indicate instead that the joy of doing work in a challenging and supportive community justifies many programmers' participation in F/OSS.[149] The Ruby language community exhibits a similarly strong collective identity. Its leader, Yukihiro Matsumoto, who goes by "Matz" online, praises the community for its cohesion: "It's surprising that people in the Ruby community, having such a wide range of variety and given its size, still continue to be nice to each other. I believe the community is Ruby's greatest strength." Matz also sees the community surrounding Ruby as essential to the popularity of the language.[150] Open-source programming projects provide a particularly resonant example of discourse communities for programming. Through them, we can see how the writing of code can be socially as well as technically influenced.

Coding Literacy Is "Leaky" Knowledge

Literacy learned in one context can spill over into others as it becomes part of an individual's identity and repertoire of practices. Deborah Brandt describes literacy as "leaky" knowledge; literacy cannot be reckoned like other business assets because corporations cannot own the knowledge housed in their personnel. Corporations can, however, attempt to cultivate and control the knowledge circulating within them.[151] They can do this by regulating writing practices and by "embed[ding] knowledge deeply within organizational routines and structures so that it does not belong to any one person."[152] Conversely, the knowledge employees gain at their jobs is also portable.[153] Brandt tells the stories of people who have learned accounting or letter writing in their workplaces and have then transferred their skills into their personal and family lives as exemplars of literacy leveraging. The Americans she studies use the literacy skills they learn in their jobs to enrich their home lives through better communication and organization.[154] Similarly, Sylvia Scribner describes ways the Vai people of Liberia transfer their literacy knowledge into writing for private communications, documenting dreams, charting family history, composing tales for children, and for keeping track of feasts and crops.[155] When people have literacy, they use it in all sorts of ways.

Like other forms of knowledge, coding literacy travels with people and spills into new contexts. As we saw in the examples of the Mozilla and Free-BSD projects, open-source software communities use committer privileges and boundary-policing of house style and values to regulate coding practices and control the product. Yet open-source projects have an incentive to encourage leaky knowledge among their participants: as noted above, a significant motivator for F/OSS participation is that skills learned in F/OSS projects can be leveraged elsewhere. The decentralization tactic of FreeBSD—Mike's assertion that no one really is in charge—can make room for what Brandt describes as "self-sponsored" learning projects. Self-sponsored projects may benefit from mentorship but they are initiated by learners and can allow learners to respond to a market putting ever-increasing demands on their literacy skills.[156]

Self-sponsored learning for coding often leans on contemporary social structures like Web forums for mentorship. On the popular Web forum Slashdot, advice about self-sponsorship was given to an Indian computer science student who wrote in looking to join an F/OSS project: "Could you suggest a road map, links to essential tools or a few projects, for people like me, who would want to improve their skills by contributing FOSS?"[157] Respondents offered him tips on how to augment his university education by pointing to particular F/OSS projects and by telling their own stories of mentorship from their project's community. One Firefox developer wrote of his first experience wanting to "patch" (contribute to) the codebase:

> I got on IRC [Internet Relay Chat] and asked for help, and a couple very patient developers helped me understand where the code was that needed to be patched, and how to fix the issue. As I found other things that were missing, or things I didn't like, I wrote more and more patches, each time with less help - probably 99% of the lines of code in my early patches were written over IRC by more experienced devs, and pasted into a text editor by me:-).[158]

The social practices and information-sharing described here enable code-learning in these spaces, but they also set the stage for coders' ability to leverage their programming skills in other contexts such as workplaces and school. Lakhani and Wolf write, "Delayed benefits to participation [in F/OSS] include career advancement ... and improving programming skills (human capital)."[159] In a sector where companies frequently fold and employment is volatile, the social and technical knowledge and skills gained through an open-source project acts as a kind of professional insurance.

In traditional workplaces, there is sometimes a conflict of interest between programmers and management over how much energy should be spent on investing in new coding skills. Brandt describes the tension that can arise when corporations seeking to control the leaky knowledge limit the opportunities for employees seeking to improve their own literacy skills through self-sponsored projects—some of them on company time. We can see the same tension with coding literacy. Jason, a game designer who has worked at several major computer game companies, said that in order to stay responsive to the ever-increasing demands on their skills, he and other programmers often invented self-improvement projects that they then pitched to management as necessary features of the software. Jason noted that this process becomes so naturalized in a fast-moving field like game programming that some programmers began to believe their self-improvement projects were really in the company's interest. He speculated that a programmer who did not follow this pattern of skill development would be perpetually stuck in the same job and unable to leverage his skills in the programming marketplace.[160] New dynamics of work, some of which I described in chapter 1, necessitate these literacy self-improvement projects. In the workplace, programmers trade on their literacy skills and must be ready to revise and augment these skills for new workplaces and contexts.

The "leakiness" we see for literacy is true for any kind of knowledge investment that a company makes in its workers or that an employee makes in herself. But literacy knowledge, because of its centrality in communication and commerce and because it can travel across information networks, can have greater value in a global marketplace than other knowledge that is confined to local materials, such as knowledge of specific company policies. The incentives to control literacy—for both individuals and groups—are high. Literacy's leaky tendencies make it possible for individuals to wrest some control over their own career trajectories despite the pressure often exerted by companies.[161] The availability of online self-sponsored learning opportunities for coding literacy makes this personal control possible. But how these self-sponsored opportunities are designed, how people learn to pitch their own literacy-improving projects to management, and how welcoming online communities are to those learning the terms of discourse are all social properties of coding literacy. The examples in this section illustrate some of the complicated ways in which literacy inheres in individuals yet is socially shaped and traded.

Conclusion

Creative programming encompasses not only the technical skills of reading and writing code on specific hardware but also social communities such as the algorave or demoscene. The F/OSS community trades and builds knowledge about code and software in complex online communities. Human audiences for code are highlighted in these creative examples, but *all* code is embedded in human social contexts. Few programmers work alone, communicating only with their computer, and many of them program in agile environments where their work is subject to regular group review or to the instant collaborative work of pair programming. Even those few programmers who do work alone use programming languages that have been shaped by the human history of programming and devices embedded in social histories. Programming—like writing—is a complex, social, expressive activity within a symbolic and technological system. In this chapter, theories of language have helped me to explain some of the ways code functions and what its affordances allow code writers to do. Affordances of both programming and writing include their creative form, discreteness, and scalability. These affordances structure how these modes can be used to create and represent knowledge. But these technical aspects of code interoperate with its social contexts and circulation. In part because of its attention to the intertwined social and technological factors of writing, diSessa's concept of material intelligences as well as New Literacy Studies theories provide a theoretically productive way of looking at code.

It is misleading, however, to consider programming and writing as separate technologies—in many practical cases, they are inseparable. As this chapter demonstrates, code, language, and culture intersect all the time. Since the advent of text-based programming languages, code is a form of writing as well as an enactment of procedures. Now that most of our writing is done with computational devices, it is no longer possible to fully extricate writing from programming, just as it is impossible to untangle writing from speech, or literacy from orality. Exploring the nature of language, action, and expression through programming allows us to think about the relationship between writing and speech differently and also to consider the ways in which technologies can combine with and foster human abilities. Computational and textual literacy are not simply parallel abilities, but intersectional, part of a new and larger version of literacy. With this framework of material intelligences and literacy, we can see both programming and writing within a longer history of technology and communication. In the next two chapters, I explore that history in greater depth.

3 Material Infrastructures of Writing and Programming

Historical studies of other technologies are important not so that historical analogies can be made, but because without such historical analyses, we cannot truly understand the nature and shape of current technologies.

—Christina Haas[1]

During the eleventh through thirteenth centuries in England, writing evolved from an occasional tool into a highly useful and infrastructural practice for the communication and recording of information. For thousands of years prior, writing had helped to record commerce and maintain redistributive economies, though it had a niche status and its importance fluctuated with vicissitudes in governance and trade.[2] But after the thirteenth century, writing in England never again waned in its central role in communication and recording of information—the power of writing "stuck."[3] Centralized government initiated this transition, but once writing began building bureaucracy, it also rippled out to restructure commerce and then individual and family life. In this process, fundamental concepts of memory, identity, and information shifted to accommodate the fact that knowledge could exist externally to individuals, travel without human proxies, and be preserved for posterity.[4] As the technology of writing transitioned from rare to common, scribes acquired a special status apart from other craftspeople. Whether or not people could read or write—and most couldn't for at least another 500 years—they saw writing infiltrate many of their everyday transactions and activities. As literacy historian Brian Stock argues, people "began to live texts."[5]

In a similar way, computer programming appears to have "stuck" in twentieth-century American society. Although the roots of computational devices extend back further, once code-controlled digital computers were widely adopted as information-processing tools by government offices and large corporations in the 1950s, code and the computational devices used to process it became increasingly infrastructural to business, bureaucratic transactions, and social practices of life in the West. Writing remade institutions and individual lives as it became infrastructural to medieval government, commerce, and social relations, and computer programming is restructuring our lives now. We e-mail each other and pay our bills online; our health, employment, marriage, credit, and tax records are recorded in computerized databases; we rely on computational algorithms to filter our news and purchases; and our free time and relationships are shaped by software such as Facebook, Twitter, Match.com, Yelp, and TripAdvisor. In developed nations such as the United States, code increasingly supports our information and communication infrastructure. As computational devices become more portable and more deeply embedded in our physical surroundings and as more spheres are subjected to computation—consumer buying habits, facial recognition, employee performance evaluations, and national security infrastructure and surveillance—we are increasingly controlled and defined by the computation enacted through computer programming. Historian Michael Mahoney writes, "From the early 1950s down to the present, various communities of computing have translated large portions of our world—our experience of it and our interaction with it—into computational models to be enacted on computers, not only the computers that we encounter directly but also the computers that we have embedded in the objects around us to make them 'intelligent.'"[6] Via ubiquitous and sometimes omnipotent computational devices and processes, computer programming has joined writing to become infrastructural to our lives as citizens, employees, and social beings.

With computer code, we have not had the luxury of time to adjust to a new material infrastructure, as was enjoyed by residents of medieval England. Stock notes that the changes he describes over the eleventh and twelfth centuries may not have been apparent within a single lifetime.[7] Across the eleventh through thirteenth centuries, historian Michael Clanchy finds "no evidence of a crisis suddenly demanding numerous literates. Because the pre-literate emphasis on the spoken word persisted, the change from oral to literate modes could occur slowly and almost imperceptibly over many generations."[8] In contrast to the centuries-long span when people gradually became accustomed to how writing could structure their lives, our embrace of computer code has been much quicker and is often painfully perceptible. As the first two chapters have shown, twenty-first-century code exhibits some of the symbolic, social, and operational features we associate with writing. Because code has been able to build on the extensive communication infrastructure already established through writing, it has itself become infrastructural much more quickly. Its role in our infrastructure renders it an important symbolic system to understand and communicate in. How can we use the history of writing to understand our society's dependence on computer code and the programming that constructs it? How might our new hybrid infrastructure of writing and code shape the institutions and lives that we build on it, as well as our composing practices?

To explore these questions, this chapter examines the period when text became central to societal infrastructure and then uses that history to understand the patterns through which we have now embraced code. This chapter works in conjunction with the next, which focuses on a second key era in the history of writing: the birth of mass literacy. The first era, described in detail below, is marked by the adoption of the material technologies of writing as central means of organizing society. In England, historians mark this transition as occurring in the eleventh through thirteenth centuries. I argue that a similar transition occurred for the technology of programming during the 1950s and 1960s in the United States. While in the first era (covered in this chapter) *inscription technologies* are adopted as material infrastructures, in the second era (chapter 4) these inscription technologies begin affecting quotidian activities of everyday citizens: *literacy* is adopted as infrastructure.

Put another way, chapters 3 and 4 use the history of writing and literacy to explore how and why writing and code have worked their way into our everyday lives. For both writing and code, the evolution from material infrastructure to literacy infrastructure follows a similar pattern. Writing and code are first adopted by centralized institutions for their communicative and information-processing and storing potentials, described in the previous chapter. Initial material costs for writing and programming are high, and centralized institutions seem better poised to absorb them. Initiatives and innovations by these institutions then push the technology out to commercial and bureaucratic spaces. Next, the technology enters homes and individual lives; it becomes domesticated. This final stage paves the way for literacy, as the technology becomes so personalized and enmeshed in people's everyday lives that to *not* know how to communicate in it becomes a disadvantage, and the naming of *illiteracy* as a concept points to an emerging mass literacy. For writing, a critical mass of people became fluent with the technology, which meant text was no longer a domain reserved just for specialists. Society could then build on the assumption that most people could read and write. For writing in Western society, this second transition happened in the long nineteenth century—the era of mass literacy campaigns by church and state. For programming, this transition to mass literacy is yet to occur. A central claim of this book is that programming is following a similar trajectory to writing, and as it does so, it changes what literacy is. This chapter tells the story of how the material infrastructure is laid for both writing and programming, ahead of the (potential) transition to mass computational literacy.

This history of text and code trickling down from centralized government to commerce to individual lives that I tell here is, like any history, both oversimplified and motivated. The adoption of writing and code as material infrastructure and the birth of literacy occurred at different times in different places, affected some demographic groups before others, and were not linear or smooth in any time or place. Their trajectories bear similarities, but their material, social, and historical conditions are different. Yet we can gain insight from history. Historians of literacy have broadly marked the two shifts I highlight in this chapter and the next.[9] Not only are the locations and moments I have chosen richly documented, but they also appear to serve as vanguards for other locations and periods in the adoption of writing and code.[10] Other historical comparisons may prompt other observations, but the particular comparisons I make in these chapters illuminate our contemporary transition, when code has become infrastructural and programming is becoming a powerful and generalizable—though not yet generalized—ability. Examining the key transition for the technologies of text and code can help us understand not only what it means to "live code"; it can also suggest something more generally about the wide-scale adoption of new communication infrastructures—who initiates an adoption, where it moves next, what kinds of pressures preceded the adoption, and what kinds of structural shifts it engenders.

To begin, we travel back in time to eleventh through thirteenth century England, when writing "stuck." Texts from that period indicate an increased reliance on the technology of writing in both church and state governance. The census, contract and common law, and the use of textual artifacts in everyday human interactions all point to writing infiltrating the everyday lives of citizens. After looking at the early infrastructures of writing established during this period, we jump forward to the 1950s, when programming "stuck" in American society. In the postwar era, rapid advances in computers and the code used to control them brought these material technologies into national defense and commercial infrastructures. These advances prefigured a later transition to programming as a domestic activity and the beginnings of a new popular mentality influenced by computation—where chapter 4 picks up the thread.

A few words about key concepts I draw on here. The concept of *infrastructure*, which I borrow in part from Susan Leigh Star, is central to understanding the historical parallels drawn in this chapter and the next. Star names several important aspects of infrastructure on the basis of her ethnographic work on people's interactions with communication technologies.[11] Infrastructures are embedded, transparent until they break down, have broad reach, are shaped by standards, and are difficult to change.[12] As Star notes, "We see and name things differently under different infrastructural regimes."[13] In other words, infrastructures fundamentally shape the way a society operates.[14] While she and her collaborators focus on infrastructures such as medical classification systems, I use these characteristics of infrastructure to understand the central roles that writing and programming play in contemporary society on a larger scale.

The words *writing* and *programming* conveniently have the same ability to refer to both a material artifact and its act of creation; I use them in this chapter to do that double-duty. I often use the word *code* when I refer solely to the material artifact of programming and *text* for the artifact of writing.

Another key concept for this chapter is that of "material intelligence," which I introduced in the previous chapter. Andrea diSessa argues that material technologies allow us to store some of our thinking processes in material forms, which then become integral to our ability to think and communicate. Because they fuse our thoughts with their materiality, these technologies become material intelligences. Writing is one of them, and programming is another, diSessa argues. A *literacy*, according to diSessa, is a more broadly distributed material intelligence: "the convergence of a large number of genres and social niches on a common, underlying representative form."[15] My historical argument syncs up with diSessa's conceptual one: chapter 2 described programming as a material intelligence, but because the ability to program is not yet generalized or universal, programming is only on the cusp of literacy.

I also draw on theories of centralized, bureaucratic governance to tell the parallel historical narratives in this chapter and the next. Effective governance of large areas relies on efficient communication, as Harold Innis writes in his influential *Empire and Communications*.[16] As the geographic area and human population of empires increases, the demand for efficient information management increases as well. Innis's work has been subject to critique for technological determinism and its simplification of the conflicting forces that apply to the centralization and distribution of government. However, his framework provides a useful way to think about communication and governance: bureaucracy relies on a degree of standardization in communication, especially as the area governed expands and the amount of information about subjects increases and diversifies. Since Innis, scholars such as Jack Goody, Walter Ong, James Beniger, and Ben Kafka have argued that modern bureaucratic governments build on sophisticated technologies of communication, specifically writing. Drawing on Max Weber, Beniger describes the system of bureaucratic control as *rationalization*—the limiting of information to be processed by a central government. Rationalization becomes necessary in eras where governments are faced with what he calls "crises of control," when "the social processing of material flows threaten[s] to exceed in both volume and speed the system's capacity to contain them."[17] Crises of control prompt shifts in the ways that information is managed and distributed. The advantages of greater standardization, translation across media,[18] and "intelligibility at a distance"[19] are some reasons centralized bureaucracies tasked with coordinating communication at a distance implemented writing and code to support their information-processing requirements.

Beniger focuses on the "control revolution" of the nineteenth century, which brought us train schedules and time zones as information technologies to manage the "control crisis" of that time. But we can trace his idea of a control revolution further back to the use of writing in the eleventh through thirteenth centuries to control the population of England.[20] When the Normans took over England, they were outsiders, and traditional methods of social- and family-based law enforcement did not serve them well. Facing a control crisis, the Normans responded by depersonalizing and consolidating government through the technology of writing. They first undertook an ambitious census to catalog the people and land. Tax records, wills, and codified laws followed, and thereby brought writing into the lives of everyday citizens around the thirteenth century. The Norman control crisis was not so much a response to information demands from outside but rather an attempt to use an inscription technology to help control a population. The documentary innovations spurred by the Norman Conquest of 1066 not only created a lasting central government, but also familiarized people with the ways texts could record actions, make promises, and define their place in society. As medieval historians Clanchy and Stock both argue, this ubiquity of writing contributed to a "literate mentality" among late medieval English people.

Like the Norman invasion, World War II was a control crisis, one that prompted America, England, and Germany to explore computation as a new information technology. The complex battlefields created a profound need for information management, and both the Axis and Allies vigorously accelerated the construction of automatic tabulation machines. Firing tables, cryptography and code-breaking, international communication, and advanced precision weaponry all pushed centralized governments, especially in the United States, Germany, and England, toward code that might help machines more efficiently process this information. Developments in digital computers and programming in the 1940s were prefigured by earlier developments in analog computation that responded to information demands from industrialization and a growing and diversifying population in the United States. The alliances between the U.S. military and universities, which began with research during the war effort and were reinvigorated after the launch of *Sputnik*, accelerated innovation in computer technology and communication. The expense and high requirements for expertise kept computers out of the hands of most individuals until the 1980s, but by then code was already an infrastructural technology for government and business. Although they were first developed as a response to the control crisis of modern warfare, population growth, and greater information complexity, computers and programming became commonplace technologies for commercial and personal transactions.

During what we might think of as control crises, then, centralized governments adopted writing and programming because of their ability to organize, process, and record information. In the eras highlighted here, writing and programming began as management techniques responding to a flood of information and became infrastructural technologies. We can see this system of written documentation scaling into infrastructure in other eras. In Revolutionary France and in the nineteenth-century British Empire, paperwork was a technology to automate bureaucracy and government. Writing made the processing of individual claims to the state less about personal relations—picture a king hearing and adjudicating cases—and more about rules and proper process. As infrastructure, writing could then be used for individual communication. According to Clanchy, "lay literacy grew out of bureaucracy."[21] Several centuries later this lay literacy helped to create the demand for print.[22]

The following section traces these historical developments in writing. In the second half of the chapter, this history of writing helps us to speculate on what the burgeoning bureaucracy of code could mean for lay programming literacy and what demands it might prompt.

The Adoption of Writing in Medieval England

The general trajectory of the inscription technologies of writing and programming began with their adoption by large-scale bureaucratic institutions, then the technologies moved to commercial entities and finally to domestic spaces. The church and the state in medieval England were the first to take advantage of the affordances of writing on a large scale, using it to keep track of subjects and their activities. Infrastructural changes in information processing and communication followed these innovations. Following this trajectory, below I begin with the church and state and then trace the movement of writing through commercial and domestic applications.

Writing in Church and State

In the eleventh century, the triumphant Norman invaders of England struggled to control a vast and strange land. The previous means of decentralized governance through social mechanisms did not favor them as outsiders. To assert the authority of the central government, they looked to writing, beginning with an ambitious census of their new territory. Throughout the eleventh through thirteenth centuries, kings and their governments instituted reforms such as contracts and laws, which were codified with written texts. In this way, the Normans were able to create a bureaucracy based on writing, propelling England "from a sophisticated form of non-modern state, managed through social mechanisms, to a crude form of modern state, organized through administrative institutions."[23] As shires and towns were caught up in these bureaucratic texts, individuals began to feel the need to understand writing.[24] By the end of the thirteenth century, English people were familiar with the functions and power of texts even though few could read or write.

The "social mechanisms" of government that greeted the Norman conquerors were based on a medieval concept of embodied memory. Established in the Greek and Roman rhetorical tradition (e.g., the *Rhetorica ad Herennium,* Cicero's *De Oratore,* Aristotle) and revived in the late medieval period,[25] embodied memory was tied to physical actions and visual aids. As historians Mary Carruthers and Jan Ziolkowski argue, memory was spatial rather than temporal, as we now think of it.[26] The medieval tactic of the memory palace, borrowed from classical tradition, best exemplifies this spatial approach to memory. By employing the spatial organization of a palace, one could memorize lengthy texts or concepts, attaching passages or ideas to rooms and imagining walking through them. For example, influential twelfth-century theologian and philosopher Hugh of St. Victor claimed that concepts should be attached to facial expressions, gestures, and physical locations in order to be memorized.[27] Memories could be codified in pictures as well—preferably an image of no more than one page so that it could be envisioned as a whole.[28] Memories could also be attached to physical performance. The physical ritual of "beating the bounds," practiced in Anglo-Saxon times, was performed every several years to remind parishioners of property boundaries. In a time before maps were common, or at least before most people could read maps, groups of people would perambulate property lines; at key markers of boundaries, they would beat trees or rocks or even young boys among the party. By literally impressing these physical bodies, they impressed the location of boundaries in people's memories. Embodied traditions of memory were also demonstrated in the York Cycle and other medieval plays, according to performance historian Jill Stevenson. These plays were performed in specific locations in order to enrich the associations of these places to religious themes and to help townspeople remember the didactic themes of the play.[29]

This physical, embodied approach may have been effective for remembering, but to the Normans it had two distinct disadvantages. First, it could not scale up to the level that a powerful centralized government required: regardless how large his mental palace was, a king could not remember all of his subjects. Second, it was difficult for outsiders to infiltrate. When the government forced the codification of land exchanges in writing in the eleventh century, the Norman outsiders were able to assert control and redraw property boundaries more easily with this writing than if they had relied on embodied memories to fail. Rather than once again pulling out their swords, they could massage documents to reflect new distributions of property. The Norman government's increased use of records and texts eroded the embodied approach to memory, and in this way a "crude form of modern state" was born—bureaucracy rather than direct rule. Writing began to supplant certain functions of human memory in cataloging and ruling people. For this reason, Clanchy calls this the shift "from memory to written record."

Many activities once impressed in human memory and social relations became codified in writing. Government documents proliferated in the twelfth century, or so the increased use of sealing wax suggests. The government was responding to a growing population, but was also relying more on writing to exercise its authority.[30] In the mid-twelfth century, for example, King Henry II displaced the Anglo-Saxon ruling style of personally settling disputes with "a system of standardized writs to automate and depersonalize the legal process."[31] Stock observes that during this time, "a complex set of human relations was eventually reduced to a body of normative legislation."[32] Feudal relationships established personally between lord and vassal were increasingly formalized in the eleventh through thirteenth centuries.[33] English common law became codified during this period as well, and in the process it homogenized and calcified certain social customs in writing.[34] Written wills were first documented in London in 1258, and only a generation later the oral witnesses to wills were no longer regularly recorded, indicating a complete transition from human to written testimony in only a few decades.[35] Edward I's *quo warranto* proceedings in the late thirteenth century forced landowners to prove "by what [written] warrant" they held their land, effectively displacing previous memory-based systems of establishing property ownership.[36]

Reflecting this shift from embodied to textual memory, the term *deed* began in the thirteenth century to refer not just to an action (e.g., a deed well done) but also to a written legal contract (e.g., a deed to a house)—suggesting that people understood actions could be carried out in text.[37] A profound example of this shift from memory to written record is the change in how the legal system coped with historical information. Customarily, the court would limit the events that could be proved in litigation to what had happened since the most recent coronation, as an acknowledgment that memory before that date was unreliable. However, Richard I's coronation date, September 3, 1189, served this referential role for the whole of the Middle Ages, indicating that documentation had surpassed human memory as the measure for legal proof. Thus, Clanchy argues that this date "marked the formal beginning of the era of official memory" and the end of government reliance on mortal memory.[38] In these ways, writing depersonalized and shored up the authority of the state.

The Catholic Church preceded the crown in many documentary innovations. Just as the crown established certain security measures for documents, the papacy began to recognize the power of scribes and to require notaries and witnesses to documents.[39] In the eleventh century, the church implemented several major changes that all served to standardize documents and make them more accessible.[40] The first complete papal register that survives was completed in the eleventh century by Pope Gregory VII, who had a profound influence on canon law and believed that written law should constitute the basis of ecclesiastical administration.[41] In the late twelfth century, there was a more consistent archival policy of Vatican documents.[42] Extensive church records were established by the Archbishop of Canterbury, Hubert Walter, who later went on to perform the same record-keeping for the crown.[43] Dominican friars had written a concordance of the Bible by 1239.[44] The church had spiritual as well as bureaucratic uses for documents: it communicated—and *ex*-communicated—via written papal bulls.[45]

Perhaps the most symbolic and well-known example of this shift to written record in England at this time was the Domesday Book, a written census commissioned by William the Conqueror in 1085. Anthropologist Jack Goody notes that, historically, written censuses have been critical for redistributive economies to keep track of people so they could pay taxes to a central authority, as in the temple and state in ancient Mesopotamia and Egypt.[46] In these times and places, as well as the one I focus on here, centralized control developed alongside writing, indicating a complex feedback loop between the two.[47] William's census attempted to codify property ownership in eleventh-century England by collecting testimonies from more than 60,000 people across the countryside. These oral testimonies were collected in vernacular languages from juries and then translated into Latin by scribes and recorded in the Domesday Book. Clanchy writes, "The jurors' verdicts, which had been oral and ephemeral in the vernacular, were converted through the skill of royal scribes into a Latin text that was durable and searchable." The reckoning of lands and assets that the Norman census undertook was called the "Domesday Book," echoing the Christian "Doomsday" because "it seemed comparable in its terrifying strictness with the Last Judgement at the end of time"[48] While laypeople considered it a powerful form of judgment, for the crown it was a dramatic way to get people under control of written law. Success using written charters to break the cycles of land inheritance and exchange may have led the Normans to think that this comprehensive written census would establish their governance more firmly.[49] In the royal treasury, where the book physically resided, it was known as the *liber judiciarious,* or "the judicial book." Its Latin title invoked Roman and papal law as well as the authority of those two powerful traditions.[50] And in this "dual process of vernacular inquiry and Latin record-making," the Domesday Book symbolized this movement from memory to written record in post-conquest England.[51]

The Domesday Book, which translated vernacular testimony into Latin record, was a largely symbolic document for the Norman government. William's ambition was frustrated by the practical difficulties of recording so many minute details. Hence, the Domesday Book is incomplete and very inconsistent across regions.[52] It was not a practical document at the time of its creation, but, along with its surveying process, it was a way to associate writing with a form of royal power.[53] Even more than its practical application for taxation, Goody claims that a census can "represent the penetration of the state into the domestic life of its subjects."[54] In chapter 4, we will see this symbolic power of the Domesday Book echoed in the symbolic power of mainframe computers in the 1950s: the huge devices had few applications but nevertheless affected public perception of computing.

Writing, from Symbolic to Practical

The symbolic power of writing in the Domesday Book translated to practical purposes as the government learned to make, store, and retrieve records more effectively.

In eleventh century England, government documents had been essentially treated as "special objects treasured in shrines," rather than as records.[55] But by the end of the twelfth century, the Exchequer had organized these documents by creating centralized treasury archives.[56] Documents produced and held by the Exchequer then became critical for the collection and redistribution of taxes.[57] Although the archives may have been at first unusable for retrieval, they indicated the increasing value placed on written records.[58] New security measures for these documents underscore this importance: copies in triplicate, and locks and keys held by multiple people.[59] By 1300, Edward I wanted documents to be retrievable for his review at any point, which meant that they needed to be indexed and organized effectively.[60] This move suggested a more practical approach to documents—writing for government *use*, rather than for symbolic power. Along with the increased quantity, the shift from symbolic to practical in the way the Exchequer's and other royal documents were treated across the eleventh through thirteenth centuries in England suggests an increasingly important role for them in governance.

In order for writing to transition from a specialized skill to a literacy, it needed to spread beyond a specialized class of citizens—beyond just clergy or gentleman, for instance. As Clanchy argues, before literacy could spread beyond these specialized classes, "literate habits and assumptions, comprising a literate mentality, had to take root in diverse social groups and areas of activity."[61] When writing is controlled by a small class of people in this way, Goody calls the uses of literacy in that society "restricted."[62] That is, writing is specialized rather than generalized—and in the terms of this book, it is still a material intelligence, not yet part of literacy.[63] But traces of the beginning of writing literacy can be found in the latter part of the period we survey here. The move from the Domesday Book in the eleventh century to thirteenth-century deeds and other functional documents in England plus the transition between writing as symbolic to writing as practical together point to a developing "literate mentality" and precede the general spread of literacy across different classes of people. As people began to treat texts as practical rather than sacred, and as they brought these texts into domestic spaces, we can see people begin to inhabit the "literate habits and assumptions" that Clanchy describes.

The circulation of documents in everyday citizens' lives was key to this transition. The government was the primary producer, user, and keeper of documents until at least the thirteenth century.[64] But by the thirteenth century, the crown required written deeds to prove the legitimacy of land transactions, written responses to censuses, and written evidence and arguments in court. Individuals and localities often had the responsibility of issuing these documents, as well as certifying, storing, and keeping track of them.[65] The proliferation of documents and bureaucracy meant that the government became more dependent on literates to carry out its functions.[66] Partly due to the state's attempts to codify financial and land transactions, rural estate managers felt economic pressures to keep records for themselves as well.[67] For instance, thirteenth-century documents exist for such mundane transactions as the purchase of livestock.[68] Stock notes that the areas of human life subject to documents at this time were limited, but significant: "birth and death, baptism and marriage, initiation, terms of service, transfers of property, and a small number of issues in public and private law."[69] Writing at this time had become useful not only for keeping track of government finances and taxes but also for small-scale accounting and personal records.

Medieval library policies are another reflection of this shift from texts as specialized or sacred to practical. Eleventh-century librarians supervised the borrowing of books once a year; each monk had one book to read for the whole year and exchanged it on a particular date under the librarian's supervision. The Dominican approach in the thirteenth century reflects a much more modern concept of libraries: books should be ready to hand and multiple.[70] The innovation of portable books, used especially by peregrinating Dominican friars, also suggests a more practical attitude toward texts.[71] This difference is critical: where monks once ruminated over one cluster of ideas, they could then peruse many portable books at once. The former scenario encourages deep reading and reverence for a particular text, whereas the latter allows for greater scrutiny of texts, as readers can bring together more wide-ranging arguments.[72] For Clanchy, "The difference in approach towards writing [in these two modes] ... is so fundamental that to use the same term 'literate' to describe them both is misleading."[73] In the later eras, historians have cited this attitudinal shift resulting from the availability of multiple, juxtaposable texts as a cause for the Enlightenment in Europe[74] as well as the dawn of mass literacy in the northeastern United States.[75] While these claims have been accused of overstatement,[76] at the very least the treatment of texts as reference material rather than as sacred seems to have helped create a more practical use for them.

Concordant with their new patterns of circulation, texts could also be found in new places by the thirteenth century. In particular, religious texts moved from monasteries into homes; the domestication of the word coincided with the domestication of the Word. This move was important in at least two ways: first, it made texts more accessible to laywomen,[77] and second, it began to integrate texts into the everyday lives of people. Women were less likely than men to have encountered texts in government and commercial transactions, and this move to domestic spaces made texts available to women, especially those of higher classes who could afford them. We know little about literacy rates among women in this period, although there are some references to nuns as literate.[78] We do know that women were more often readers than writers; for spiritual enlightenment, both women and men in higher classes were expected to read in Latin, French, and English, as well as to be able to interpret religious images.[79]

Regardless of the degree to which they could read them, however, elite women in the thirteenth century commissioned Books of Hours, often with illustrations and elaborate, jewel-encrusted covers as indicators of wealth.[80] These Books of Hours not only made books more accessible to women but also brought a culture of reading into the home. This culture of reading was then passed on to children in the household, paving the way for more extensive cultures of literacy in subsequent generations. Literacy was often learned in the home, from mothers,[81] a pattern repeated elsewhere in history.[82] Clanchy goes so far as to argue that "the 'domestication' of ecclesiastical books by great ladies, together with the ambitions of mothers of all social classes for their children, were the foundations on which the growth of literacy in fourteenth- and fifteenth-century Europe were constructed."[83] As we will see in the second half of this chapter, the domestication of computers also set the stage for the spread of programming. When books and computers became available for home use, people could interact with them and find ways to fit them into their lives. They became personalized.

Books of Hours were both objects and texts. They contained writing as well as images and memory maps to help individuals read and retain their religious import. They were constructed of animal skin, containing annotations and images sewn in by previous owners. All texts are material of course, but the physical traces of previous owners and personal modifications heighten the palpability of Books of Hours, according to Jill Stevenson. In a particular text, the Pavement Hours, she points out sewn-in insertions of images of a female saint reading a book and of Saint

Christopher (the protector of travelers and also associated with merchants), which both mirror the user/reader of the book and "literally thread the book's owner into each prayer's use."[84] As objects, Books of Hours could be physically present during worship, functioning much like souvenirs to help people remember key events.[85] Their material qualities and the spaces they inhabited meant that Books of Hours helped to bridge the gaps between memory and writing and between sacred and practical literacy. In the Middle Ages, traditions of reading aloud and illuminated texts served as bridges between the oral and written, aiding those who depended on writing but were unable to read or write themselves. In this way, writing subtly wove itself into existing patterns of orality and images.[86]

Other Janus-faced artifacts witnessed this transition from a memory-based to a document-based society. For example, knives with inscriptions that date from the twelfth century connected material memory to new documentary methods of recording land exchanges. Ironically, the Normans appear to have imported this tactic of material exchange to signify land transactions, along with their importation of more established documentation. A memorable (though possibly apocryphal) story of William the Conqueror from 1069 has him dramatically brandishing a knife during a land exchange and saying, "That's the way land ought to be given," alluding to the way that he acquired English land by force several years earlier. The document that records this transaction says, "'By this evident sign, this gift is made by the testimony of many nobles standing at the king's side.'" Pointing to the material object and performance as evidence, witnesses could attest from memory that the transaction had occurred.[87]

The signatory seal was another material symbol of this shift from memory to written record. To participate in a new world of written contracts and deeds, individuals needed to learn to sign their names to indicate their acquiescence to the contracts. Many people learned to read during this period, although those who could read could not necessarily write because the medieval technology of writing—the paper, ink, writing instruments, and scripts—was difficult to master.[88] Those who could not sign their names could use seals. Once possessed only by kings and nobles, the seal became a commonplace possession even of serfs, who were required by statute to own one by the end of the thirteenth century.[89] For this reason, Clanchy calls the signatory seal "the harbinger of literacy, as it was the device which brought literate modes even into remote villages."[90]

Religious representations of reading and writing also imply the growing power of text at this time. Prior to the thirteenth century, the virgin Mary is generally shown spinning at the Annunciation. Afterward, she is often shown reading piously when the angels interrupt her. This representation served as a model for contemporary women who owned the Books of Hours in which she was depicted.[91] As in other eras, the virtue of reading contrasts with the dangers of writing. Clanchy notes from religious depictions that "the devil ... became literate in the thirteenth century; he also established a hellish bureaucracy to match that of the king or pope." In light of the thirteenth-century Inquisition, which depended on written depositions, this depiction was particularly sinister.[92] Other images show devils recording mispronounced prayers in church and using those deformed words for ill.[93] As this portrayal of the devil suggests, writing's relationship to truth caused some anxiety among medieval people, a theme we pick up on in the next chapter.

Images combined with text, the material and textual Books of Hours, inscribed knives, and signatory seals served as "boundary objects" between a society organized by memory and one organized by documents. According to Geoffrey Bowker and Susan Leigh Star, "boundary objects" are those that make infrastructures legible to each other, especially during times of transition. They serve as translators across contexts.[94] Immaterial practices such as reading aloud also bridged gaps between oral and literate culture.[95] Through these boundary objects and other ways, literates and nonliterates alike could participate in the burgeoning written culture. But by end of the thirteenth century, this was no longer an option: bureaucratic initiatives by the state and church had driven written documents into the very life cycle of English people—their birth, marriage, and death records as well as their religious and domestic spaces.

Prior to the eleventh century, when writing was only occasional and not central to business or legal transactions, the ability to read and write was a craft not so different from the ability to carve wood or make pottery. Scribes or clerks could be employed when necessary, but business and governance were generally conducted through personal contact. The concept of literacy did not exist because knowing how to read and write were highly specialized skills. But as writing became infrastructural in the early fourteenth century—that is, when writing became so important that institutions such as government and commerce began to depend on it—texts were no longer set apart as special, and literacy was no longer a specialized skill. As texts became more embedded in the general activities of everyday life, they prefigured another transition, which we will explore in more detail in the next chapter: the transition toward a *literate mentality*. This literate mentality signals not widespread literacy, but a mindset about the world that is shaped by the ubiquity of texts. The pervasive technology of writing affected methods of understanding the world, ways of presenting the self, and understanding the relationship of humans and nature—similar to the influence of the technology of computation once it became more widespread.

The Adoption of Computation in Twentieth-Century America

In medieval England, the "twin bureaucracies" of church and state mobilized over several centuries to develop sophisticated documentation systems. In twentieth-century America, what we might think of as the "triplet bureaucracies" of government, industry, and university mobilized to further their computational information-management systems. We moved from governments of writing to governments of writing and computation. Rather than religious and government bureaucracy in medieval England, it was primarily national defense that encouraged computation to spread in the United States. During World War II, the U.S. government experienced a Beniger-style "control crisis"[96]; accurate weapons tables, effective espionage, and compressed time frames pushed human and analog calculators to their limits. Wartime budgets were the primary funders of research in the early years of computers, and the American government, in particular the military, was the greatest user of computers during the 1940s and 1950s.[97] After computers became indispensable to governance and defense in the 1950s, corporations such as American Airlines discovered they could get a competitive edge using computation. Computers were miniaturized and personalized beginning in the 1970s. From the 1980s on, they began to work their way into everyday life in America: households played computer games, kept financial records in spreadsheets, and used modems and other hardware to connect to others through networks. We might think of this moment as parallel to what Clanchy called the shift "from memory to written record"—we have experienced a shift from written to *computational* record. But just as texts never completely displaced orality in everyday life, computation has not superseded writing across the board. Instead, we live in a world where written language and code interact in complicated ways.

The second half of this chapter focuses on computation and follows a similar trajectory we just traced with writing: from large-scale, centralized uses to small-scale, domestic uses. As with writing, the big, initial investments in computer technology were made by centralized governments; afterward, computers were taken up by businesses and universities, and finally, people invited them into their homes and daily lives. Massive, expensive, batch-processed machines are necessarily tools for dedicated specialists, as John Kemeny and Thomas Kurtz observed when they set out to make programming accessible to Dartmouth undergraduates.[98] When machines are inexpensive, portable, and one doesn't have to be an engineer to use them, the kinds of people who can learn to program change. Each generation of computer called for a different kind of programming; by following the hardware as it became more accessible and practical, we can see a development parallel to the history of programming languages we encountered in chapter 2. Only when computation could happen on cheap, small, and personal devices could a concept of computational or coding literacy be possible, so this half of the chapter necessarily pairs the institutional forces supporting the material intelligence of programming with the computational technologies they developed to do so. It therefore focuses on a history of hardware and infrastructure development as a necessary precursor to computational literacy. While the quest for a perfect language for novices has been ongoing since BASIC, this movement of computational devices into homes and our everyday lives removed many of the material barriers to computational literacy.

Government Spurs Computational Research

Although World War II was the most immediate cause of the development of code and computers in the United States, the information pressures of the nineteenth-century census foreshadowed those of World War II. Just as the Domesday Book attempted to catalog the newly conquered English population, the American census helped to recruit soldiers and to tax citizens of the new United States. The first accounting of the new republic's population, conducted in 1790, required census-takers to personally visit every household in the new nation, taking note of all residents. But the task of visiting and collecting data from every household was sustainable only for a smaller U.S. population, in the same way that personal relationships could not scale up for a more centralized government in the Middle Ages. As the nation grew commensurately with its ambitions for data, human-implemented writing and mathematics reached their limit. Thus, the census once again became an impetus for a more sophisticated literacy technology. The Domesday Book largely took advantage of a technology already present, but the American census prompted the development of a brand-new technology: automated computation.

As the American census became more ambitious and larger in scale during the nineteenth century, the government looked to more efficient data-processing techniques to collect and make use of the information.[99] The 1830 census implemented standardized, printed forms for collecting data to simplify the tabulating process. Streamlined forms made more cataloging possible: "social statistics" (e.g., information about jobs and class) and information from corporations were then collected.[100] But the standardization of data collection could only aid the tabulation process so much. Struggling with data analysis, the Census Office implemented a rudimentary tallying machine in 1870. Even with this machine, by 1880 the population had grown so much that the calculations of its collected data took most of the decade.[101]

Anticipating the onslaught of information that would come from the 1890 census, Herman Hollerith, a mechanical engineer and statistician who worked for the Census Office during the 1880 census, devised an analog, electronic computer. The "Hollerith machine" processed cards with various data points punched out, and when hand-fed by operators it calculated data much faster than statisticians could. Variations of the Hollerith machine were used from the 1890 through the 1940 census. By 1940, there were many analog calculating machines designed to solve specific classes of mathematical problems such as the census presented, but there existed no general-purpose computer as either Charles Babbage or Alan Turing had imagined. By 1950, the U.S. Census Office was one of the first customers of a commercially available digital computer—the UNIVAC I.[102] As this dramatic change in technology for the census suggests, between 1940 and 1950 research in automated computation was greatly accelerated.

World War II was an information war; it pushed much of the Western world into a "control crisis" that necessitated faster and more efficient processing of information. Specifically, the acute need for weapons and strategic data tabulation led to advances in computation on both sides of the conflict. In Germany, isolated from other development in computers, Konrad Zuse developed a series of computers beginning in the late 1930s. The most important of these was the Z3, which performed sophisticated arithmetic and was in operation from 1941 to 1943, when it was destroyed in an Allied raid on Berlin.[103] The British, including Alan Turing, focused on cryptography and used computation to crack the code used by the Germans to transmit critical information during the war.[104] In 1944, they completed the code-breaking Colossus and put ten of these computers in operation at Bletchley Park, reducing the time to break codes from weeks to hours. The male cryptographers and Women's Royal Naval Service (Wren) operators worked together to decode messages from the German Lorenz machine. In advance of D-Day, they revealed that Hitler was unaware of the Allied plans, a key bit of knowledge that General Eisenhower claimed may have shortened the war significantly.[105] The Colossus project was classified until the

1970s, however, and so it and many of its operators did not significantly influence or participate in later development of computers.[106]

The Americans, spurred by Vannevar Bush as head of the U.S. Office of Scientific Research and Development during World War II, were interested in increasing the speed and power of tabulating machines, particularly for the use of calculating firing and navigation tables. Firing tables were the limiting factor in advances in artillery technology at the time: each new gun required a firing table for the gunner to account for ammunition trajectories and moving targets, and each firing table took a hundred people a month to calculate.[107] Analog computers were occasionally used for this tabulation, although the pressure for more rapid results drove research on electronic, digital computation. The Mark I (1944), designed at Harvard and built by IBM to perform calculations for the Navy, was an automatic and electromechanical computer that was driven by a 50-foot rotating shaft.[108] John von Neumann used it for atomic bomb calculations during the war. The ENIAC (1946) was the first successful electronic computer. Underwritten by the U.S. government during World War II, the ENIAC was developed at the University of Pennsylvania Moore School, exemplifying the collaboration between government and universities in this phase of computational research. Although the computer was finished a few months too late to help the war effort, its underlying research paved the way for subsequent developments in computers.[109]

One problem with the ENIAC was the time it took to reprogram it: it needed to be physically reconfigured for every new problem it solved. Subsequently, John von Neumann and the Moore School team worked on the concept of a "stored program computer"—a computer that would store its programs in the same way that it stored its data. As discussed in chapter 2, this design allowed computers to be general purpose machines because they could be reprogrammed without being rewired. Crucially, historians Martin Campbell-Kelly and William Aspray mark the completion in 1949 of the EDSAC, the first successful stored program computer, as "the dawn of the computer age."[110] Beyond stored programs, countless other developments occurred in the wake of World War II: magnetic storage, transistors, direct keyboard input, compilers, break points for debugging, and programming languages. Like innovations in late medieval England that allowed the government to store and access documents more easily, these material improvements made computers more useful and easier for people to work with.

The Cold War of the 1950s led to further development of computer technology within government, industry, and universities, embedding the new technology more deeply within the bureaucratic systems of each of these institutions. The SAGE (Semi Automatic Ground Environment) missile defense system, begun in the 1950s, illustrates the ways that military forces encouraged the spread of code in the infrastructure of American government after the war. The SAGE defense project, an ambitious, multisite, integrated computational system designed to defend the United States against a potential Soviet missile attack, was the most extensive software project of the 1950s and, like the research on computation during World War II, it relied on the merged efforts of industry, government, and universities in its development. Postwar computers were batch-controlled, a method that was useless for feedback during real-time flight and combat situations. MIT and IBM had worked on a computer (Project Whirlwind) that would help give real-time feedback to Navy bombers, and this real-time technology was integrated into the SAGE project.[111] SAGE was significant for its level of complexity; it combined communications, computation, and weaponry to detect, evaluate, and intercept a potential airborne attack (figures 3.1 and 3.2).

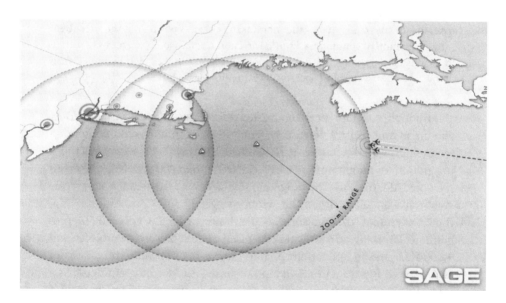

Figure 3.1

The SAGE system linked radar towers and fed the information back to a SAGE Direction Center, where it would be processed by an AN/FSQ-7 computer. SAGE simulation by Chester Beals, 2009. Reprinted with permission of MIT Lincoln Laboratory, Lexington, Massachusetts.

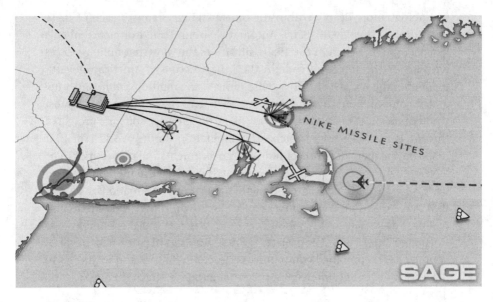

Figure 3.2
If an enemy aircraft was detected, the SAGE Direction Center would designate air bases to launch counterattacks and monitor the aircraft's position. If the aircraft got through the initial counterattacks, the Direction Center would trigger Nike surface to air missiles to launch. SAGE simulation by Chester Beals, 2009. Reprinted with permission of MIT Lincoln Laboratory, Lexington, Massachusetts.

Although developments in missile technology made it an imperfect command and control defense system,[112] SAGE's influence on computing technology was tremendous, particularly in the way that it served as a training ground for programmers.[113] In 1955, fewer than 200 people in the country could do the kind of programming necessary to build a large-scale system like SAGE. By 1960, the Systems Development Corporation (SDC), the RAND spinoff that did software development for SAGE, had 3,500 programmers working on SAGE and other Department of Defense projects, and 4,000 had already left to join private industry.[114] The nonprofit status of SDC allowed it to function as a kind of "university for programmers": as a rule, SDC didn't oppose the recruitment of their personnel, which allowed programmers to diffuse throughout commercial industry in the 1950s and 1960s.[115] The massive scope and manpower of SAGE—a total of 1,800 programmer-years were spent on the project—meant that programmers who trained on SAGE were present on every other large software project in the 1960s and 1970s.[116] Along with personnel, technological and organizational innovations from SAGE were also diffused throughout the early computing industry.[117] Beyond its influence on other computational projects and personnel in the 1960s and 1970s, SAGE also marked a significant step in the government's infrastructural reliance on computer programming. The many programmers of the SAGE defense system wrote code that protected the integrity of Canadian and American governments quite literally. The SAGE system was operational at multiple sites in the United States and Canada from 1963 until the early 1980s, when it was finally dismantled.[118]

While Soviet missiles posed a threat to American physical safety and led to the SAGE defense system, the 1958 launch of *Sputnik* symbolized the Soviet threat to American scientific and technological prowess. To combat this intellectual threat, the U.S. Advanced Research Projects Agency (ARPA) was launched in the United States and allocated a budget from defense funding lines in order to promote scientific and technological "blue-sky" research.[119] The first project of the new agency was to facilitate communication and information exchange and share computational resources across research and government institutions. Computers at the time ran unique, specialized operating systems and had widely varying interfaces, so connecting them across a standardized network was a challenge.[120] J. C. R. Licklider, who directed the ARPA division working on networking, imagined an "intergalactic network" that would bring humans and computers together in symbiosis[121] by relying on standardized "message processors."[122] Under his direction, the networking efforts of ARPA led eventually to the development of the ARPANET, first implemented in 1969. At the time, ARPANET, which relied on protocol and standardized code to exchange packets of information between nodes across a network, had no commercial application. But it was the precursor to the Internet, and its basic packet-switching protocol is key to the architecture of our current World Wide Web.

Directly or indirectly, much of the current technology and the human expertise for programming can be traced back to midcentury, large-scale, American government projects such as ARPANET, SAGE, and ENIAC. Several generations of programmers learned their trade on major government-funded software projects in the 1950s and 1960s like SAGE and ARPANET, and then circulated out into large commercial projects with IBM, Remington Rand, or smaller companies, disseminating their knowledge of code writing further. As historian Kenneth Flamm points out, government funding tends to support basic research and infrastructure such as ARPANET, which then has long-term benefits for industry.[123] Post-*Sputnik* government funding allowed IBM to set up an official research arm in 1961.[124] In 1965, government funding supplied roughly half of all computer research and development budgets in the United States.[125] Government funding for computer research continued to be significant in the 1960s and 1970s but surged again in the 1980s with the chilling of the Cold War, as the United States maneuvered against the Soviets on the battleground of space exploration, technological research, education, and defense.[126]

More than just funding for large projects, the organizational structures of government helped to support computational research. For example, ARPANET's protocol to connect disparate computers across networks may have been possible only with the muscle of centralized institutions such as the U.S. government to enforce it. ARPA's famously short chain of command under J. C. R. Licklider in the early 1960s allowed it to pursue radical projects such as ARPANET.[127] This organizational structure was then emulated by Licklider's successor, Robert Taylor, when he went to Xerox PARC in the 1970s to influence another round of computational research. Centralized organization helped to facilitate the big projects of midcentury computation, but computation also emulated this structure. The traditional bureaucratic structure of centralized government was an analog precursor to the computer, argues Jon Agar. For Agar, the British Empire's embrace of the "symbolic abstraction of writing and the surveillance of facts" led to the concept of the computer as a means to systematize government bureaucracy.[128] Government funding, organization, and enforcement helped boost the technologies of code and computation through modeling and funding, just as it had with writing. In turn, adoption of these means allowed governments to scale up and systematize information processing through written or computational bureaucracy. This systemization was incomplete and problematic in some ways, as I describe in chapter 4, but it did lead to more pervasive and embedded uses of writing or computation in everyday lives of citizens.

Commerce Embraces Computers and Code

In the latter half of the twentieth century, industry followed the U.S. government in adopting computation to handle information-processing tasks that they were (barely) managing through other means. Several computational projects from the 1960s through 1980s serve as illustration: the influential SABRE airline reservation system, IBM's problematic and innovative OS/360 operating system, and the commercially popular VisiCalc spreadsheet program for the minicomputer. SABRE, one of the first major nongovernmental software projects and built by some of the programmers of SAGE, showed how computation could manage the growing information problem of airline reservations. The OS/360 was IBM's attempt to make an operating system that would run the same software across an entire line of computers. The project represented the burgeoning market for computers in commercial spaces as well as a response to increased demand for software functionality and reliability. Finally, VisiCalc was part of other developments that made computation necessary and useful for smaller-scale businesses. The calculating spreadsheet program was the first "killer app" for home computers; it also illustrated an expansion in the personal uses for commercial software. These software projects provide a snapshot of how computation filtered out from large and central information-management projects to small businesses and individuals.

Like missile defense, the airline reservation process had grown in complexity in the postwar era. Technological advancements and increasing wealth led more people to choose travel by air; more travelers traveled on more planes. However, American Airlines' system to keep track of reservations had evolved very little from what had been first implemented in the 1920s, when plane travel was a luxury reserved for the few. Human agents kept track of flights and passengers on paper cards. Once airline travel became more popular and these agents could no longer share one file and one table, a giant screen posted the flights and seats available in a room full of agents. At this point, American Airlines' manual reservation system hit a wall: one in every 12 reservations had errors.[129] In the midst of this massive information-management problem in 1953, the president of American Airlines found himself on a flight sitting next to a high-ranking salesman from IBM who had been working on the SAGE defense project. When the two struck up a conversation, they realized the potential for collaboration on the airline reservation problem. The reservation problem, after all, was a command and control problem: a network of distributed agents needed to send and receive data from a central reservation system. By 1960, the first experimental airline reservation system, built by IBM and named Semi-Automated Business Research Environment (SABRE, inspired by SAGE), was operational. By 1964, all of American Airlines' reservations were handled by the SABRE system. To keep up with their competition, Delta and PanAm both contracted with IBM to implement their own reservation systems.[130] Drawing on resources and knowledge generated by government defense funding, the SABRE project was critical to American Airlines and air travel more generally, but also to the general infrastructure of business that had begun to rely on air travel to conduct people from office to office in an increasingly nationalized corporate landscape.

The 1960s saw computers entering many more businesses and corporate applications; major corporations used computers, and software was devised for grocery warehousing, hotel and flight reservations, and other business contexts.[131] Periodicals such as *Datamation, Data Systems,* and *Data Processing,* launched in the United States and United Kingdom in the late 1950s, aimed to explain computers to top management and help them choose systems to manage their businesses.[132] Computers had been essentially a service industry in the 1950s, with the cost of software folded into the cost of hardware. This setup allowed IBM, the most established manufacturer of hardware, to dominate software as well. Because code per se wasn't yet monetized, IBM's SHARE program, launched in 1955 to help IBM clients share computer programs and operating systems and procedures, took advantage of the company's vast user base and connected otherwise competitive businesses.[133] IBM's SHARE program was later emulated by other manufacturers. As software techniques developed rapidly in the 1960s, software became a product separate from hardware. The first software company went public in 1960, and others followed with high capital investments that reflected the public's faith in the booming industry.[134]

Despite the debut of lower-cost manufacturers and independent software houses, IBM had a huge first-mover advantage: the most extensive services and a massive, free, shared codebase. But they still faced market pressures.[135] IBM sought to keep its edge on the growing market for computers in the 1960s by releasing an integrated hardware and software line. At the time, each computer model had a unique operating system and method of programming it. IBM's System/360 was an impressive engineering feat: a full line of computers that could be similarly programmed, allowing businesses to upgrade computers without the huge expense of rewriting their software. The operating system that was slated to run the line of computers—the OS/360—pointed the way forward to more standardized computer interfaces. Its innovation as well as the infamous challenges encountered in the development of the OS/360 make it the poster child for software development in the 1960s. Enterprise software projects such as the OS/360 were designed to solve one kind of information overload problem but created a new one: How does one manage the communication demands of a massive programming project with millions of lines of code and hundreds of programmers working together?[136] As the project's manager Frederick Brooks famously asserted, "there is no silver bullet" for managing software projects such as the OS/360; even with good management and tools, the information problems that software presents remain difficult.[137]

Despite the challenges of budgets and bugs, by the 1960s large businesses had begun to rely on software to organize their daily operations. The demand for sophisticated software and programmers to write it increased, but there were not enough programmers to write the software that was increasingly central to business. Large software projects like the OS/360 went over budget and missed deadlines. A "software crisis" emerged—the first of many.[138] As a 1995 *Scientific American* article on the snafus of the baggage-routing software at the Denver International Airport points out, the software industry has been in perennial crisis since the 1960s.[139] The fact that the 1960s launched the "software crisis"—that is, a critical shortage of programmers necessary to write the software demanded by industry— indicates the centrality of programming and programmers from that time forward.

Programmers in this era struggled to develop and learn programming languages that would be comprehensible to the computer yet also stretch their human capacity (see chapter 2 for a more detailed account of these trade-offs). New methods of programming were developed to help alleviate the crisis. The Garmisch Conference on Software Engineering in 1968 sought to reform software practices into predictable engineering protocols. "Structured design methodology," the most widely adopted of the software engineering practices at the time, helped the programmer manage complexity by limiting his view of the code, and gradually directing attention down to lower and lower levels of detail.[140] Programs such as Autoflow helped to automate the software planning process. Compilers and the "automatic programming" approach, developed by Grace Hopper in the 1950s, contributed to this effort to make programming easier. This premium on programmer time echoes an earlier moment when scribe time was highly valuable, when pressure on writing led to time-saving innovations such as cursive.

Advertisements for computer programmers in the 1960s reflect this labor crisis; they called not for experienced programmers, but instead for people with particular skills and personality traits willing to take tests to indicate whether they would make good programmers.[141] In 1966, 68% of employers used aptitude tests, and a cottage industry of training for these tests was born.[142] These ads also sometimes appealed directly to women—another possible sign of a labor shortage. One 1963 ad encouraged women programmers, saying that they could "pep up" the office, as well as be logical. Janet Abbate notes that this rhetoric suggests a low-skilled female programmer wouldn't disrupt the regular hierarchy of a company.[143] The software crisis threatened to make programmers more powerful through leverage in business, but the extensive recruiting tactics and language development mitigated that power.

As programmers working in universities and industry developed languages to represent problems and solutions more effectively, and as technology dropped in price, more businesses could afford to integrate computers into their workflow. For smaller businesses, however, the benefits of computers were not necessarily worth the cost until the late 1970s. Cash registers had handled monetary transactions, calculators had dropped in price and increased in capacity enough to accommodate most mathematical needs, and typewriters were still the best available technology for word processing. But in 1979, the VisiCalc spreadsheet program changed the equation.[144] Businesses that wrote invoices, calculated payroll, or had incoming and outgoing flows of resources—in other words, most of them—could then see the value of computers, and some began to integrate them into their workflow. They finally had a compelling reason to adopt computers and commercial software for the management of preexisting information problems.[145] Consequently, computers began showing up in smaller businesses in the late 1970s, and companies that made lower-cost commercial machines competed intensely for business.[146] Word processing programs were also in development at this time, although computer-based word processing did not become integral to businesses until the combination of cheaper printers and user-friendly programs like WordStar emerged in the early 1980s. These affordable computers and useful software packages brought the computer into the home as well.

Another commercial development in the 1970s brought computers to smaller businesses with significant consequences to commercial infrastructure: the Universal Product Code (UPC). The UPC symbol, a collectively designed and code-based label for retail products, streamlined sales and stock but also forced retailers to invest in computers to scan and manage their goods. Larger retailers were more prepared to absorb these costs. This transition remade the industry by consolidating retailers and pushing small grocery stores out of business, but it also indicated something more profound about the computerization of everyday life, claim Campbell-Kelly et al.:

> Alongside the physical movement of goods there is now a corresponding information flow that enables computers to track the movement of this merchandise. Thus the whole manufacturing-distribution complex has become increasingly integrated. ... In a sense, there are two systems coexisting, one physical and one virtual. The virtual information system in the computers is a representation of the status of every object in the physical manufacturing and distribution

environment—right down to an individual can of peas. This would have been possible without computers, but it would not have been economically feasible because the cost of collecting, managing, and accessing so much information would have been overwhelming.[147]

The UPC system remade sales through the way it symbolically merged physical and informational flows in commercial contexts, but it also made this virtual-material hybrid part of everyday life. Even more than with their airline reservations, people interacted with computers through their groceries.

Commerce helped to promote the development and adoption of writing in medieval England, from the centralized taxation system to rural estate managers, and in similar ways American businesses promoted the spread of computation. From the management of complex travel and global business to standardized operating systems to personal accounting, commercial programming was a fact of life by the 1980s, which further embedded code into the infrastructure of U.S. society. The trickle-down from government to industry to small businesses led next to the domestication of computers, which we investigate in the next section.

Computers Get Personal

Writing in the twelfth and thirteenth centuries moved from the church and government and began to touch individuals practically and personally through contracts, charters, writs, and other forms of documentation; similarly, computers emerged from universities and government and entered elementary schools and homes in the early 1980s. This move brought computation home, practically and personally, to many Americans. Prior to that point, computers were critical for certain sectors of the U.S. government and business, but their utility for individuals was not apparent. Computers were relegated to information-management situations such as censuses, wars, and large-scale corporate databases but were not a daily reality for most people. Had that continued to be the case, programming could have remained simply a specialized skill, operating tacitly—although still powerfully—in the background. But, instead, software has made its way into most Americans' lives—our workplaces, communication methods, and social lives are saturated with the work of programmers. For writing, this domestication presaged the need to communicate with the technology—the need to be literate. What does it presage for computation? This is not yet known, but in this section we will look at the domestication of computational technologies with an eye to this parallel.

The seeds for personal interactions with computers were sown in the 1960s. At universities, students were sometimes exposed to computers and occasionally wrote their own punch-card routines. At Dartmouth, math professors John Kemeny and Thomas Kurtz developed BASIC as an accessible programming language as well as a time-sharing system that made expensive computer time available to undergraduates (Dartmouth Time-Sharing System; DTSS). In the 1960s, many students at Dartmouth and several other places, like New York University's School of Business, were taught BASIC and used the innovative DTSS.[148] Both of these innovations proved highly influential to individual access to computation in later decades. While BASIC has been derided by computer scientists such as Edsger Dijkstra,[149] it created an entirely new group of computer users "who could develop their own programs and for whom the computer was a personal-information tool."[150] As chapter 1 described, BASIC profoundly influenced the popular programming movement.

In terms of hardware, spaces such as Dymax, led by People's Computer Company founder Bob Albrecht, made machines available to the public in a revolutionary spirit.[151] Given the cost of computer time during the early 1970s, this was impressive and not particularly common. Until the mid 1970s, high expense and expertise mostly relegated computers to government, university, and business applications. The development of minicomputers in this decade signaled a new era, bringing the computer not only to small businesses but also to hobbyists and other individuals.

We might mark the beginning of the minicomputer's appeal to home users with the Altair 8800, famously announced in a 1975 *Popular Electronics* issue: "THE HOME COMPUTER IS HERE!" The editor's introduction notes, "For many years, we've been reading about how computers will one day be a household item." Finally, the Altair is here, a "within-pocketbook-reach sophisticated minicomputer system." He compares it to another home machine people were familiar with: "Unlike a calculator—and we're presenting an under-$90 scientific calculator in this issue, too—computers can make *logical* decisions." Uses listed for the "home computer" (note that it is not yet called the *personal* computer) were as nebulous as they were various: it could be a home alarm, robot brain, autopilot, or recipe database. Advertisements invited owners to invent their own uses as well.[152] The Altair required technical skills to assemble and program, and it did not come equipped with software, so it appealed to hobbyists interested in tinkering with the machine and eager to own a computer like those they had read about or experienced at work or university. It was wildly successful for hobbyists, but its steep technical learning curve meant the Altair could not capture a larger market; it sold only a few thousand units in 1975.[153] More important than its sales figures, however, the Altair augured explosive growth in the home computer market. It also inspired a young Bill Gates and Paul Allen to write a version of the Dartmouth BASIC language for the computer, making its programming much easier—and, in the process, launching the software behemoth Microsoft.[154]

Also setting the scene for the early 1980s computer boom was research on user interaction. Douglas Englebart at Stanford had wowed the audience at the 1968 Joint Computer Conference when he presented his On-Line System, including the use of a mouse, networking, and a windowed screen interface. Some of this research was embraced by Xerox PARC,[155] a venture made possible by the Xerox Corp's domination of the photocopy market. Although PARC was not able to commercialize much of its technology, it incubated the development of object-oriented programming languages, the desktop metaphor, and the laptop. Steve Jobs and Steve Wozniak were able to poach and re-create some of the technology developed at PARC when they developed their Lisa and Macintosh computers in the early 1980s.[156] Much of PARC's research was driven by the visionary Alan Kay, who developed the influential object-oriented language Smalltalk and pioneered thinking about personal computers. Kay's so-called KiddiComp, or Dynabook, a personal computer easy enough for kids to use, was considered a far-out idea even at the innovative PARC in the early 1970s.[157] In 1972, Kay introduced an internal memo on "A Personal Computer for Children of All Ages" explaining that "it should be read as science fiction."[158] That Kay's ideas about computing being *personal* were "science fiction" in the early part of the decade is one indication of how radical was the paradigm shift to come during the 1970s microcomputer revolution.[159]

In 1977, the Apple II was released, and for the first time a ready-made computer was affordable for middle-class families in the United States. Its success was due, in part, to its form and packaging; unlike the Altair, its components (keyboard, CPU, and CRT screen) were preassembled.[160] A 1977 *Scientific American* ad announces that the Apple II is "The home computer that's ready to work, play, and grow with you," and its accompanying image suggests that the best place for the Apple II to be used is on the kitchen table—at the center of American family life.[161] Later the same year, other affordable personal computers such as the Commodore PET and TRS-80 were released, each targeting a slightly different market.[162] Popular magazines such as *Compute!* focused on these consumer computer models and helped people choose and write software for them.[163] By 1980, there were more than 100 different (and incompatible) computer platforms.[164]

Computers were becoming more popular, although a 1980 interview with Atari's marketing vice president noted that "Atari's competitors in the personal computer market chuckle at what they see is the company's attempt to develop the 'home' computer market, in the face of extensive market research that says the home market won't 'happen' for another 4–5 years."[165]

The home computer became more appealing with applications like Visi-Calc in 1979, which made the computer useful to businesses, to families keeping track of personal budgets, and to people working from home. Because it was only available on the Apple at first, it helped to sell those computers. VisiCalc was part of a juggernaut of software and applications made available to minicomputer owners in the early 1980s. IBM's PC, released in 1981 along with Lotus 1-2-3 and MS-DOS, made the minicomputer a serious system for productivity.[166] But the burgeoning game industry also made the machine fun.[167] Arcade games such as Frogger, Space Invaders, and Pac-Man could be played at home. In 1982, the summer blockbuster *Tron*, the first movie to use computer animation for its special effects, portrayed a scrappy hacker fighting with a computer in a stylish and iconic video-game scenario. *Time* magazine declared the computer "Machine of the Year" for 1982, and sales for home computers skyrocketed. The August 1982 issue of *Compute!* had a feature article on "The New Wave of Home Computers," noting that IBM and Apple had adjacent booths at a recent electronics show, where "it was impossible to tell which company was the establishment giant and which was the cocky upstart. The home/personal computer firms ... finally have achieved their place in the sun."[168] Speaking to the rapid developments in the PC market, they said "no fiction writer would come up with the developments we have seen in the personal computer industry in the past few months."[169]

The Commodore 64 (C64), released in 1982, dominated the market because of its affordability and accessibility. Television and print advertising for the C64 suggested that the computer would benefit families with spreadsheets and word processing, kids could get an edge in school, and the whole family would enjoy the games they could play on it (figure 3.3). (This also is the year that a used C64 made its way into my house, along with dozens of floppy disks of pirated games.)

As Campbell-Kelly and Aspray explain, in the early 1980s the tipping point with computers was reached "so that people of ordinary skill would be able to use them and want to use them. The graphical user interface made computers much easier to use, while software and services made them worth owning."[170]

The educational applications of computers grew dramatically in the early 1980s, as marketing and educational games made claims, and as parents saw their kids use computers in schools. In 1980, computers were in 15% of elementary schools and 50% of secondary schools. By 1985, the numbers were up to 82% and 93%, and there were national, state, and locally mandated computer literacy courses.[171] Computers entered schools in the 1980s in part because they were getting relatively inexpensive but also because the escalation of the Cold War and the economic threat from Japan increased funding to prepare a future workforce to work with computers.[172] The most popular model in schools was the Apple II because Apple donated many to schools in a brilliant move to corner the educational computer market. Educational typing and math and spelling games were popular, as was the nominally historical game Oregon Trail. But programming was also par for the course at the time. Inspired in part by Seymour Papert's educational claims for programming in the popular book *Mindstorms* (1980), the Logo language was taught in schools (such as mine) in the early 1980s. Logo for the Apple II was focused on graphics and allowed students to program a small triangle called a "turtle" to make multicolored patterns on the screen (see chapter 1).

As the Logo initiatives indicate, when computers moved into homes and schools, so did computation and programming. Computer magazines from the time reflect the home computer's status as a programmable object as well as a platform for applications. Ads for programming tools filled magazines such as *Compute!* For instance, a 1982 ad by educational publisher John Wiley & Sons said, "Because you didn't buy your Apple to practice your typing," they offered "Practical manuals that show you how to program your Apple for business, learning and pleasure."[173] In 1980, an Atari spokesman emphasized that Atari computers were meant for people interested in programming or just applications: "More and more of the younger generation are learning to program and work with more sophisticated applications."[174]

BASIC was often the language the younger generation learned on because it was included with many of the computers that made their way into homes in the early 1980s, including the C64 and PET, the Apple II series, and the Atari 400 and 800.[175] Interaction with these machines often required typing in BASIC commands, and therefore users had to have at least a rudimentary knowledge of how code controlled these machines. For those who wanted to move beyond these rudiments, books on BASIC were available beginning in the mid-1970s.[176] A culture of printing BASIC code in magazines, plus sharing it at computer fairs and among friends, contributed to

Figure 3.3
This 1985 advertisement portrays the Commodore 64 as a family computer with multiple uses. Advertisement from Archive.org. Reprinted courtesy of Cloanto Corporation, rights holder for Commodore Computer.

It's 6 a.m. Do you know where your husband is?

It's 8 a.m. Do you know where your daughter is?

It's 11 a.m. Do you know where you are?

We do.

We make the Commodore 64,™ the computer that's in more homes , businesses and schools than any other computer.

With its 64K memory, its high fidelity sound and its high resolution sprite graphics, it's one powerful computer. With its price—about one third that of

the 64K IBM PCjr™ or the Apple IIe™—it's one affordable computer. (In fact, you can add a disk drive, a printer or a modem and get a powerful computing system for just about the price of those other computers alone.)

And with all the Commodore software programs we make for it, it's one useful computer.

What can you use it for? Just about anything you want to. For fun or profit, for homework or housework, for

higher game scores or higher S.A.T. scores, for words or music. For all hours of the day. And night.

So if you're looking for a computer, it pays to look into the Commodore 64.

You'll definitely have enough money for it. Just make sure you have enough time for it.

COMMODORE 64

IT'S NOT HOW LITTLE IT COSTS,
IT'S HOW MUCH YOU GET.

Figure 3.3 (continued)

the circulation of knowledge about programming home computers. Consequently, BASIC was the first language of many casual programmers at the time, and it became "the lingua franca of home computing" in the 1980s.[177] So while software applications such as VisiCalc made computers practical for families and small businesses, BASIC introduced many of them to the language of programming.

After computers and computation entered many people's everyday lives in the 1980s, computers began to shape who we were. The widespread applicability of programming and the experience of computation as central to everyday life has changed the ways that we perceive ourselves and our world. We can call this emerging shift in perception a *computational mentality*, after the *literate mentality* that people experienced in thirteenth-century Britain. What this mentality means for programming and literacy and the affective implications of the domestication of computers and texts are explored in the next chapter.

Conclusion: From Symbolic to Practical, Centralized to Distributed

Keeping track of populations, collecting money from them, and defending them all put pressure on the information-management systems of government. In response to these information challenges, we see a deliberate movement toward more systematic bureaucratic organization in eleventh-through thirteenth-century England and in nineteenth- and twentieth-century America. This organizational shift involved the adoption of an inscription system that would better facilitate the necessary increase in the systematicity of communication and information management. The government's embrace of this inscription system—writing or code—helped popularize it with commerce and individuals.

Writing as a way of keeping track—bureaucracy—may have initially taken hold in centralized religion and government because they were faced with the most complex and copious information. In Beniger's terms, churches and governments hit the "control crisis" first. But centralized institutions are also perhaps the only forces large and powerful enough to command the resources to set this infrastructural transition in motion. This becomes clear in the more recent history of code. As suggested by the American and British governments' investment in "blue-sky" research on computation, the high-risk, high-reward nature of the venture could perhaps only be absorbed by very powerful, rich, and stable institutions with already established organizational infrastructure, such as government and (often government-sponsored) university and industry research centers. While writing may have had lower (but still significant) material costs than computing, centralized institutions still supplied the organizational structure to support the transition.

We can see that after some groundwork had been laid and the government began to rely on the technology, it forced commerce to adopt either writing or code through changes it made in bureaucratic requirements. The uses of writing or code technology in governance influenced citizens' adoption of the technology to organize their own affairs and began to establish the technology's associated literacy as a desired skill to have. As Furet and Ozouf write of the spread of French literacy in the seventeenth through nineteenth centuries, "The spread of literacy was born of the market economy." This "market economy, backed by and relying upon the machinery of the centralized state, expanded the role of writing as a necessary condition of modernization."[178] In other words, these bureaucratic requirements set the stage for the inscription technology to become infrastructural to people's everyday lives.

At first, these uses of writing were often symbolic rather than functional, as in the case of the Domesday Book. However, the increasingly central role of writing in people's interactions with the state and commerce underscored the importance of writing—and following that, the importance of literacy, or understanding and responding to such uses of writing. Likewise, computers and programming began as practical solutions to complex governmental information problems, and they remained distant from the general American public through the 1950s. For both writing and programming, then, what began as a technology for information management by centralized institutions such as governments then came to structure individual lives and promise more diverse uses for individuals. At this point, the ability to write in that inscription technology is, in Andrea diSessa's terms, a "material intelligence." In the next chapter, we explore the point when a writing technology becomes so ubiquitous that it leads to a "mentality" among those who can use it as well as those who cannot. For writing, a widespread literate mentality prefigured literacy as an essential life skill. What will a computational mentality lead to?

The story I have told here and continue in the next chapter may strike some as too teleological or too adherent to a progress narrative in which bureaucracy employs technology for the benefit of citizens. The information-processing strategies of governments as they intersect with technology have, of course, been extensively critiqued. Because my objective is to trace threads across history to help us "understand the nature and shape of current technologies" as Christina Haas recommends, rather than rehash these critiques I will name a few salient problems with governmental uses of technology to "rationalize" citizens.

In his critique of "computationalism" as a form of Foucauldian "governmentality"—a neoliberal method of decentralizing government control and insidiously embedding it in individuals—David Golumbia offers one caution about our story of government and technology. For Golumbia, "computationalism" is a set of beliefs that the world is fully subject to computation and that this is a good thing; for example, Thomas Friedman's much-maligned characterization of the world as "flat."[179] Computation is often presented as a way to liberate individuals from heavy bureaucracy (e.g., the "freedom" rhetoric surrounding talk about the Internet[180]). But Golumbia notes that computation has long been advantageous to the state, especially for war, and therefore it effectively consolidates rather than distributes power.[181] Wendy Hui Kyong Chun also fears the coupling of the illusion of "freedom" and the Internet; for her, this computational network may promise freedom but has overwhelming capabilities of surveillance and control.[182] Although I note that standardization allows for scaling-up information collection, storage, and transfer in a way that governments required during the periods I examine, it also can mean a loss of humanity, a mechanization of personal qualities and processes. To return to Beniger's account of "rationalization" as a response to control crises, the reduction and standardization of information and peoples can delete complex social contexts and implement tacit power structures.

Indeed, for those subject to them, transitions from personal to bureaucratic systems of organization have inevitably caused anxiety about the relationship between humans and technology. Our focal period of medieval England was perhaps the first of these moments when government processes previously performed by people were automated in writing, but there were subsequent ones. In post-Revolutionary France, according to Ben Kafka, the government instantiated a complex bureaucracy to depersonalize and make transparent its processes and thereby achieve greater *liberté, égalité, fraternité*. But citizens could become so tangled up in this process that Kafka argues any sane person would be aggrieved were they able to see the system as a whole.[183] Jon Agar argues that as nineteenth-century British government moved from personal dealings and positions based on social status to protocols and merit-based appointments, "changes were all marked by moves from the personal to the impersonal, from practices contingent on the individual to the systemic. Trust in the gentleman was being transferred, partially, to trust in the system," with corresponding unsettling feelings of mechanization.[184] Agar helps us make the connection between written bureaucracy and computation. The "government machine" of bureaucracy reached its "apotheosis" in the twentieth century with the computer, he argues, as computers mechanized government functions in a way that human civil servants were designed for, but never quite capable of.[185] Twentieth and twenty-first-century science fiction provides a window on anxieties about depersonalization through computation: out-of-control mainframes (*2001: A Space Odyssey; Colossus*); digitization of humans in dystopian networks (*Snow Crash; The Matrix Trilogy*); and pervasive surveillance (*Minority Report; Little Brother; Super Sad True Love Story*).

These anxieties are well founded: computation is ascendant. We now find ourselves subject to the "Regime of Computation," in Katherine Hayles's language,[186] in the ways that our personhood is translated into data to be surveilled, collected, and leveraged to control us or market to us. Computers make decisions that were once the province of humans, sometimes with disastrous consequences—flash crashes of the stock market, accidental bombings by drones, NSA flags on travelers with names similar to those of wanted terrorists, and so forth. But, as I described in chapter 2, the affordances of computation make its dominance in our lives perhaps inevitable. Powerlessness in the face of a new information technology ordering the world is one source of these anxieties. Another source of anxiety is ignorance: many people know that code and the people who write it are powerful, but because they don't understand the medium, they don't know what to do about the problem or even recognize that it could be a problem. Together, this ignorance and anxiety reflects the transitional nature of computation in our current moment. My goal is not to critique this ascendancy of computation, as Golumbia does, but instead to name a historical precedent for it, perhaps opening the possibility that we could alter its course and make it more humane. The next chapter's continued examination of historical precedents in writing for our contemporary moment in programming takes us further in that direction.

4 Literacy for Everyday Life

Our twentieth century western form of literacy is not an invariable norm; it is as culture-bound and shaped by available technologies (computers, most obviously) as medieval manuscript literacy was. Comparing medieval norms with modern ones puts current questions about literacy in perspective. The best way of understanding the modern western literate mentality is to see where it came from.

—Michael Clanchy, *From Memory to Written Record*[1]

Our contemporary society can be characterized as a *software society* and our culture can be justifiably called a *software culture*—because today software plays a central role in shaping both the material elements and many of the immaterial structures which together make up "culture."

—Lev Manovich, *Software Takes Command*[2]

By the end of the thirteenth century, everyday English citizens were familiar with the ways texts could shape the world: their birth, marriage, and death records as well as their religious and domestic spaces were saturated with writing. This bloom of bureaucracy meant that "literacy fingered its way into every corner of domestic life, providing a formidable instrument of control over family affairs," according to Jack Goody.[3] Documentation in everyday life externalized and formalized personal relationships that were previously dominated by interpersonal interactions. Nonliterates drew on the resources of literates to gain control of their affairs. People began to see their place in the world a bit differently: the world could be a kind of text, subject to interpretation. Regardless of their literacy skills, people recognized that they could be represented in writing.

This was the beginning of a "literate mentality": a widespread worldview reflecting the power of writing among literates and nonliterates alike. As it became apparent that literacy was advantageous and as education became more readily available, people sought out literacy for themselves and their children. Governments and churches encouraged literacy in their flocks to strengthen collective spiritual and economic health. Literacy rates climbed. More institutions could build on the assumption that people were literate. Then, as institutions such as schools, the church, and the law began to assume literacy for participation, *nonliterates* became *illiterates*—defined by lack rather than difference. Illiteracy thus became a marked condition as early as the thirteenth century, although it was not until the nineteenth century when it could be assumed that most people in the West were literate. During the nineteenth century, *literacy* became part of the infrastructure of writing in government, education, and commerce. William Gilmore calls this the point where "literacy becomes a necessity for life."[4]

The history of textual literacy—beginning with the domestication of writing, proceeding through its power to influence worldviews, and then becoming a material basis for literacy—provides a foil for our contemporary relationship with programming and computation, as it did for an earlier shift in chapter 3. That chapter followed the trajectory of computation and writing as they made their way into domestic spaces and lives. This chapter turns from the technology itself to the people who use it. When these technologies enter people's everyday lives, how do ways of thinking and living in the world change? Medieval historians such as Brian Stock claim that a literate mentality accompanied the everyday use of texts, as communities formed around textual interpretations. Literacy scholar David Olson argues that ways of reading texts in several different eras led to revolutions in thinking, including the Reformation and early modern science, as well as the postmodern turn.[5] Elizabeth Eisenstein has made a similar claim for the era of print.[6] Deborah Brandt argues that in our current moment, as "writing is eclipsing reading as the literacy of consequence," people are thinking differently about their reading and writing practices.[7] Daniel Punday traces the intertwined metaphors for computing and writing that have shaped literary works since the twentieth century.[8] That technologies other than writing shape our thought has also long been recognized; for example, Lewis Mumford's idea that the clock produced a new concept of time that facilitated the Industrial Revolution or Martin Heidegger's claim that technology "enframes" our world as resources to be processed.[9] Significant public commentary on technology is devoted to the ways that human relationships and thinking have shifted with modern technology; for instance, the work of Nicholas Carr and Sherry Turkle.[10] My claim that human society is undergoing a new "mentality" because of its extensive engagement with the technology of computation is preceded by many others.

First, a word about what it might mean to describe a "mentality." The concept of "mentalities" comes from midcentury French thinkers such as Robert Mandrou, George Duby, Lucien Febvre, Marc Bloch, and, later, Jacques Le Goff, who together extended Durkheim's "modes of thought" to describe a widely held collection of beliefs characteristic of an era.[11] A history of mentalities gives flesh to bare economic and rational histories of peoples by describing the habits and patterns of thoughts that cut across individuals. As a method, the tracing of mentalities is imprecise; it deals with the "*je ne sais quoi* of history," as Le Goff puts it.[12] Although the mentalities method has been critiqued for offering a homogeneous style of thinking for a given era, Roger Chartier points out that historians tracing mentalities never claimed that thinking was the same across classes or that mentalities offered a perfect window into the thought patterns of a civilization.[13] Mentalities are shared across a population, yet they interplay with the social realities of class and culture, Le Goff insists, and so we must understand them as reflecting social realities imperfectly.[14]

Because imprecision could make this method an "alibi for epistemological laziness,"[15] historians must pay attention to the material sources from which they construct their history of mentality, Le Goff says.[16] But historians must also attend to the social structures that support mentalities: "the history of cultural systems, systems of beliefs, values and intellectual equipment within which they were given shape, lived and evolved."[17] For Lucien Febvre, there were three critical assumptions for a history of mentalities: "that methods of reasoning and forms of thinking are not universal; that they depend above all on the material instruments and conceptual categories associated with a particular era; and that the development of mental tools is not marked by any continuous or necessary progress."[18] In the work of these historians, we can see an emphasis on the materials from which mentalities were constructed.

Here, as I frame my previous chapters' technological histories, linguistic parallels, and social contexts with this concept of mentalities, I am mindful of the overbroad claims possible with this frame. Indeed, broad consequences for literacy on individual and societal mentalities, as claimed by writing scholars such as Walter Ong, Eric Havelock, Jack Goody, and Ian Watt, have been heavily critiqued, and justifiably so.[19] No empirical evidence has been found to corroborate the huge claims of those earlier accounts proposing a "great divide" between oral and literate societies. It is difficult to separate schooling from literacy, and literacy by itself seems only to have isolated cognitive effects.[20] Writing may *facilitate* a kind of objectivity or a certain kind of thinking, but it does not cause or guarantee it. What I describe as the "literate mentality" (and below, the "computational mentality") is not an empirical phenomenon; it is, following Febvre and Le Goff, located broadly in culture rather than in individual literates.

As Chartier suggests, historians of mentalities often saw language and technology as platforms upon which beliefs were mounted.[21] Andrea diSessa's concept of "material intelligences," which we explored in chapter 2, helps to describe the thinking that writing as a technology facilitates. David Olson elaborates:

> If literacy is thought of as simply the basic skill of recognizing emblems or decoding letters to sound or words to meanings, the implications of literacy, while important, are bound to be limited. But if we regard literacy in the classical sense, as the ability to understand and use the intellectual resources provided by some three thousand years of diverse literate traditions, the implications of learning to exploit these resources may be enormous.[22]

In extending the literate mentality to the computational one in this chapter, I take cues from Olson's later work, as well as from Michael Clanchy, who deliberately avoids the question of whether literacy restructures thought at the level of individual psychology or cognition. Clanchy uses the term "the literate mentality" "simplistically to describe the cluster of attitudes which literates in medieval England shared, and expressed in all sorts of ways in surviving records."[23] More recently, Brandt explicitly draws on Durkheim and the French tradition of mentalities in order to describe how a shifting emphasis in literacy from reading to writing affects the conditions of everyday writers in America.[24] Similarly, I see the literate mentality as a kind of zeitgeist, a shared rather than individual pattern of thought.

We see this literate mentality emerge when the technology of writing begins to affect personal lives. Government uses of writing—or later, computation—redefine what it means to be a citizen. People using writing or computation in domestic and personal contexts begin to reflect its influences in theories of the world and self. These resulting theories are cultural phenomena and are shared independently of literacy status. As a mentality begins to emerge, and as texts or code become central to everyday activities, communities form around uses of the technology. Members can draw on what Norma González and Luis Moll have called a community's "funds of knowledge," pooling their collective human resources to navigate the spaces governed by the technology.[25] But, in the case of writing, community funds no longer suffice when everyday life becomes saturated with the technology. Not only communities but also their members become marked by their uses of the technology: individuals can be labeled "illiterate." The marking of individual reading and writing skills as present or absent sig-naled an eventual transition to mass literacy, and a point where reading and writing became a "necessity for life." Now that some will admit to or are marked as being "computationally illiterate," might we be headed into an era where computational skills could be a "necessity for life?" A point where computational literacy augments what we now think of as literacy more broadly?

Because a literate mentality or computational mentality is not an all-or-nothing state, the several examples of historical moments that I offer below can illustrate different degrees and kinds of literacy or computation operating in society. We look at the influence of writing on people in thirteenth-century England, eighteenth century France, and the long nine-teenth century, when mass education and religious movements drove mass literacy across the West. I argue that a computational mentality began to emerge in America in the 1950s, at the point when the American public became aware of computers. It grew along with the influence of computers in public and private life. In the 1980s, when computers entered many middle-class American homes, and again in the 1990s, when they allowed people to communicate on the World Wide Web, we see significant jumps in their influence on everyday lives. Now that computers are embedded in handheld devices that travel with us everywhere, computation has quite literally become personal. Since the 1950s, philosophies of mind, social spheres, and fundamental concepts of self appear to increasingly reflect a feeling that we are "computed." With the increasing ubiquity of computers, we are developing a computational mentality that parallels the literate mentality that emerged with the pervasiveness of texts. These shifts in cul-ture and identity accompanying the penetration of writing and computa-tion in everyday lives coincide with an integrated and personal relationship to the technology.

The impingements of computation and writing on daily lives lay the groundwork for people to understand the power of the technology and for them to desire and seek out literacy—prerequisites to a successful mass lit-eracy movement.[26] A literate mentality signaled a society's dependence on text, and it also presaged a wider role for literacy in everyday life. What does a computational mentality suggest? Although few are now computationally literate—that is, able to read and write code—most people in the West are cognizant of the ways computation shapes our everyday life. Certain popu-lations are already feeling the pressure of computational literacy on their professions and everyday lives; unless they learn to write code, they feel computationally *illiterate*. In light of a shift to a literate mentality, this chapter highlights the anxieties and ambitions associated with this new computational mentality, which, I argue, signals a move toward computation becoming the material basis for a new literacy. In the final sections of this chapter, I outline how an emerging computational mentality might presage a greater need for individuals to be able to read and write code, the language of computation.

Surrounded by Writing

How did it feel to be a subject of Edward I at the end of the thirteenth century in England? Experiences varied greatly for men, women, Jews, Christians, knights, serfs, craftsmen, and clergy, so it is impossible to describe the feelings of an "average" medieval subject. But chances are good that no matter who you were in late thirteenth century England, you were surrounded by writing. If you had been summoned to court, it would have been in writing. While there, you needed an attorney to prepare your written statement, and a written transcript would have documented the hearing.[27] If you had bought or sold property, you would have used a charter to mark the transfer. If you couldn't sign the document, you would have used a seal instead. If you were a serf and therefore unlikely to buy or sell property, your rights and obligations to your master might have been documented in writing.[28] If you were an estate manager, you probably used writing to keep track of your affairs.[29] If you were part of the king's administration, you would have been able to access royal records because they were written and stored, and you might have been aware that their value for posterity and proof depended on their accessibility.[30] If you were a monk, you would have had access to more than one book at a time, such that you could juxtapose and compare them in addition to meditating on them.[31] If you were a nun, you might have been literate, as you would have lived like a (male) monk. But since women's lives were circumscribed by the home and poorly documented, we don't know much about medieval women's literacy generally.[32] However, if you were a woman of a higher class, you would have been immersed in writing, and you might have been able to read in Latin, French, and English. You even may have owned a precious Book of Hours, which was both a text and an aesthetic, devotional object, and demanded an extraverbal, visual and meditative kind of reading. But you were less likely to have been able to read alphabetic text, and much less likely to write, than your brother or husband.[33] Regardless of your specific place in society, your experiences of writing probably would have been strange to your grandparents, who would have conducted more of their business face to face, on personal terms. This section explores what it might have meant to be surrounded by writing at this time. In a literate era, written documentation can codify lives, defining relationships, movement, and even the self-presentation of individual bodies.

Participation in Collective Literacy

As described in the previous chapter, writing began to replace human memory and social mechanisms of community and trust in the eleventh through thirteenth centuries. Because bureaucratic and commercial uses of writing circumscribed everyone, everyday English citizens were forced to acknowledge writing in their lives. Medieval historian Brian Stock claims that the twelfth century is the point when writing became so integrated into daily life that people began feeling compelled to engage with the technology.[34] Through the proliferation of documents in archives, the spread of literate skills, and the general penetration of writing into ordinary lives, people began to absorb the functions and importance of documents into their modes of thinking and interacting. Clanchy claims that by the end of Edward I's reign in 1307, "writing [was] familiar throughout the country-side. ... This is not to say that everyone could read and write by 1307, but that by that time literate modes were familiar even to serfs, who used charters for conveying property to each other and whose rights and obligations were beginning to be regularly recorded in manorial rolls. Those who used writing participated in literacy, even if they had not mastered the skills of a clerk."[35]

It is critical to note that *participation* in literacy is different from individual literacy or mass literacy. It signals a point when people are surrounded by and affected by writing. Because people knew their lives were shaped by texts, medieval historians generally consider English society to be literate at this time, despite low individual literacy rates. Franz Bäuml writes, "At all levels of society, the majority of the population of Europe between the fourth and fifteenth centuries was, in some sense, illiterate. Yet medieval civilization was a literate civilization; the knowledge indispensable to the functioning of medieval society was transmitted in writing: the Bible and its exegesis, statutory laws, and documents of all kinds."[36] Stock describes "textual communities" that pooled their literacy resources and navigated this literate civilization.[37] Nicholas Orme claims that medieval English society was "collectively literate" at the end of the thirteenth century: "Everyone knew someone who could read, and everyone's life depended to some extent on reading and writing."[38] A new category of person emerged: the "quasi-literate," a person who couldn't read or write but who had access to someone who could.[39] Because of these circulation patterns of literacy, it is difficult to determine who had ready access to text through their personal connections, that is, was *effectively* literate.[40] For example, Bäuml reminds us that the signature, often used as a historical measure of literacy, is a socially conditioned artifact. Even literates might have had professional scribes sign documents on their behalf, just as secretaries now sometimes sign documents on behalf of their bosses.[41] And because literacy in medieval England was complicated by the circulation of three languages—English, French, and Latin—it would be impossible to assess an individual's literacy without taking into account complex contexts for its multiple uses and forms. Looking at the same phenomenon of collective literacy hundreds of years later, David Vincent notes that we cannot look at individual literacy in the eighteenth and nineteenth centuries to determine access to text. A whole family or social unit could function in a literate society if just one member could read or write.[42]

The pooling of resources to navigate literacy challenges is a contemporary phenomenon, too, and well documented in ethnographic research. Norma González and Luis Moll show working-class Mexican communities in Arizona drawing on collective "funds of knowledge" to solve problems and support education of their members.[43] Shirley Brice Heath describes residents of one Carolina Piedmont community interpreting important school and health documents together.[44] Marcia Farr tracks the sharing of literacy and language skills among an extended family network of Chicanos in Chicago, showing that they can together respond to a number of documentary situations that might have challenged any one member alone.[45] Kate Vieira demonstrates a similar collective coping strategy for written documents among Portuguese-speaking immigrants in Massachusetts.[46] The fact that communities across time and space can draw on community resources to surmount the obstacles that their documentary societies throw at them means that we must consider literacy a social rather than individual phenomenon. What it means to be literate at any given time will always be shaped by dominant and niche uses of literacy, languages, genres, and community resources. Below, we will see how this collective literacy functions for current computational challenges as well.

Bureaucracy and Anxiety: Substituting Personal Relations with Writing

As described in chapter 3, the uses of writing for governance accelerated greatly at the end of the thirteenth century in England. But we can trace this phenomenon to other eras and places, including eighteenth-century France and nineteenth-century England. In all of these moments, attempts to increase the scope and efficiency of governance led to bureaucratic expansion and greater dependence on writing. For people during these times, however, textual changes were not limited to government. Texts began to substitute for human action, as in the case of written deeds or wills replacing corporal memory tactics. Through this substitution, texts became a kind of truth in themselves, rather than reflecting or recording some truth outside of them. For example, we now perceive written surveys of land as the authoritative description of property; if there are conflicts between neighbors about boundaries, the written legal description presides. But this was not always the case. Stock explains this transition: "People began to think of facts not as recorded in texts, but as embodied in texts, a change in mentality of major importance in the rise of methods for classifying, encoding and retrieving written information."[47]

Similar to the Norman Conquest, the French Revolution was an impetus for a different kind of government. Ben Kafka describes the state's shift from personal dealings to written ones. Under the ancien régime, civil service positions were obtained through personal connections; you got to where you were because of whom you knew.[48] The Revolution's violent distaste for nepotism abolished that system and looked to writing to achieve greater *liberté*, *égalité*, and *fraternité*. The new system presumed that writing could render the state more efficient as well as more democratic by making its operations more transparent. For example, Kafka cites a 1793 order containing provisions for efficiency, stipulating "All relations between all public functionaries can no longer take place except in writing." Paperwork could facilitate surveillance. Surveillance of government would abolish corruption, and surveillance of citizens would ensure efficiency and fairness in governance. At least, these were the ostensible objectives of this emphasis on documentation. As Kafka points out, it seems impossible that *all* relations among public servants could have occurred in writing.[49]

A similar automation of governance through writing happened at the height of the British Empire. Inspired by the systematic management they saw in the American government, British government "mechanizers" sought to streamline administration and collect more statistical information about British citizens.[50] These reformers wanted to divide labor and make the government into an efficient and transparent machine. Charles Babbage successfully used this management philosophy in his 1852 bid for funding his Difference and Analytical Engines: "There is no reason why mental, as well as bodily Labour, should not be economized by the aid of machinery."[51] Although his engines were important precursors to the computer, they did not help systematize governance; instead, what answered the call for systemization was a steady increase in civil service personnel as well as documentation and standardization of their duties. Reformers imposed what Jon Agar calls "a Domesday compilation of landholdings in which land was measured and rights were visibly assigned in written documents."[52] The goal was to make things simpler and systematic.[53] These depersonalizing influences were particularly pronounced in British colonial India, where utilitarian philosophers such as Jeremy Bentham and James Mill wanted to replace the local tradition of personal rule with automated administration, "in which what governed was the symbolic abstraction of writing and the surveillance of facts."[54]

These transitions from oral to written communication allowed government to scale up and avoid some aspects of nepotism and class preference. Governments could record, process, and store a greater quantity of information about their citizens or enemies. But the ideals of increased documentation failed to match reality. The twelfth-century Domesday Book, nineteenth-century British surveys of landholdings, and Revolutionary France's attempts at comprehensive and authoritative documentation all had greater aspirations than applications. This was, in part, because the volume of information collected in these efforts was immense and impossible to fully process.[55] Looking back at the Revolution, nineteenth-century French encyclopedist Pierre Larousse wrote about the problem of drowning in paperwork: thousands of clerks were generating and signing documents like automatons, without reading them, without their content passing through their minds at all.[56] Ben Kafka offers an interesting account of an eighteenth century civil servant on trial who claimed that he signed but did not read a document because of "the physical impossibility of doing otherwise": the volume of documents that came across his desk was too great to read.[57] The hope that governments had for written documentation, however unachievable, suggests the power of writing and its association with knowledge during these eras.[58]

The substitution of paper for personal relations may have denigrated aspects of humanity even as it failed to achieve complete transparency or surveillance. The danger bureaucracy poses to humanity is, of course, a common theme taken up by writers from Franz Kafka to Max Weber. In the eras we observe, the idea that writing could stand in for a person was jarring. Writing can be forged, can disrupt established power structures, and can appear to assume a kind of autonomous power. The shifting boundary between the duties of humans and their technologies can even change perceptions of humanity itself. Such ruptures in the social fabric reveal a society growing increasingly dependent on writing.

Forgery can be a major social problem for a society learning to depend on writing. Writing can claim untrue things long after they have been disproved, as Socrates observed in Plato's *Phaedrus*. This seems especially true in the twelfth century, when writing was becoming authoritative yet was also subject to manipulation; at that time, writing "implied distrust, if not chicanery, on the part of the writer."[59] For example, as a particularly literate class, twelfth-century monks knew that "a document which stated something untrue or unverifiable would continue to state it—and make it look authentic and proven—as long as that document existed."[60] Monks became notorious forgers; although they often framed these forgeries as translations of God's will, they established ownership of land and property under dubious terms.[61] Contemporary, widely distributed propaganda against the pope's attempts to show overlordship of France at the turn of the fourteenth century through a series of papal bulls demonstrate a tension between the fact that writing was thought to be authoritative, and the fact that it could be manipulated: "[The pope] can easily acquire a right for himself over anything whatever: since all he has to do is write, and everything will be his as soon as it is written." The "knight" in this fictional dialogue claims not to be familiar with letters and big words, but he knows that one cannot issue written decrees where one lacks jurisdiction.[62] When truth can be embodied in texts, truth can be massaged through forgery or misrepresentation.[63] Forgeries such as those written by monks or property documents required by new Norman laws were also good reasons for medieval people not to trust writing as it came to affect their lives more thoroughly. A literate society such as ours might trust documents because we believe individual human memory to be more fickle than our established social institutions and technologies that verify documents: standardized forms, indelible signatures, laws against forgeries, watermarks, digital passwords, and cryptography. Without these supports, societies shifting to writing wrestled with problems of verity and forgery.

Another anxiety about the shift to a writing-centered governance is located in the fact that it can disrupt traditional hierarchies. Writing allows new kinds of people to make decisions. Many medieval nobles were displeased with policy changes regarding written documentation because the new policies subjected them to legalistic seizures that had previously affected only the powerless.[64] Ben Kafka notes that clerks in the new French state were able to combine the newly central role of writing with their access to paperwork to achieve "a degree of power out of proportion to their social and political status."[65] Because documentation of qualifications substituted for personal recommendations, this disparity between position and power was heightened. Agar sees a similar anxiety in nineteenth-century Britain. As civil servants were no longer selected because of their breeding and judgment but rather on an ostensibly meritocratic basis, men of lower birth—or even women—could use the power of writing to make decisions. Contemporaries wondered: without proper cultural training, would they make decisions in the "right" way?[66]

Perhaps most disconcerting about written bureaucracy was the idea that the technology itself might be in charge, fully displacing humans. Ben Kafka traces the origin of the word *bureaucracy* in eighteenth-century France as a critique of a system using technology to replace human roles in governance: while *demo*-cracy describes rule by the people, *bureau*-cracy describes "rule by a piece of office furniture."[67] Projecting forward from nineteenth-century Britain, Agar claims that the computer is "the apotheosis of the civil servant" because it does everything exactly as told, with no room for personal discretion.[68] The boundaries between humans and technology are blurred through this substitution, first as writing replaces human memory, relationships, and discretion and again as computers replace humans doing the work of writing.[69] Friedrich Kittler identifies mass education as one source of the blurring between the work of humans and texts—education being a budding bureaucracy of its own as well as an important contributor to the steep rise in literacy rates in the nineteenth century. He writes, "Compulsory education engulfed people in paper … Whatever they emitted and received was writing. And because only that exists which can be posted, bodies themselves fell into the regime of the symbolic."[70] As people became more literate and more enmeshed in bureaucracy, texts became more central in their lives as well as *to* their lives. The interpenetration of the technology of writing and human social structures led people to think of themselves differently.

For good reasons, writing was not immediately accepted as authoritative or as a valid alternative to traditional social interactions, just as the use of computation in place of those interactions is often viewed with skepticism now. There was often a generation gap between when a form of documentation was developed and when it was accepted.[71] As David Levy argues, documents and writing could not serve as proxies for human witnesses without complex structures to support them and give them context,[72] and those structures took considerable time and effort to build. Support structures must be built not only through material methods such as indexing, verification, and archives, but also in the culture that relies on writing. The mere presence of writing or literacy does not imply an understanding of legal codes or the other potential functions of writing, as Olson observes.[73]

Only when cultures begin to accept writing as a form of authority and learn to work with it can we can think of them as possessing a collective "literate mentality."

This textual dominance continues, of course. The areas of life that were subjected to written documentation during the Middle Ages are still subjected to them now: marriage certificates, birth certificates, citizenship documents, and property deeds. Perhaps these forms of documentation have worn their way into our bureaucratic system so deeply that they are the most resistant to change.[74]

Shifts in Ways of Reading

A developing literate mentality in the Middle Ages influenced scientific methods and philosophical ideas as well as governance. Text allowed for some distance between speaker and idea; in science, this meant that methods could be scrutinized apart from their actor. Traditional cosmologies became distinct from scientific explanations of the world and nature. In philosophy, the way records could time-shift events highlighted the distinction between what was really happening and what was thought to be happening.[75] The organizing structures that arose around texts in the medieval era made possible the "classifying, sifting, and encoding" of reality. Events could be edited and ordered, and differences between codified rules for behavior and actual behavior emerged.[76] Stock demonstrates that certain interpretations of medieval heresies arose from these disparities between texts and actuality.[77]

The acknowledgment that text could embody a truth was a marked change over earlier ways of reading, argues Olson. Before that, when texts were scarcer and literacy rarer, the paradigm of reading was meditation on a text: a person would read one text over and over, allowing multiple meanings to emerge. We might think of the Books of Hours, discussed in chapter 3, as many elite women probably could not read but could contemplate the symbolic images and decorative text in their books. The proliferation of meanings that individuals could glean from texts became dangerous to religious authority over scripture, however, and there was a move originating from church factions to pin textual meaning down. Olson points to twelfth-century Hugh of St. Victor as pioneering the concept of literal interpretation, later embodied in Thomas Aquinas's thirteenth-century *Summa Theologica* and eventually leading to Martin Luther's complaint against what "truth" had become for the church.[78] Thus, the twelfth century marks a key transition in literacy: the move from writing as *reminder* of truth to writing as *representation* of truth. Once the literal truth is thought to be represented in a text, it becomes discoverable with careful reading of that text.[79] Olson says this way of "reading the Book of Scripture" for an inherent truth led to "reading the Book of Nature" in early modern science, which sought to peel scientific fact away from subjective interpretation. Robert Boyle's scientific experiments serve as examples. Just as anyone could, with effort, look through a written text to see its "correct" meaning, Boyle's witnesses could "read" the events all alike.[80]

The printing press's facilitation of standard texts reinforced this notion of literal truth. Because the early print period is well studied, I will provide just a few illustrative and canonical examples here. Clanchy notes that there are many variations in texts of Magna Carta, indicating that exactness was not necessary or even possible in documents at the time. He writes, "Insistence on absolute literal accuracy is a consequence of printing, compounded by photocopying and computing."[81] Jay David Bolter points out that whereas writing practices like calligraphy draw attention to the text itself, print typography can standardize a text and deemphasize its materiality.[82] Consequently, the typographic letter appears to lead to a more authoritative text and to an idea of reliable, standardized interactions with texts. Olson notes that the Latinate neologism *verbatim* was coined in the fifteenth century, coincident with the invention of printing.[83] These standardized interactions with printed texts contributed directly to the Enlightenment, according to Eisenstein. The verbatim interpretation of texts is reflected in shifts in contract law as well, as courts moved from enforcing the perceived intent of a contract to its literal text in the nineteenth century.[84]

In his broad historical survey of shifts in ways of reading, Olson claims that cultural understandings of our world, science, and psychology are all "by-products of our ways of interpreting and creating written texts, of living in a world on paper."[85] Historical details of how different forms of text and textual practices shape different modes of thinking are important to acknowledge. Written texts provide fewer cues than oral delivery about how to "take" them; for example, ironically, sincerely, or jokingly. Readers must interpret texts, supplying the illocutionary force of the text themselves. Ways of reading have changed with the availability and style of texts, Olson argues, leading to broader changes about how we interpret the world. He argues that this perspective is different from the so-called great-divide theories of Levy-Bruhl, who tried to characterize a "primitive mind," or of McLuhan, who tried to distinguish between "oral man," "literate man," and "electronic man." The mentality that Olson exposes lies not in individual cognition, but in a cultural mindset and shared ways of thinking about the self and the world. Olson explains: humans could always reason, but literacy and its cultural contexts allow them to reason about reason.[86] Texts as representations, whether of truth (modernism) or of other representations (postmodernism), allow for abstract reasoning. The result is different "theor[ies] of literacy and mind" corresponding with different ways of reading.[87]

The Limits of Collective Literacy: Literacy as a "Necessity for Life"

Prodded by government policies and aided by the domestication of books and technology of the printing press, reading and writing increasingly became generalized skills from the Middle Ages through the Renaissance in the West. But it was not until the eighteenth century that we saw something like mass literacy, in particular among women and people of the lower classes. Beginning around the late eighteenth century, literacy began to be so widely needed in everyday life that people increasingly sought it out, and consequently it began to be widely possessed. As people became literate across regions, sexes, and classes, literacy became even more necessary. As Lawrence Cremin observed of nineteenth- and twentieth-century America, "In an expanding literacy environment, literacy tends to create a demand for more literacy."[88] In other words, literacy amplifies itself. William Gilmore, who explored the transition to mass literacy in eighteenth- and nineteenth-century Vermont, called this the point where reading became a "necessity of life" because reading was embedded in the day-to-day activities of most people.[89] Reading's importance generally precedes that of writing because reading meant one could understand and participate, especially in religion. When the ability to participate in this world of letters—through reading and perhaps even through writing—becomes a "necessity of life," we can see the beginnings of what we can consider *literacy*. Reading and, later, writing distinguish themselves from other important skills because of their widespread, powerful, and now infrastructural nature.

As forms of reading and writing become more useful because the scope of their application increases, people begin to perceive them as essential personal skills, not simply something for which one can lean on family or hire out. Here we can see the rhetorical layer of literacy forming, as discussed in chapter 1. Deborah Brandt's ethnographic studies of literacy as it is lived in individual lives highlight this rhetorical shift. As the social and material systems that give literacy its value change, so does the value placed on various kinds of literacies.[90] The skills that people have are no longer thought to be sufficient. Concepts of what literacy is morph in concert with actual and perceived shifts in demands on people's skills.

When literacy is widely thought to be a necessity of life, it becomes essential for people to know certain forms of reading and writing to carry out their daily lives as citizens and workers or to maintain their social positions. In colonial New England, colonists wishing to maintain a higher social status began to need literacy in the eighteenth century, argues Kenneth Lockridge.[91] Information management and commercial transactions increasingly demanded literacy. As in medieval England, business once conducted face to face, such as land purchases, became documented in writing. Few men were literate in New England in the seventeenth century, but there also wasn't much need for literacy—the gap between literacy demand and literacy supply was narrow. But after the American Revolution, when adult male literacy in New England was almost universal, the gap was widened by voting requirements, commerce, and other demands of the new citizenry.[92] As literacy became more common, it became more necessary—and vice versa.

The necessity of literacy for civic participation—one of the main justifications for national literacy campaigns (see chapter 1)—began to manifest itself in voting procedures, legal proceedings, and interpretations of contract law in the nineteenth century. As other voting requirements were gradually stripped away—location of birth, property ownership, race, and later sex—literacy and education began to stand in for those qualities in defining what it meant to be an American citizen.[93] Until the Voting Rights Act of 1965, literacy tests were used to disenfranchise many African Americans, especially in the South. These tests were often administered prejudicially and so were not tests of reading per se. However, they reflect the way that the civic value of literacy established in the nineteenth century could provide cover for racial disenfranchisement.

Assuming they made it past any literacy tests in their state, illiterate voters encountered another challenge in the secret ballot. Edward Stevens quotes from a court's interpretation of a late nineteenth-century Pennsylvania statute that the secret ballot "was well calculated to promote the cause of general education by compelling the masses to learn to read and write as a condition precedent to the exercise of the right to suffrage." Moreover, this ballot would also "punish the illiterate by compelling them to admit their ignorance in public, by asking aid in preparation of their ballots."[94] A number of late nineteenth century cases basically said "tough luck" to illiterate voters: because their ballots were the same as everyone else's, their personal deficits were their own misfortune.[95] The secret ballot assumed individual literacy as a default. This literate default was a reflection of higher literacy rates among American voters, but it also marked illiterates and may have driven them to seek literacy.

Illiteracy was not only a misfortune at the ballot box, but also in contract law beginning in the nineteenth century. Through the eighteenth century, paternalism in the courts had protected illiterates who had unwittingly agreed to unfair contractual terms. But at the same time the idea of a *verbatim* contract became dominant, signing a bad contract became an individual's responsibility. This shift was connected to rising literacy rates, as courts began to assume that parties could all execute their "freedom of contract," regardless of their literate status. In the seventeenth century, it was not uncommon for documents to be drawn up with half of the signers using a mark in place of a signature, suggesting that literates and illiterates mixed in business and legal affairs.[96] Through cases in the nineteenth century, illiterates were not thought of as infirm or incapable of assenting to contracts; however, their degree of knowledge about *literal* terms of a contract were unclear. Courts that once had acted as though illiterates needed to be protected began to assume the illiterate party's obligation to find someone to read the contract to them. Those who did not were negligent, and negligence is not protected under the law.[97] Stevens notes that this made illiteracy an ethical problem for courts, in terms of contract enforcement as well as jury selection. In the later nineteenth century, there were cases that marked illiterate jurors as potentially incompetent.[98] Currently in the United States, not being able to fill out the juror form or understand and speak English can disqualify jurors.[99]

The growing importance of literacy does not mean that people who were illiterate could not survive in a literate society or that literacy was or has ever been fully universal. As Furet and Ozouf lament, "Wherever we look, in every period, social stratification presides over the history of literacy."[100] The demands and supply of literacy varied widely across echelons of wealth and between men and women. Lockridge notes that "literacy was intimately connected with sex, wealth, and occupation, and that to an appreciable degree such forces determined literacy," at least until the rise of mass schooling.[101] Upper-class Bostonian men were all literate by the end of the seventeenth century, whereas women's literacy rates at that time appear to have plateaued at 45%.[102] Not until the mid-eighteenth century did rural men catch up somewhat to urban men.[103] Stratifications were much more pronounced in England, Pennsylvania, and Virginia. In France, literacy rates lagged in rural areas, in the southwest, and among women at least until the late nineteenth century.[104] In industrial areas, children left school at younger ages—before they were taught to write—and so factories had a depressing effect on literacy.[105] Even now, literacy is not evenly distributed in most societies and across the globe, nor is the need for it. Women's literacy levels lag behind men's in underdeveloped countries,[106] and even in a country with near-universal literacy like the United States, race and class disparities mark literacy skills.[107] Even when literacy becomes a "necessity of life," it is more necessary and more accessible for some than for others.

As this section has outlined, beginning in the late eighteenth century and accelerating in the nineteenth century, literacy—especially reading literacy—grew more common throughout Europe and North America because of mass schooling and mass literacy campaigns, the rhetoric of building the nation, increased economic activity, and personal motivation. Increased literacy levels corresponded to an increased importance of texts in people's daily lives—newspapers that cataloged both local and global events, almanacs that offered advice to farmers, and accounts that kept track of debts. The pervasiveness of texts created a kind of collective literate mentality among people, regardless of individual literacy levels. As texts became a central conduit for culture and knowledge, reading became not just useful, but necessary. This appears to have become the case, at least to varying degrees, across much of the West in the nineteenth century. In the next section, we look at the potential indications and implications of a transition to mass computational literacy in light of this history of the transition to mass literacy.

Surrounded by Computation

Since at least the 1980s, computers and software have been part of most Americans' daily lives; together, they shape how we work, play, and maintain relationships. Behind the paper tokens of our identities and relationships such as photo IDs and marriage certificates are massive digital databases held by our governments, social networks, and employers. And many of our other daily transactions are now built on systems running computer code—personnel records, bank accounts, e-mail communication.

At the parallel point in the history of writing, writing's pervasive presence prodded individuals to be literate. And, indeed, computation has now become so ubiquitous that skills in working with it—most obviously in the physical form of computers but also in responding to its bureaucratic and commercial manifestations—can no longer be safely bracketed into specialized professions. Although these skills are still a material intelligence rather than a full-fledged literacy because they are not yet a "necessity of life," they are increasingly in demand. To navigate many professions and the demands of life in the twenty-first century, we need to have computational skills, or at least know someone who does.

In chapter 3, our historical survey traced computers' increasing prominence in American professional and personal lives from the 1940s to the 1980s, when computation was tied to physical computers. Above, we explored the eras when writing was so pervasive that people began to have a "literate mentality," regardless of whether or not they were literate. In this half of the chapter, I argue that just as people developed a literate mentality in an era saturated with texts, today we can see a "computational mentality" in our society so dominated by computers. This computational mentality manifests itself in dominant theories and discussions of mind and self and society as well as in our language and habits. It also suggests that we are rapidly approaching a limit to our collective computational literacy and a horizon for when this literacy might be needed for everyday life.

Computers Enter Public Consciousness

Government-sponsored research in the heady years after World War II heightened computational capacities for war, defense, and other information-processing pressures. This period also brought computers into the public and inspired both optimism and skepticism about where computation could go. Exemplifying the optimism associated with this period is Vannevar Bush's canonical "As We May Think," published in the *Atlantic* in 1945. Bush generated excitement about computers when he claimed that a future device called a "Memex" would be "an enlarged intimate supplement to ... memory" and would help to catalog and retrieve the collected knowledge of civilization.[109]

The Mark I had caught the imagination of the general population in 1944 and was "an icon for the computer age," according to Campbell-Kelly and Aspray.[110] Depictions of computers in the 1950s echo the assertion by Edmond Berkeley in his popular 1949 book that computers weren't automatons but *"Giant Brains, or Machines that Think."* Building on ideas from scientific management and intelligence testing in the 1920s, as well as his background in Boolean algebra and symbolic logic, Berkeley imagined computers would be able to answer complex social questions in systematic and rational ways.[111] Then came the UNIVAC I, the commercially available computer designed by the team that developed the ENIAC at the Moore School. The UNIVAC was used by the U.S. Census Bureau in 1950[112] and was famously showcased on CBS as a television publicity stunt to predict election results in 1952, which it did—more accurately than the pollsters. Campbell-Kelly et al. note that "the appearance of the UNIVAC on election night was a pivotal moment in computer history."[113] Although people may have heard about computers before, they were unlikely to have seen one before the broadcast.[114] *New Yorker* cartoon editor Robert Mankoff writes, "When Univac correctly predicted the results of the 1952 Presidential election, the public became aware of 'thinking machines,' and *New Yorker* cartoonists began to endow what were then called 'electronic brains' with the ability to manage more than numbers."[115] In one cartoon, a computer manages a baseball team (figure 4.1).

In another popular depiction of computers, the 1957 movie *Desk Set* starring Spencer Tracey and Katherine Hepburn, a computer that takes over a television network research department goes haywire and fires everyone. Bernadette Longo notes that the metaphors of both brain and robot obtained for computers in this era. Robots—a concept made publicly prominent through the play *R.U.R.* in the 1920s—had already captured the idea

"Shift the outfield to the left, play the third baseman deep, and
feed the batter a curve—low, and on the inside."

Figure 4.1
In this 1955 *New Yorker* cartoon, a computer coaches a baseball team, showing that computers were thinking as well as calculating machines. Joseph Mirachi, *New Yorker*, June 18, 1955. Reprinted with permission from Condé Nast.

that automation to improve human life could also supplant it. When combined with the metaphor of the brain, computers became both fearsome and awesome: "We feared these new electronic helpers even as we embraced them," she writes.[116]

The U.S. government's SAGE missile defense project represents another facet of this era's computational fantasies. For example, the *Pittsburgh Press* presented SAGE in 1956 with the headline "U.S. Unveils Push-Button Defense" and called its central computer "a flashing, clicking monster larger than the average home."[117] The terminals were controlled with light guns pointed at screens, accentuating the system's futuristic military applications.[118] A promotional video produced by IBM's Military Products Division titled "On Guard!" tells us, over footage of technical equipment and personnel, "You are listening to the heartbeat of the SAGE computer. Every instrument in this room is constantly monitoring, testing, pulse-taking, controlling. For this is the programming and operations center for the SAGE computer, which surrounds it."[119] Over an image of a little girl sleeping and her parents watching over her, the film concludes, "And as long as we're on guard, as long as we're ready to look ahead and move ahead, the future of America is secure." At the height of the Cold War, SAGE must have been reassuring but also alien to the American public.

These were the years of Big Science, both comforting and intimidating in its authority. Science fiction writers such as Arthur C. Clarke and Isaac Asimov probed the power as well as the dangers of computers. The film *2001: A Space Odyssey* (1968), based on a Clarke story from 1951, intertwines exploration of the frontier of space with the problems of computers that can make decisions. Less commercially successful, though still revealing, was *Colossus: The Forbin Project* (1970, based on a 1966 story), which pitches American and Soviet sentient supercomputers against each other with disastrous results.

J. C. R. Licklider's work with ARPANET in the early 1960s augured a new approach in human-computer interaction against the dominant and dominating visions of command and control systems. He posited the computer as an aid to human communication in his visionary essays "Man-Computer Symbiosis" (1960) and "The Computer as Communication Device" (1968, with Robert Taylor).[120] The cartoon above serves as an early example of the ways computers were portrayed as artificial brains that threatened the human monopoly on rational thought. In these accounts, the fundamental qualities of what it means to be human were called into question. In contrast, Licklider carved out an important role for computers while preserving human exceptionalism:

In the anticipated symbiotic partnership, men will set the goals, formulate the hypotheses, determine the criteria, and perform the evaluations. Computing machines will do the routinizable work that must be done to prepare the way for insights and decisions in technical and scientific thinking. Preliminary analyses indicate that the symbiotic partnership will perform intellectual operations much more effectively than man alone can perform them.[121]

As computers began to pierce the public consciousness of Americans, theories began to emerge in both academic and popular venues about how these "thinking machines" and humans should interact. Anxiously or optimistically, these midcentury visions imagined a necessary relationship between humans and computers in the division of intellectual labor.

These representations of the mainframe era suggest the uneasy but increasingly pervasive relationship between humans and computation. We might think of this stage as parallel to that of the early twelfth century in England, when the Domesday Book and other documentary innovations made writing familiar to many, although intimidating and perhaps even world-ending. The uses of writing and computation were still relatively limited; however, most people would have seen or heard of some of what the technologies were capable of doing. Computers began to be part of the landscape of human thought, and in these examples, we can see the horizon of a computational mentality.

Computational Models of the World

The midcentury ideas that spawned research and development in code and computation led to new ways of thinking about and modeling the world. While these models may have circulated among scientists, technologists, and philosophers, they nonetheless reflect a trajectory toward a more popular computational mentality. For example, in 1943, Erwin Schrödinger proposed that the basis of life was a "genetic code-script," not unlike Morse code.[122] A code-script was his answer to the question of how life was able to seemingly defy the second law of thermodynamics; it could allow for both variation and order. While the genetic code is quite different from what Schrödinger suggested, his code model was key to unlocking some of the mystery of genetics.[123]

Also reflecting influence from early theories of code and computation, the theory of "cellular automata"—individual computational units that follow programmed rules—has been used to explain various phenomena from biological systems to group behavior. Automata have simple individual rules, but when grouped together they emulate "emergent" behavior. The simple rules and grouping of cellular automata make them particularly amenable to computation—and, conversely, theories of computation helped to spawn the concept of cellular automata. The theory of cellular automata has multiple links to computational research: it was inspired by Turing's 1936 model of the "Turing machine," described more explicitly by John von Neumann in 1951 and extended in the 1980s by Stephen Wolfram.[124] Mathematician John Conway proposed his "game of life" in 1970, which models this complex behavior emerging from simple rules. Simulating the game of life is a now common programming exercise.[125] Benoit Mandelbrot's fractal generation relies on similar principles of simple equations and high processing power to result in complex mathematical structures. Konrad Zuse—the German inventor of the computer and innovator of programming languages—suggested that physical models of the world could be influenced by ideas from computation in his *Rechnender Raum* ("Calculating Space"). He proposed "digital physics" in 1967, based on the idea that the universe itself is a computer.[126] Years later, as N. Katherine Hayles details, this idea of a "universal computer" was taken up by Seth Lloyd, Edward Fredkin, and others.[127]

For systems such as the universal computer, fractals, and cellular automata, there is no shortcut via an equation for determining an end result of a process. Only by letting the system run—by computing it—can we see what emerges. Because this computational model cannot be described ahead of its enactment, it runs counter to Enlightenment ideals of being able to describe systems perfectly as well as the presupposition of a "transcendental signified," which Derrida names as logos, or God.[128] It is a stepwise way of viewing and analyzing the world: lots of little independent entities and calculations accrete into complex systems, rather than complexity being designed or described top-down. For this reason, cognitive scientists Francisco Varela, Evan Thompson, and Eleanor Rosch argue that this computational model signals a Kuhnian revolution in the way we think about the world.[129] Wolfram calls it "a new kind of science."

There is an important tension underlying the work of Wolfram and others: is computation a *model* for the world or does it *constitute* the world? For Hayles, this tension is more interesting than its potential resolution. It tells us "what it means to be situated at a cultural moment when the question remains undecidable—a moment, that is, when computation as means and metaphor are inextricably entwined as a generative cultural dynamic."[130] She notes that computation deployed as metaphor has real effects in the world, and thereby becomes ontological. For instance, American military strategy evolved from "command and control" to "network-centric warfare" in parallel with similar developments in computation. The results of this strategy were, of course, not simply metaphorical, though they began that way.[131] For David Golumbia, this elevation of computation from metaphor to model—what he calls "computationalism"—is dangerous and totalizing.[132] If everything from DNA to the shape of space-time is influenced by computation, Golumbia notes, "The power and universal application of computation has made it look to us as if, quite literally, *everything* might be made of computation."[133] This is a bad thing, Golumbia argues, because it means that we are substituting a *model* of the world for the world itself. Treating this ontological phenomenon more neutrally, Hayles calls the means-and-metaphor model of the world the "computational universe."

Regardless of its veracity or moral valence, I would argue that the mere existence of this model of the world reflects a computational mentality at work, at least in scientific sectors of society. Even if metaphors are not operationalized as military strategy or models for DNA as Hayles mentions, they nevertheless reflect a mindset. We "live by" metaphors, as George Lakoff and Mark Johnson argue: "our conceptual system is largely metaphorical [and so] the way we think, what we experience, and what we do every day is very much a matter of metaphor."[134] Because computers have become everyday objects and computation an everyday process, their metaphors have entered our everyday language. Sherry Turkle pins this uptick in computer metaphors to the 1980s, the personal computing era.[135] Wendy Hui Kyong Chun observes that, more recently, computer code, software, and hardware have become metaphors for genetics, culture, nature, memory, and cognition.[136] Although Chun resists these metaphors, especially the metaphorical conflation of computer storage and human memory, her wide-ranging discussion of the various metaphors to which computers have been subjected suggests how thoroughly they have become embedded in our ways of thinking about our bodies, brains, and behaviors. Computers are now evident in the language and models we use to describe our worlds.

Computational Models for Mind and Self

Immediately following their military applications, computers also became integral to the simulation of human thought, to scientific models for the functions of the human brain. As Turkle explains, research in artificial intelligence (AI) and human psychology converged in interesting ways beginning in the 1950s: the top-down Freudian model of ego, superego, and id were displaced by newer models of distributed cognition, inspired by concepts of computer engineering.[137] In linguistics, Noam Chomsky proposed algorithmic approaches to language acquisition. Chomsky's "universal grammar" operated like a computer chip, programmed by a human's early linguistic environment. It is no coincidence that Chomsky's theory was developed along with a flurry of research on computers and artificial intelligence at MIT.[138] Analytic philosophy offered theories of mind influenced by this branch of linguistics and the rise of the computer. The idea was that by discovering certain things about algorithms, we would also understand aspects of human thought.[139] According to Hilary Putnam, philosophers began asking, "Are thinking and referring identical with computational states of the brain?" Putnam himself proposed the computer as a model for the mind.[140]

Consolidating some of these threads of academic inquiry and centered on the computer as a model for the mind, cognitive science emerged.[141] Cognitivism—a branch of cognitive science often mistaken for the whole—posits that cognition "is the manipulation of symbols after the fashion of digital computers." It works from the premise that both humans and computers operate only with *representations* rather than "reality."[142] Connectionism, another area of cognitive science, specifies that the way human brains cope with the representation of reality is distributed across a network.[143] For instance, the theory of "perceptrons" describes the ways that small chunks of thought can be networked across the brain and how a computer might be able to simulate that thought.[144] Like Chomsky's linguistics, connectionism has close ties to the computer: it was developed by Seymour Papert and Marvin Minsky, who worked in artificial intelligence at MIT and used the computer as a model.[145] Varela, Thompson, and Rosch point out that in cognitive science, the computer is both a model of mind and a tool of research to learn more about the mind.[146] As Hayles suggested with her idea of the "computational universe," the mind and the computer have served as models and simulations of each other in cognitive science and AI research since the 1950s.

Ideas about the computational mind are not isolated to academic inquiry. Varela, Thompson, and Rosch point to Turkle's best-selling work on how people see themselves reflected in computers to indicate the popularity of computational ideas about human cognition. Turkle reflected in 2005 that her 1984 book "*The Second Self* documents a moment in history when people from all walks of life (not just computer scientists and artificial intelligence researchers) were first confronted with machines whose behavior and mode of operation invited psychological interpretation and that, at the same time, incited them to think differently about *human* thought, memory and understanding."[147]

The form that computation took in each era influenced the models of the self that were generated. Turkle claims that in contrast to monolithic mainframe computers, minicomputers and windowing operating systems that took hold in the 1980s encouraged people to think of themselves as multiple.[148] This concept of a multiple, fragmented self was paralleled in theories of postmodernism and of cognitive science.[149] Turkle's later work traces shifting concepts of self as distributed across networks such as MUD (multi-user dungeon) game platforms in the 1990s and social media sites in the early 2000s.[150] Extending her theory, we can perhaps trace mobile computational devices to the genesis of the "quantified self" movement, adherents of which aim to collect massive quotidian data from themselves. With a goal of "optimizing" brain or body performance, self-trackers chart minutiae of their diet, exercise, sleep, and performance to find patterns. This movement has gone mainstream with commercial computational devices such as the popular FitBit or Apple Watch or software applications to facilitate this tracking. Many self-trackers report that they conceive of themselves and the way they spend their time quite differently when quantifying and processing it as multiple, discrete data points rather than as ephemeral and subjective sensations.[151]

The massive online databases of personal information held by Facebook, LiveJournal, Orkut, Twitter, and other social media websites also enable new forms of self-presentation. In the medium of Facebook, for instance, relationships are formalized on the basis of the programmatic structure the site provides. "Friending" is binary—someone is or is not a friend—and means something different from making friends in person. "Facebook friends" can be business acquaintances, celebrities, or others one has never met "IRL" (in real life). Facebook has recently expanded the ways that gender and relationships can be designated, but they are still definitively encoded. A status of "In a relationship" marks a social relationship that may not have been so starkly and publicly formalized offline. Even the newer "It's complicated" designation for relationships erects borders around the previously amorphous beginnings and endings of romantic entanglements.

The ubiquity of smartphones that can rapidly post text, video, and images to globally accessible social media sites such as Facebook means that the identities and relationships people construct there are deeply integrated with "real life."[152] Online social networks travel with us, and our real-life networks are echoed online. Teens largely use these online social networks to augment their social experiences in their local communities, observes danah boyd.[153] Nathan Jurgenson argues that, at least for the generation of people used to cataloging their lives online, it is no longer possible to separate their online and offline lives. We learn to see with a "Facebook eye": "Facebook fixates the present as always a future past. ... Social media users have become always aware of the present as something we can post online that will be consumed by others."[154] We choose our words in terms of what is potentially reportable on Facebook or Instagram or Twitter, we report our physical locations and habits through Yelp and Foursquare, and we see the activities of our children and friends as videos or pictures to be viewed on Instagram or Vine. The "shock" video site World Star Hiphop serves as an interesting and disturbing example; videos sometimes feature bystanders chanting "World Star," anticipating the action's later appearance on the site. As the *Gothamist* commented, "The site's popularity has created a sort of voyeuristic feedback loop, in which disassociated bystanders immediately videotape violent incidents and act as if they're *already* watching a video on the Internet."[155] Diamond Reynolds's choice to live-stream the shooting death of her boyfriend Philando Castile on Facebook Live on July 6, 2016 led to immediate and widespread outrage and protest over police brutality. Even in the heat of that tragic moment, Reynolds was savvy enough to know the affordances of live-streaming to "get out the truth."[156]

Because the popularity of these social sites changes regularly, these specific examples may already be dated when this book is published. But as long as some of the work of relationships is carried across online social networks, the corporate policies of these sites will affect the status of real relationships and self-presentation: we think of ourselves in their terms, according to their affordances. That corporate entities controlling social media networks have so much influence on the ways we see ourselves should perhaps be a concern. The external, formal, global expression of the self—particularly on social networking sites—leads to a kind of self-editing for presentation in the new medium, just as documentation has done. The people who saw texts move into their lives in the Middle Ages developed a pattern of thinking, habits, and assumptions of a literate mentality. These examples of the shifting ways we see ourselves, our worlds, and our relationships suggest that we have developed a computational mentality as computational devices have become integrated into our professional and personal lives. Although few people know how to program the devices on which code and computation ride into our lives, their manifestations influence us anyhow. In various ways, we have learned to see ourselves as "computed" by the devices and networks on which we depend.

From Computational Mentality to Literacy?

As people now think of themselves as "computed," they are also beginning to need to know how to compute. Surrounded by all of this computation, many people find themselves needing to access or acquire new computational skills to navigate their personal and professional lives. As with writing, the requirements for these skills vary widely, from what we might think of as basic skills to highly complex compositions and niche knowledge. Because computational skills can often be shared between people and across social groups, we are not yet to the point where every individual must be computationally literate. As we saw earlier, however, this social borrowing of literacy skills to navigate essential demands of life, along with a collective literate mentality that was based on the pervasiveness of texts in everyday life, presaged a time when textual literacy was demanded of individuals. Code has only recently become central to our lives, but the diversity and number of people who can program has increased dramatically since the birth of computer code. Writing also became a more widely held skill as it grew in importance. The ability to program is useful to not only computer specialists but also a variety of professions. And there are hints of the kinds of institutions that might be built on the assumption that many people know how to program. We are also seeing evidence of the consequences of individuals not knowing how to read or write code, especially in spheres of government and commerce. Has programming become "a necessity for life?" Not yet perhaps, but the disadvantages of a lack of computational literacy are beginning to manifest themselves. I discuss a few of these indications of our potential turn to mass computational literacy below.

The Limits of Collective Computational Literacy

Like skills with reading and writing, computational skills are often loaned from one community or family member to another. The Pew Internet and American Life Project reports that 48% of technology users need help fixing their phones, computers, and other devices when they break down. Eighteen percent of people with computer failures seek help from family and friends.[157] In many social or family groups, there are often one or two "go-to" people who come to the rescue, who are more skilled than others at problem solving or communication with computers. They serve as tech support for parents or friends whose computers are saddled with viruses or need reorganizing or replacing. Skills in making websites, databases, and image editing are also loaned across groups.[158] While these fix-it sessions may not require programming per se, they do require a more intimate knowledge of file systems, memory organization, and software conventions and available capabilities. Individuals called on to perform these tasks can compound their computational literacy as they learn to perform each new complex task.

Within groups, one or two people's skills can facilitate access to computational literacy for everyone, just as those who can read might read aloud for their families and thus share their access to text. This loaning of skills within groups is possible because people of varying levels of computational literacy mix easily, especially within families. People with different levels of textual literacy also mixed freely in eras where literacy was stratified by sex and age; however, this is no longer common in areas with near-universal literacy. Now, textual literacy levels stratify by class and race and tend to accumulate in some groups more than others. Mixing can happen more easily across languages; for instance, bilingual children of immigrants often serve as interpreters for their families or communities.[159] Although various levels mix now in computational literacy, it appears to be collecting in affluent or already advantaged groups—a phenomenon related to what is sometimes called the "digital divide." Consequently, some groups have greater "funds of knowledge" to draw on than others.

When collective literacy strained under the weight of a society so fully enmeshed in writing, it incentivized individual literacy. Now that we are fully enmeshed in computation, is our collective computational literacy hitting its limits? Perhaps the promises of natural language programming, robust and easy-to-use code libraries, WYSIWYG interfaces, and career specialization will prevent computational literacy from becoming a necessity of life.[160] But the precedent set by writing suggests otherwise. The shift in mentality and the pervasiveness of computation suggest that it is changing what it means to be literate. Computation and coding are now skills upon which many other forms of communication and knowledge are built. Computation is increasingly used as a model of the world and self. The next section looks at how a computational mentality might lead to computational literacy.

Programming Is No Longer a Specialized Skill

What does it look like for other skills to be built on top of computational literacy, for it to move from a specialized and niche ability to something relevant to a diversity of fields and applications? With the rise of interest in programming among artists, journalists, and others, programming is no longer a domain solely for computer scientists. Indeed, programming never was a domain exclusively for specialists. As I described in chapter 1, programming demonstrated potential to be more generally useful from the outset, which John Kemeny and Thomas Kurtz capitalized on at Dartmouth College in the 1960s. What does it mean for computational literacy to become a *platform literacy*?

Although we do not have figures on programming in the general population, the audience and demand for the learn-to-code materials now available online indicate that a wide variety of people are teaching themselves to code. One reason people are driven to learn programming is that it is becoming more useful across a number of professions. Clay Shirky describes this pressure of programming on employment as "downsourcing," a twist on outsourcing; downsourcing is "the movement of programming from a job description to a more widely practiced skill."[161] Just as the need to use software has begun to permeate job descriptions, the need to couple programming with domain knowledge in jobs is accelerating. Scientists, economists, statisticians, media producers, or journalists who also know something about programming can streamline or enrich their research and production.

Journalism is one of the professions most acutely affected by this downsourcing of programming. Online journalism—whether on blogs or traditional news organizations' websites—now involves the integration of visual, audio, and programmatic elements, echoing Deborah Brandt's finding that workplace literacies have become more complex throughout the twentieth century.[162] Alongside traditional writing, interactive graphics and information displays are now ubiquitous on websites such as the *New York Times*, *Vox*, and *FiveThirtyEight*, leading the way toward a code-based approach to conveying the news.

The press, anxiously experiencing as well as reporting on their own state of affairs, has picked up on this shift in information conveyance from alphabetic text to code-based digital media. An article on the Web magazine *Gawker* describes the "Rise of the Journalist Programmer": "Your typical professional blogger might juggle tasks requiring functional knowledge of HTML, Photoshop, video recording, video editing, video capture, podcasting, and CSS, all to complete tasks that used to be other people's problems, if they existed at all. ... Coding is the logical next step down this road. ... You don't have to look far to see how programming can grow naturally out of writing."[163] In other words, the tasks that once belonged to other people's job descriptions have now been "downsourced" into the daily routines of today's typical journalist.[164] The kinds of functional knowledge that *Gawker* lists differ in their technical requirements; for example, HTML is a way of formatting text for display and not a full programming language. But this knowledge is related to computational literacy: how to issue formal commands to the computer, work with various protocols, and build chained procedures that process data.

As programming moves into more domains and professions, it has diversified in appearance. Defining someone who "knows how to program" is as difficult as defining someone who "knows how to write." As literacy studies has taught us, it is notoriously difficult to measure literacy. Literacy resources can be shared among family groups, allowing many people the benefit of one contributor's literacy. Historical studies of signatures are only a proxy for a limited concept of functional literacy, and in contemporary studies we must ask: literate in what genre? With what audience? For what purpose? People can be literate at different levels in the different fields of academic writing, journalism, technical writing, short stories, novels, writing for social media, letter writing, and so forth, and the genre conventions of each of these areas mean that literate skills do not translate perfectly across them. In the same way, the proliferating genres of programming complicate our ability to measure who is computationally literate: designing and programming an operating system, computer game, website, or mobile phone app, scripting an Excel datasheet or writing a Firefox plug-in draw on vastly different skills and even call on different kinds of programming languages. And yet, as with writing, we may consider these skills as part of the same constellation of programming abilities. As Jack Goody suggested with his concept of "restricted literacy," and as the social turn of New Literacy Studies (NLS) reflects, societies and cultures all construct and use literacy in different ways. The diversifying applications for programming, which shape its practices in different ways, are one indication of its more widespread and literacy-like behavior.

Computational Literacy for Civic Contexts

Computational literacy has become useful in civic contexts, again indicating its relevance beyond specialized applications. For instance, Michele Simmons and Jeff Grabill examine civic organizations, catalog how a community group can struggle and succeed with code-based technology to get their messages out, and conclude that programmatic database manipulation can no longer be relegated to technical disciplines. They suggest that computational literacy appears to have a growing role in new forms of civic organizations and expression as they assert: "Writing at and through complex computer interfaces is a required literacy for citizenship in the twenty-first century."[165] To extend Simmons and Grabill's claims about civic literacy, we can look to the "crisis camps" set up in major world cities after the 2010 earthquake in Haiti, where teams of programmers used geographic data available from Google maps and NASA to write a Craigslist-style database that would match donations with needs and help locate missing persons.[166] Along these lines, the organization Code for America (launched in 2009) uses the Teach for America model to embed programmers within local city governments to help streamline some of their specific bureaucratic processes. Adopt-a-hydrant, one of the apps designed by Code for America fellows, matches up fire hydrants in cities like Chicago with local volunteers who agree to keep them clear of snow in case of emergency.[167] Code for America "brigades" have sprouted in many major cities, including my own—Pittsburgh—where meetings collect people with various interests and skills around the use of city data. Some of these civic activities do not require extensive skills in programming, but all draw on concepts of database construction and simple code-based procedures. In other words, elements of programming support writing that can make a difference in the world.

These widespread uses for programming in individual and civic applications display some of the promise that it brings to personal lives and governmental structures. With the integration of programming into more aspects of our lives, we can also see some of the hazards of ignorance about code, especially in terms of legislation. In 1993, Bonnie Nardi argued that it is important for end users to know how to program "so that the many decisions a democratic society faces about the use of computers, including difficult issues of privacy, freedom of speech, and civil liberties, can be approached by ordinary citizens from a more knowledgeable standpoint."[168] In moments like the congressional debates on anti-spam laws for e-mail in the mid 1990s[169] and the proposed Stop Online Piracy Act (SOPA) of 2012, we saw what happens when U.S. public officials do not have the general knowledge Nardi argued for. In those cases, fundamental misunderstandings of how computer code works obscured the terms of debate and nearly led to crippling or unenforceable laws.

Debates around "net neutrality," the Apple Store developer license and data storage, and sharing on social networking sites also foist techno-ethical quandaries onto voters. What does preferential data packet-switching mean for one's home broadband service? Is it censorship to restrict the programming languages in which people can write for particular platforms? Do I have the right to program a computational device that I own? What rights does Facebook have to my network of friends when I trust my data to them? Is using a programmatic script to scrape data from websites on a massive scale something people should be allowed to do, and, if not, how would we prevent it? What constitutes online security and illegal hacking? What does it matter if public officials use private or public servers for their e-mail?

Twenty-first-century American citizens and lawmakers are forced to consider such sophisticated technological questions daily.

One of the justifications of nineteenth century mass literacy campaigns was that a democratic society needed to read in order to consider the questions they were asked to vote on. Should we know enough about the operations of programming in order to recognize and regulate these practices? We must now, for example, understand and trust the technology of writing in order to accept the ways that quotidian bureaucratic documents govern our lives. As we have seen, however, this trust was not always warranted or freely given by a citizenry when the bureaucratic applications of writing were innovated. The ways that texts began to shape the social and political relations of individuals suggests that we will also need to pay greater attention to the ways that code is cataloging and surveilling our lives. We are now seeing critical gaps in governance and communication when lawmakers and citizens are not knowledgeable enough about programming and computational architecture to understand what is possible or desirable to regulate about it. If citizens and lawmakers respond in the way they did to the pressures of texts in governance, we may see computational literacy added to the complex mix of skills we now think of as literacy.

Conclusion

Just as writing was propelled from a specialized to a generalized skill by initiatives from centralized institutions and its adoption into commerce and personal lives, programming—once highly specialized and limited to big-budget operations—is now central to government, large- and small-scale commerce, education, and personal communications. The penetration of text into everyday lives meant that people participated in literacy regardless of their own literate status. People began to acknowledge the way texts are able to shape lives and actions and redefine what it means to be a human in the world. As we are being surrounded by computation in the same way people were once surrounded by writing, we are developing a computational mentality. We are recognizing the role that computation plays in our lives and adjusting our models of the world and ourselves to reflect that role.

A literate mentality was one result of writing becoming an infrastructural technology in society; an increased pressure on individual literacy was another. As writing became so pervasive and as the ability to read and write was increasingly called upon for everyday activities, these skills could no longer be shared by social groups. Collective literacy hit its limits, and now it appears as though collective computational literacy might be doing the same thing. Although code is embedded in the infrastructure of our workplaces, government, and daily communications, programming is not yet a skill required for participation in social, civic, and commercial life in America; it is not yet a "necessity of life." But diversifying applications for programming, the critical need to understand aspects of computation in order to understand proposed laws and privacy rights, and the individual interest in learning programming that reflects those phenomena all seem to point to an increased role for programming in everyday life—perhaps even to a future of computational literacy.

What might a world with mass computational literacy look like? We might begin to see practices and institutions being built on the assumption that everyone can program. We might see computational solutions to organizational problems that have previously been addressed by bureaucracy. These shifts might decrease the relative value of textual literacy. In big and small ways, mass computational literacy could destabilize the institutions built on textual literacy and the hierarchies established along textual literacy lines (e.g., education). And, as it turns out, we can see glimmers of these effects already. Code-based networks, in various forms, are the most prominent examples of our reliance on computation as infrastructure. But a few of these networks signal something more: they are deeply disruptive of current hierarchies that are based on literacy and bureaucracy. Because it is difficult to regulate code across international boundaries, these networks can even undermine or challenge sovereign states. While most of these networks are reasonably accessible to those without computational literacy, they still order their participants according to what I would call their literate skills, and they rely on significant numbers of participants who are computationally literate.

The World Wide Web is the most obvious example of a code-based network that relies on widespread distribution of computational literacy and which has disrupted literate hierarchies. Since its inception in the early 1990s, the Web has allowed people to put information online using simple forms of code: HTML, or Hypertext Markup Language. More recent developments in HTML and Web standards, and interfaces with more complex programming languages such as Javascript, allow for interactions between users and complex databases and algorithms. Templates allow people to put things on the Web without knowing programming, of course, and people hire Web design firms to build sites just as people would hire scribes to take care of their writing needs when its applications were still restricted. But someone who can build her own site or even customize a Wordpress template to make a unique site retains more control and may have an advantage in certain areas over those who outsource these tasks, especially as the economy shifts toward contract and contingent labor, where people must promote their work to participate. The Web has so far fallen short of being the mass code-writing platform that Tim Berners-Lee originally envisioned it as,[170] but it has instead become a mass text-writing platform.[171] And as a platform that combines text and code, it has ruffled enough feathers to inspire a raft of handwringers lamenting the ways it has decreased textual literacy skills and upset hierarchies that are based on them.[172]

Networks built on top of the Web and Internet have been destabilizing in political ways, too: consider the roles of Facebook and Twitter in the Moldovan and Iranian elections of 2009 and the Arab Spring beginning in Tunisia in 2010. These networks helped people organize both physical and online protests across national borders and largely without high-profile leaders. And despite trying to block Internet traffic, states were unable to fully shut down these lines of communication. The U.S. State Department even intervened to ask Twitter to delay network maintenance so that Iranian protestors could keep tweeting.[173] While it was possible for individuals to post to Facebook and Twitter without computational literacy, it appears to have taken a significant number of people on the ground setting up alternative networks to route around the attempted state controls. The legacies of these protests have been mixed, but they did generally succeed in their immediate objectives to overthrow established governance, and they certainly succeeded in getting publicity out on global networks. More recently, Internet conferencing, live-streaming, and Twitter have helped to disseminate word about government disruption with the short-lived July 2016 coup in Turkey and the June 2016 sit-in over gun control in the U.S. House of Representatives.[174]

The cryptocurrency Bitcoin presents another code-network-based disruption to state sovereignty and to the hierarchies of the international monetary system. Bitcoins are virtual, digital currency, unique numerical codes that circulate through networks in transactions computationally verified peer-to-peer, across multiple Bitcoin users. A central registry of transactions is designed to prevent fraud while the lack of international regulation and anonymity of the transactions facilitate almost any kind of purchase (see, for instance, the Tor-based Silk Road market that ran in the period 2011–2013). Its legality in certain countries is tenuous, but its mathematical and computational basis means that it is resistant to regulation. Governments can curb official exchanges with their own currencies, but to effectively ban Bitcoin one would need to ban computational networks altogether. In this way, Bitcoin undermines a major function of centralized governments and the hierarchy of international banks.[175] Gaining ground on the heels of the 2008 financial collapse and widespread outrage about the way investment banks deal with the money supply, it is hard not to see Bitcoin as a code-based critique of the international banking system and a potentially disruptive economic—and thus political—force. Because Bitcoin relies on trust in computational systems and speculation and market tools, it thus favors computational literates and even implies a kind of computational mentality. It is not surprising that Bitcoin has a strong following among programmers.

As the ways that programming can be used are diversifying, and as more people appear to be learning to program for their jobs or personal interests, we can begin to see some initiatives and institutions being built on the platform of more widespread computational literacy. While historical findings indicate that literacy does not, independent of other factors, empower people or lift them out of lower incomes or social classes, *illiteracy* can be an impediment in a world where text and literacy is infrastructural to everyday life. The illiterate person is "less the maker of his destiny than the literate person," as Stevens observed about colonial New England.[176] Now, it seems that people who are not *computationally literate* must, in growing numbers of cases, rely on others to help them navigate their lives. As more communication, social organization, government functions, and commerce are being conducted through code, we are seeing an increased value on the skills to use and compose software. We cannot collapse the various affordances, technologies, and histories of writing into a perfect parallel with programming. However, the historical patterns of literacy that I've outlined in the past two chapters gesture toward answers to these essential questions about code's critical role in our daily lives.

Conclusion: Promoting Coding Literacy—Lessons from Reading and Writing

> Code has been my life, and it has been your life, too. It is time to understand how it all works.
> —Paul Ford, "What Is Code?"

Literacy has always been in flux. What it entails, who is expected to have it, and to what degree they should have it to be considered literate has varied throughout regions, cultures, and history. Although the contemporary rhetoric around literacy education is often about supposedly declining rates of reading or writing, literacy is a moving target. Depending on how we define literacy and our baseline measure, we could point to either rising or declining literacy rates at almost any place or time.

But despite—or maybe because of—its fluctuations, literacy is a powerful concept. The use of the concept and term *literacy* can support educational initiatives or inspire public handwringing. Literacy has rhetorical force, and what is considered literacy affects any society that values literacy. Sylvia Scribner argues that the ways we define literacy determine our evaluation of the problem of illiteracy and the objectives of educational programs we design to combat it.[1] Given the high stakes of defining literacy, Scribner supplies some salient questions for us to consider: "What activities are carried out with written symbols? What significance is attached to them, and what status is conferred on those who engage in them? Is literacy a social right or a private power?"[2] We must also ask: How should these skills be taught, and to whom? The questions posed by Scribner are empirical, and we can answer them through careful cultural analysis. But how or to whom skills should be taught is a question of values. We might rephrase these questions as: How *should* we define literacy? In this book, I have argued that coding *should* be part of our definition of literacy.

Because defining literacy is both an empirical and ethical endeavor, I have used a concept of literacy composed of both material and rhetorical components in this book: *Literacy is a widely held, socially useful and valued set of practices with infrastructural communication technologies.* The various practices of literacy offer material advantages for individuals and groups functioning in society: people use reading and writing to understand and sign contracts, learn in schools, keep track of expenditures, interact with governments, read news about important events, or write editorials and blog posts. These activities can be valuable to individuals or social groups without being "widely held"; they are, then, in Andrea diSessa's terms, "material intelligences." Whether literacies are widely held or useful are material questions. The work of rhetoric is to ask whether or not we value them, whether or not we consider these activities part of literacy and thus whether we should enfold them into literacy's matrix of status and education. What we consider literacy and what values we attach to those literacies are choices with real effects on our educational agendas. Scribner's analysis of the values we have ascribed to literacy suggests that "an ideal literacy is simultaneously adaptive, socially empowering, and self-enhancing."[3] Can a perspective from literacy studies help us to get closer to this ideal with coding?

I hope so. I have given both rhetorical and material reasons that we might need to consider the programming of computers as part of a new and enlarged literacy. Code is central to most lives and infrastructures in the developed world and widely recognized as such. The ability to program is powerful, and assertions that coding is a "new literacy" abound in popular discourse. Thus, coding has both the material and rhetorical factors that compose a literacy.

But is coding *really* a new literacy, as so many of the popular articles ask? Rather than answering that question with a "yes" or "no," I argue that we need to begin treating coding as a literacy. Whether or not coding *is* a literacy, coding is part of computational literacy and a more complex idea of what literacy *should* be. Acknowledging that there is something called "coding literacy," or "computational literacy," or the many other names this literacy goes by, can help us think more carefully about—and perhaps change—how code is written and by whom. This concept gives us access to the rhetorical force of the term and concept of *literacy*, ways of looking at the social aspects of coding practices, historical lessons of mass literacy efforts, barriers to access, and also the well-developed tools and theories of literacy education. Below, I consider what this book's exploration of computational literacy might mean for those who want to encourage it.

Promoting Computational Literacy

The social properties of computational literacy remind us that many different factors will affect the ways people learn it, their motivations for doing so, what they might do with that literacy when they have it, and how it might be valued by others. Thus, understanding the social properties of computational literacy is critical for any educational project seeking to promote it. Studying textual literacy in international contexts, Brian Street advises understanding first what the context for literacy is, and what people want to use it for, and then afterward establishing a curriculum to support and respect those uses.[4] Following this advice from literacy researchers, then, would mean that computational literacy campaigns can aim for certain outcomes, but they must also solicit and respond to the aspirations, ideas, and established practices of their audiences. Such campaigns must also be prepared for the inevitability that, for better or worse, people will apply their computational literacy skills in unpredictable ways.

We may also observe from research in the social aspects of literacy that widespread computational literacy is unlikely to be a panacea for disparities in economic or cultural opportunities. Contrary to the rhetoric of literacy campaigns that reading can improve one's life, research in literacy has shown that literacy does not necessarily help people rise up.[5] In fact, literacy education tends to shore up inequality because it is generally taught in ways that preserve hegemonic structures. The need for literacy rises along with literacy rates, and already-advantaged groups tend to accrue literacy more quickly, thus tracking more closely along with that rising demand. Formal education—one of several structures in which children acquire literacy—tends to benefit the middle and upper classes most because it reflects the cultural values and practices of those cultures. For children coming from disadvantaged backgrounds, the structure of school is often alienating. Why do teachers ask questions to which they already know the answer? Why do all the kids have to sit and follow schedules together? School is indeed strange! But for kids used to parents asking them questions and following schedules for work and play, it feels more natural, and they can learn more easily. These are often the same kids that have lots of resources supporting literacy at home through extracurricular activities and supplemental learning opportunities. As Mizuko Ito et al. have pointed out, the gap in extracurricular learning opportunities is widening among school-aged children in the United States, especially in the area of digital literacies.[6] In this way, literacy education can tend to benefit those who already have it, rather than those who need it. Even wide-scale literacy campaigns explicitly focused on political and social participation, often inspired by the work of revolutionary educator Paolo Freire, do little to combat class disparities. Instead, the massive social change these campaigns engender lead to different distributions and types of literacies, and disparities remain.[7] And yet we can't exactly wage *antiliteracy* campaigns to stem rising inequality. How might we promote coding literacy without exacerbating social inequities?

Because literacy is a socially contingent concept that takes a different shape in each group and individual, diverse educational approaches are necessary. A monolithic plan for computational literacy is likely to exacerbate established gaps in literacy skills among groups. The good news is that organizations such as #YesWeCode, Code.org, Globaloria, and Black Girls Code, as well as languages such as BASIC, Logo, Python, Processing, and Scratch, all offer different approaches to coding literacy, and some are specifically focused on closing those gaps. Many of the founders of these organizations, including Kimberly Bryant (Black Girls Code), Hadi and Ali Partovi (Code.org), Van Jones (#YesWeCode), Idit Harel Caperton (Globaloria), and the Scratch team (including Mitchel Resnick and Yasmin Kafai), have stated their personal interest in leveling the playing field for programming as well as making it easier for people from underrepresented groups to be a part of the profession. As I noted in chapter 1, each of these efforts makes some implicit arguments about what computational literacy might be for; any educational effort aimed at literacy is bound to be prescriptive in some way.[8]

Many of these efforts straddle the line between formal schooling and informal learning. MIT's Scratch, for example, hosts a community where people can independently share and comment on projects, as well as a community geared specifically toward educators; they also promote after-school computer clubs focused on the language.[9] Their explicit focus on the social aspects of learning and the value of code in circulation make it a robust model for computational literacy.[10] Codecademy offers lessons directly on its website, along with more extensive curricula for educators. These curricula are making their way into formal schooling, from the U.K.'s adoption of the Codecademy curriculum, to Estonia's use of Scratch and Logo in their elementary school initiative, to Silicon Valley schools' embrace of Code.org's curriculum, and to codeSpark's game The Foos aimed at preschools.[11]

As coding-for-everyone moves into the classroom, we can look to the history of literacy for guidance. Jenny Cook-Gumperz warns of the homogenizing of literacy once it became coupled with mass schooling in the nineteenth century. Prior to mass schooling, "popular literacy" accommodated a diversity of values and practices and intertwined people's home and work lives; school standardized these *literacies* into *literacy*, foreclosing many practical uses for literacy and devaluing any literacy practice that did not fit neatly into the hierarchical and factory-modeled classroom.[12] Currently, many of these coding literacy initiatives help to diversify and open up social networks that encourage people to learn and improve their programming skills: will computational literacy's current diversity be curtailed if it is converted into a standardized computer science curriculum? If greater access is a goal for computational literacy initiatives, how does this conflict or synchronize with formal schooling partnerships? Given the history of literacy and schooling, we may want to give the push for a standard computational literacy curriculum some greater scrutiny. Formal schooling can make literacy more accessible to students, but it can also privilege some students over others and consolidate literacy around a narrow band of practices.

There appears to be widespread political support for these organizations' campaigns for computational literacy. However, their efforts rely on broader engagement with digital technologies, and this engagement is sometimes poorly supported or even discouraged. Digital technologies can be seen as expensive extras in districts with tight budgets and pressures to teach to standardized tests in reading and math. Ito et al. lament the political and societal resistance to children's engagement with digital media: "Despite its power to advance learning, many parents, educators, and policymakers perceive new media as a distraction from academic learning, civic engagement, and future opportunity." This lack of public support for digital media in public schools "threaten[s] to exacerbate growing inequities in education," they argue, because public school cuts, especially in districts serving nonaffluent populations, tend to affect courses that offer meaningful engagement with digital technologies. Students then miss out on the kind of critical engagement with these technologies that might be supported in schools, and those with fewer resources at home are denied one especially crucial place they might have engagement with digital technologies. Because students across the socioeconomic class spectrum still use these technologies (cell phones, games, social media) outside of school, they can find school less relevant to their daily lives when it ignores these technologies. Echoing the lessons we learn from shifts in literacy often benefitting populations already literacy-rich, Ito et al. assert that to avoid further alienating those students most disconnected from schools, an educational agenda must "begin with questions of equity, leverage both in-school and out-of-school learning, and embrace the opportunities new media offer for learning."[13] Their "connected learning" approach embraces rather than resists students' digital media use outside of school, potentially providing the kind of engagement necessary to encourage computational literacy.

The same political forces that denigrate young people's engagement with digital media such as computer games and social networking have promoted computational literacy. For example, President Obama has often used video games as a negative example of how kids can spend time,[14] but he encouraged kids to make games in his video statement promoting Code. org's Hour of Code: "Don't just buy a new video game; make one. Don't just download the latest app; help design it."[15] Playing games and making them are, of course, different activities, but the disparity in their value for the nation is striking. As we saw in chapter 1, when literacy is a raw material for production, it is a generator of wealth for a society. (President Obama also echoes this national economic benefit of literacy in his video statement by emphasizing the value of having sufficient programmers for the nation.) Consequently, coding literacy can be prized at the same time that its products—for example, video games and social media networks—are, paradoxically, blamed for obesity, laziness, or underachievement.

Computational literacy is not so easily separated from the use of media such as games. Informal engagement with these technologies can *lead* people into more sustained engagement: a gamer can get interested in what computers do and want to learn programming to tweak settings or write her own game. This process can lead toward computational literacy.[16] Even John Kemeny and Thomas Kurtz defended the connection of programming and gaming on mainframes in the 1960s: "People feel that it is frivolous to use these giants to play games. We do not share this prejudice. There is no better way of destroying fear of machines than to have the novice play a few games with the computer. … And most of the games have been programmed by our students, which is an excellent way to learn programming."[17] No one learns programming solely in order to learn programming; motivations for computational literacy matter, and they can derive from uses of digital technologies that are not always socially sanctioned. Thus, the connected learning agenda promoted by Ito et al., which emphasizes these links between the social uses of digital media and deeper engagement with the media, is a useful guide for the promotion of computational literacy.

Access has been a key challenge and area of inquiry for mass literacy promotion efforts: access to education, to the material artifacts of reading and writing, and to the models for reading and writing practices with whom students can identify. Computational literacy efforts often focus on the technical and social barriers to learning programming—making available education, materials, and role models. Black Girls Code, for example, is focused on helping young black women connect with each other and meet other black women programmers and computer scientists as role models. The Scratch community sponsors after-school computer clubhouses modeled in part on Seymour Papert's observation of Brazilian Samba Schools—extracurricular spaces where novices and experts mix freely in the expressive potential of a medium.[18] "Makerspaces" now popping up in public libraries often include computers or physical computing materials.[19] Yasmin Kafai and Quinn Burke discuss eCrafting circles, gatherings focused on wearable computing and "etextiles," which tend to appeal more to young women.[20]

One additional barrier to coding literacy is that code can sometimes be difficult to access for technical and legal reasons. Only some kinds of software include ways of modifying it or accessing its code, and even when those options are available they can be deeply hidden. At the rise of the graphical user interface (GUI), Neal Stephenson lamented that the GUI hid the command line, and, with it, the obvious connection of software to code.[21] Free and open-source software can offer users these connections, but it remains intimidating to many users. Commercial Web-based software often offers application program interfaces (APIs), which allow users to write software that builds on the functionality of those programs. Many of these APIs have good documentation and communities to support people writing these supplemental programs. But Web-based software that runs on commercial servers also hides a lot of its workings, and all or most of its code. We have seen a lot of discussion about what these hidden but pervasive programs mean for our communication and privacy, but very little on how they might impact the ways that people become motivated to learn programming or how they might access the means to do so. If the seamlessness of our heavily trafficked Web software such as search engines and social networking sites dampens people's cognizance of the workings of code or their motivations for learning to write it, should open algorithms and code be incentivized or legally required? If we consider coding a literacy, what arguments might we make for better access to proprietary software code and algorithms?

Laws about software can also bar people's material access to code as well as the procedures that code represents. Under patent law in the United States and many other countries, it is possible to patent software processes and thus bar others from writing code that enacts the same processes.[22] Because patent law was designed with engineering contexts in mind, it prevents people from "designing around" patents, or creating products that do the same thing but in different ways. Only in the past several decades has it been possible to patent processes and, in particular, processes in software. Software patents are notoriously low-quality, meaning that they sometimes cover processes already widely known or they are so unspecific in their description that they could theoretically cover a whole host of processes. The aggressive behavior of so-called patent trolls and companies who vigorously defend their patents with cease-and-desist letters threatening costly legal battles can make it potentially dangerous for people to write and publish code. While big software companies battle patent lawsuits daily and have the patent portfolios and legal teams to do so, open-source projects and independent programmers are not immune from these threats and are less prepared to fight legal battles over code.[23] Many coding literacy efforts seek to support the kind of code written by small companies or individuals or open-source projects, and so the legal regime of software patents can potentially undermine their efforts. These legal barriers to accessing or writing code echo Lawrence Lessig's argument that legal access to creative raw material is necessary for encouraging creative work in art and writing. With copyrights currently extended beyond the "limited times" guaranteed by the Constitution of the United States, Lessig claims that access is unduly restricted.[24] His efforts with Creative Commons, which were modeled on free and open-source software, also seek to increase the freedom of writers to create new works through generous licensing. Overbearing intellectual property laws are well-known barriers to accessing raw material for any creative endeavor, including programming, but arguments against these barriers rarely note the ways they impede a novice's ability to learn. Given the persistent emphasis on computational literacy as a national asset, we may want to begin making these connections in arguments about both coding literacy and the intellectual property of software.

Research on literacy shows us the importance of "access" in literacy education, which entails material access to reading and writing implements, spaces in which to learn, plus cultural access to familiar practices and people with whom the learner can identify. These types of access are all relevant to computational literacy as well, although the technical nature and legal treatment of software complicates material access to reading or writing code. Code needs to be legally, technically, and socially accessible to support coding literacy promotion efforts, and because this access is complex, the responsibility for this access lies in several different areas. Educators in both formal and informal learning spaces have some responsibility to introduce code as an important form of contemporary writing. Those already computationally literate can make it socially welcoming to a wider range of people and recognize that programming is not the perfect meritocracy it is sometimes imagined to be. Students should have access to the digital media that feels relevant and connected to their lives outside of school. Media and cultural influencers can branch out from the exclusionary and unappealing stereotypes of coders as "geeks," who are often presented and popularly imagined as white males. And the intellectual property law regimes for software need to accommodate the kind of informal programming that results from computational literacy promotional efforts. A concept of coding literacy helps to support these efforts alongside the "transformative" access to programming that Adam Banks describes, which allows people "*to both* change the interfaces of that system *and* fundamentally change the codes that determine how the system works."[25] If coding literacy promotional efforts can open up access in this way, what coding literacy is and does can be transformed in positive ways.

Looking Forward

This book was designed to provide the historical, rhetorical, and conceptual evidence to support the argument for computational literacy; that is, an argument that a concept of computational literacy should exist. About this kind of literacy, Matthew Fuller asserts that for educators, "What such a literacy might be returns always as a question, and not as a program. In order to ask that question well, however, it is useful to have access to vocabularies which allow one to do so."[26] As Fuller suggests, "What is computational literacy?" is still and always will be an open question. Any answer I or anyone else might give is provisional. Consequently, I have avoided outlining any specific program to promote computational or coding literacy. However, for educators of both literacy and programming, I hope to have provided some vocabulary to ask that question well.

The vocabulary I have provided here is derived largely from literacy research. In chapter 1, I told a history of how coding literacy has been promoted through languages, hardware, and educational campaigns since the 1960s, and I used a parallel history of efforts to promote reading literacy to highlight the rhetorical and ideological aspects of these efforts for coding. The communicative and informational affordances of writing and programming were my focus in chapter 2. Historical research in literacy was the foil for my explorations of how coding literacy has been and could be functioning in society. As I explained in chapter 3, the technology of writing became infrastructural in government and commerce first, making the ability to read or write valuable skills. Once these skills were more widely distributed and affected collective mentalities, the idea emerged that reading and writing were something called *literacy*, and that concept gathered rhetorical force. We are, as I argued in chapters 3 and 4, at the point where code is infrastructural and the reading and writing of it are valuable skills. But although we may have developed a computational mentality to match our code-based infrastructure, these skills are not so widely held that they are part of literacy. And yet, thinking of coding as literacy—treating *coding literacy* as a real thing—allows us to anticipate this time and prepare for it with better and more inclusive educational approaches.

One might argue that coding literacy is only important to the cultures and groups that are technologically ensconced in it. But the network effects of code means that it recruits cultures and people regardless of whether or not they participate in it actively or whether or not they even want to.[27] Our contemporary communication networks are built with code, a fact that makes it *and* writing more globally relevant. Through fund-raising, governance, warfare, education, and a globalized labor force, networks built with code ensnare groups that might not have any direct access to computers or even writing. If "literate practices depend on powerful and consolidating technologies," as Deborah Brandt and Katie Clinton assert,[28] the powerful and consolidating properties of code make coding not only a literate practice but also a very influential one. What do we lose when only a small and relatively homogeneous population designs and controls these literacy technologies? If we want a more inclusive and equal society, the writing of code should not be left to a handful of elite or isolated groups. A concept of coding literacy can help us to understand the stakes for who codes and how.

I have argued that the ability to read and write code appears to be augmenting literacy—a historically and socially contingent concept about symbol manipulation. What might it look like if many people become literate in this technology or if institutions build on the assumption that many people are literate in it? How might we shape the education for these skills to help them be equitably distributed? We cannot collapse the various affordances, technologies, and histories of writing into a perfect parallel with programming. However, the historical and cultural patterns of literacy that I have outlined in this book gesture toward answers to these critical, contemporary questions about code and computation's roles in our daily lives. We need to understand how programming shapes our composition and communication environments. This does not mean that we need to acquire the source code for every program we use as well as an ability to read it or write it, but we do need to learn how the procedures implemented in code shape and constrain the ways that we compose and communicate: What assumptions about information, texts, and people are embedded in the software programs in which we compose? What control do software programs wrest from us through their collection of our data? The scrutiny of computational procedures can help us to understand the affordances and actions of the various programs on which we now depend.

The roles that literacy has always played in our lives—the acquisition and communication of information, the central role in citizenship and education—are now changed by computers, code, and programming. Because programming is intertwining itself with writing in our composition environments, laws, social networks, and communications, it appears to be changing what it means to be literate in the twenty-first century. Computer programming is re-coding literacy.

Notes

Introduction

1. Stephanie Simon, "Seeking Coders, Tech Titans Turn to Schools," *Politico*, December 9, 2014, www.politico.com/story/2014/12/hour-of-code-schools-obama-113408.html; Yasmeen Khan, "City Wants to Spend Millions to Make School Kids Tech Savvy," WNYC, accessed September 18, 2015, www.wnyc.org/story/mayors-plan-will-require-all-nyc-schools-offer-computer-science/.

2. "Computers Are The Future, But Does Everyone Need to Code?" *All Tech Considered* (NPR), January 25, 2014, www.npr.org/blogs/alltechconsidered/2014/01/25/266162832/computers-are-the-future-but-does-everyone-need-to-code; Tasneem Raja, "Is Coding the New Literacy?" *Mother Jones*, June 2014, www.motherjones.com/media/2014/06/computer-science-programming-code-diversity-sexism-education; "Teaching Code in the Classroom," *New York Times*, May 12, 2014, www.nytimes.com/roomfordebate/2014/05/12/teaching-code-in-the-classroom/.

3. Katie Nelson, "Google Is Putting $50 Million Toward Getting Girls to Code," Mashable, June 20, 2014, http://mashable.com/2014/06/20/google-made-with-code/#6WOwloNGyPqn/.

4. "Scratch," Massachusetts Institute of Technology, accessed September 28, 2015, https://scratch.mit.edu; "CodeSpark Academy with The Foos," codeSpark, accessed October 21, 2016, http://thefoos.com; "Dash and Dot, Robots That Help Kids Learn to Code," Wonder Workshop, accessed September 28, 2015, www.makewonder.com.

5. Anya Kamenetz, "Coding Class, Then Naptime: Computer Science for the Kindergarten Set," NPR.org, accessed September 18, 2015, www.npr.org/sections/ed/2015/09/18/441122285/learning-to-code-in-preschool/.

6. The Raspberry Pi founder, Clive Beale, said: "We're not trying to make everyone a computer scientist, but what we're saying is, 'this is how these things work, it's good for everyone to understand the basics of how these things work.'" Beth Gardiner,

"Adding Coding to the Curriculum," *New York Times*, March 23, 2014, http://www.nytimes.com/2014/03/24/world/europe/adding-coding-to-the-curriculum.html.

7. John Trimbur, "Literacy and the Discourse of Crisis," in *The Politics of Writing Instruction: Postsecondary*, Richard Bullock and John Trimbur, Eds. (Portsmouth, NH: Heinemann, 1991), 277–295.

8. Daniel P. Resnick and Lauren B. Resnick, "The Nature of Literacy: An Historic Exploration," *Harvard Educational Review* 47, no. 3 (1977): 370–385; Deborah Brandt, "How Writing Is Remaking Reading," in *Literacy and Learning, Reflections on Reading, Writing and Society* (San Francisco, CA: Jossey-Bass/John Wiley & Sons, 2009), 161–176.

9. Sylvia Scribner claims that when George McGovern pointed to this problem of literacy's lack of definition in 1978, he was following a tradition of frustration about it. Sylvia Scribner, "Literacy in Three Metaphors," *American Journal of Education* 93, no. 1 (1984): 6–21.

10. I've chosen this title primarily for its dual functionality for my argument, but I'm also aware of similar titles of work by technology scholars I deeply admire: Janet Abbate, *Recoding Gender: Women's Changing Participation in Computing* (Cambridge, MA: MIT Press, 2012); E. Gabriella Coleman, *Coding Freedom: The Ethics and Aesthetics of Hacking* (Princeton, NJ: Princeton University Press, 2012).

11. For example, how different technologies change writing and reading has been central to Christina Haas's research in literacy. Deborah Brandt traces literacy technologies as they are laminated in individual lives. Specifically focused on programming as a literacy technology, Andrea diSessa presents a theory of literacy supported by cognitive, social, and technological "pillars," which I discuss in more detail in chapter 2. Christina Haas, *Writing Technology: Studies on the Materiality of Literacy* (Mahwah, NJ: Lawrence Erlbaum, 1996); Deborah Brandt, *Literacy in American Lives* (Cambridge, UK: Cambridge University Press, 2001); Andrea diSessa, *Changing Minds: Computers, Learning and Literacy* (Cambridge, MA: MIT Press, 2000).

12. Scribner, "Literacy in Three Metaphors."

13. Jenny Cook-Gumperz, "Literacy and Schooling: An Unchanging Equation?" In *The Social Construction of Literacy*, 2nd ed. (Cambridge, UK: Cambridge University Press, 2006), 19–49.

14. Brandt, *Literacy in American Lives*; Sylvia Scribner and Michael Cole, *The Psychology of Literacy* (Cambridge, MA: Harvard University Press, 1981).

15. Code.org co-founder Hadi Partovi wrote in a comment to a post on my blog, "Our organizational brand name is 'code.org', because that was a short URL ..." Hadi Partovi, December 24, 2013, comment on "Is coding the new literacy everyone should learn? Moving beyond yes or no," *Nettework* (blog), December 11, 2013,

http://www.annettevee.com/blog/2013/12/11/is-coding-the-new-literacy-everyone
-should-learn-moving-beyond-yes-or-no/.

16. Brenda Glascott proposes to use "literacy" as a Williams-like keyword for the
field of composition, arguing that it allows us to re-see previous research. Brenda
Glascott, "Constricting Keywords: Rhetoric and Literacy in Our History Writing,"
Literacy in Composition Studies 1, no. 1 (2013), http://licsjournal.org/OJS/index.php/
LiCS/article/view/6/.

17. Abbate, *Recoding Gender*, 4.

18. The New Literacies Studies was first named as such by James Paul Gee, *Social
Linguistics and Literacies: Ideology in Discourses* (London: Falmer Press, 1990).

19. Brian V. Street, *Literacy in Theory and Practice* (Cambridge, UK: Cambridge University Press, 1984), 180.

20. James Paul Gee, *Social Linguistics and Literacies*, 2nd ed. Critical Perspectives on
Literacy and Education (New York: Routledge Falmer, 1996), 42–45.

21. Shirley Brice Heath, *Ways with Words: Language, Life and Work in Communities
and Classroom* (New York: Cambridge University Press, 1983).

22. Victoria Purcell-Gates, *Other People's Words: The Cycle of Low Literacy* (Cambridge, MA: Harvard University Press, 1997).

23. J. Elspeth Stuckey, *The Violence of Literacy* (Portsmouth, NH: Boynton/Cook,
1991).

24. Adam Banks, *Race, Rhetoric, and Technology* (Mahwah, NJ: Lawrence Erlbaum,
2006).

25. Banks, *Race, Rhetoric, and Technology*, 45 (emphasis in original). His computer-
inspired metaphors reflect his interest in both literacy and technology in the book.

26. See Abbate, *Recoding Gender*, 3 n.5 for a list of excellent work on women and
participation in computer science; also see William Aspray, *Participation in Computing: The National Science Foundation's Expansionary Programs*. History of Computing
(Basel, Switzerland: Springer, 2016), in particular the appendix, which lists NSF
grants focused on women in computing 1989–2003; a business perspective from
Google, "Women Who Choose Computer Science—What Really Matters," Google,
May 26, 2014, https://static.googleusercontent.com/media/www.wenca.cn/en/us/
edu/pdf/women-who-choose-what-really.pdf. See also Jane Margolis and Allan
Fisher, *Unlocking the Clubhouse: Women in Computing* (Cambridge, MA: MIT Press,
2003); Thomas Misa, Ed., *Gender Codes: Why Women Are Leaving Computing* (Hoboken, NJ: Wiley–IEEE Computer Society, 2010).

27. Ian Bogost, *Persuasive Games: The Expressive Power of Videogames* (Cambridge,
MA: MIT Press, 2007); Michael Mateas, "Procedural Literacy: Educating the New

Media Practitioner," *On The Horizon* (Special Issue on Future of Games, Simulations and Interactive Media in Learning Contexts) 13, no. 1 (2005): 1–15.

28. diSessa, *Changing Minds*.

29. Jeannette Wing, "Computational Thinking," *Communications of the ACM* 49, no. 3 (2006): 33–35.

30. Annette Vee, "Proceduracy: Writing to and for Computers," Watson Conference, University of Louisville, October 2008.

31. Wing, "Computational Thinking."

32. Bogost, *Persuasive Games*, 245.

33. Bogost, *Persuasive Games*, 29.

34. Bogost, *Persuasive Games*, 257.

35. Mateas, "Procedural Literacy."

36. Mateas, "Procedural Literacy," 101.

37. diSessa, *Changing Minds*.

38. Mark Guzdial, "Anyone Can Learn Programming: Teaching > Genetics," Blog@ CACM, October 14, 2014, http://cacm.acm.org/blogs/blog-cacm/179347-anyone -can-learn-programming-teaching-genetics/fulltext.

39. Comment on Mark Guzdial, "Definitions of 'Code' and 'Programmer': Response to 'Please Don't Learn to Code,'" Computing Education Blog, December 20, 2012, https://computinged.wordpress.com/2012/12/20/definitions-of-code-and -programmer-response-to-please-dont-learn-to-code/; Mark Guzdial, *Learner-Centered Design of Computing Education: Research on Computing for Everyone*. Synthesis Lectures on Human-Centered Informatics (San Rafael, CA: Morgan & Claypool Publishers, 2015).

40. Guzdial, *Learner-Centered Design of Computing Education*, 2–3.

41. Ed Lazowska and David Patterson, "Students of All Majors Should Study Computer Science," *Chronicle of Higher Education*, November 26, 2013, http://chronicle .com/blogs/letters/students-of-all-majors-should-study-computer-science/.

42. Wing, "Computational Thinking," 33.

43. One more: The UK government issued statutory guidance for the "National Curriculum in England: Computing Programme of Study" in 2013, which suggests an approach to computing influenced by literacy. Their stated purpose is a nice encapsulation of many of the ideas in circulation about computational literacy, and it includes an emphasis on programming and acknowledgment that CS is the core rather than the rights holder of computing:

A high-quality computing education equips pupils to use computational thinking and creativity to understand and change the world. Computing has deep links with mathematics, science and design and technology, and provides insights into both natural and artificial systems. The core of computing is computer science, in which pupils are taught the principles of information and computation, how digital systems work and how to put this knowledge to use through programming. Building on this knowledge and understanding, pupils are equipped to use information technology to create programs, systems and a range of content. Computing also ensures that pupils become digitally literate—able to use, and express themselves and develop their ideas through, information and communication technology—at a level suitable for the future workplace and as active participants in a digital world.

UK Department for Education, "National Curriculum in England: Computing Programmes of Study." Statutory Guidance (2013), https://www.gov.uk/government/publications/national-curriculum-in-england-computing-programmes-of-study/national-curriculum-in-england-computing-programmes-of-study [sic].

44. Caitlin Kelleher and Randy Pausch, "Lowering the Barriers to Programming: A Taxonomy of Programming Environments and Languages for Novice Programmers," *ACM Computing Surveys* 37, no. 2 (2005): 83–137.

45. Kafai and Burke, *Connected Code,* 55. These concepts circulate widely. Low floors and high ceilings have been around since BASIC; the "wide walls" were added in 2005 by Resnick et al., and Kafai and Burke add the open windows with their idea of "connected code." Mitchel Resnick, Brad Myers, Kumiyo Nakakoji, Ben Shneiderman, Randy Pausch, Ted Selker, and Mike Eisenberg, "Design Principles for Tools to Support Creative Thinking." Working Paper, Research Showcase @ CMU, Carnegie Mellon Institute for Software Research and School of Computer Science, Pittsburgh, PA, October 30, 2005, http://repository.cmu.edu/cgi/viewcontent.cgi?article=1822&context=isr.

46. Quoted in Donald Knuth, *Literate Programming*. CSLI Lecture Notes (Stanford, CA: Center for the Study of Language and Information, 1992), 2.

47. Matti Tedre, *The Science of Computing: Shaping a Discipline* (Boca Raton, FL: CRC Press, Taylor & Francis Group, 2015), 56.

48. Mary Shaw, "Progress toward an Engineering Discipline for Software," presented at the SPLASH/PLoP [Pattern Languages of Programs] Conference, Pittsburgh, PA, October 26, 2015, http://2015.splashcon.org/event/plop2015-plop-keynote-mary-shaw. This talk referenced and extended her earlier, influential paper, "Prospects for an Engineering Discipline of Software," *IEEE Software* 7, no. 6 (November 1990): 15–24.

49. Abbate, *Recoding Gender,* 53–54.

50. On the term: David Alan Grier, "The ENIAC, the Verb 'to Program' and the Emergence of Digital Computers," *IEEE Annals of the History of Computing* 18, no. 1 (1996): 51–55; on the profession: Nathan Ensmenger, *The Computer Boys Take Over:*

Computers, Programmers, and the Politics of Technical Expertise (Cambridge, MA: MIT Press, 2010).

51. Ensmenger, *The Computer Boys Take Over.*

52. Bonnie Nardi, *A Small Matter of Programming: Perspectives on End User Computing* (Cambridge, MA: MIT Press, 1993); Christopher Scaffidi, Mary Shaw, and Brad Myers, "An Approach for Categorizing End User Programmers to Guide Software Engineering Research," *ACM SIGSOFT Software Engineering Notes* 30, no. 4 (2005): 1–5; Andrew J. Ko, Brad Myers, Mary Beth Rosson, Gregg Rothermel, Mary Shaw, Susan Wiedenbeck, Robin Abraham, Laura Beckwith, Alan Blackwell, Margaret Burnett, Martin Erwig, Chris Scaffidi, Joseph Lawrance, and Henry Lieberman, "The State of the Art in End-User Software Engineering," *ACM Computing Surveys* 43, no. (2011): 1–44.

53. "Codecademy," Codecademy, accessed July 21, 2016, https://www.codecademy.com; "About Us," *Code.org*, accessed July 21, 2016, https://code.org.

54. "#YesWeCode," #YesWeCode, accessed July 17, 2016, www.yeswecode.org/; "Black Girls Code," Black Girls Code, accessed July 17, 2016, www.blackgirlscode.com/what-we-do.html; "Girl Develop It," Girl Develop It, accessed July 17, 2016, https://www.girldevelopit.com; "Made with Code_Google," Made W/ Code, accessed July 17, 2016, https://www.madewithcode.com.

55. Kelly Field, "New Players Could Be in Line to Receive Federal Student Aid," *Chronicle of Higher Education* (July 2, 2015), http://chronicle.com/article/New-Players-Could-Be-in-Line/231333/.

56. Below, I have made the mentions of computer science and computer programming boldface to highlight the use of the two terms in their mission statement from July 2014:

Code.org® is a non-profit dedicated to expanding participation in **computer science** by making it available in more schools, and increasing participation by women and underrepresented students of color. Our vision is that every student in every school should have the opportunity to learn **computer programming**. We believe **computer science** should be part of the core curriculum in education, alongside other science, technology, engineering, and mathematics (STEM) courses, such as biology, physics, chemistry and algebra.

Our goals include:
• Bringing **Computer Science** classes to every K-12 school in the United States, especially in urban and rural neighborhoods.
• Demonstrating the successful use of online curriculum in public school classrooms.
• Changing policies in all 50 states to categorize C.S. as part of the math/science "core" curriculum.
• Harnessing the collective power of the tech community to celebrate and grow **C.S. education** worldwide.
• To increase the representation of women and students of color in the field of **Computer Science**.

(Source: July 1, 2014, wayback machine: https://web.archive.org/web/2014070 1080436/http://code.org/about/)

By early August 2014, they had removed the bulleted points and brought computer science and programming together (again, emphasis added):

Launched in 2013, Code.org® is a non-profit dedicated to expanding participation in **computer science** by making it available in more schools, and increasing participation by women and underrepresented students of color. Our vision is that every student in every school should have the opportunity to learn **computer science**. We believe **computer science and computer programming** should be part of the core curriculum in education, alongside other science, technology, engineering, and mathematics (STEM) courses, such as biology, physics, chemistry and algebra.
   (Source: August 9. 2014, wayback machine: https://web.archive.org/web/20140809084421/ http://code.org/about/)

Between July and August 2015, they had settled on the goal of promoting computer science rather than computer programming (emphasis added):

Launched in 2013, Code.org® is a non-profit dedicated to expanding access to **computer science**, and increasing participation by women and underrepresented students of color. Our vision is that every student in every school should have the opportunity to learn **computer science**. We believe **computer science** should be part of core curriculum, alongside other courses such as biology, chemistry or algebra.
   (Source: August 18, 2015, wayback machine: https://web.archive.org/web/20150818231636/ https://code.org/about/)

57. August 14, 2013, wayback machine: https://web.archive.org/web/201308140 53107/http://www.code.org/about; September 22, 2013, wayback machine: https:// web.archive.org/web/20130922162459/http://www.code.org/about.

58. Annette Vee, "Is Coding the New Literacy? Moving Beyond Yes or No," Nettework, December 11, 2013, www.annettevee.com/blog/2013/12/11/is-coding-the -new-literacy-everyone-should-learn-moving-beyond-yes-or-no/.

59. Ibid.

60. He reiterates this claim in a blog post just a month afterward:

Our organization is called Code.org, but our focus is on computer science. If we could fit EverySchoolShouldOfferComputerScience.org in one word, we'd do it. I believe most people don't care about the difference between code and computer science. They just feel technology is passing them by quickly, and they don't want their kids to suffer the same fate.
   As a computer scientist, I know the coding languages we teach now may be out of date in 25 years. But the concepts are fundamental: conditionals, loops, abstraction, these concepts span all languages. I learned them 25 years ago, and they're relevant today. That's why our intro curriculum teaches these concepts with visual programming, without any language.

Hadi Partovi, "The 'Secret Agenda' of Code.org," Anybody Can Learn, January 20, 2014, http://blog.code.org/post/73963049605/the-secret-agenda-of-codeorg.

Between July and August 2015, they eliminated the mention of computer programming altogether and just focused on computer science. July 22, 2015, wayback machine: https://web.archive.org/web/20150722085355/http://code.org/about/;

August 18, 2015, wayback machine: https://web.archive.org/web/20150818231636/
https://code.org/about/.

61. Jeff Atwood, "Please Don't Learn to Code," Coding Horror, May 12, 2012,
https://blog.codinghorror.com/please-dont-learn-to-code/, para. 4, emphasis in
original. Atwood's invocation of Java—the language that dominates professional
software contexts—is another indication of his assumptions that the "'everyone
should learn programming' meme," as he calls it, is referring to professional and not
casual programming contexts.

62. Mark Guzdial, "Definitions of 'Code' and 'Programmer': Response to 'Please
Don't Learn to Code,'" Computing Education Blog, December 20, 2012, https://
computinged.wordpress.com/2012/12/20/definitions-of-code-and-programmer
-response-to-please-dont-learn-to-code/.

63. Jeremy Hsu and Innovation News Daily, "Secret Computer Code Threatens Science," *Scientific American*, April 13, 2012, www.scientificamerican.com/article/secret-
computer-code-threatens-science/.

64. "jordanb," comment on "Secret Computer Code Threatens Science (scientificamerican)," *Hacker News*, April 13, 2012, https://news.ycombinator.com/item?id
=3844910/.

65. Jeff Atwood, "Code Smells," Coding Horror, May 18, 2006, https://blog
.codinghorror.com/code-smells/.

66. Shaw, "Progress toward an Engineering Discipline for Software."

67. Margolis and Fisher, *Unlocking the Clubhouse*, 53–57.

68. Sherry Turkle and Seymour Papert, "Epistemological Pluralism: Styles and Voices
within the Computer Culture," *Signs* 16, no. 1 (Autumn 1990): 128–157. More
recently, Alan Liu echoes this reference to Levi-Strauss's bricoleur in his response to
Stephen Ramsay's controversial argument that digital humanists needed to build
things and code. Alan Liu, "Comment on 'On Building,'" Stephen Ramsay [blog],
January 11, 2011, http://stephenramsay.us/text/2011/01/11/on-building/#comm
ent-223113606/. Drawing on Turkle and Papert's concept of epistemological pluralism, Resnick et al. describe design principles for software user interfaces that can
foster creative programming ("Design Principles for Tools to Support Creative
Thinking").

69. Noah Wardrip-Fruin, *Expressive Processing: Digital Fictions, Computer Games, and
Software Studies* (Cambridge, MA: MIT Press, 2009); Mateas, "Procedural Literacy"; N.
Katherine Hayles, *Electronic Literature: New Horizons for the Literary* (South Bend, IN:
University of Notre Dame Press, 2008), 157; Fox Harrell, *Phantasmal Media: An
Approach to Imagination, Computation, and Expression* (Cambridge, MA: MIT Press,
2013); Stephen Ramsay, *Reading Machines: Toward an Algorithmic Criticism* (Urbana:
University of Illinois Press, 2011).

70. Nick Montfort, *Exploratory Programming for the Arts and Humanities* (Cambridge, MA: MIT Press, 2016).

71. Ensmenger, *The Computer Boys Take Over*; Abbate, *Recoding Gender*.

72. Katie Hafner, "Giving Women the Access Code," *New York Times,* April 2, 2012, www.nytimes.com/2012/04/03/science/giving-women-the-access-code.html; Steve Henn, "When Women Stopped Coding," *Planet Money* (NPR), October 21, 2014, www.npr.org/blogs/money/2014/10/21/357629765/when-women-stopped-coding/.

73. In software development and applications, 19.7% were women, and in Web development, 39.5% were women. "Labor Force Statistics from the Current Population Survey," Bureau of Labor Statistics, U.S. Department of Labor, February 26, 2014, www.bls.gov/cps/cpsaat11.htm.

74. Cecilia Kang and Todd C. Frankel, "Silicon Valley Struggles to Hack Its Diversity Problem," *Washington Post,* July 16, 2015, www.washingtonpost.com/business/economy/silicon-valley-struggles-to-hack-its-diversity-problem/2015/07/16/0b0144be-2053-11e5-84d5-eb37ee8eaa61_story.html; Kaya Thomas, "Invisible Talent," NewCo Shift, July 14, 2016, https://shift.newco.co/invisible-talent-409a085bee9c/.

75. Tasneem Raja, "'Gangbang Interviews' and 'Bikini Shots': Silicon Valley's Brogrammer Problem," *Mother Jones,* April 26, 2012, www.motherjones.com/media/2012/04/silicon-valley-brogrammer-culture-sexist-sxsw/.

76. Ensmenger, *The Computer Boys*, 69–70.

77. Guzdial, "Anyone Can Learn Programming: Teaching > Genetics."

78. Margolis and Fisher, *Unlocking the Clubhouse*, 75ff.

79. Alexandria Lockett, "I am Not a Computer Programmer," in "The Role of Computational Literacy in Computers and Writing," *Enculturation*, October 12, 2012, www.enculturation.net/node/5270/.

80. Raja, "Silicon Valley's Brogrammer Problem"; Anastasia Salter, "Code Before Content? Brogrammer Culture in Games and Electronic Literature," presented at the Electronic Literature Organization, Vancouver, BC, June 10, 2016, http://www.slideshare.net/anastasiasalter/code-before-content-elo-slides/.

81. See also: Misa, Ed., *Gender Codes*; Margolis and Fisher, *Unlocking the Clubhouse*.

82. Mark Guzdial, "How to Teach Computing across the Curriculum: Why Not Logo?" Computing Education Blog, April 13, 2012, https://computinged.wordpress.com/2012/04/13/how-to-teach-computing-across-the-curriculum-why-not-logo/; Guzdial, *Learner-Centered Design of Computing Education*.

83. See, for instance, Alison Langmead and David Birnbaum, "Task-Driven Programming Pedagogy in the Digital Humanities," *New Directions for Computing Education: Embedding Computing across Disciplines*, Samuel B. Fee, Amanda M. Holland-Minkley,

and Thomas Lombardi, Eds. (New York: Springer, forthcoming); Stephen Ramsay, "On Building," Stephen Ramsay, January 11, 2011, http://stephenramsay.us/text/2011/01/11/on-building/.

84. John G. Kemeny, "The Case for Computer Literacy," *Daedalus* (Special Issue on Scientific Literacy) 112, no. 2 (1983): 228.

85. As a global lingua franca, English is the basis of most programming languages, even those written outside of English-dominant contexts (e.g., Ruby, written by Japanese programmer Yukihiro Matsumoto). This English influence has historical roots as well, as English-speaking contexts dominated early computer research and software development. The historical and social influence of English on programming language design is some indication that code is constructed with technological considerations only.

86. Many programs can translate for several different kinds of machines so that a programmer can write just one version of source code to deploy to many different machines; the Java language compiler is one example of these more versatile translating programs.

87. For a lucid explanation of the multiple layers of code written by programmers and parsed by computers, see Ed Felton, "Source Code and Object Code," Freedom to Tinker, September 4, 2002, https://freedom-to-tinker.com/blog/felten/source-code-and-object-code/.

88. Bogost, *Persuasive Games*, 4.

89. Alexander Galloway, *Protocol: How Control Exists after Decentralization* (Cambridge, MA: MIT Press, 2006), 165.

90. Wendy Hui Kyong Chun, *Programmed Visions: Software and Memory*. Software Studies (Cambridge, MA: MIT Press, 2011), 22–23 and 54.

91. This places it in an interesting position in the eyes of the law. See Annette Vee, "Text, Speech, Machine: Metaphors for Computer Code in the Law," *Computational Culture* 2 (2012), http://computationalculture.net/article/text-speech-machine-metaphors-for-computer-code-in-the-law/.

92. Tedre, The Science of Computing, 97.

93. This is sometimes referred to as "von Neumann architecture," after John von Neumann, a member of the ENIAC team at the University of Pennsylvania and the named author of the groundbreaking "First Draft of a Report on the EDVAC." Because the origin of this design was collaborative and complicated, I do not refer to it as "von Neumann architecture" here.

94. Grier, "The ENIAC, the Verb 'to Program' and the Emergence of Digital Computers."

95. Paul Graham, *Hackers and Painters: Big Ideas from the Computer Age* (Sebastopol, CA: O'Reilly, 2004).

96. In an introductory lecture to the Structure and Interpretation of Computer Programs at MIT, Abelson says: "Now the reason that we think computer science is about computers is pretty much the same reason that the Egyptians thought geometry was about surveying instruments: when some field is just getting started and you don't really understand it very well, it's very easy to confuse the essence of what you're doing with the tools that you use." Hal Abelson, "SICP/What Is Computer Science?" YouTube video, 10:00, posted by "LarryNorman," September 12, 2006, https://www.youtube.com/watch?v=zQLUPjefuWA/. The quote "Computer science is no more about computers than astronomy is about telescopes" is often attributed to Edsger Dijkstra. Ian Parberry makes a compelling case that it should be attributed to Michael R. Fellows instead. Ian Parberry, "Computer Science Education," June 10, 2010, https://larc.unt.edu/ian/research/cseducation/. See also chapter 2 of this volume.

97. A fuller explanation of the evolution of programming languages can be found in chapter 2 of this volume.

98. David Nofre, Mark Priestley, and Gerard Alberts, "When Technology Became Language: The Origins of the Linguistic Conception of Computer Programming, 1950–1960," *Technology and Culture* 55 no. 1 (2014): 40–75.

99. Alan Perlis, "The Computer in the University," in *Computers and the World of the Future,* Martin Greenberger, Ed. (Cambridge, MA: MIT Press, 1962), 203. Thanks to Mateas's "Procedural Literacy," which pointed me to this book of important discussions about programming in the early 1960s.

100. From a statement made in 1980, quoted by Abbate, *Recoding Gender,* 85.

101. Brandt, Literacy in American Lives.

102. Marc Andreessen, "Marc Andreessen on Why Software Is Eating the World," *Wall Street Journal,* August 20, 2011, www.wsj.com/news/articles/SB1000142405311 19034809045765122509915629460/.

103. Walter Ong, "[Review Of] The Implications of Literacy," *Manuscripta* 28, no. 2 (1984): 108–109.

104. This was a key point missed by Vilem Flusser when he argues that writing will be replaced by communication in new media such as computer programming. Vilem Flusser, *Does Writing Have a Future?* Trans. Nancy Ann Roth (Minneapolis: University of Minnesota Press, 2011).

105. Howard Berkes, "Booting Up: New NSA Data Farm Takes Root in Utah," *All Things Considered* (NPR), September 23, 2013, http://www.npr.org/sections/alltechco

nsidered/2013/09/23/225381596/booting-up-new-nsa-data-farm-takes-root-in
-utah/.

106. Tom Lauricella, Kara Scannell, and Jenny Strasburg, "How a Trading Algorithm
Went Awry," *Wall Street Journal*, October 2, 2010, www.wsj.com/articles/SB1000142
4052748704029304575526390131916792/.

107. "Our Mission," *Sunlight Foundation*, accessed October 9, 2016, http://sunlight
foundation.com/about/.

108. Sunlight Foundation, "Tools," accessed October 9, 2016, https://sunligh
tfoundation.com/tools/.

109. "City Announces Open Data Platform Launch," *Office of [Pittsburgh] Mayor William Peduto*, July 2, 2014, http://pittsburghpa.gov/mayor/release?id=3255/.

110. "Showcase," Western Pennsylvania Regional Data Center, October 9, 2016,
http://www.wprdc.org/category/showcase/.

111. W. Michele Simmons and Jeffrey Grabill, "Toward a Civic Rhetoric for Technologically and Scientifically Complex Places: Invention, Performance, and Participation," *College Composition and Communication* 58, no. 3 (2007): 419–448.

112. James Brown, Jr., *Ethical Programs: Hospitality and the Rhetorics of Software* (Ann
Arbor: University of Michigan Press, 2015).

113. Nick Montfort et al., *10 PRINT CHR$(205.5+RND(1)); : GOTO 10* (MIT Press,
2014), 153.

114. Montfort et al., *10 PRINT*, 186.

115. Montfort et al., *10 PRINT*, 186.

116. Kate Vieira, *American by Paper: How Documents Matter in Immigrant Literacy*
(Minneapolis: University of Minnesota Press, 2016).

117. Aneesh Aneesh, *Virtual Migration: The Programming of Globalization* (Durham,
NC: Duke University Press, 2006).

118. Alice Marwick and danah boyd call this "context collapse." Alice E. Marwick
and danah boyd, "I Tweet Honestly, I Tweet Passionately: Twitter Users, Context
Collapse, and the Imagined Audience," *New Media & Society* 20, no. 10 (2010): 1–20.
doi: 10.1177/1461444810365313.

119. Scribner, "Literacy in Three Metaphors."

120. David Barton points out, "The trouble with metaphors for literacy … is that
they are limited in scope and do not capture the breadth of what is involved in reading and writing." David Barton, *Literacy: An Introduction to the Ecology of Written
Language* (Oxford, UK: Blackwell Publishers, 1994), 14.

121. Susan Leigh Star, "The Ethnography of Infrastructure," *American Behavioral Scientist* 43, no. 3 (1999): 381–382. The full list of properties of infrastructure Star provides is embeddedness, transparency, reach or scope, learned as part of membership, links with conventions of practice, embodiment of standards, built on an installed base, becomes visible upon breakdown, is fixed in modular increments, not all at once or globally.

122. Star, "The Ethnography of Infrastructure," 380.

123. Commenting on Jack Goody's legacy, Charles Bazerman explains that although each society turns out differently, "each evolving way of life incorporates an infrastructure based on literacy … The scholar's task then is not to find the universal social consequences of literacy but to understand how each society has elaborated a way of life on the matrix of literacy, with the consequence that each participant in the society to some degree participates in the particularized literate systems, whether or not each participant reads or writes." Charles Bazerman, "The Writing of Social Organization and the Literate Situating of Cognition: Extending Goody's Social Implications of Writing," in *Technology, Literacy, and the Evolution of Society: Implications of the Work of Jack Goody*, David R. Olson and Michael Cole, Eds. (Mahwah, NJ: Lawrence Erlbaum, 2006), 218.

124. Anne Frances Wysocki and Johndan Johnson-Eilola, "Blinded by the Letter: Why Are We Using Literacy as a Metaphor for Everything Else?" in *Passions, Pedagogies, and Twenty-First Century Technologies*, Gail Hawisher and Cynthia Selfe, Eds. (Logan: Utah State University Press, 1999), 349–368; see also Mariolina Salvatori, "New Literacy Studies: Some Matters of Concern," *Literacy in Composition Studies* 1, no. 1 (2013), http://licsjournal.org/OJS/index.php/LiCS/article/view/18/.

125. diSessa, *Changing Minds*, 5.

126. diSessa, *Changing Minds*, 7.

127. "A literacy is the convergence of a large number of genres and social niches on a common, underlying representational form" is one definition diSessa provides (*Changing Minds*, 24).

128. diSessa, *Changing Minds*, 8.

129. diSessa, *Changing Minds*, 5.

130. Jack Goody and Ian Watt, "The Consequences of Literacy," *Comparative Studies in Society and History* 5, no. 3 (1963): 304–345.

131. Marshall McLuhan, *The Gutenberg Galaxy* (Toronto: University of Toronto Press, 1962).

132. Janet Emig, *The Composing Processes of Twelfth Graders* (Urbana, IL: National Council of Teachers, 1971); Linda Flower and John R. Hayes, "A Cognitive Process

Theory of Writing," *College Composition and Communication* 32, no. 4 (1981): 365–387. I thank Lauren Rae Hall for the background on B. F. Skinner.

133. Street, *Literacy in Theory and Practice.*

134. Shirley Brice Heath, *Ways with Words.*

135. James Paul Gee, "The New Literacy Studies: From 'Socially Situated' to the Work of the Social," in *Situated Literacies: Reading and Writing in Context,* David Barton, Mary Hamilton, and Roz Ivanic, Eds. (New York: Routledge, 2000), 180.

136. Jenny Cook-Gumperz, "The Social Construction of Literacy," in *The Social Construction of Literacy,* 2nd ed. (Cambridge, UK: Cambridge University Press, 2006), 3.

137. Harvey Graff, *The Labyrinths of Literacy: Reflections on Literacy Past and Present,* Revised Edition (Pittsburgh: University of Pittsburgh Press, 1995), 27.

138. Harvey Graff, *The Literacy Myth: Cultural Integration and Social Structure in the Nineteenth Century* (New Brunswick, NJ: Transaction Publishers, 1991).

139. David Barton and Mary Hamilton, "Literacy Practices," in *Situated Literacies: Reading and Writing in Context,* David Barton, Mary Hamilton, and Roz Ivanic, Eds. (New York: Routledge, 2000), 10.

140. Barton and Hamilton, "Literacy Practices," 12.

141. Street, *Literacy in Theory and Practice,* 97.

142. Graff, *Labyrinths,* 144.

143. Graff, *Labyrinths,* 143.

144. Scribner and Cole, *The Psychology of Literacy,* 236.

145. The New London Group, "A Pedagogy of Multiliteracies: Designing Social Futures," in *Multiliteracies: Literacy Learning and the Design of Social Futures,* Bill Cope and Mary Kalantzis, Eds. (London: Routledge, 2000), 9–38.

146. James Paul Gee, *What Video Games Have to Teach Us about Learning and Literacy* (New York: Palgrave Macmillan, 2003).

147. The New London Group, "A Pedagogy of Multiliteracies," 6.

148. This is what David Vincent gets at when he writes, in exasperation at the push against literacy as unique: "Rather than refighting the battle against what Brian Street termed the 'autonomous model' of literacy, the challenge now is to exploit with more rigour and imagination the implications of the functional approach. If it is seen as a purely critical exercise, there is a danger of the entire issue disappearing below the waves, weighed down with an ever-increasing freight of qualifications and contradictions. If the larger claims for literacy are falsified, if the traditional dichotomies of oral and literate, educated and uneducated, rational and irrational,

collapse into a complex series of interactions and relativities, there seems little point in the further study of the subject as a particular domain of human activity." This suggests that we must revisit the "functional" approach to literacy as not simply negative, and then expand beyond the boundaries of instrumental approaches to literacy. David Vincent, *The Rise of Mass Literacy: Reading and Writing in Modern Europe* (Cambridge, UK: Polity, 2000), 23.

149. Gail Hawisher and Cynthia Selfe, Eds., *Critical Perspectives on Computers and Composition Instruction* (New York: Teachers College Press, 1989).

150. Haas, *Writing Technology*, 3.

151. Deborah Brandt and Katie Clinton, "Limits of the Local: Expanding Perspectives of Literacy as a Social Practice," *Journal of Literacy Research* 34, no. 3 (September 2002), 337. doi: 10.1207/s15548430jlr3403_4

152. Brandt and Clinton, "Limits of the Local."

153. Brandt and Clinton, "Limits of the Local," 338.

154. For the example of the role undersea cables play in global networks, see Nicole Starosielski, *The Undersea Network* (Durham, NC: Duke University Press, 2015).

155. Bazerman, "The Writing of Social Organization and the Literate Situating of Cognition," 216.

156. Kate Vieira, "On the Social Consequences of Literacy," *Literacy in Composition Studies* 1, no. 1 (2013), http://licsjournal.org/OJS/index.php/LiCS/article/view/7/.

157. Vieira, *American by Paper*.

158. Vincent, *The Rise of Mass Literacy*, 25.

159. William J. Gilmore, *Reading Becomes a Necessity of Life: Material and Cultural Life in Rural New England, 1780–1835* (Knoxville: University of Tennessee Press, 1989), 181.

160. Daniel Kohanski, *The Philosophical Programmer: Reflections on the Moth in the Machine* (New York: St. Martin's Press, 1998), 188.

161. Rob Kitchin and Martin Dodge, *Code/Space: Software and Everyday Life* (Cambridge, MA: MIT Press, 2014); Blake Hallinan and Ted Striphas, "Recommended for You: The Netflix Prize and the Production of Algorithmic Culture," *New Media and Society* (2014), doi: 10.1177/1461444814538646; Tarleton Gillespie, "The Relevance of Algorithms," in *Media Technologies*, Tarleton Gillespie, Pablo Boczkowski, and Kirsten Foot, Eds. (Cambridge, MA: MIT Press, 2014), 167–194; Anne Helmond, "The Algorithmization of the Hyperlink," *Computational Culture* 3 (2013), http://computationalculture.net/article/the-algorithmization-of-the-hyperlink/.

162. Randall Munroe, "Research Ethics," xkcd [comic], July 4, 2014, http://xkcd
.com/1390/.

163. "See the Moments You Care About First," Instagram Blog, June 2, 2016, http://
blog.instagram.com/post/145322772067/160602-news/.

164. Michael Nunez, "Former Facebook Workers: We Routinely Suppressed Conservative News," Gizmodo, May 9, 2016, http://gizmodo.com/former-facebook-
workers-we-routinely-suppressed-conser-1775461006/; Safiya Umoja Noble, "Google
Search: Hyper-Visibility as a Means of Rendering Black Women and Girls Invisible,"
InVisible Culture: An Electronic Journal for Visual Culture 19 (2013), http://ivc.lib
.rochester.edu/google-search-hyper-visibility-as-a-means-of-rendering-black
-women-and-girls-invisible/.

165. Aneesh, Virtual Migration, 110.

166. Bryce Goodman and Seth Flaxman, "EU Regulations on Algorithmic Decision-
Making and a 'right to Explanation,'" arXiv, June 26, 2016, https://arxiv.org/
pdf/1606.08813v1.pdf.

167. James Brown, Jr., and Annette Vee, "Rhetoric and Computation," Computational Culture, Issue 5 (Special Issue on Rhetoric and Computation), Jan. 15 (2016),
http://computationalculture.net/editorial/rhetoric-special-issue-editorial-
introduction; James Brown, Jr., Ethical Programs.

168. David Olson, The World on Paper: The Conceptual and Cognitive Implications of
Writing and Reading (Cambridge, UK: Cambridge University Press, 1994), xvi, quoting Ernest Gombrich, who is citing Kohler.

169. Peter Denning, "The Profession of IT: Voices of Computing," Communications
of the ACM 51, no. 8 (2008): 19–21.

170. Examples of scholars working in this area include Noah Wardrip-Fruin, N.
Katherine Hayles, Matthew Kirschenbaum, and Mark Marino in literature; Ian
Bogost, James Brown, Jr., Tarleton Gillespie, Elizabeth Losh, and Kevin Brock in
rhetoric; Michael Mateas and Fox Harrell in game design; E. Gabriella Coleman in
cultural anthropology; and Zeynep Tufekci in sociology. There are many more.
While these scholars do not always declare their interest in transcending disciplines
with their work on computer programming, their work is often taken up outside of
their home discipline.

Chapter 1

1. Edward Stevens, Literacy, Law and Social Order (DeKalb: Northern Illinois University Press, 1988), 8–9.

2. John Kemeny, "The Case for Computer Literacy," Daedalus 112, no. 2 (1983):
216.

3. Python is a popular language engineered to be broadly accessible and used often in education.

4. Guido van Rossum, *Computer Programming for Everybody (Revised Proposal)* (Reston, VA: Corporation for National Research Initiatives, 1999), http://legacy.python.org/doc/essays/cp4e.html.

5. Mark Guzdial, *Learner-Centered Design of Computing Education: Research on Computing for Everyone* (San Rafael, CA: Morgan & Claypool Publishers, 2015), 5.

6. Douglas Rushkoff, *Program or be Programmed*, Kindle ed. (New York: OR Books, 2010), 1.

7. Marc Prensky, "Programming Is the New Literacy," *Edutopia* (January 13, 2008), www.edutopia.org/literacy-computer-programming.

8. Lesley Chilcott, "Code: The New Literacy" [Code.org promotional video], Code.org, August 27, 2013, https://www.youtube.com/watch?v=MwLXrN0Yguk/

9. "De Blasio Announces Computer Science Program, Other Initiatives For NYC Public School Students," accessed September 18, 2015, http://newyork.cbslocal.com/2015/09/16/computer-science-nyc-schools/.

10. John Naughton, "Why All Our Kids Should Be Taught How to Code," *Guardian*, March 31, 2012, https://www.theguardian.com/education/2012/mar/31/why-kids-should-be-taught-code/.

11. Naughton cites the fact that code governs our communication and world to support his argument, and claims that C. P. Snow's "two cultures" problem has "blindsided us" to the relevance of computational processes in the humanities.

12. Tim Mansel, "How Estonia became E-stonia," *BBC News*, May 16, 2013, www.bbc.com/news/business-22317297/.

13. "Bootstrap," Bootstrap, accessed September 29, 2015, www.bootstrapworld.org; "Scratch," MIT, accessed September 29, 2015, https://scratch.mit.edu; "CodeCombat—Learn How to Code by Playing a Game," CodeCombat, accessed September 29, 2015, https://codecombat.com/; "Dash and Dot, Robots That Help Kids Learn to Code," Wonder Workshop, accessed September 28, 2015, https://www.makewonder.com.

14. Sylvia Scribner, "Literacy in Three Metaphors," *American Journal of Education* 93, no. 1 (1984): 8.

15. Jenny Cook-Gumperz, "The Social Construction of Literacy," in *The Social Construction of Literacy*, 2nd ed. (Cambridge, UK: Cambridge University Press, 2006), 1–18.

16. Brenda Glascott, "Constricting Keywords: Rhetoric and Literacy in our History Writing," *Literacy in Composition Studies* 1, no. 1 (2013): 18, http://licsjournal.org/OJS/index.php/LiCS/article/view/6/.

17. The brevity of this overview of literacy's values means that it downplays differences between nations as well as differences in literacy expectations for men and women and people of different backgrounds. In practice, schooling, and in particular schooling in writing, has almost always been more accessible to boys than girls, resulting in persistent gaps between male and female literacy rates. Exceptions occur, as in seventeenth-century Sweden, when matching standards for literacy resulted in relatively matching literacy levels for men and women. Women's roles in personal letter writing as well as educators of children were strong literacy motivators both for individual women and for schooling policies, although not much more than basic literacy was needed for those domestic activities. Generation gaps in literacy are also stubborn. As literacy's values have become more tied to economics and technologies, older generations have fewer incentives to expand their literacy skills. Those who are motivated have fewer resources to do so, as adult education programs are rarely as widespread as those for children. Finally, the differences between literacy levels and rates across race and class are sometimes profound. For American slaves of African descent in the nineteenth century, literacy schools supported learning but could not fully combat the de jure and de facto discrimination against African Americans learning to read in both the South and the North. The "Achievement Gap" persists, with significantly lower reading levels among African-American and Latin-American children, sometimes leading to different inscriptions of value to literacy than in populations with historically greater access to it.

18. David Barton, *Literacy: An Introduction to the Ecology of Written Language* (Oxford, UK: Blackwell Publishers, 1994), 20–21.

19. Jenny Cook-Gumperz, "Literacy and Schooling: An Unchanging Equation?" in *The Social Construction of Literacy*, 2nd ed., Jenny Cook-Gumperz, Ed. (Cambridge, UK: Cambridge University Press, 2006), 19–49.

20. Barton, *Literacy*, 21.

21. Barton, *Literacy*, 10–11.

22. Barton notes that the metaphors for literacy can never capture its richness and are always problematic in some way. *Literacy*, 14.

23. Barton, *Literacy*, 12.

24. Scribner, "Three Metaphors."

25. Scribner, "Three Metaphors," 9–11.

26. Scribner, "Three Metaphors," 11.

27. Scribner, "Three Metaphors," 18.

28. Deborah Brandt, *Literacy in American Lives* (Cambridge, UK: Cambridge University Press, 2001); Deborah Brandt, "Accumulating Literacy," *College English* 57, no. 6 (1995): 649–668.

29. Merrill Sheils, "Why Johnny Can't Write," *Newsweek,* December 8, 1975: 58–65.

30. Daniel P. Resnick and Lauren B. Resnick, "The Nature of Literacy: An Historical Explanation," *Harvard Educational Review* 47, no. 3 (1977): 370–385.

31. John Trimbur, "Literacy and the Discourse of Crisis," in *The Politics of Writing Instruction: Postsecondary*, Richard Bullock and John Trimbur, Eds. (Portsmouth, NH: Heinemann, 1991), 277–295.

32. Trimbur, "Literacy and the Discourse of Crisis," 280.

33. Mariolina Salvatori, "New Literacy Studies: Some Matters of Concern," *Literacy in Composition Studies* 1, no. 1 (2013): 66–69; Anne Wysocki and Johndan Johnson-Eilola, "Blinded by the Letter: Why Are We Using Literacy as a Metaphor for Everything Else?" in *Passions, Pedagogies, and 21st Century Technologies,* Gail Hawisher and Cynthia Selfe, Eds. (Logan: Utah State University Press, 1999), 349–368.

34. A nod to Wayne Booth, "rhetoric makes realities, however temporary." Wayne C. Booth, *The Rhetoric of Rhetoric* (Malden, MA: Blackwell Publishing, 2004), 16.

35. From a Google search, March 7, 2014: https://twitter.com/paulroetzer/status/333998199423520768/; https://moodle.org/mod/forum/discuss.php?d=245221/; https://twitter.com/djp1974/status/420342598566309888/; for example, "For a non-coder and a rank website beginner, how difficult is Twitter/Facebook syndication using BBEdit (or anything else)?"

36. François Furet and Jacques Ozouf, *Reading and Writing: Literacy in France from Calvin to Jules Ferry* (Cambridge, UK: Cambridge University Press, 1982), 59.

37. Furet and Ozouf, *Reading and Writing,* 60.

38. David Vincent, *The Rise of Mass Literacy: Reading and Writing in Modern Europe* (Cambridge, UK: Polity, 2000).

39. Furet and Ozouf, *Reading and Writing,* 60.

40. Resnick and Resnick, "The Nature of Literacy," 379.

41. Lee Soltow and Edward Stevens, *The Rise of Literacy and the Common School in the United States: A Socioeconomic Analysis to 1870* (Chicago: University of Chicago Press, 1982).

42. William McKinley, "First Inaugural Address of William McKinley," Yale Law School Lillian Goldman Law Library, accessed October 12, 2016, http://avalon.law.yale.edu/19th_century/mckin1.asp.

43. Harvey Graff, *Labyrinths of Literacy* (Pittsburgh, PA: University of Pittsburgh Press, 1995), 191–194.

44. Egil Johansson, "Literacy Campaigns in Sweden," *Interchange* 19, no. 3/4 (1988): 157. This is an interesting parallel to the Middle Ages, when the benefit of clergy to

escape criminal punishment could be exercised by the laity if they could read a written passage in Latin. Michael T. Clanchy, *From Memory to Written Record: England 1066–1307*, 3rd ed. (Somerset, NJ: John Wiley & Sons, 2012). ProQuest ebrary.

45. North America: Graff, *Labyrinths*, 194. Europe: Johansson, "Literacy Campaigns," 157.

46. Furet and Ozouf, *Reading and Writing*, 118.

47. Stevens, *Literacy, Law and Social Order*, 12.

48. Samantha NeCamp, *Adult Literacy and American Identity: The Moonlight Schools and Americanization Programs* (Carbondale: Southern Illinois University Press, 2014), 32.

49. Paul McBride, "Peter Roberts and the YMCA Americanization Program 1907—World War I," *Pennsylvania History: A Journal of Mid-Atlantic Studies* 44, no. 2 (1977): 150.

50. Europe: Thomas Laqueur, "The Cultural Origins of Popular Literacy in England: 1500-1850," *Oxford Review of Education* 2, no. 3 (1976): 255–275. America: Cook-Gumperz, "Literacy and Schooling."

51. Cook-Gumperz, "Literacy and Schooling," 26.

52. Cook-Gumperz, "Literacy and Schooling," 32.

53. R. P. Dore, quoted in Graff, *Labyrinths*, 182.

54. Furet and Ozouf, *Reading and Writing*, 254.

55. Quoted in Stevens, *Literacy, Law and Social Order*, 14.

56. Graff, *Labyrinths*, 182.

57. Richard Ohmann, "Literacy, Technology, and Monopoly Capital," *College English* 47, no. 7 (1985): 677.

58. Laqueur, "The Cultural Origins of Popular Literacy in England," 270.

59. Cook-Gumperz, "Literacy and Schooling," 39.

60. Soltow and Stevens, *The Rise of Literacy*.

61. Ohmann, "Literacy, Technology, and Monopoly Capital," 677. According to Ohmann, the first measurement of literacy was in 1870 by Edwin Leigh: *Illiteracy in the United States*, Annual Report of the Commissioner of Education. More detail is provided in chapter 4.

62. Egil Johansson, "Literacy Campaigns in Sweden," *Interchange* 19, no. 3/4 (1988): 135–162.

63. Vincent, *The Rise of Mass Literacy*, 6.

64. Furet and Ozouf, *Reading and Writing*, 7.

65. Ohmann, "Literacy, Technology, and Monopoly Capital," 677.

66. NeCamp, *Adult Literacy and American Identity*, 26.

67. Deborah Brandt, "Drafting U.S. Literacy," *College English* 66, no. 5 (2004): 485–502.

68. U.S. Department of Education, *A Nation at Risk* (1983), http://www2.ed.gov/pubs/NatAtRisk/risk.html.

69. Vincent, *The Rise of Mass Literacy*, 7.

70. Brandt, "Drafting U.S. Literacy," 485.

71. Of this "takeoff," Brian Street writes that it is "a hypothesis that occurs with apparent authority in many literacy programme outlines. What is not specified is what specific literacy practices and concepts 40% of the population are supposed to acquire. Yet comparative material, which Anderson himself provides, demonstrates that such practices and conceptions are very different from one culture to another." Brian V. Street, *Literacy in Theory and Practice* (Cambridge, UK: Cambridge University Press, 1985), 2.

72. Brandt, "Drafting U.S. Literacy," 487–488. The connection of literacy to national economic development is also apparent in the 2002 National Adult Literacy Survey:

> In the past, the lack of ability to read and use printed materials was seen primarily as an individual problem, with implications for a person's job opportunities, educational goals, sense of fulfillment, and participation in society. Now, however, it is increasingly viewed as a national problem, with implications that reach far beyond the individual. Concerns about the human costs of limited literacy have, in a sense, been overshadowed by concerns about the economic and social costs. (xii)

Irwin S. Kirsch et al., *Adult Literacy in America: A First Look at the Findings of the National Adult Literacy Survey* (Washington, DC: U.S. Department of Education Office of Educational Research and Improvement, 2002), https://nces.ed.gov/pubs93/93275.pdf.

73. Cook-Gumperz, "The Social Construction of Literacy," 1.

74. Richard Ohmann writes, "Literacy *tests* and census questions become evidence to fix the literacy *rate* of a society." Ohmann, "Literacy, Technology, and Monopoly Capital," 677.

75. R. F. Arnove and H. J. Graff, *National Literacy Campaigns* (New York: Plenum Press, 1987), 7.

76. Soltow and Stevens, 10. Ohmann expresses similar ideas: "Technique is less important than context and purpose in the teaching of literacy; and the effects of literacy cannot be isolated from the social relations and processes within which

people become literate." Ohmann, "Literacy, Technology, and Monopoly Capital,"
687. Robert F. Arnove and Harvey Graff extend this idea as well: "Whether the materials and methods of literacy and postliteracy campaigns are truly designed to equip
people to play more active roles in shaping the direction of their societies, or, to the
contrary, are intended to induct people into roles predetermined by others is a telling indication of ideology and intent." Arnove and Graff, *National Literacy Campaigns*, 27.

77. Maria Bibbs, *The African American Literacy Myth: Literacy's Ethical Objective during
the Progressive Era, 1890-1919* (Ph.D. dissertation, University of Wisconsin-Madison,
2011). ProQuest 3488549.

78. Arnove and Graff, *National Literacy Campaigns*, 5.

79. Arnove and Graff, *National Literacy Campaigns*, 4.

80. Sarah Robbins, *Managing Literacy, Mothering America* (Pittsburgh, PA: University
of Pittsburgh Press, 2004).

81. Arnove and Graff, *National Literacy Campaigns*, 5.

82. Arnove and Graff, *National Literacy Campaigns*, 11–12.

83. Arnove and Graff, *National Literacy Campaigns*, 7.

84. Arnove and Graff, *National Literacy Campaigns*, 20.

85. Arnove and Graff, *National Literacy Campaigns*, 8.

86. Arnove and Graff, *National Literacy Campaigns*, 15.

87. Arnove and Graff, *National Literacy Campaigns*, 14.

88. Richard R. Fagen, *The Transformation of Political Culture in Cuba* (Stanford, CA:
Stanford University Press, 1969), 56–58.

89. Arnove and Graff, *National Literacy Campaigns*, 27.

90. Arnove and Graff, *National Literacy Campaigns*, 9.

91. Julie Nelson Christoph, "Each One Teach One: The Legacy of Evangelism in
Adult Literacy Education," *Written Communication* 26, no. 1 (2009): 89. doi:
10.1177/0741088308327478.

92. U.S. Department of Education, Office of Vocational and Adult Education,
An American Heritage—Federal Adult Education: A Legislative History 1964–2013
(Washington, DC: U.S. Department of Education, 2013), 18, http://lincs.ed.gov/
publications/pdf/Adult_Ed_History_Report.pdf.

93. *An American Heritage—Federal Adult Education*, 20.

94. "National Institute for Literacy," *Federal Register*, accessed June 19, 2015, https://
federalregister.gov/agencies/national-institute-for-literacy/.

95. Rab Houston, "The Literacy Campaigns in Scotland, 1560-1803," in *National Literacy Campaigns*, Robert F. Arnove and Harvey J. Graff, Eds. (New York: Plenum Press, 1987), 52.

96. Graff and Arnove, *National Literacy Campaigns*, 25.

97. Furet and Ozouf, *Reading and Writing*, 66. Vincent makes a similar point that trends in education followed demand. Vincent, *The Rise of Mass Literacy*, 25.

98. Furet and Ozouf, *Reading and Writing*, 65–68.

99. NeCamp, *Adult Literacy and American Identity*, 19–29.

100. Deborah Brandt, *The Rise of Writing: Redefining Mass Literacy* (Cambridge, UK: Cambridge University Press, 2014).

101. Furet and Ozouf, *Reading and Writing*, 167.

102. Deborah Brandt, "Remembering Writing, Remembering Reading," *College Composition and Communication* 45, no. 4 (1994): 459–479. doi: 10.2307/358760.

103. Brandt, "Drafting U.S. Literacy," 45.

104. Brandt, "Accumulating Literacy," 660.

105. "The primary goal motivating our development of DTSS [Dartmouth Time-Sharing System] was the conviction that knowledge about computers and computing must become an essential part of liberal education. Science and engineering students obviously need to know about computing in order to carry on their work. But we felt exposure to computing and its practice, its powers and limitations must also be extended to nonscience students, many of whom will later be in decision-making roles in business, industry and government. The administration and the Board of Trustees of Dartmouth gave us their full support as they, too, realized and accepted the goal of 'universal' computer training for liberal arts students." John Kemeny and Thomas Kurtz, "Dartmouth Time-Sharing," *Science*, 162 (1968): 162, 223–228.

106. "One Laptop per Child," accessed September 29, 2015, http://one.laptop.org/.

107. Mitchel Resnick and David Siegel, "A Different Approach to Coding: How Kids Are Making and Remaking Themselves from Scratch," Medium.com, November 10, 2015, https://medium.com/bright/a-different-approach-to-coding-d679b06d83a; Guzdial, *Learner-Centered Design of Computing Education*.

108. George E. Forsythe, "The Role of Numerical Analysis in an Undergraduate Program," *American Mathematical Monthly* 66, no. 8 (Oct., 1959): 655. I'd like to thank Matti Tedre and Peter Denning for introducing me to this early source on computer education.

109. Forsythe, "The Role of Numerical Analysis in an Undergraduate Program," 657.

110. Donald L. Katz, "Conference Report on the Use of Computers in Engineering Education," *Communications of the ACM* 3, no. 10 (1960): 522–527. I'd like to thank Matti Tedre and Peter Denning for introducing me to this conference report.

111. Mark Guzdial and Eliot Soloway still find this vision influential for current approaches to introductory computer science courses. "Computer Science Is More Important Than Calculus: The Challenge of Living Up to Our Potential," *Inroads—The SIGCSE Bulletin* 35, no. 2 (2003): 5–8.

112. Alan Perlis, "The Computer in the University," in *Computers and the World of the Future*, Martin Greenberger, Ed. (Cambridge, MA: MIT Press, 1962), 188.

113. "It was finally realized that it was much more sensible to teach a machine a language that is easier for human beings to learn than to force every human user to learn the machine's own language." John Kemeny, *Man and the Computer* (New York: Scribner, 1972), 8.

114. For more on Fortran and end-user programming, see Wendy Hui Kyong Chun, *Programmed Visions: Software and Memory*. Software Studies (Cambridge, MA: MIT Press, 2011), 44–45.

115. Kemeny and Kurtz, "Dartmouth Time-Sharing," 225.

116. Kemeny and Kurtz, "Dartmouth Time-Sharing," 223.

117. Steven Levy, *Hackers: Heroes of the Computer Revolution*. New York: Dell Publishing, 1984.

118. Theodore Holm Nelson, *Computer Lib/Dream Machines* (Redmond, CA: Microsoft Press, 1987), 6.

119. Nick Montfort et al., *10 PRINT CHR$(205.5+RND(1)); : GOTO 10* (Cambridge, MA: MIT Press, 2014), 184.

120. Howard F. Fehr, "The Secondary School Mathematics Curriculum Improvement Study: A Unified Mathematics Program," *The Mathematics Teacher* 67, no. 1 (Jan., 1974): 25–33. Notably, Estonia's current mass programming campaign has direct roots to this experimental math program in the United States in the late 1960s. The Estonian president, Toomas Hendrik Ilves, grew up as an Estonian expatriate in Leonia, New Jersey, where he was part of an experimental math and programming campaign funded by Columbia University. Ilves said in 2008: "That Estonia is one of the most Interneted countries is due to Mrs. Cummings' programming class," referring to his teacher at Leonia High, Christine Cummings. In 2012, Ilves helped drive the campaign to teach programming to first-graders, recognizing the value of these skills. Herb Jackson, "'From Estonia to Leonia,' The Record, 23 April 2008," President Ilves Media, Interviews, April 23, 2008, https://web.archive.org/web/20151231223413/https://www.president.ee/en/media/interviews/3304-qfrom-estonia-to-leoniaq-the-record-23-april-2008/index.html. I'd like to thank

Jonathan Schilling, a student of the program alongside Ilves, for some of the history on this program and pointing me to Fehr's report.

121. Seymour Papert and Cynthia Solomon, "Twenty Things to Do with the Computer," Artificial Intelligence Laboratory, MIT, June 1971, http://www.stager.org/articles/twentythings.pdf.

122. Alan Kay, "A Personal Computer for Children of All Ages," Xerox Palo Alto Research Center, August 1972, www.mprove.de/diplom/gui/Kay72a.pdf.

123. Nick Montfort et al., *10 PRINT*, 168.

124. Ed Edelson, "Fast-Growing New Hobby, Real Computers You Assemble Yourself," *Popular Science*, December 1976, 82–83; 146–147.

125. "Scientific American Volume 237, Issue 3 - Scientific American," *Scientific American*, accessed September 28, 2015, www.scientificamerican.com/magazine/sa/1977/09-01/.

126. Notably, *Tron* appears to have a legacy connected to Ted Nelson. A cowriter of the screenplay, Bonnie MacBird, claims to have bought *Computer Lib/Dream Machines* in Los Angeles in 1980, read about Alan Kay there, and then hired him on as a consultant on *Tron*. Bonnie MacBird, "Seminal Work and Instrumental in the Creation of TRON," Amazon user review, August 21, 2011, www.amazon.com/review/R36QFVARF6SWA1/ref=cm_cr_dp_title?ie=UTF8&ASIN=B003LOB14Q&channel=detail-glance&nodeID=283155&store=books/.

127. Nick Montfort et al., *10 PRINT*, 179.

128. Nick Montfort et al., *10 PRINT*, 158.

129. For a good review of the 1980s computer games copyright cases, see Greg Lastowka, "Copyright Law and Video Games: A Brief History of an Interactive Medium," in *The SAGE Handbook of Intellectual Property*, Matthew David and Debora Halbert, Eds. (Thousand Oaks, CA: Sage Publications Ltd., 2015), http://knowledge.sagepub.com/view/the-sage-handbook-of-intellectual-property/i3554.xml.

For more on the development of software as a commodity separate from hardware, see Steve Weber, *The Success of Open Source* (Cambridge, MA: Harvard University Press, 2004).

130. Stallman describes his inspiration here: Richard Stallman, "The GNU Project," GNU Operating System, 1998, www.gnu.org/gnu/thegnuproject.html.

131. "Logo History," Logo Foundation, n.d., http://el.media.mit.edu/logo-foundation/what_is_logo/history.html.

132. Alan Kay and Adele Goldberg, "Personal Dynamic Media," *Computer* 10, no. 3 (1977): 31–41.

133. Kemeny, "The Case for Computer Literacy," 228.

134. Jim Ferguson, "Computing across the Curriculum," *The Social Studies* 80, no. 2 (1989): 69–72. doi: 10.1080/00220973.1945.11019944.

135. A successful example of this implementation is at Georgia Tech, which in 2003 switched from a one-size-fits-all required computing course for all students (where pass rates were low and the course was dreaded by faculty and students alike) to several different courses focused on liberal arts, engineering, and computer science. Mark Guzdial, "Teaching Computing to Everyone," *Communications of the ACM* 52, no. 5 (2009): 31. doi: 10.1145/1506409.1506420.

136. Tim Berners-Lee, *Weaving the Web: The Original Design and Ultimate Destiny of the World Wide Web* (San Francisco: HarperBusiness, 2000).

137. Nick Montfort et al., *10 PRINT*, 192.

138. whytheluckystiff, "The Little Coder's Predicament," Advogato, June 11, 2003, www.advogato.org/article/671.html.

139. Oracle, after acquiring Sun in 2007, released parts of Java as open source although the status of Java as open or closed source is complex. Robert McMillan, "Oracle Makes Java More Relevant Than Ever—For Free," *WIRED*, September 25, 2013, www.wired.com/2013/09/oracle_java/.

140. Ed Lazowska, Eric Roberts, and Jim Kurose, "Tsunami or Sea Change? Responding to the Explosion of Student Interest in Computer Science," presented at the National Center for Women & Information 10th Anniversary Summit/Computing Research Association Conference at Snowbird, Utah, May 2014, http://lazowska .cs.washington.edu/NCWIT.pdf.

141. Adam Banks, *Race, Rhetoric, and Technology* (Mahwah, NJ: Lawrence Erlbaum Associates, 2006); Yasmin Kafai and Quinn Burke, *Connected Code: Why Children Need to Learn Programming*. MacArthur Foundation Series on Digital Media and Learning (Cambridge, MA: MIT Press, 2014), chapter 1.

142. Lazowska, Roberts, and Kurose, "Tsunami or Sea Change?"

143. "Sugar—OLPC," accessed September 29, 2015, http://wiki.laptop.org/go/ Sugar/.

144. Taylor Soper, "Analysis: The Exploding Demand for Computer Science Education, and Why America Needs to Keep up," GeekWire, June 6, 2014, www.geekwire. com/2014/analysis-examining-computer-science-education-explosion/.

145. Quinn Burke engages in a similar project of analyzing the metaphors used for promoting programming in K–12 schools. He reviewed 67 sources arguing for students to learn programming at the K–12 level and concluded that three arguments predominate: code is "grounded mathematics," code is language/literacy, and code

is a technical skill. Quinn Burke, "Mind the metaphor: charting the rhetoric about introductory programming in K–12 schools," *On the Horizon* 24, no. 3 (2016): 210–220.

146. The bio and statistics as well as some background on recruiting big names and making the Code.org video are described here by cofounders Hadi and Ali Partovi: "Iam Hadi Partovi, Co-Founder of Code.org, Here with My Identical Twin Brother Ali Partovi. Ask Us Anything. • /r/IAmA," Reddit, accessed June 19, 2015, https://www.reddit.com/r/IAmA/comments/19eqzm/iam_hadi_partovi_cofounder_of_codeorg_here_with/.

147. Code.org, "The 2015 Hour of Code," YouTube, December 21, 2015, https://www.youtube.com/watch?v=Ofze6CWUCx8/.

148. "About Us," Code.org, accessed September 14, 2015, https://code.org/about/.

149. "About Us," Code.org.

150. Lesley Chilcott, "What Most Schools Don't Teach" [Code.org promotional video], Code.org, February 26, 2013, https://www.youtube.com/watch?v=nKIu9yen5nc/. See also the longer version of the video: Lesley Chilcott, "Code Stars" [Code.org promotional video], Code.org, February 26, 2013, https://www.youtube.com/watch?v=dU1xS07N-FA/.

151. "Does Universal Programming Even Make Sense?" Ken's Blog, February 24, 2008, http://blog.kenperlin.com/?p=97/.

152. Code.org, "The 2015 Hour of Code."

153. Rushkoff, *Program or be Programmed*, 1.

154. Stevens, *Literacy, Law, and Social Order*, 19.

155. For example, literacy classes for women in Uganda appear to help them keep accounts, improve sanitation and hygiene, and improve family nutrition. "Uganda—Empowerment of Rural Women Through Functional Adult Literacy," IFAD [The International Fund for Agricultural Development, a Specialized Agency of the United Nations], n.d., https://www.ifad.org/topic/tools/tags/gender/gender/knowledge_note/2594004/.

156. "Iam Hadi Partovi," Reddit.

157. "Black Girls Code: What We Do," Black Girls Code, n.d., accessed June 23, 2015, www.blackgirlscode.com/what-we-do.html.

158. Taylor Gordon, "Combating Racism with Coding: Van Jones Discusses Teaching 100,000 Low-Income Kids How to Code," *Atlanta Blackstar*, January 21, 2015, http://blerds.atlantablackstar.com/2015/01/21/combating-racism-coding-van-jones-discusses-teaching-100000-low-income-kids-code/.

159. Forsythe, "The Role of Numerical Analysis in an Undergraduate Program," 655.

160. J. C. R. Licklider and Robert W. Taylor, "The Computer as a Communication Device," *Science and Technology* 76, no. 2 (1968): 40.

161. Seymour Papert, *Mindstorms: Children, Computers, and Powerful Ideas* (New York: Basic Books, 1980).

162. In an online essay that held up Smalltalk and Logo as excellent examples of programming systems that focused on learning rather than syntax, prominent user interface expert Bret Victor wrote, "The canonical work on designing programming systems for learning, and perhaps the greatest book ever written on learning in general, is Seymour Papert's *Mindstorms.* ... If you are going to design anything whatsoever related to learning, then you literally *need* to read *Mindstorms*." Bret Victor, "Learnable Programming: Designing a Programming System for Understanding Programming," Worry Dream [blog], September 2012, http://worrydream.com/#!/ LearnableProgramming.

163. See Kafai and Burke, *Connected Code*, chapter 6, for more on the connection between Papert and the Maker Movement.

164. Kay, "A Personal Computer for Children of All Ages."

165. Kemeny, *Man and the Computer*, 43.

166. Kemeny, "The Case for Computer Literacy," 230.

167. Alan Kay, "User Interface: A Personal View," in *The Art of Human–Computer Interface Design*, Brenda Laurel, Ed. (Reading, MA: Addison-Wesley, 1990), 193.

168. Chilcott, "What Most Schools Don't Teach."

169. Sylvia Scribner and Michael Cole, *The Psychology of Literacy* (Cambridge, MA: Harvard University Press, 1981).

170. Stephen Ramsay, "On Building," Stephen Ramsay [blog], January 11, 2011, http://stephenramsay.us/text/2011/01/11/on-building/.

171. Mitchel Resnick et al., "Scratch: Programming for All," *Communications of the ACM* 52, no. 11 (2009): 62.

172. Resnick et al., "Scratch," 67.

173. Kafai and Burke, *Connected Code*.

174. Cook-Gumperz, "Literacy and Schooling"; Laqueur, "The Cultural Origins of Popular Literacy."

175. Stevens, *Literacy, Law, and Social Order*, 65.

176. Stevens, *Literacy, Law, and Social Order*, 66.

177. Kemeny and Kurtz, "Dartmouth Time-Sharing," 223. In their final report on the grant, they wrote, "It is vitally important that the leaders of government,

industry and education should know both about the potential and limitations of the use of computers, and be aware of the respective roles of Man and machine in the partnership." John Kemeny and Thomas Kurtz, *The Dartmouth Time-Sharing Computing System Final Report*. Course Content Improvement Program (Dartmouth, NH: Dartmouth College, 1967), 1.

178. Kemeny, *Man and the Computer*, 58.

179. Kemeny, "The Case for Computer Literacy," 216.

180. Nelson, *Computer Lib/Dream Machines*, 5.

181. Beth Gardiner, "Adding Coding to the Curriculum," *New York Times*, March 23, 2014, www.nytimes.com/2014/03/24/world/europe/adding-coding-to-the -curriculum.html.

182. Herb Jackson, "From Estonia to Leonia."

183. Hadi Partovi, "The 'Secret Agenda' of Code.org," Anybody Can Learn, January 20, 2014, http://blog.code.org/post/73963049605/the-secret-agenda-of-codeorg/.

184. "Training 100,000 Low-Income Youth to Code: A Q&A with Van Jones [and Angela Glover Blackwell]," PolicyLink, August 6, 2014, www.policylink.org/focus -areas/equitable-economy/at/van-jones-on-yes-we-code/.

185. Lawrence Lessig, *Code: And Other Laws of Cyberspace* (New York: Basic Books, 2000).

186. Nathan Ensmenger, *The Computer Boys Take Over: Computers, Programmers, and the Politics of Technical Expertise* (Cambridge, MA: MIT Press, 2010).

187. Alison Griswold, "When It Comes to Diversity in Tech, Companies Find Safety in Numbers," *Slate*, June 27, 2014, www.slate.com/blogs/moneybox/2014/06/27/ tech_diversity_data_facebook_follows_google_yahoo_in_releasing_the_stats.html.

188. "Training 100,000 Low-Income Youth to Code."

189. "Made with Code_Google," Made W/ Code, accessed June 23, 2015, https:// www.madewithcode.com.

190. Aneesh Aneesh, *Virtual Migration: The Programming of Globalization* (Durham, NC: Duke University Press, 2006).

191. Lesley Chilcott, "Code Stars" [Code.org promotional video], Code.org, February 26, 2013, https://www.youtube.com/watch?v=dU1xS07N-FA.

192. "Code.org Stats: What's Wrong with This Picture?" Code.org, n.d., accessed June 23, 2015, https://code.org/stats. Source data are from the U.S. Bureau of Labor Statistics and linked from the infographic.

193. Gardiner, "Adding Coding to the Curriculum."

194. Office of the Mayor [Bill de Blasio], "Computer Science for All: Fundamentals for Our Future," Official Website of the City of New York, accessed September 18, 2015, www1.nyc.gov/office-of-the-mayor/education-vision-2015-computer-science.page/.

195. Megan Smith, "Computer Science For All," The White House [blog], January 30, 2016. https://www.whitehouse.gov/blog/2016/01/30/computer-science-all/.

196. Ibid.

197. Arnove and Graff, *National Literacy Campaigns*, 25.

198. Grace Conyers, "The ProgeTiiger Initiative," AAAS MemberCentral, March 13, 2013, http://membercentral.aaas.org/blogs/aaas-serves/progetiiger-initiative/.

199. Christopher Scaffidi, Mary Shaw, and Brad Myers, "An Approach for Categorizing End User Programmers to Guide Software Engineering Research," *ACM SIGSOFT Software Engineering Notes* 30 no. 4 (2005), 1–5.

200. Arnove and Graff, *National Literacy Campaigns*, 7.

201. Resnick and Seidel, "A Different Approach to Coding"; Guzdial, *Learner-Centered Design of Computing Education*; Matti Tedre and Peter Denning, "The Long Quest for Computational Thinking," Proceedings of the 16th Koli Calling Conference on Computing Education Research, November 24–27, 2016, Koli, Finland.

202. Kevin Brooks and Chris Lindgren, "Responding to the Coding Crisis: From Code Year to Computational Literacy," in *Strategic Discourse: The Politics of (New) Literacy Crises*, Lynn Lewis, Ed. (Logan: Computers and Composition Digital Press/Utah State University Press, 2015), http://ccdigitalpress.org/strategic/.

203. Ohmann, "Literacy, Technology, and Monopoly Capital," 685. He relies on James Donald's concept of "literacy from above" (government-driven literacy) and "literacy from below" (popular literacy) to make this point.

204. Aneesh, *Virtual Migration*.

205. Daniel M. Zuckerman, "All Pittsburgh Students Should Learn Computer Programming" [op-ed], *Pittsburgh Post-Gazette*, September 8, 2013, www.post-gazette.com/opinion/Op-Ed/2013/09/08/All-Pittsburgh-students-should-learn-computer-programming/stories/201309080158/.

206. Jennifer Miller, "Teacher's Vision, but Done New York City's Way," *New York Times*, March 29, 2013, http://www.nytimes.com/2013/03/31/nyregion/software-engineering-school-was-teachers-idea-but-its-been-done-citys-way.html.

207. Kafai and Burke, *Connected Code*, 52.

208. Yasmeen Khan, "De Blasio Says to Tackle Inequities, School Kids Must Go Back to the Basics," WNYC, accessed September 18, 2015, www.wnyc.org/story/de-blasio-tackles-inequity-nyc-schools-computer-science/.

209. Lyndsey Layton, "Bill Gates Calls on Teachers to Defend Common Core," *Washington Post*, March 14, 2014, www.washingtonpost.com/local/education/bill -gates-calls-on-teachers-to-defend-common-core/2014/03/14/395b130a-aafa-11e3 -98f6-8e3c562f9996_story.html.

210. Issie Lapowsky, "The Startup That's Bringing Coding to the World's Class-rooms," *WIRED*, May 22, 2014, www.wired.com/2014/05/codecademy/.

211. Elizabeth Losh, *The War on Learning* (Cambridge, MA: MIT Press, 2014).

212. Vincent, *The Rise of Mass Literacy*, 24.

213. Paul Ford, "What Is Code?" *Bloomberg Business*, June 11, 2015, www.bloomberg .com/graphics/2015-paul-ford-what-is-code/.

214. "Leaders from across the political spectrum have stepped forward to ask students everywhere to learn computer programming. This is literally the one idea that 100% of politicians agree on." Hadi Partovi, "With Support from Obama to Shakira, Apple to Zuckerberg, the Hour of Code Is Here," Anybody Can Learn, December 8, 2013, http://blog.code.org/post/69469632752/hourofcodeishere/.

215. Nitasha Tiku, "How to Get Girls Into Coding," *New York Times*, May 31, 2014, www.nytimes.com/2014/06/01/opinion/sunday/how-to-get-girls-into-coding.html.

216. Harvey Graff, "The Literacy Myth at 30," *Journal of Social History* 43, no. 3 (2010): 652.

Chapter 2

1. Jack Goody, *The Domestication of the Savage Mind* (Cambridge, UK: Cambridge University Press, 1977); Walter Ong, "Writing Is a Technology That Restructures Thought," in *Literacy: A Critical Sourcebook*, Ellen Cushman et al., Eds. (Boston: Bedford/St. Martins Press, 2001), 19–31; Marshall McLuhan, *Understanding Media: The Extensions of Man*, 1st MIT Press ed. (Cambridge, MA: MIT Press, 1994).

2. Andrea diSessa, *Changing Minds: Computers, Learning and Literacy* (Cambridge, MA: MIT Press, 2000), 6.

3. diSessa, *Changing Minds*, 5. The next two chapters in the current volume chart the historical circulation of these technologies and skills in order to explore this distinction between literacies and material intelligences more carefully.

4. diSessa, *Changing Minds*, 11.

5. Mark Poster, "Introduction," in *Does Writing Have a Future?* by Villem Flusser, trans. Nancy Ann Roth (Minneapolis: University of Minnesota Press, 2011), x.

6. Vannevar Bush, "As We May Think," *Atlantic*, July 1945, www.theatlantic.com/ magazine/archive/1945/07/as-we-may-think/303881/.

7. Martin Greenberger, "The Computers of Tomorrow," *Atlantic*, May 1964, www
.theatlantic.com/past/docs/unbound/flashbks/computer/greenbf.htm.

8. Vannevar Bush, "Memex Revisited" in *New Media Old Media: A History and Theory
Reader*, Wendy Hui Kyong Chun and Thomas Keenan, Eds. (New York: Routledge,
2005), 85.

9. J. C. R. Licklider, "Man-Computer Symbiosis," *IRE Transactions on Human Factors
in Electronics* HFE-1, no. 1 (1960): 4–11. doi: 10.1109/THFE2.1960.4503259.

10. Martin Heidegger, "The Question Concerning Technology," in *Basic Writings
from Being and Time (1927) and the Task of Thinking (1964)*, David Farrell Krell, Ed.
(New York: Harper and Row, 1977), 283–317.

11. Quoted in Martin Greenberger, Ed., *Computers and the World of the Future* (Cambridge, MA: MIT Press, 1962), 211.

12. Quoted in Greenberger, Ed., *Computers and the World of the Future*, 213.

13. Ian Bogost, *Persuasive Games: The Expressive Power of Videogames* (Cambridge,
MA: MIT Press, 2010), 5.

14. Hal Abelson and Gerald Jay Sussman with Julie Sussman, *The Structure and Interpretation of Computer Programs*, 2nd ed. (Cambridge, MA: MIT Press, 1996), xviii.

15. Hal Abelson, "SICP/What is Computer Science?" YouTube video, 10:00, posted
by "LarryNorman," September 12, 2006, https://www.youtube.com/watch?v=zQLUP
jefuWA/.

16. Augusta Ada (Countess of) Lovelace, "Notes on the Sketch of The Analytical
Engine Invented by Charles Babbage," 1842, https://www.fourmilab.ch/babbage/
sketch.html.

17. Seymour Papert, *Mindstorms: Children, Computers, and Powerful Ideas* (New York:
Basic Books, 1980).

18. For a description of Piagetian learning principles and Logo, see Cynthia Solomon, *Computer Environments for Children: A Reflection on Theories of Learning and
Education* (Cambridge, MA: MIT Press, 1986).

19. Papert responded to this critique in 1997 by saying that they weren't seeing the
big picture. Their critique "was in the spirit of those who dismissed the Wright
brothers' flight on the grounds that a hop of 22 feet was of no serious importance."
Seymour Papert, "Educational Computing: How Are We doing?" *T H E Journal (Technological Horizons in Education)* 24, no. 11 (1997): 78–80.

20. Roy Pea and D. Midian Kurland, "On the Cognitive Effects of Learning Computer Programming," *New Ideas in Psychology* 2, no. 2 (1984): 138.

21. Pea and Kurland, "On the Cognitive Effects," 144.

22. Harold A. Innis, *Empire and Communications* (Toronto: University of Toronto Press, 1972).

23. McLuhan, *Understanding Media*.

24. Ong, "Writing Is a Technology That Restructures Thought."

25. Jack Goody and Ian Watt, "The Consequences of Literacy," *Comparative Studies in Society and History* 5, no. 3 (1963): 304–345.

26. Brian V. Street, *Literacy in Theory and Practice* (Cambridge, UK: Cambridge University Press, 1985).

27. Sylvia Scribner and Michael Cole, *The Psychology of Literacy* (Cambridge, MA: Harvard University Press, 1981).

28. Kate Vieira, too, admits that she has "sympathy for the bold, and currently unpopular, question that anthropologist Jack Goody and literary critic Ian Watt posed in 1963: What are the consequences of literacy?" By literacy, Vieira means a material thing, a thing with social origins but with material effects on people in the world. Kate Vieira, "On the Social Consequences of Literacy," *Literacy in Composition Studies* 1, no. 1 (2013): 26–32, http://licsjournal.org/OJS/index.php/LiCS/article/view/7/.

29. Lisa Gitelman, *Paper Knowledge: Toward a Media History of Documents* (Durham, NC: Duke University Press, 2014); Matthew Kirschenbaum, *Mechanisms: New Media and the Forensic Imagination* (Cambridge, MA: MIT Press, 2008); Lori Emerson, *Reading Writing Interfaces: From the Digital to the Bookbound* (Minneapolis: University of Minnesota Press, 2014); Tim Laquintano, "Sustained Authorship: Digital Writing, Self-Publishing, and the Ebook," *Written Communication* 27, no. 4 (2010): 469–493. doi: 10.1177/0741088310377863.

30. Bruno Latour, *Reassembling the Social: An Introduction to Actor-Network Theory* (Oxford, UK: Oxford University Press, 2005).

31. For instance, although Brian Street dedicated a sizable chunk of his introduction to *Literacy in Theory and Practice* to tearing down what he calls the "autonomous model of literacy," represented by Jack Goody's work and that of others, Street's own "ideological model of literacy" synthesizes the complex interactions between literacy's social *and* technological factors. He writes, "Literacy, of course, is more than just the 'technology' in which it is manifest. No one material feature serves to define literacy itself. It is a social process, in which particular socially constructed technologies are used within particular institutional frameworks for specific social purposes." Brian Street, *Literacy in Theory and Practice* (Cambridge, UK: Cambridge University Press, 1984), 97. Another central figure in NLS, Harvey Graff, has devoted much of his historical work in literacy to dispelling what he calls the "literacy myth"—the common contention that literacy leads to social uplift—yet he also points to the social value of particular literacy technologies. He writes, "Literacy,

though not actually *causing* politicization or collective action, did prove a valued, useful vehicle for presenting, airing and gaining larger audiences for grievances. [Literature, religious action, and scholarship were] all amplified in important new, innovative ways with the addition of printing's technology." Harvey Graff, *Labyrinths of Literacy: Reflections on Literacy Past and Present*, Revised Edition (Pittsburgh, PA: University of Pittsburgh Press, 1995), 143–144.

32. We might say the same for Marc Prensky's popular concept of "digital natives" and "digital immigrants," which is sometimes invoked in discussions of programming as a literacy. Marc Prensky, "Digital Natives, Digital Immigrants," *On the Horizon* 9, no. 5 (2001): 1–6. doi: 10748120110424816.

33. David Olson, *World on Paper: The Conceptual and Cognitive Implications of Writing and Reading* (Cambridge, UK: Cambridge University Press, 1994), 37.

34. Deborah Brandt, *Literacy in American Lives* (Cambridge, UK: Cambridge University Press, 2001); Deborah Brandt, *The Rise of Writing: Redefining Mass Literacy* (Cambridge, UK: Cambridge University Press, 2014); Niko Besnier, *Literacy, Emotion and Authority: Reading and Writing on a Polynesian Atoll* (Cambridge, UK: Cambridge University Press, 1995); Christina Haas, *Writing Technology: Studies on the Materiality of Literacy* (Mahwah, NJ: Lawrence Erlbaum, 1996); Kate Vieira, *American by Paper: How Documents Matter in Immigrant Literacy* (Minneapolis: University of Minnesota Press, 2016); Timothy Laquintano, *Mass Authorship and the Rise of Self-Publishing* (Iowa City: University of Iowa, 2016).

35. Ruth Schwartz Cowan, *Social History of American Technology* (Oxford, UK: Oxford University Press, 1986).

36. Thomas Misa, "How Machines Make History, and How Historians (and Others) Help Them to Do So," *Science, Technology, & Human Values* 13, no. 3/4 (1988): 322.

37. diSessa, *Changing Minds*, 6.

38. John von Neumann, "First Draft of a Report on the EDVAC," Michael D. Godfrey, Ed., *IEEE Annals of the History of Computing* 15, no. 4 (1993): 27–75.

39. Friedrich A. Kittler, *Gramophone, Film, Typewriter* (Stanford, CA: Stanford University Press, 1999). Because of World War II, Zuse's computer—designed in Germany—was not as influential to computer design in Britain and America.

40. Example and explanation from Daniel Kohanski, *The Philosophical Programmer: Reflections on the Moth in the Machine* (New York: St. Martin's Press, 1998), 83.

41. Kathleen Broome Williams tells a story that Grace Hopper once couldn't balance her checkbook, and her brother discovered the error: she would occasionally record figures in octal rather than decimal. From that mix-up, Hopper concluded that the computer should bend to the way people are already trained to think, in

decimal. Kathleen Broome Williams, *Grace Hopper: Admiral of the Cyber Sea* (Annapolis, MD: Naval Institute Press, 2004), 70.

42. The program they wrote, called "Initial Orders," was the first assembler program. Martin Campbell-Kelly and William Aspray, *Computer: A History of the Information Machine*, 2nd ed. (Boulder, CO: Westview Press, 2004), 166. For a succinct summary of programming the EDSAC, see Martin Richards, "EDSAC Initial Orders and Squares Program," University of Cambridge Computer Laboratory, n.d., www .cl.cam.ac.uk/~mr10/edsacposter.pdf.

43. Code excerpted here was written by Nathan McKenzie (August 8, 2007), and given to me for the purpose of this example.

44. Janet Abbate, *Recoding Gender: Women's Changing Participation in Computing* (Cambridge, MA: MIT Press 2012), 75–83. Quoting Grace Murray Hopper, "The Education of a Computer," in *Proceedings of the 1952 ACM National Meeting* (Pittsburgh, PA: ACM, 1952), 243.

45. Michael Mahoney, "Finding a History for Software Engineering," *IEEE Annals of the History of Computing* 26, no. 1, (2004): 16.

46. Abbate, *Recoding Gender*, 79–80.

47. Kohanski, *The Philosophical Programmer*, 90.

48. Kohanski, *The Philosophical Programmer*, 90.

49. Kohanski, *The Philosophical Programmer*, 91.

50. As work in organization science has demonstrated, standards are always political, especially at their inception. See Geoffrey C. Bowker and Susan Leigh Star, *Sorting Things Out: Classification and Its Consequences* (Cambridge, MA: MIT Press, 1999).

51. Nathan Ensmenger, *The Computer Boys Take Over: Computers, Programmers, and the Politics of Technical Expertise* (Cambridge, MA: MIT Press, 2010), 100–103.

52. Although ALGOL was by all accounts a better language, by that time COBOL had such wide distribution that ALGOL struggled to cut into its dominance. Ensmenger notes that COBOL is still a major legacy language, because so many software systems were originally built in it. The Y2K crisis was connected, in part, to the way that COBOL rendered dates, and by that time there were an estimated 70 billion lines of code in COBOL in use. Ensmenger, *The Computer Boys Take Over*, 103.

53. Campbell-Kelly et al., *Computer*, 3rd ed.

54. Sherry Turkle, *Life on the Screen: Identity in the Age of the Internet* (New York: Simon and Schuster, 1995), 56.

55. John McCarthy, "LISP—Notes on Its Past and Future—1980," John McCarthy's Home Page (Stanford University), March 22, 1999, www-formal.stanford.edu/jmc/ lisp20th.pdf.

56. Richard Gabriel, "The Art of Lisp and Writing [Foreword to *Successful Lisp: How to Understand and Use Common Lisp* by David B. Lamkins]," *Dreamsongs*, 2004, www.dreamsongs.com/ArtOfLisp.html.

57. Paul Graham, *Hackers & Painters: Big Ideas from the Computer Age* (Sebastopol, CA: O'Reilly, 2004).

58. An extensive taxonomy of approaches for novice programming languages can be found in Caitlin Kelleher and Randy Pausch, "Lowering the Barriers to Programming: A Taxonomy of Programming Environments and Languages for Novice Programmers," *ACM Computing Surveys* 37, no. 2 (2005): 83–137.

59. See here for a detailed explanation and examples: "Visual Programming Guide," Postscapes, n.d., http://postscapes.com/iot-visual-programming-tools/.

60. See Casey Alt, "Objects of Our Affection," for a lucid and interesting description of the ways that object-oriented programming languages have helped make computers ubiquitous in modern life. Casey Alt, "Objects of Our Affection: How Object Orientation Made Computation a Medium," in *Media Archaeology*, Erkki Huhtamo and Jussi Parikka, Eds. (Berkeley: University of California Press, 2011), 278–301.

61. Infamously, the Twitter service was originally built in Ruby on Rails and needed to scale up once it became more popular in 2009. Users frequently saw the "fail whale" that indicated an overload on the Twitter platform. Developers then switched the structure to Scala in order to handle the load. Victor Luckerson, "How Twitter Slayed the Fail Whale," *Time*, November 6, 2013, http://business.time.com/2013/11/06/how-twitter-slayed-the-fail-whale/.

62. See for instance قلب, a programming language in Arabic. Its creator, Ramsay Nasser, says, "If we are going to really push for coding literacy, which I do; if we are going to push to teach code around the world, then we have to be aware of what the cultural biases are and what it means for someone who doesn't share that background to be expected to be able to reason in those languages" (quoted in Neil McAllister, "Meet قلب, the Programming Language That Uses Arabic Script," *Register,* January 25, 2013, www.theregister.co.uk/2013/01/25/arabic_programming_language/.

The fact that English is a lingua franca for code—both in terms of programming languages and in online discussions of programming—is connected to a larger phenomenon of English as a global language. This is just one (obvious) indication that code is, at least in part, a socially constructed linguistic artifact.

63. Alexander Galloway, *Gaming: Essays on Algorithmic Culture* (Minneapolis: University of Minnesota Press, 2006), 5. He is paraphrasing Friedrich Kittler.

64. John Langshaw Austin, *How to Do Things with Words* (Cambridge, MA: Harvard University Press, 1962); Kenneth Burke, *Language as Symbolic Action* (Berkeley: University of California Press, 1966).

65. Kenneth Burke, quoted in William A. Covino, "The Eternal Return of Magic-Rhetoric: Carnak Counts Ballots," in *Rhetoric and Composition as Intellectual Work*, Gary Olson, Ed. (Carbondale: Southern Illinois University Press, 2002), 221.

66. Gabriel, "The Art of Lisp and Writing."

67. Austin, *How to Do Things with Words*, 149.

68. See Geoff Cox and Alex McLean, *Speaking/Code: Coding as Aesthetic and Political Expression* (Cambridge, MA: MIT Press, 2012), for another perspective on what speech act theory can tell us about code and speech.

69. Austin, *How to Do Things with Words*, 99.

70. Austin, *How to Do Things with Words*, 149.

71. John R. Searle, *Speech Acts: An Essay in the Philosophy of Language* (Cambridge, UK: Cambridge University Press, 1969), 37.

72. Searle, *Speech Acts*, 17.

73. Yasmin Kafai and Quinn Burke, *Connected Code: Why Children Need to Learn Programming* (Cambridge, MA: MIT Press, 2014).

74. Terry Winograd and Fernando Flores, *Understanding Computers and Cognition* (Norwood, NJ: Ablex Publishing Corporation, 1986), 78.

75. Winograd and Flores often refer to the ineluctable combination of locutionary and illocutionary forces in language in *Understanding Computers and Cognition*.

76. Linda Flower and John R. Hayes, "Images, Plans, and Prose: The Representation of Meaning in Writing," *Written Communication* 1, no. 1 (1984), 130.

77. Lovelace, "Notes on the Sketch of The Analytical Engine Invented by Charles Babbage," Note G.

78. Alan Turing, "Computing Machinery and Intelligence," *Mind* 59, no. 236 (1950): 450.

79. Here, I picture Stanley Fish's scenario of defining "class," "text," and the practice of hand-raising in the absence of "interpretative communities" that share basic assumptions of context. Stanley Fish, *Is There a Text in This Class? The Authority of Interpretive Communities* (Cambridge, MA: Harvard University Press, 1980).

80. Walter Ong, *Orality and Literacy: The Technologizing of the Word* (New York: Routledge, 2002), 7.

81. Jay David Bolter, *Writing Space: Computers, Hypertext, and the History of Writing* (Hillsdale, NJ: Lawrence Erlbaum, 1991), 203.

82. Joel Haefner, "The Politics of the Code," *Computers and Composition* 16 (1999): 329.

83. Bogost, *Persuasive Games*, 7.

84. Ong, "Writing Is a Technology That Restructures Thought," 22.

85. Wendy Hui Kyong Chun takes issue with this idea of perfect execution in code, arguing that it elides differences between machine and source code and ignores the materiality of computer memory, which has been elaborated by Matthew Kirschenbaum. She also argues, via Judith Butler, that an application of speech act theory suggests a desire to map code onto simple power structures (*Programmed Visions*, 23–28). While I agree that the materiality of computers affects the execution of code (which I elaborate later), I think that too much attention to the "power structures" in code can erase the real differences between code and human language. Wendy Hui Kyong Chun, *Programmed Visions: Software and Memory* (Cambridge, MA: MIT Press, 2013); Kirschenbaum, *Mechanisms*.

86. Although see Adrian Johns for argument that print wasn't as uniform as is often claimed (e.g., by Elizabeth Eisenstein). Adrian Johns, *The Nature of the Book* (Chicago: University of Chicago Press, 1998).

87. Notably, the legal fate of software was tied up in copyright debates about photocopiers and even overshadowed by them because the technology of software and photocopiers became critical to commerce around the same time. See the CONTU report, commissioned by President Lyndon Johnson. United States National Commission on New Technological Uses of Copyrighted Works (CONTU), "Final Report of the National Commission on New Technological Uses of Copyrighted Works," *Computer/Law Journal* 3, no. 1 (1981), 53–104.

88. Bernard Stiegler, "Interobjectivity and Transindividuation," open! Platform for Art, Culture & the Public Domain, September 28, 2012, http://www.onlineopen.org/interobjectivity-and-transindividuation/.

89. Stiegler, "Interobjectivity and Transindividuation."

90. Bernard Stiegler, "Die Aufklärung in the Age of Philosophical Engineering," trans. Daniel Ross, *Computational Culture* 2 (2012), http://computationalculture.net/comment/die-aufklarung-in-the-age-of-philosophical-engineering/.

91. Stiegler, "Die Aufklärung."

92. Bernard Stiegler, *Technics and Time, 1: The Fault of Epimetheus*, trans. Richard Beardsworth and George Collins (Stanford, CA: Stanford University Press, 1998).

93. Stiegler, "Die Aufklärung."

94. Kohanski, *The Philosophical Programmer*, 4.

95. Stiegler, "Die Aufklärung"; Ong, *Orality and Literacy*, 81.

96. Annette Vee, "Text, Speech, Machine: Metaphors for Computer Code in the Law," *Computational Culture* 2 (2012), http://computationalculture.net/article/text -speech-machine-metaphors-for-computer-code-in-the-law/.

97. Jacques Derrida, *Of Grammatology*, corrected ed., trans. Gayatri Chakravorty Spivak (Baltimore, MD: Johns Hopkins University Press).

98. N. Katherine Hayles, *My Mother Was a Computer: Digital Subjects and Literary Texts* (Chicago: University of Chicago Press, 2005), chapter 2.

99. She calls the reciprocal influences of writing and programming "intermediation." Hayles, *My Mother Was a Computer.*

100. Gabriel, "The Art of Lisp and Writing [Foreword to *Successful Lisp*]."

101. Cristina Videira Lopes, *Exercises in Programming Style* (Boca Raton, FL: Chapman and Hall/CRC, 2014).

102. Michael Mateas and Nick Montfort, "A Box, Darkly: Obfuscation, Weird Languages, and Code Aesthetics," *Proceedings of the 6th Digital Arts and Culture Conference, IT University of Copenhagen* (2005), 144–153, NickM.com, http://nickm.com/ cis/a_box_darkly.pdf.

103. The restricted form of code has proved generative to writers who compose poems evoking the logic and expressions of programming, yet are meant only for human readers. Examples include Susan Wheeler, mez, and Sharon Hopkins. Combining code conventions with words meaningful in human languages was explored creatively as early as 1968, with the publication of Noël Arnaud's *Algol*. Arnaud's poems, although not executable by the ALGOL compiler, were composed with key words in the ALGOL programming language (Mateas and Montfort, "A Box, Darkly").

104. Frederick P. Brooks, *The Mythical Man-Month: Essays on Software Engineering* (Reading, MA: Addison-Wesley, 1982), 47.

105. Brooks, *Mythical Man-Month,* 5.

106. Brooks, *Mythical Man-Month,* 7.

107. Donald Knuth, *Literate Programming* (Stanford, CA: Center for the Study of Language and Information, 1992), ix.

108. Mateas and Montfort, "A Box, Darkly."

109. Karl Hasselström and Jon Åslund, "Shakespeare Programming Language," SourceForge, August 21, 2001, http://shakespearelang.sourceforge.net/report/ shakespeare/shakespeare.html#sec:hello/.

110. Mateas and Montfort, "A Box, Darkly." See Hasselström and Åslund, "Shakespeare Programming Language," for a description of their objectives for SPL.

111. Cox and McLean, *Speaking Code*, 6.

112. Example from Mateas and Montfort, "A Box, Darkly."

113. "Malbolge," Esolang, the Esoteric Programming Languages Wiki, accessed November 12, 2013, http://esolangs.org/wiki/Malbolge/.

114. Example from Mateas and Montfort, "A Box, Darkly."

115. Mateas and Montfort, "A Box, Darkly." In the author's description of the code, he writes, "incidentally, i've come to hate malbolge. no doubt that was the author's intention." He also notes that he doesn't have a computer science degree, but works as a freelance software engineer. Andrew Cooke, "Malbolge: Hello World," Andrew Cooke (personal website), accessed May 18, 2015, http://acooke.org/malbolge.html.

116. Stephen Fortune, "What on Earth Is Livecoding," DazedDigital, May 2013, www.dazeddigital.com/artsandculture/article/16150/1/what-on-earth-is-livecoding/.

117. Fortune, "What on Earth Is Livecoding."

118. Michael Mateas, "Procedural Literacy: Educating the New Media Practitioner," *On The Horizon* (Special Issue on the Future of Games, Simulations and Interactive Media in Learning Contexts) 13 (2005); Noah Wardrip-Fruin, *Expressive Processing: Digital Fictions, Computer Games, and Software Studies* (Cambridge, MA: MIT Press, 2009).

119. Espen Aarseth, *Cybertext: Perspectives on Ergodic Literature* (Baltimore, MD: Johns Hopkins University Press, 1997).

120. David M. Rieder, "Scripted Writing() Exploring Generative Dimensions of Writing in Flash Actionscript," in *Small Tech: The Culture of Digital Tools*, Byron Hawk, David M. Rieder, and Ollie O. Oviedo, Eds. (Minneapolis: University of Minnesota Press, 2008), 80–94.

121. N. Katherine Hayles, "Print Is Flat, Code Is Deep: The Importance of Media-Specific Analysis," *Poetics Today* 25, no. 1 (2004): 67–90. doi: 10.1215/03335372-25-1-67.

122. Mateas, "Procedural Literacy."

123. Paul Ford, "What Is Code?" *Bloomberg Business*, June 11, 2015. www.bloomberg.com/graphics/2015-paul-ford-what-is-code/.

124. For a more thorough exploration of the sociality of software, see Adrian Mackenzie, *Cutting Code: Software and Sociality*. Digital Formations (Bern, Switzerland: Peter Lang International Academic Publishers, 2006).

125. Nathan Ensmenger, "Software as History Embodied," *IEEE Annals of the History of Computing* 31, no. 1 (2010): 86–88.

126. Brooks, *Mythical Man-Month*, 42.

127. Mikhail M. Bakhtin, "The Problem of Speech Genres," In *Speech Genres and Other Late Essays*, C. Emerson and M. Holquist, Eds., translated by Vern W. McGee (Austin: University of Texas Press, 1986), 69.

128. James Paul Gee, *Social Linguistics and Literacies*, 2nd ed. Critical Perspectives on Literacy and Education (New York: Routledge Falmer, 1996), 132.

129. Gee, *Social Linguistics and Literacies*, 132.

130. Gee, *Social Linguistics and Literacies*, 138–143.

131. As one programmer I interviewed says, "with Internet-linked stuff, I don't think anyone's going to be programming in a vacuum anymore" (Mike Silbersack, personal interview, Skype, September 9, 2009).

132. I know that this discussion is reductive and is likely to set off alarm bells for anyone more familiar with these development processes. Agile development has been critiqued for being too heavy-handed, too: too much testing, and so forth. But for the scope of this discussion, these agile practices serve to illustrate some of the social factors in collaborative coding.

133. "Code Review FAQ," MDN [Mozilla Developer Network], March 14, 2013, https://developer.mozilla.org/en-US/docs/Code_Review_FAQ/.

134. Not all workplaces have code with consistent style, of course. One programmer told me of working at a company where its disorganization was apparent in the way each programmer had a section of the codebase as his or her "fiefdom." No one seemed to read or work on each other's code effectively. This provides a negative example of social effects on code—the antisocial nature of the code affected its efficiency and maintainability. This programmer was thankful that he had already cut his programming teeth on a much "tighter" code base.

135. "Code Review FAQ," MDN [Mozilla Developer Network].

136. Karim R. Lakhani and Robert Wolf, "Why Hackers Do What They Do: Understanding Motivation and Effort in Free/Open Source Software Projects," in *Perspectives on Free and Open Source Software*, Joseph Feller et al., Eds. (Cambridge, MA: MIT Press, 2005), 7.

137. Jeff Atwood, "Pair Programming vs. Code Reviews," Coding Horror, November 18, 2007, https://blog.codinghorror.com/pair-programming-vs-code-reviews/.

138. In response to Atwood's column, J. Stoever writes, "I personally don't really like to talk a lot. I picked an office job in programming in part because it lets me spend most of my day in silence and concentration. Having to work that closely with someone else all day would certainly put a dent in job attractivity for me."

139. Bryan Arendt, comment on Atwood, "Pair Programming vs. Code Reviews."

140. Lakhani and Wolf, "Why Hackers Do What They Do."

141. Lakhani and Wolf, "Why Hackers Do What They Do," 5.

142. E. Gabriella Coleman, "Three Ethical Moments in Debian," Working Paper Series, Center for Critical Analysis, Rutgers University, 2005. Social Science Research Network, http://dx.doi.org/10.2139/ssrn.805287/.

143. Mike Silbersack, personal interview, Skype, September 9, 2009.

144. "FAQ: Chapter 1. Introduction," FreeBSD, n.d., https://www.freebsd.org/doc/faq/introduction.html.

145. Jean Lave and Etienne Wenger, *Situated Learning: Legitimate Peripheral Participation* (Cambridge, UK: Cambridge University Press, 1991).

146. Weber, *The Success of Open Source*.

147. Lave and Wenger, *Situated Learning,* 93.

148. Coleman, "Three Ethical Moments," 28.

149. Lakhani and Wolf, "Why Hackers Do What They Do."

150. Bruce Stewart, "An Interview with the Creator of Ruby [Yukihiro Matsumoto]," O'Reilly Linux Devcenter, November 29, 2001, www.linuxdevcenter.com/pub/a/linux/2001/11/29/ruby.html.

151. Deborah Brandt, "Writing for a Living: Literacy and the Knowledge Economy," *Written Communication* 22, no. 2 (2005): 188.

152. Brandt, "Writing for a Living," 189.

153. Brandt, "Writing for a Living," 191.

154. Brandt, *Literacy in American Lives*.

155. Scribner, "Literacy in Three Metaphors," 16.

156. Brandt, "Writing for a Living," 191.

157. Tathagata, "Good Ways To Join an Open Source Project?" Slashdot, June 22, 2007, https://ask.slashdot.org/story/07/06/22/1526234/good-ways-to-join-an-open-source-project/.

158. "CTho9305," comment on Tathagata, "Good Ways To Join an Open Source Project?"

159. Lakhani and Wolf, "Why Hackers Do What They Do," 7.

160. Jason (a video-game designer), in conversation with the author, September 2009.

161. Brandt, *Literacy in American Lives*.

Chapter 3

1. Christina Haas, *Writing Technology: Studies on the Materiality of Literacy* (Mahwah, NJ: Lawrence Erlbaum, 1996), 221.

2. Jack Goody, Ed., *The Logic of Writing and the Organization of Society* (Cambridge, UK: Cambridge University Press, 1986).

3. Brian Stock, *The Implications of Literacy: Written Language and Models of Interpretation in the Eleventh and Twelfth Centuries* (Princeton, NJ: Princeton University Press, 1983).

4. Michael Clanchy, *From Memory to Written Record: England, 1066–1307*, 2nd ed. (Malden, MA: Blackwell Publishing, 1993); Stock, *The Implications of Literacy*.

5. Stock, *The Implications of Literacy*, 4.

6. Michael Mahoney, "The Histories of Computing(s)," *Interdisciplinary Science Reviews* 30, no. 2 (2005): 127.

7. Stock, *The Implications of Literacy*, 9.

8. Clanchy, *From Memory to Written Record*, 2nd ed., 272.

9. See especially Goody, *The Logic of Writing*.

10. Although Clanchy says that "the shift from memory to written record" was probably occurring across Western Europe at this time, it was best documented in England. Clanchy, *From Memory to Written Record*, 2nd ed., 5. For other periods, see Jon Agar, *The Government Machine: A Revolutionary History of the Computer* (Cambridge, MA: MIT Press, 2003), "Colonial Great Britain"; Ben Kafka, *The Demon of Writing: Powers and Failures of Paperwork* (Cambridge, MA: MIT Press, 2012), "Revolutionary France."

11. Susan Leigh Star, "The Ethnography of Infrastructure," *American Behavioral Scientist* 43, no. 3 (1999): 377–391.

12. Star, "The Ethnography of Infrastructure," 381–382.

13. Star, "The Ethnography of Infrastructure," 380.

14. Here, infrastructures might seem similar to Kuhnian paradigms, as both influence the ways we think and operate. But I think of infrastructures as material and paradigms as conceptual.

15. Andrea diSessa, *Changing Minds: Computers, Learning and Literacy* (Cambridge, MA: MIT Press, 2000), 24.

16. Harold A. Innis, *Empire and Communications* (Toronto: University of Toronto Press, 1972), 7.

17. James R. Beniger, *The Control Revolution: Technological and Economic Origins of the Information Society* (Cambridge, MA: Harvard University Press, 1986), 219.

18. Beniger, *The Control Revolution*, 15.

19. Charles Bazerman, "The Writing of Social Organization and the Literate Situating of Cognition: Extending Goody's Social Implications of Writing," in *Technology, Literacy, and the Evolution of Society: Implications of the Work of Jack Goody*, David R. Olson and Michael Cole, Eds. (Mahwah, NJ: Lawrence Erlbaum, 2006), 235.

20. In fact, we can trace it even earlier: as Denise Schmandt-Besserat has demonstrated, the first uses of writing in ancient Egypt and Mesopotamia were for commercial purposes, to keep track of accounts and goods: Denise Schmandt-Besserat, *Before Writing: From Counting to Cuneiform*, Vol. 1 (Austin: University of Texas Press, 1992). See also Goody, *Logic of Writing*, 67.

21. Clanchy, *From Memory to Written Record*, 2nd ed., 19.

22. Clanchy, *From Memory to Written Record*, 2nd ed., 1.

23. W. L. Warren, "The Myth of Norman Administrative Efficiency," *THRS* 5th Series XXXIV (1984), 132, quoted in Clanchy, *From Memory to Written Record*, 2nd ed., 66.

24. Clanchy, *From Memory to Written Record*, 2nd ed., 19.

25. Mary Carruthers and Jan M. Ziolkowski, "General Introduction," in *The Medieval Craft of Memory*, Mary Carruthers and Jan M. Ziolkowski, Eds. (Philadelphia: University of Pennsylvania Press, 2002), 1–31.

26. Carruthers and Ziolkowski, "General Introduction," 13.

27. Mary Carruthers, *The Book of Memory: A Study of Memory in Medieval Culture*, 2nd ed. (Cambridge, UK: Cambridge University Press, 2008), 94–95.

28. Carruthers and Ziolkowski, "General Introduction," 11–12. Similarly, computation was popularly performed on the fingers (11).

29. Jill Stevenson, *Performance, Cognitive Theory, and Devotional Culture* (New York: Palgrave Macmillan, 2010), 101.

30. Clanchy, *From Memory to Written Record*, 2nd ed., 62.

31. Clanchy, *From Memory to Written Record*, 2nd ed., 67.

32. Stock, *The Implications of Literacy*, 48. Ben Kafka (*The Demon of Writing*) provides a compelling account of this depersonalization of government through increased documentation in Revolutionary France.

33. Stock, *The Implications of Literacy*, 48.

34. Clanchy, *From Memory to Written Record*, 2nd ed.; Stock, *The Implications of Literacy*.

35. Clanchy, *From Memory to Written Record*, 2nd ed., 254.

36. Clanchy, *From Memory to Written Record*, 2nd. ed., 35–37.

37. Clanchy, *From Memory to Written Record*, 2nd ed., 52.

38. Clanchy, *From Memory to Written Record*, 2nd ed., 152.

39. Stock, *The Implications of Literacy*, 40–41.

40. "The form of papal bulls was clarified; the offices of writing and dating were combined; the curial script was abandoned and along with it reliance on the Roman *scriniarii* [i.e., there was finally a standardized hand in the eleventh century]; and the rules for the *cursus* were standardized." Stock, *The Implications of Literacy*, 35.

41. Stock, *The Implications of Literacy*, 36.

42. Stock, *The Implications of Literacy*, 35.

43. Clanchy, *From Memory to Written Record*, 2nd ed., 152.

44. Clanchy, *From Memory to Written Record*, 2nd ed., 181.

45. Stock, *The Implications of Literacy*, 37; Clanchy, *From Memory to Written Record*, 2nd ed., 5.

46. Goody, *The Logic of Writing*, 63.

47. Goody, *The Logic of Writing*, 63–64; 91.

48. Clanchy, *From Memory to Written Record*, 3rd ed., 25.

49. Clanchy, *From Memory to Written Record*, 2nd ed., 34.

50. As suggested by the two titles for the Norman census—Domesday Book and *liber judiciarious*—there was a complex relationship between vernacularity, writing, authority, and class during this period. Two vernaculars circulated at this time, versions of French and English sometimes called Anglo-Norman and Old/Middle English. A third language, Latin, circulated as the language of the church, but also as a language of official record in both church and state. Anglo-Norman was a native language for some of the aristocracy, at least in the early period of the time we survey here. (When it became primarily a learned, elite language is a subject of much debate among scholars of Anglo-Norman. Richard Ingham, Ed. *The Anglo-Norman Language and Its Contexts* [York, UK: York Medieval Press, 2010].) English appears to have superseded Anglo-Norman as a native language during this period, although correspondence among the aristocracy often continued to be written in Anglo-Norman. English became a literary language, popular for texts designed to circulate among a wider audience. Written records required literacy of those who dealt with

them, of course, but specifically literacy in Latin. It's not just the ability to read and write that facilitates the shift from memory to written record, then, but also the ability to work in Anglo-Norman or Latin, the languages of written records at the time. As countless studies of literacy demonstrate, the ability to read and write cannot be removed from social context, and in the period we survey here, these social contexts were marked by differences among vernacular and ruling languages.

51. Clanchy, *From Memory to Written Record*, 3rd ed., 26.

52. This pattern is echoed in Revolutionary France, where Ben Kafka (*The Demon of Writing*) describes a tension between the new state's desire for surveillance as well as efficiency in its documentary procedures.

53. Clanchy, *From Memory to Written Record*, 2nd ed., 32.

54. Goody, *The Logic of Writing*, 63–64.

55. Clanchy, *From Memory to Written Record*, 2nd ed., 161.

56. Clanchy, *From Memory to Written Record*, 2nd ed., 69.

57. Collection and redistribution, which are complex information tasks, also drove the use of writing in the "twin bureaucracies" of temple and palace according to Goody. In ancient Mesopotamia and Egypt, the census established a basis for more elaborate records of what subjects owed or were owed by these central powers. In this way, the bureaucratic and economic uses of writing were entangled, diffusing writing from governmental out to commercial contexts. Goody, *The Logic of Writing*, 45–67.

58. As Clanchy writes, "It was easier to make records than to use them efficiently." Clanchy, *From Memory to Written Record*, 2nd ed., 70.

59. Clanchy, *From Memory to Written Record*, 2nd ed., 71.

60. Clanchy, *From Memory to Written Record*, 2nd ed., 161.

61. Clanchy, *From Memory to Written Record*, 2nd ed., 185.

62. Jack Goody, Ed. *Literacy in Traditional Societies* (Cambridge, UK: Cambridge University Press, 1968). Although Goody's specific concept of literacy has been critiqued for adhering too closely to the paradigm of the Greeks, Charles Bazerman claims that the idea of "restricted literacy" opens up ways of thinking about how societies use literacy in different ways. Bazerman, "The Writing of Social Organization."

63. diSessa, *Changing Minds*.

64. Clanchy, *From Memory to Written Record*, 2nd ed.

65. Goody, *The Logic of Writing*, 160. This was true in England, whereas elsewhere in Europe at that time, including Italy and France, there was a system of village notaries to perform those duties.

66. Clanchy, *From Memory to Written Record*, 2nd ed., 46.

67. Clanchy, *From Memory to Written Record*, 2nd ed., 65.

68. Clanchy, *From Memory to Written Record*, 2nd ed., 48.

69. Stock, *The Implications of Literacy*, 17.

70. Clanchy, *From Memory to Written Record*, 2nd ed., 160.

71. Clanchy, *From Memory to Written Record*, 2nd ed., 135.

72. We might wonder what headlines a thirteenth-century Nicholas Carr would write in the wake of this change: "Are Libraries Making Us Stoopid?" As outlined in the introduction to this book, reading practices have changed dramatically through the history of text, and societal changes appear to have accompanied these changes. David Olson's *The World on Paper: The Conceptual and Cognitive Implications of Writing and Reading* (Cambridge, UK: Cambridge University Press, 1996) describes some of these broad changes.

73. Clanchy, *From Memory to Written Record*, 2nd ed., 160.

74. Although she is concerned with an era several hundred years after the one focused on here, Elizabeth Eisenstein makes a similar point. She posits that the printing press contributed to the new, empirical way of thinking evidenced in the Renaissance because of the way it made texts widely available. Texts could then be circulated widely and juxtaposed, even on a larger scale than Dominican friar librarians could enable. Elizabeth Eisenstein, *The Printing Press as an Agent of Change*, Vols. 1 and 2. (New York: Cambridge University Press, 1980).

75. William Gilmore, *Reading Becomes a Necessity of Life: Material and Cultural Life in Rural New England, 1780–1835* (Knoxville: University of Tennessee Press, 1989).

76. For a specific critique of Eisenstein, see Adrian Johns, *The Nature of the Book: Print and Knowledge in the Making* (Chicago: University of Chicago Press, 2000).

77. Texts would also have been somewhat less available to women monastics than to their male counterparts, but the real contrast was in lay life. (I thank my colleague Ryan McDermott for pointing this out to me.)

78. Clanchy, *From Memory to Written Record*, 2nd ed., 252.

79. Clanchy, *From Memory to Written Record*, 2nd ed., 194.

80. Clanchy, *From Memory to Written Record*, 2nd ed., 194.

81. Clanchy, *From Memory to Written Record*, 2nd ed., 15–16.

82. Sarah Robbins, *Managing Literacy, Mothering America: Women's Narratives on Reading and Writing in the Nineteenth Century* (Pittsburgh, PA: University of Pittsburgh Press, 2004).

83. Clanchy, *From Memory to Written Record*, 2nd ed., 252.

84. Stevenson, *Performance*, 110.

85. Stevenson, *Performance*, 110–111.

86. As Walter Ong argued, "Writing does not take over immediately when it first comes in. It creates various kinds of interdependence and interaction between itself and underlying oralities." Walter Ong, "[Review of] *The Implications of Literacy* ..., by Brian Stock," *Manuscripta* 28, no. 2 (1984): 108.

87. Clanchy, *From Memory to Written Record*, 3rd ed., 38.

88. Clanchy, *From Memory to Written Record*, 2nd ed., 115.

89. Clanchy, *From Memory to Written Record*, 2nd ed., 2.

90. Clanchy, *From Memory to Written Record*, 3rd ed., 318.

91. Clanchy, *From Memory to Written Record*, 3rd ed., 194.

92. Clanchy, *From Memory to Written Record*, 3rd ed., 190.

93. Clanchy, *From Memory to Written Record*, 3rd ed., 190.

94. Geoffrey C. Bowker and Susan Leigh Star, *Sorting Things Out: Classification and Its Consequences* (Cambridge, MA: MIT Press, 1999), 297.

95. Clanchy, *From Memory to Written Record*, 2nd ed., 308.

96. Beniger, *The Control Revolution*. See especially chapter 2.

97. In 1953, the U.S. government owned 54% of the computers then in use; if we include government contractors, the number is closer to 70%. In 1955, a cheaper IBM model appeared on the market, and as more businesses began adopting them, the government's dominance as a consumer dropped. By 1966, only 10% of computers were owned by U.S. government agencies (Kenneth Flamm, *Targeting the Computer: Government Support and International Competition* [Washington, DC: The Brookings Institution, 1987], 107). However, government funding for computer R&D remained high throughout the twentieth century. In 1965, government funding backed roughly half of all computer R&D, it dropped to 25% in the mid-1970s, dropped further to 15% in 1979, and then surged again to more than 20% in 1983, as defense spending increased during the Reagan era (Flamm, *Targeting the Computer*, 103). Some computer R&D was funded through the Department of Energy and NASA, but DARPA's strategic computing initiative in 1984 and other defense-related funding accounted for much of it.

98. John Kemeny and Thomas Kurtz, "Dartmouth Time-Sharing," *Science* 162 (1968): 223–228.

99. U.S. Census Bureau, "History: Overview," accessed January 5, 2010, www.census .gov/history/www/through_the_decades/overview/index.html.

100. Jon Agar notes that the British government followed closely behind. "Mecha-nizers," as Agar calls them, took up American systematic management and merged it with British public service. Statisticians called for more data and more order, to make Britain more like other nations (*The Government Machine*, 10).

101. U.S. Census Bureau, "History: Overview."

102. U.S. Census Bureau, "History: Overview"; U.S. Census Bureau, "UNIVAC I," accessed April 23, 2010, www.census.gov/history/www/innovations/technology/univac_i.html.

103. "Timeline of Computer History: 1941," Computer History Museum, n.d., acces-sed January 3, 2017, www.computerhistory.org/timeline/1941/. Zuse also designed a programming language for these computers, Plankalkül (F. L. Bauer and H. Wössner, "The 'Plankalkül' of Konrad Zuse: A Forerunner of Today's Programming Languages," The Retrocomputing Museum [reprinted from the *Communications of the ACM*, 1972], www.catb.org/retro/plankalkuel/). His computers and programming language were not influential to later language and machine development, however, because post-war Germany did not have the resources to pursue further development, and the Americans and British were pursuing their own lines of computer development.

104. The British government classified this project until the 1970s, and so while the project was critical to the Allies' victory, the advances made in computers there did not influence other computer projects much. Martin Campbell-Kelly and William Aspray, *Computer: A History of the Information Machine*, 2nd ed. The Sloan Technol-ogy Series (Boulder, CO: Westview Press, 2004).

105. Janet Abbate, *Recoding Gender: Women's Changing Participation in Computing* (Cambridge, MA: MIT Press, 2012), 15–16.

106. "Timeline of Computer History: 1944," Computer History Museum, n.d., accessed January 3, 2017, www.computerhistory.org/timeline/1944/.

107. Campbell-Kelly and Aspray, *Computer*, 73. The use of teams of human comput-ers stretches back at least to the eighteenth century, for instance in solving the "lon-gitude problem" of sea navigation in eighteenth-century Britain (Mary Croarken, "Eighteenth Century Computers," *Computer Resurrection: Bulletin of the Computer Conservation Society* 39 [2007], www.cs.man.ac.uk/CCS/res/res39.htm#h/). Once again, we can attribute this innovation to a kind of "control crisis," in this case, the limits of navigation for the aspiring British Empire.

108. "Harvard Mark I/IBM ASCC," Computer History Museum, accessed September 30, 2015, www.computerhistory.org/revolution/birth-of-the-computer/4/86/350/.

109. Campbell-Kelly and Aspray, *Computer*, 107–108; U.S. Census Bureau, "UNIVAC I."

110. Campbell-Kelly and Aspray, *Computer*, 88. The authors note that the Manches-ter Baby Computer, developed in the United Kingdom and finished in 1948, was the first demonstration of the stored program concept.

111. MIT's Lincoln Laboratory has an excellent background and history of the SAGE project, including contemporary promotional videos and interviews with programmers on the project ("SAGE: Semi-Automatic Ground Environment Air Defense System," Lincoln Laboratory, MIT, 2015, www.ll.mit.edu/about/History/SAGE _TOCpage.html). See also "Funding a Revolution: Government Support for Computing Research," National Academies Press, 1999, www.nap.edu/read/6323/page/92/.

112. Campbell-Kelly and Aspray, *Computer,* 151.

113. Flamm, *Targeting the Computer,* 122.

114. Flamm, *Targeting the Computer,* 122.

115. "Funding a Revolution," 95, quoting Claude Baum, *The System Builders: The Story of SDC* (Santa Monica, CA: System Development Corporation, 1981), 47–51.

116. Campbell-Kelly and Aspray, *Computer,* 151.

117. "Funding a Revolution," 94.

118. Martin Campbell-Kelly, William Aspray, Nathan Ensmenger, and Jeffrey Yost. "Chapter 7: Reaping the Whirlwind," in *Computer: A History of the Information Machine,* 3rd ed. (Boulder, CO: Westview Press, 2013), e-book.

119. Katie Hafner and Matthew Lyon, *Where Wizards Stay Up Late: The Origins of the Internet* (New York: Simon and Schuster, 1996), 20–24.

120. Hafner and Lyon, *Where Wizards Stay Up Late.*

121. "Connections: Global Networks," Computer History Museum, 2006, www .computerhistory.org/revolution/networking/19/374/.

122. J. C. R. Licklider and Robert W. Taylor, "The Computer as Communication Device," *Science and Technology* 76, no. 2 (1968), 32.

123. Flamm, *Targeting the Computer,* 100.

124. "Funding a Revolution," 97.

125. Flamm, *Targeting the Computer,* 103.

126. Government funding had a lower bound of 25% of all research funding on computers in the mid-1970s, hit a low of 15% in 1979, and rose again to more than 20% in 1983. Flamm, *Targeting the Computer,* 103.

127. "Funding a Revolution," 102.

128. Agar, *The Government Machine,* 48.

129. Campbell-Kelly and Aspray, *Computer,* 153. It was so fallible that business travelers wanting to be certain of catching a flight booked two flights to account for these errors.

130. Campbell-Kelly and Aspray, *Computer,* 157.

131. Campbell-Kelly and Aspray, *Computer,* 185–204.

132. Chris Hipwell, "The Mainframe Years in the Computer Press," *Computer Resurrection: Bulletin of the Computer Conservation Society* 39 (2007), www.cs.man.ac.uk/CCS/res/res39.htm#e/.

133. Atsushi Akera, "Voluntarism and the Fruits of Collaboration: The IBM User Group, Share," *Technology and Culture* 42, no. 4 (2001): 710–736.

134. Campbell-Kelly and Aspray, *Computer,* 175.

135. IBM dominated so thoroughly that the Justice Department filed an antitrust suit against the company in 1969, Campbell-Kelly et al., *Computer,* "The Maturing of the Mainframe: The Rise of IBM"; "Software Becomes a Product," Computer History Museum, accessed September 27, 2015, www.computerhistory.org/revolution/mainframe-computers/7/172/.

136. For a detailed history of OS/360s development, see Frederick P. Brooks, *The Mythical Man-Month: Essays on Software Engineering* (Reading, MA: Addison-Wesley, 1982).

137. Frederick P. Brooks, "No Silver Bullet: Essence and Accidents of Software Engineering," *IEEE Computer* 20, no. 4 (1987): 10–19.

138. Mahoney, "The Histories of Computing(s)," 128.

139. W. Wayt Gibbs, "Software's Chronic Crisis," *Scientific American,* September 1994, 86–95. A more recent articulation of this crisis shows up in the 2013 promotional video for Code.org, which encourages people to learn programming because doing so will increase their employability (see chapter 1). Code.org illustrates this claim with graphs showing huge disparities between programmer demand and supply.

140. Campbell-Kelly and Aspray, *Computer,* 181–182.

141. Ensmenger, *The Computer Boys Take Over: Computers, Programmers, and the Politics of Technical Expertise* (Cambridge, MA: MIT Press, 2010). For a compelling story of an African-American woman who aced these tests and was, after much resistance from the company, allowed to train as a programmer, see Reginald Braithwaite, "A Woman's Story," Raganwald [blog], March 29, 2012, http://braythwayt.com/posterous/2012/03/29/a-womans-story.html.

142. Abbate, *Recoding Gender,* 50.

143. Abbate, *Recoding Gender,* 61.

144. Campbell-Kelly and Aspray, *Computer,* 224.

145. For a contemporary review that captures the enthusiasm and significance of VisiCalc, see Joseph H. Budge, "Visicalc: A Software Review," *Compute*, August 1980, 19, Archive.org.

146. For a compelling and contemporary account of the development of these machines in the 1970s, see Tracy Kidder, *The Soul of a New Machine* (New York: Back Bay Books / Little, Brown and Company, 2000).

147. Campbell-Kelly et al., *Computer*, "Real Time: Reaping the Whirlwind."

148. Nick Montfort, Patsy Baudoin, John Bell, Ian Bogost, Jeremy Douglass, Mark C. Marino, Michael Mateas, Casey Reas, Mark Sample, and Noah Vawteret, *10 PRINT CHR$(205.5+RND(1));: GOTO 10* (Cambridge, MA: MIT Press), 185.

149. Edsger Dijkstra, "How Do We Tell Truths That Might Hurt?" in *Selected Writings on Computing: A Personal Perspective* (New York: Springer-Verlag, 1982), 129–131.

150. Campbell-Kelly et al., *Computer*, "New Modes of Computing."

151. Steven Levy, *Hackers: Heroes of the Computer Revolution* (New York: Dell Publishing, 1984).

152. Art Salsberg, "THE HOME COMPUTER IS HERE!" [Editorial], *Popular Electronics*, January 1975; H. Edward Roberts and William Yates, "ALTAIR 8800 The Most Powerful Minicomputer Project Ever Presented—Can Be Built for under $400," *Scientific American*, January 1975.

153. Jeremy Reimer, "Total Share: 30 Years of Personal Computer Market Share Figures," *Ars Technica*, December 15, 2005, http://arstechnica.com/features/2005/12/total-share/.

154. Montfort et al., *10 PRINT*.

155. "Funding a Revolution," 109.

156. "Funding a Revolution," 110.

157. Michael Hiltzik, *Dealers of Lighting: Xerox PARC and the Dawn of the Computer Age* (New York: HarperBusiness, 2000), 94–96.

158. Alan Kay, "A Personal Computer for Children of All Ages," Xerox Palo Alto Research Center, August 1972, www.mprove.de/diplom/gui/Kay72a.pdf.

159. See also Alan Kay and Adele Goldberg, "Personal Dynamic Media," *Computer* 10, no. 3 (1977): 31–41.

160. Campbell-Kelly et al., *Computer*, "The Shaping of the Personal Computer."

161. Apple Computer, "Introducing Apple II," *Scientific American* 237, no. 3 (1977): 98–99.

162. Campbell-Kelly et al., *Computer*, "The Shaping of the Personal Computer."

163. *Compute!* magazine archive, Archive.org, accessed December 10, 2014 https://archive.org/details/compute-magazine/.

164. Reimer, "Total Share."

165. Michael Tomczyk, "Atari's Marketing Vice President Profiles the Personal Computer Market (Interview with Conrad Jutson)," *Compute*, August 1980, 16.

166. "Funding a Revolution," 108.

167. See Levy, *Hackers*, for a lively account of the game industry in the late 1970s and early 1980s.

168. Tom R. Halfhill, "The New Wave of Home Computers," *Compute*, August 1982, 18.

169. David Thornburg, "A Monthly Column: Computers and Society," *Compute*, August 1982, 14.

170. Campbell-Kelly and Aspray, *Computer,* 231.

171. Marlaine E. Lockheed and Ellen B. Mandinach, "Trends in Educational Computing: Decreasing Interest and the Changing Focus of Instruction," *Educational Researcher* 15, no. 5 (1986): 21–26.

172. Cynthia Selfe, *Technology and Literacy in the 21st Century: The Importance of Paying Attention* (Carbondale: Southern Illinois University Press, 1999).

173. "Book/Disk Combinations" [Ad for John Wiley & Sons], *Compute*, August 1982, 25, Archive.org.

174. Tomczyk, "Atari's Vice President Profiles the Personal Computer Market," 16–17.

175. Montfort et al., *10 PRINT*, 181.

176. Montfort et al., *10 PRINT*, 183–184.

177. Montfort et al., *10 PRINT*, 159.

178. François Furet and Jacques Ozouf, *Reading and Writing: Literacy in France from Calvin to Jules Ferry* (Cambridge, UK: Cambridge University Press, 1982), 304.

179. David Golumbia, *The Cultural Logic of Computation* (Cambridge, MA: Harvard University Press), 9.

180. See Coleman, *Coding Freedom* for an extended analysis of this rhetoric and set of practices surrounding programming.

181. Golumbia, *Cultural Logic*, 10–11.

182. Wendy Hui Kyong Chun, *Control and Freedom: Power and Paranoia in the Age of Fiber Optics* (Cambridge, MA: MIT Press, 2006).

183. Kafka, *The Demon of Writing*. Ben Kafka acknowledges the irony of his last name and his chosen research subject.

184. Agar, *The Government Machine*, 47.

185. Agar, *The Government Machine*, 3.

186. Hayles, *My Mother Was a Computer*.

Chapter 4

1. Michael T. Clanchy, *From Memory to Written Record: England 1066–1307*, 3rd ed. (Somerset, NJ: John Wiley & Sons, 2012), 197–198.

2. Lev Manovich, *Software Takes Command*, Software Studies Initiative, 2008, 16–17, http://softwarestudies.com/softbook/manovich_softbook_11_20_2008.pdf.

3. Jack Goody, *The Logic of Writing and the Organization of Society* (Cambridge, UK: Cambridge University Press, 1986), 161.

4. William Gilmore, *Reading Becomes a Necessity of Life: Material and Cultural Life in Rural New England, 1780–1835* (Knoxville: University of Tennessee Press, 1989).

5. David Olson, *The World on Paper: The Conceptual and Cognitive Implications of Writing and Reading* (Cambridge, UK: Cambridge University Press, 1994).

6. Elizabeth Eisenstein, *The Printing Press as an Agent of Change*, Vols. 1 & 2 (New York: Cambridge University Press, 1980).

7. Deborah Brandt, *The Rise of Writing: Redefining Mass Literacy* (Cambridge, UK: Cambridge University Press, 2014), 3.

8. Daniel Punday, *Computing as Writing* (Minneapolis: University of Minnesota Press, 2015).

9. Lewis Mumford, *Technics and Civilization*, with a New Foreword by Langdon Winner (Chicago: University of Chicago Press, 2010); Martin Heidegger, "The Question Concerning Technology," in *Basic Writings from Being and Time (1927) and the Task of Thinking (1964)*, David Farrell Krell, Ed. (New York: Harper and Row, 1977), 283–317.

10. For example: Nicholas Carr, "Is Google Making Us Stupid?" *Atlantic*, August 2008, www.theatlantic.com/magazine/archive/2008/07/is-google-making-us-stupid/306868/. I address Sherry Turkle's work in more detail later on.

11. Roger Chartier, "Histoire Des Mentalités," in *The Columbia History of Twentieth-Century French Thought*, Lawrence D. Kritzman, Brian J. Reilly, and M. B. DeBevoise, Eds. (New York: Columbia University Press, 2007), 54–58.

12. Jacques Le Goff, "Mentalities: A New Field for Historians," trans. Michael Fineberg, *Social Science Information* 13, no. 1 (1974): 81–97, 81.

13. Chartier, "Histoire Des Mentalités," 58.

14. He writes, "Born to a large extent from a reaction to the imperialism of economic history, the history of mentalities should not serve as a vague excuse for the resurgence of an outmoded spiritualism in, for instance, the vague and illusory shape of an indefinable collective *mind,* nor should it be an attempt to prolong the life of crude marxism by seeking at little cost the definition of superstructures mechanically produced by socio-economic infrastructures." Le Goff, "Mentalities," 93.

15. Le Goff, "Mentalities," 94.

16. Le Goff, "Mentalities," 91.

17. Le Goff, "Mentalities," 93.

18. Chartier, "Histoire Des Mentalités," 55.

19. For example, Walter Ong, *Orality and Literacy* (London: Routledge, 1982); Eric Havelock, *Preface to Plato* (Cambridge, MA: Harvard University Press, 1963); Jack Goody and Ian Watt, "The Consequences of Literacy," *Comparative Studies in Society and History* 5, no. 3 (1963): 304–345.

20. Sylvia Scribner and Michael Cole, *The Psychology of Literacy* (Cambridge, MA: Harvard University Press, 1981).

21. Chartier, "Histoire Des Mentalités."

22. Olson, *The World on Paper,* 17.

23. Clanchy, *From Memory to Written Record,* 3rd ed., 188.

24. Brandt, *The Rise of Writing,* 137.

25. Luis Moll and Norma González, "Lessons from Research with Language Minority Children," in *Literacy: A Critical Sourcebook,* Ellen Cushman et al., Eds. (Boston: Bedford/St. Martins Press, 2001), 156–171.

26. François Furet and Jacques Ozouf, *Reading and Writing: Literacy in France from Calvin to Jules Ferry* (Cambridge, UK: Cambridge University Press, 1982).

27. Clanchy, *From Memory to Written Record,* 3rd ed., 276–278.

28. Clanchy, *From Memory to Written Record,* 3rd ed., 2.

29. Clanchy, *From Memory to Written Record,* 3rd ed., 67.

30. Clanchy, *From Memory to Written Record,* 3rd ed., 153–155.

31. Clanchy, *From Memory to Written Record,* 3rd ed., 162.

32. Clanchy, *From Memory to Written Record,* 3rd ed., 253.

33. Clanchy, *From Memory to Written Record,* 3rd ed., 195–196.

34. Brian Stock, *The Implications of Literacy: Written Language and Models of Interpretation in the Eleventh and Twelfth Centuries* (Princeton, NJ: Princeton University Press, 1983), 17.

35. Clanchy, *From Memory to Written Record*, 3rd ed., 2.

36. Franz Bäuml, "Varieties and Consequences of Medieval Literacy and Illiteracy," *Speculum* 55, no. 2 (1980): 237.

37. Stock, *The Implications of Literacy*. But see Clanchy's review of the book for a critique of this concept. Michael T. Clanchy, "The Implications of Literacy: Written Language and Models of Interpretation in the Eleventh and Twelfth Centuries, by Brian Stock [Review]," *Canadian Journal of History* 18, no. 3 (1983): 403–404.

38. Quoted in Clanchy, *From Memory to Written Record*, 3rd ed., 40.

39. Bäuml, "Varieties and Consequences of Medieval Literacy and Illiteracy," 246.

40. Bäuml, "Varieties and Consequences of Medieval Literacy and Illiteracy," 243–234.

41. Bäuml, "Varieties and Consequences of Medieval Literacy and Illiteracy," 240–241.

42. David Vincent, *The Rise of Mass Literacy: Reading and Writing in Modern Europe*. Themes in History (Cambridge, UK: Polity, 2000), 16.

43. Moll and González, "Lessons from Research with Language Minority Children."

44. Shirley Brice Heath, *Ways with Words: Language, Life and Work in Communities and Classroom* (New York: Cambridge University Press, 1983).

45. Marcia Farr, "En Los Dos Idiomas: Literacy Practices Among Chicago Mexicanos," in *Literacy Across Communities*, Beverly J. Moss, Ed. (Cresskill, NJ: Hampton Press, 1994), 9–47.

46. Kate Vieira, *American by Paper: How Documents Matter in Immigrant Literacy* (Minneapolis: University of Minnesota Press, 2016).

47. Brian Stock, *Listening for the Text: On the Uses of the Past* (Baltimore, MD: Johns Hopkins University Press, 1990), 126.

48. Ben Kafka, *The Demon of Writing: Powers and Failures of Paperwork* (Cambridge, MA: MIT Press / Zone Books, 2012), 47.

49. Kafka, *The Demon of Writing*, 58.

50. Jon Agar, *The Government Machine: A Revolutionary History of the Computer* (Cambridge, MA: MIT Press, 2003), 10.

51. Quoted in Agar, *The Government Machine*, 43.

52. Agar, *The Government Machine*, 49.

53. Agar, *The Government Machine*, 47.

54. Agar, *The Government Machine*, 48.

55. For this reason, Michael Clanchy divides documentation in medieval governance into three major eras: making, storing, and using. He writes, "Making documents for administrative use, keeping them as records, and using them again for reference were three distinct stages of development which did not automatically and immediately follow from each other." Clanchy, *From Memory to Written Record*, 3rd ed., 156.

56. Kafka, *The Demon of Writing*, 107.

57. Kafka, *The Demon of Writing*, 63.

58. Kafka makes this specific point in connection with the 1793 order mentioned above, but his observation is valid for the other eras I discuss as well. Kafka, *The Demon of Writing*, 58.

59. Clanchy, *From Memory to Written Record*, 3rd ed., 195.

60. Clanchy, *From Memory to Written Record*, 3rd ed., 195.

61. Clanchy, *From Memory to Written Record*, 3rd ed., 150.

62. The knight says to the cleric, "Those are big words, and I am a layman, and though I learned a few letters as a boy I never got deep enough to understand words so high" (200). Although the knight's language and mixed metaphors indeed suggest his lack of learning, his reasoning in the dispute is sound and based on relevant biblical passages. Tierney writes that "It was the kind of argument that any French noble or merchant could understand and the work enjoyed very wide circulation at the time of the dispute between [King Philip IV] and [Pope Boniface VIII]" (195). *Disputatio inter Clericum et Militem* ["Dispute between a Cleric and a Knight"], 1296–1298, trans. E. Lewis, *Medieval Political Ideas*, II (New York: Knopf, 1954), 567–573; reprinted in Brian Tierney, *The Crisis of Church and State, 1050–1300* (Englewood Cliffs, NJ: Prentice Hall, 1964), 201. I was introduced to this piece of medieval propaganda by Clanchy, *From Memory to Written Record*, 3rd ed., 183.

63. Stock, *The Implications of Literacy*, 62.

64. Goody, *Logic of Writing*, 159.

65. Kafka, *The Demon of Writing*, 80.

66. Agar, *The Government Machine*, 47, 65.

67. Kafka, *The Demon of Writing*, 77–81.

68. Agar, *The Government Machine*, 3.

69. Walter Ong makes this parallel, arguing that Plato saw writing as inhuman in the same way that people thought of computers as inhuman at that time. Walter Ong, "Writing Is a Technology That Restructures Thought," in *Literacy: A Critical Sourcebook*, Ellen Cushman et al., Eds. (Boston: Bedford/St. Martins Press, 2001), 19–31.

70. Friedrich A. Kittler, *Gramophone, Film, Typewriter* (Stanford, CA: Stanford University Press, 1999), 8.

71. Clanchy, *From Memory to Written Record*, 3rd ed., 77.

72. David Levy, *Scrolling Forward* (New York: Arcade Publishing, 2001).

73. Olson, *The World on Paper*, 41.

74. This documentation still works to sort bodies, as Kate Vieira's work with Lusophone immigrants demonstrates. Vieira, *American by Paper*.

75. Stock, *The Implications of Literacy*, 4.

76. Stock, *The Implications of Literacy*, 4.

77. Stock, "The Making of 'Heresies,'" *The Implications of Literacy*, 145–151.

78. Olson, *The World on Paper*, 148–154.

79. Olson, *The World on Paper*, 177.

80. Olson, *The World on Paper*, 167. But eventually, conflicts among readers' interpretations of texts led to a new kind of mentality, Olson argues; modernism gave way to postmodernism. Descartes was an early precursor in his assertion that thinking was inseparable from knowledge (245). In this account, modernism was a way of coping with interpretation, and postmodernism was the realization that interpretations could never be pinned down (117).

81. Clanchy, *From Memory to Written Record*, 3rd ed., 267.

82. Jay David Bolter, *Writing Space: The Computer, Hypertext and the History of Writing* (Hillsdale, NJ: Lawrence Erlbaum, 1991).

83. Olson, *The World on Paper*, 105.

84. Edward Stevens, *Literacy, Law, and Social Order* (DeKalb: Northern Illinois University Press, 1988), 153.

85. Olson, *The World on Paper*, 19.

86. Olson, *The World on Paper*, 35.

87. Olson, *The World on Paper*, 18.

88. Lawrence Cremin, *American Education: The National Experience 1783–1876* (New York: Harper and Row, 1982), 493.

89. Gilmore, *Reading Becomes a Necessity of Life.*

90. Deborah Brandt, *Literacy in American Lives* (Cambridge, UK: Cambridge University Press, 2001), 1; Brandt, *The Rise of Writing.*

91. Kenneth Lockridge, *Literacy in Colonial New England: An Enquiry into the Social Context of Literacy in the Early Modern West* (New York: W.W. Norton, 1975), 68.

92. Lockridge, *Literacy in Colonial New England,* 37.

93. Stevens, *Literacy, Law, and Social Order,* 65.

94. Stevens, *Literacy, Law, and Social Order,* 89–90.

95. Stevens, *Literacy, Law, and Social Order,* 90.

96. Stevens, *Literacy, Law, and Social Order,* 62.

97. Stevens, *Literacy, Law, and Social Order,* 175.

98. Stevens, *Literacy, Law, and Social Order,* 95.

99. United States Courts, "Juror Qualifications," Services and Forms (n.d.), www.uscourts.gov/services-forms/jury-service/juror-qualifications.

100. Furet and Ozouf, *Reading and Writing,* 303.

101. Lockridge, *Literacy in Colonial New England,* 57.

102. Lockridge, *Literacy in Colonial New England,* 38.

103. Lockridge, *Literacy in Colonial New England,* 22.

104. Furet and Ozouf, *Reading and Writing.*

105. Furet and Ozouf, *Reading and Writing,* 188.

106. Lalita Ramdas, "Women and Literacy: A Quest for Justice," in *Literacy: A Critical Sourcebook,* Ellen Cushman et al., Eds. (Boston: Bedford/St. Martins Press, 2001), 629–643.

107. Irwin S. Kirsch et al., "Adult Literacy in America: A First Look at the Findings of the National Adult Literacy Survey," U.S. Department of Education Office of Educational Research and Improvement, April 2002, https://nces.ed.gov/pubs93/93275.pdf.

109. Vannevar Bush, "As We May Think," *Atlantic,* July 1, 1945, www.theatlantic.com/magazine/archive/1945/07/as-we-may-think/303881/.

110. Martin Campbell-Kelly and William Aspray, *Computer: A History of the Information Machine.* The Sloan Technology Series (Boulder, CO: Westview Press, 2004), 65.

111. Bernadette Longo, "Edmund Berkeley, Computers, and Modern Methods of Thinking," *IEEE Annals of the History of Computing* 26, no. 4 (2004): 4–18. doi: 10.1109/MAHC.2004.28.

112. Remington Rand, the manufacturer of the UNIVAC I, sold 46 machines in 1951, at $1 million each. "Timeline of Computer History: 1951," Computer History Museum, n.d., accessed January 3, 2017, www.computerhistory.org/timeline/1951/.

113. Martin Campbell-Kelly, William Aspray, Nathan Ensmenger, and Jeffrey Yost. Computer: A History of the Information Machine. 3rd ed. [e-book] (Boulder, CO: Westview Press, 2013).

114. "Timeline of Computer History: People & Pop Culture," Computer History Museum, n.d., accessed January 3, 2017, www.computerhistory.org/timeline/popular-culture/. Opinion polls had predicted a win for Stevenson, but the computer's analysis of early returns was so far from them, they withheld its—ultimately more accurate—results.

115. Robert Mankoff, "Computer Games," *From the Desk of Bob Mankoff* [blog], *The New Yorker,* February 23, 2011, http://www.newyorker.com/from-the-desk-of-bob-mankoff/computer-games/.

116. Bernadette Longo, "Metaphors, Robots, and the Transfer of Computers to Civilian Life," *Comparative Technology Transfer and Society* 3, no. 5 (2007): 253–273.

117. Albert M. Colegrove, "U.S. Unveils Push-Button Defense," *Pittsburgh Press,* January 18, 1956, https://news.google.com/newspapers?nid=1144&dat=19560118&id=hUEqAAAAIBAJ&sjid=5k0EAAAAIBAJ&pg=6449,383706/.

118. "Timeline of Computer History: 1958," Computer History Museum, n.d., accessed January 3, 2017, www.computerhistory.org/timeline/1958/.

119. IBM Military Products Division, "On Guard" [video], Lincoln Laboratory, MIT, Sage Missile Defense System (n.d.), accessed December 8, 2014, www.ll.mit.edu/about/History/SAGEairdefensesystem.html.

120. J. C. R. Licklider, "Man-Computer Symbiosis," *IRE Transactions on Human Factors in Electronics* HFE-1, no. 1 (1960): 4–11. doi: 10.1109/THFE2.1960.4503259; J. C. R. Licklider and Robert W. Taylor, "The Computer as a Communication Device," *Science and Technology* 76, no. 2 (1968): 21–41.

121. Licklider, "Man-Computer Symbiosis," 4.

122. Wendy Hui Kyong Chun, "Programmability," in *Software Studies: A Lexicon,* Matthew Fuller, Ed. (Cambridge, MA: MIT Press, 2008), 224–229.

123. Matthew Cobb, "What Is Life? The Physicist Who Sparked a Revolution in Biology," *Guardian,* February 7, 2013, https://www.theguardian.com/science/blog/2013/feb/07/wonders-life-physicist-revolution-biology/.

124. N. Katherine Hayles, *My Mother Was a Computer: Digital Subjects and Literary Texts* (Chicago: University of Chicago Press, 2005), 15–38. See also Francesco Berto and Jacopo Tagliabue, "Cellular Automata," in *The Stanford Encyclopedia of Philosophy,* Edward N. Zalta, Ed., 2012, http://plato.stanford.edu/archives/sum2012/entries/cellular-automata/.

125. The simulation is widely available online, such as here: Pedro Vam, "Conway's Game of Life," accessed July 1, 2015, http://pmav.eu/stuff/javascript-game-of-life -v3.1.1/.

126. Konrad Zuse, *Calculating Space, Translation of Rechnender Raum*, trans. Aztec School of Languages (Cambridge, MA: MIT Project MAC, 1970), ftp://ftp.idsia.ch/ pub/juergen/zuserechnenderraum.pdf. I found a lucid explanation of Zuse's work as well as a PDF scan of "Calculating Space" here: Jürgen Schmidhuber, "Zuse's Thesis: The Universe Is a Computer," Jürgen Schmidhuber's Home Page, n.d., http://people .idsia.ch/~juergen/digitalphysics.html.

127. Hayles, "Intermediation: Textuality and the Regime of Computation," *My Mother Was a Computer*, 15–38.

128. Hayles, *My Mother Was a Computer*, 23.

129. Francisco J. Varela, Evan Thompson, and Eleanor Rosch, *The Embodied Mind: Cognitive Science and Human Experience* [first MIT Press paperback] (Cambridge, MA: MIT Press, 1993).

130. Hayles, *My Mother Was a Computer*, 20.

131. Hayles, *My Mother Was a Computer*, 21.

132. David Golumbia, *The Cultural Logic of Computation* (Cambridge, MA: Harvard University Press, 2009), 9.

133. Golumbia, *The Cultural Logic of Computation*, 19.

134. George Lakoff and Mark Johnson, *Metaphors We Live By* (Chicago: University of Chicago Press, 2008), 3.

135. Sherry Turkle, *Life on the Screen* (Cambridge, MA: MIT Press, 1995).

136. Wendy Hui Kyong Chun, *Programmed Visions: Software and Memory*. Software Studies (Cambridge, MA: MIT Press, 2011).

137. Turkle, *Life on the Screen*.

138. For more on the influence of computation on Chomsky's theories of grammar, see Golumbia, *The Cultural Logic of Computation*, Parts I and II.

139. Golumbia, *The Cultural Logic of Computation*, 7.

140. Josh Harlan, "Hilary Putnam: On Mind, Meaning and Reality, Interview with Josh Harlan," *Harvard Review of Philosophy* (Spring 1992): 21.

141. For a recent review of different computational approaches in cognitive science, see: Nir Fresco, "The Explanatory Role of Computation in Cognitive Science," *Minds and Machines* 22, no. 4 (2012): 353–380. doi: 10.1007/s11023-012-9286-y.

142. Varela et al., *The Embodied Mind*, 8.

143. Varela et al., *The Embodied Mind*, xvii.

144. Marvin Minsky and Seymour Papert, *Perceptrons: An Introduction to Computational Geometry*, Expanded Edition (Cambridge, MA: MIT Press, 1987).

145. Turkle, "The Quality of Emergence," *Life on the Screen*, 125–148.

146. Varela et al., *The Embodied Mind*, 5.

147. Sherry Turkle, *The Second Self: Computers and the Human Spirit*, 20th anniversary ed. (Cambridge, MA: MIT Press, 2005), 1.

148. Turkle, *Life on the Screen,* 49.

149. Turkle, *Life on the Screen,* 49.

150. Turkle, *The Second Self*; Sherry Turkle, *Alone Together: Why We Expect More from Technology and Less from Each Other* (New York: Basic Books, 2012).

151. Gary Wolf, "Know Thyself: Tracking Every Facet of Life, from Sleep to Mood to Pain, 24/7/365," *Wired*, June 22, 2009, www.wired.com/2009/06/lbnp-knowthyself/.

152. As the Pew Internet and American Life project reports from 2015, 92% of American teens aged 12–17 go online daily, 24% are "almost constantly" online, and 89% use at least one social media tool such as Facebook or Snapchat (Amanda Lenhart, "Teens, Social Media & Technology Overview 2015," Pew Research Center, April 2015, www.pewinternet.org/2015/04/09/mobile-access-shifts-social-media-use -and-other-online-activities/). Even older adults are on Facebook: 71% of Internet-using adults use Facebook, and 56% over age 65 are on the site (Maeve Duggan et al., "Social Media Update 2014," Pew Research Center, January 2014, www.pewinternet .org/2015/01/09/social-media-update-2014/). As of April 2015, Facebook reports that there were 936 million users active on the site daily, and 1.44 billion monthly. Approximately 87% of these users access the site from their mobile devices (Emil Protalinski, "Facebook Passes 1.44B Monthly Active Users and 1.25B Mobile Users; 65% Are Now Daily Users," VentureBeat, April 22, 2015, http://venturebeat .com/2015/04/22/facebook-passes-1-44b-monthly-active-users-1-25b-mobile-users -and-936-million-daily-users/).

153. danah boyd, *It's Complicated: The Social Lives of Networked Teens* (New Haven, CT: Yale University Press, 2014), www.danah.org/books/ItsComplicated.pdf.

154. Nathan Jurgenson, "The Facebook Eye," *Atlantic*, January 13, 2012, www .theatlantic.com/technology/archive/2012/01/the-facebook-eye/251377/.

155. John Del Signore, "Police Seek 3 Men for Beating L Train Rider Who Scolded Them for Spitting," *Gothamist*, November 16, 2011, http://gothamist.com/2011/11/ 16/police_search_for_men_in_beating_of.php.

156. Brian Stelter, "Philando Castile and the Power of Facebook Live," *CNN Money*, July 7, 2016, http://money.cnn.com/2016/07/07/media/facebook-live-streaming -police-shooting/.

157. John B. Horrigan and Sydney Jones, "When Technology Fails," Pew Research Center, November 2008, www.pewinternet.org/2005/07/06/computer-problems-vex -millions/.

158. The phenomenon of holiday family computer-fixing is so familiar to those skilled with computers that the popular LifeHacker blog often runs a post on Thanksgiving to advise them on their holiday duties. Before providing readers with the best tools of the year to optimize old or virus-clogged machines, editor Gina Trapani writes, "You're headed home next week to a turkey feast with all the trimmings - and Mom and Dad's computer. You know what's going to happen. ... The annual Family Computer Fixing event is upon us, and *you* are the emcee." Gina Trapani, "Geek to Live: How to Fix Mom and Dad's Computer," LifeHacker, November 18, 2005, http://lifehacker.com/138113/geek-to-live--how-to-fix-mom-and-dads -computer/.

159. Vieira, *American by Paper.*

160. For an example of the promises of code libraries, see Paul Katsen, "Programming! = Writing Code," accessed July 14, 2015, http://katsenblog.com/post /119256226994/programming-writing-code/.

161. Clay Shirky, "Situated Software," Clay Shirky's Writings about the Internet, March 30, 2004, http://shirky.com/writings/herecomeseverybody/situated_software .html.

162. Brandt, *Literacy in American Lives.*

163. Ryan Tate, "Hack to Hacker: Rise of the Journalist-Programmer," Gawker, January 14, 2010, http://gawker.com/5448635/hack-to-hacker-rise-of-the-journalist -programmer/.

164. Responding to this shift in the profession, journalism schools have focused attention on training a new crop of journalists to be writers of code as well as text. For example, Columbia University offers a dual-degree program in Journalism and Computer Science that integrates their traditional journalism program with computer programming, and Northwestern University's Medill School of Journalism offers classes where students work together to develop software applications for journalism. "Journalism and Computer Science," Columbia University, n.d., https:// journalism.columbia.edu/journalism-computer-science; Jasmine Rangel, "Class Pairs Journalism, Computer Science Students to Develop Projects," Medill School of Journalism, Northwestern University, December 9, 2013, www.medill.northwestern .edu/experience/news/2013/fall/news-class-pairs-journalism-computer-science -students-to-develop-projects.html.

165. Simmons and Grabill, "Toward a Civic Rhetoric," 441.

166. Brett Neely, "Devising Aid Programs on Their Laptops," Marketplace, January 18, 2010, www.marketplace.org/topics/your-money/devising-aid-programs-their -laptops/.

167. "Adopt-a-Hydrant," Code for America, n.d., https://www.codeforamerica.org/apps/adopt-a-hydrant/.

168. Bonnie Nardi, *A Small Matter of Programming: Perspectives on End User Computing* (Cambridge, MA: MIT Press, 1993), 3–4.

169. Paul Graham, *Hackers & Painters: Big Ideas from the Computer Age* (Sebastopol, CA: O'Reilly Media, 2004).

170. Tim Berners-Lee, *Weaving the Web: The Original Design and Ultimate Destiny of the World Wide Web* (San Francisco: HarperBusiness, 2000).

171. Brandt, *The Rise of Writing*.

172. Carr, "Is Google Making Us Stupid?"; Naomi Baron, *Always On: Language in an Online and Mobile World* (Oxford: Oxford University Press, 2010).

173. Damien McElroy, "Twitter Maintained Service during Iranian Elections after US State Dept Request," *Telegraph*, June 16, 2009, www.telegraph.co.uk/technology/twitter/5552733/Twitter-maintained-service-during-Iranian-elections-after-US-State-Dept-request.html.

174. David Folkenflik, "House Democrats Deliver Gun Control Sit-In Via Periscope, Facebook Live," *All Tech Considered* (NPR), June 23, 2016, www.npr.org/sections/allt echconsidered/2016/06/23/483205687/house-democrats-deliver-sit-in-via-digital -platforms/; Zeynep Tufekci, "How the Internet Saved Turkey's Internet-Hating President," *New York Times*, July 18, 2016, www.nytimes.com/2016/07/20/opinion/how-the-internet-saved-turkeys-internet-hating-president.html.

175. But Bitcoin is subject to many of the same problems of state-backed currencies: speculation, politics, volatility, bad traders, and fraud or irregularities in trading sites. In the ways that it circumvents traditional markets and identity-verification systems verified by central states, Bitcoin is not subject to current bureaucratic systems of governance and identification. After the implosion of the trading site Mt. Gox, coin exchanges are now backed by venture capital firms, offering an alternative governance, and making Bitcoin essentially *doubly* backed by code. Jon Russell, "Mt. Gox Customers Can Now File Claims for Their Lost Bitcoins," TechCrunch, April 22, 2015, https://techcrunch.com/2015/04/22/mt-gox-claims/.

176. Stevens, *Literacy, Law, and Social Order*, 64.

Conclusion

1. Sylvia Scribner, "Literacy in Three Metaphors," *American Journal of Education* 93, no. 1 (1984): 6.

2. Scribner, "Literacy in Three Metaphors," 8.

3. Scribner, "Literacy in Three Metaphors," 18.

4. Brian V. Street, *Literacy in Theory and Practice* (Cambridge, UK: Cambridge University Press, 1985): 220–226. Scribner makes a similar argument: Literacy education efforts "need [to] understand the great variety of beliefs and aspirations that various people have developed toward literacy in their particular historical and current life circumstances." Scribner, "Literacy in Three Metaphors," 17.

5. Harvey Graff, *The Literacy Myth: Cultural Integration and Social Structure in the Nineteenth Century* (New Brunswick, NJ: Transaction Publishers, 1991).

6. Mizuko Ito et al., *Connected Learning: An Agenda for Research and Design* (Irvine, CA: Digital Media and Learning Research Hub, 2013).

7. Scribner, "Literacy in Three Metaphors," 12.

8. Jenny Cook-Gumperz, "Literacy and Schooling: An Unchanging Equation?" in *The Social Construction of Literacy*, 2nd ed. (Cambridge, UK: Cambridge University Press, 2006), 21.

9. "Scratch," MIT, n.d., https://scratch.mit.edu.

10. See Yasmin Kafai and Quinn Burke, *Connected Code: Why Children Need to Learn Programming*. MacArthur Foundation Series on Digital Media and Learning (Cambridge, MA: MIT Press, 2014).

11. Grace Conyers, "The ProgeTiiger Initiative," *AAAS MemberCentral*, March 13, 2013, http://membercentral.aaas.org/blogs/aaas-serves/progetiiger-initiative/; Beth Gardiner, "Adding Coding to the Curriculum," *New York Times*, March 23, 2014, www.nytimes.com/2014/03/24/world/europe/adding-coding-to-the-curriculum.html; Anya Kamenetz, "Coding Class, Then Naptime: Computer Science for the Kindergarten Set," NPR.org, accessed September 18, 2015, www.npr.org/sections/ed/" 2015/09/18/441122285/learning-to-code-in-preschool/.

12. Jenny Cook-Gumperz, "Literacy and Schooling"; Thomas Laqueur, "The Cultural Origins of Popular Literacy in England: 1500–1850," *Oxford Review of Education* 2, no. 3 (1976): 255–275.

13. Ito et al., *Connected Learning*, 6-7.

14. For example, he connected video games to childhood obesity in a talk he gave to the American Medical Association. "Text of Obama's Speech to the AMA," WSJ Blogs—Health Blog, June 15, 2009, http://blogs.wsj.com/health/2009/06/15/text-of-obamas-speech-before-the-ama/.

15. Mark Deloura and Randy Paris, "Don't Just Play on Your Phone, Program It," Whitehouse.gov, December 9, 2013, https://www.whitehouse.gov/blog/2013/12/09/don-t-just-play-your-phone-program-it/.

16. Constance Steinkuehler and Barbara Z. Johnson, "Computational Literacy in Online Games: The Social Life of Mods," *International Journal of Gaming and Computer-Mediated Simulations* 1, no. 1 (2009): 53–65.

17. John Kemeny and Thomas Kurtz, *The Dartmouth Time-Sharing Computing System Final Report*. Course Content Improvement Program (Dartmouth, NH: Dartmouth College, 1967), 8.

18. Kafai and Burke, *Connected Code*, 52.

19. Kafai and Burke, *Connected Code*, 91.

20. Kafai and Burke, *Connected Code*, 101–102.

21. Neal Stephenson, *In the Beginning Was the Command Line* (New York: Avon Books, 1999).

22. Annette Vee, "Software Patent Law in Global Contexts: A Primer for Technical Writing Specialists," in *Legal Issues in Global Contexts: Perspectives on Technical Communication in an International Age*, Martine Courant Rife and Kirk St. Amant, Eds. (Amityville, NY: Baywood Publishing, 2014), 169–190.

23. Annette Vee, "Carving up the Commons: How Software Patent Law Impacts Our Digital Composition Environments," *Computers and Composition* 27, no. 3 (2010): 179–192; "When Patents Attack!" *This American Life*, July 22, 2011, www.thisamericanlife.org/radio-archives/episode/441/when-patents-attack/.

24. Lawrence Lessig, *Free Culture: The Nature and Future of Creativity* (New York: Penguin Books, 2004).

25. Adam Banks, *Race, Rhetoric, and Technology* (Mahwah, NJ: Lawrence Erlbaum, 2006), 45.

26. Matthew Fuller, Ed., *Software Studies: A Lexicon* (Cambridge, MA: MIT Press, 2008), 10.

27. As Manuel Castells notes, the logic of the network has subsumed "every domain of activity, every context, and every location that could be electronically connected." Manuel Castells, *The Rise of the Network Society*, 2nd ed. (West Sussex, UK: John Wiley & Sons, 2010), 52.

28. Deborah Brandt and Katie Clinton, "Limits of the Local: Expanding Perspectives on Literacy as a Social Practice," *Journal of Literacy Research* 34, no. 3 (2002): 338.

Bibliography

Aarseth, Espen. *Cybertext: Perspectives on Ergodic Literature*. Baltimore, MD: Johns Hopkins University Press, 1997.

Abbate, Janet. *Recoding Gender: Women's Changing Participation in Computing*. Cambridge, MA: MIT Press, 2012.

Abelson, Hal. "SICP/What Is Computer Science?" [posted by "LarryNorman"] YouTube video, 2006. https://www.youtube.com/watch?v=zQLUPjefuWA/.

Abelson, Hal, and Gerald Jay Sussman with Julie Sussman. *The Structure and Interpretation of Computer Programs*. 2nd ed. Cambridge, MA: MIT Press, 1996.

"About Us." Code.org, accessed July 21, 2016. https://code.org/about/.

"Adopt-a-Hydrant." Code for America, n.d. http://www.adoptahydrant.org.

Agar, Jon. *The Government Machine: A Revolutionary History of the Computer*. Cambridge, MA: MIT Press, 2003.

Akera, Atsushi. "Voluntarism and the Fruits of Collaboration: The IBM User Group, Share." *Technology and Culture* 42, no. 4 (2001): 710–736.

Alt, Casey. "Objects of Our Affection: How Object Orientation Made Computation a Medium." In *Media Archaeology*, edited by Erkki Huhtamo and Jussi Parikka, 278–301. Berkeley, CA: University of California Press, 2011.

Andreessen, Marc. "Marc Andreessen on Why Software Is Eating the World." *Wall Street Journal*, August 20, 2011. www.wsj.com/news/articles/SB100014240531119034 80904576512250915629460/.

Aneesh, Aneesh. *Virtual Migration: The Programming of Globalization*. Durham, NC: Duke University Press, 2006.

Apple Computer. "Introducing Apple II." *Scientific American* 237 (3) (1977): 98–99.

Arnove, Robert F., and Harvey J. Graff. *National Literacy Campaigns*. New York: Plenum Press, 1987.

Aspray, William. *Participation in Computing: The National Science Foundation's Expansionary Programs. History of Computing*. Basel, Switzerland: Springer, 2016.

Atwood, Jeff. "Code Smells." Coding Horror [blog], May 18, 2006. http://blog.codinghorror.com/code-smells/.

Atwood, Jeff. "Pair Programming vs. Code Reviews." Coding Horror [blog], November 18, 2007. https://blog.codinghorror.com/pair-programming-vs-code-reviews/.

Atwood, Jeff. "Please Don't Learn to Code." Coding Horror [blog], May 12, 2012. http://blog.codinghorror.com/please-dont-learn-to-code/.

Austin, John Langshaw. *How to Do Things with Words*. Cambridge, MA: Harvard University Press, 1962.

Bakhtin, Mikhail M. "The Problem of Speech Genres." In *Speech Genres and Other Late Essays*, edited by C. Emerson and M. Holquist, translated by Vern W. McGee, 60–102. Austin: University of Texas Press, 1986.

Banks, Adam. *Race, Rhetoric, and Technology*. Mahwah, NJ: Lawrence Erlbaum Associates, 2006.

Baron, Naomi. *Always On: Language in an Online and Mobile World*. 1st ed. Oxford, UK: Oxford University Press, 2010.

Barton, David. *Literacy: An Introduction to the Ecology of Written Language*. Oxford, UK: Blackwell Publishers, 1994.

Barton, David, and Mary Hamilton. "Literacy Practices." In *Situated Literacies: Reading and Writing in Context*, edited by David Barton, Mary Hamilton and Roz Ivanic, 7–15. New York: Routledge, 2000.

Bauer, F. L., and H. Wössner. "The 'Plankalkül' of Konrad Zuse: A Forerunner of Today's Programming Languages." The Retrocomputing Museum (reprinted from the Communications of the ACM, 1972). www.catb.org/retro/plankalkuel/.

Baum, Claude. *The System Builders: The Story of SDC*. Santa Monica, CA: System Development Corporation, 1981.

Bäuml, Franz H. "Varieties and Consequences of Medieval Literacy and Illiteracy." *Speculum* 55, no. 2 (1980): 237–265.

Bazerman, Charles. "The Writing of Social Organization and the Literate Situating of Cognition: Extending Goody's Social Implications of Writing." In *Technology, Literacy, and the Evolution of Society: Implications of the Work of Jack Goody*, edited by David R. Olson and Michael Cole, 215–239. Mahwah, NJ: Lawrence Erlbaum, 2006.

Beniger, James R. *The Control Revolution: Technological and Economic Origins of the Information Society*. Cambridge, MA: Harvard University Press, 1986.

Berkes, Howard. "Booting Up: New NSA Data Farm Takes Root in Utah." *All Things Considered* (NPR), September 23, 2013. http://www.npr.org/sections/alltechconside red/2013/09/23/225381596/booting-up-new-nsa-data-farm-takes-root-in-utah/.

Berners-Lee, Tim. *Weaving the Web: The Original Design and Ultimate Destiny of the World Wide Web.* San Francisco: HarperBusiness, 2000.

Berto, Francesco, and Jacopo Tagliabue. "Cellular Automata." In *The Stanford Encyclopedia of Philosophy*, edited by Edward N. Zalta, 2012. http://plato.stanford.edu/archives/sum2012/entries/cellular-automata/.

Besnier, Nico. *Literacy, Emotion and Authority: Reading and Writing on a Polynesian Atoll.* Cambridge, UK: Cambridge University Press, 1995.

Bibbs, Maria. *The African American Literacy Myth: Literacy's Ethical Objective during the Progressive Era, 1890-1919.* Ph.D. dissertation, University of Wisconsin-Madison, 2011. ProQuest 3488549.

"Black Girls Code: What We Do." Black Girls Code, n.d., accessed June 23, 2015. www.blackgirlscode.com/what-we-do.html.

Bogost, Ian. *Persuasive Games: The Expressive Power of Videogames.* Cambridge, MA: MIT Press, 2007.

Bolter, Jay David. *Writing Space: The Computer, Hypertext and the History of Writing.* Hillsdale, NJ: Lawrence Erlbaum, 1991.

Booth, Wayne C. *The Rhetoric of Rhetoric.* Malden, MA: Blackwell Publishing, 2004.

Bowker, Geoffrey C., and Susan Leigh Star. *Sorting Things Out: Classification and Its Consequences.* Cambridge, MA: MIT Press, 1999.

boyd, danah. *It's Complicated: The Social Lives of Networked Teens.* New Haven, CT: Yale University Press, 2014. www.danah.org/books/ItsComplicated.pdf.

Braithwaite, Reginald. "A Woman's Story," accessed September 27, 2015. http://braythwayt.com/posterous/2012/03/29/a-womans-story.html.

Brandt, Deborah. "Accumulating Literacy." *College English* 57, no. 6 (1995): 649–668.

Brandt, Deborah. "Drafting U.S. Literacy." *College English* 66, no. 5 (2004): 485–502. doi: 10.2307/4140731.

Brandt, Deborah. "How Writing Is Remaking Reading." In *Literacy and Learning, Reflections on Reading, Writing and Society*, 161–176. San Francisco: Jossey-Bass/John Wiley & Sons, 2009.

Brandt, Deborah. *Literacy in American Lives.* Cambridge, UK: Cambridge University Press, 2001.

Brandt, Deborah. "Remembering Writing, Remembering Reading." *College Composition and Communication* 45, no. 4 (1994): 459–479. doi: 10.2307/358760.

Brandt, Deborah. *The Rise of Writing: Redefining Mass Literacy.* Cambridge, UK: Cambridge University Press, 2014.

Brandt, Deborah. "Writing for a Living: Literacy and the Knowledge Economy." *Written Communication* 22, no. 2 (2005): 166–197. doi: 10.1177/0741088305275218.

Brandt, Deborah, and Katie Clinton. "Limits of the Local: Expanding Perspectives on Literacy as a Social Practice." *Journal of Literacy Research* 34, no. 3 (2002): 337–356.

Brooks, Frederick P. "No Silver Bullet: Essence and Accidents of Software Engineering." *IEEE Computer* 20 (4) (1987): 10–19.

Brooks, Frederick P. *The Mythical Man-Month: Essays on Software Engineering.* Reading, MA: Addison-Wesley, 1982.

Brooks, Kevin, and Chris Lindgren. "Responding to the Coding Crisis: From Code Year to Computational Literacy." In *Strategic Discourse: The Politics of (New) Literacy Crises*, edited by Lynn Lewis. Logan: Computers and Composition Digital Press/Utah State University Press, 2015. http://ccdigitalpress.org/strategic/.

Brown, James, Jr. *Ethical Programs: Hospitality and the Rhetorics of Software.* Ann Arbor: University of Michigan Press, 2015.

Brown, James, Jr., and Annette Vee. "Rhetoric and Computation." Computational Culture (Special Issue on Rhetoric and Computation), January 15, 2016. http://computationalculture.net/editorial/rhetoric-special-issue-editorial-introduction/.

Budge, Joseph H. "Visicalc: A Software Review." *Compute*, August 1980. Archive.org.

Burke, Kenneth. *Language as Symbolic Action.* Berkeley, CA: University of California Press, 1966.

Bush, Vannevar. "As We May Think." *Atlantic*, July 1945. www.theatlantic.com/magazine/archive/1945/07/as-we-may-think/303881/.

Bush, Vannevar. "Memex Revisited." In *New Media Old Media: A History and Theory Reader*, edited by Wendy Hui Kyong Chun and Thomas Keenan, 85–95. New York: Routledge, 2005.

Campbell-Kelly, Martin, and William Aspray. *Computer: A History of the Information Machine.* 2nd ed. The Sloan Technology Series. Boulder, CO: Westview Press, 2004.

Campbell-Kelly, Martin, William Aspray, Nathan Ensmenger, and Jeffrey Yost. *Computer: A History of the Information Machine.* 3rd ed. [e-book]. Boulder, CO: Westview Press, 2013.

Carr, Nicholas. "Is Google Making Us Stupid?" *Atlantic*, August 2008. www.theatlantic.com/magazine/archive/2008/07/is-google-making-us-stupid/306868/.

Carruthers, Mary. *The Book of Memory: A Study of Memory in Medieval Culture.* 2nd ed. Cambridge, UK: Cambridge University Press, 2008.

Carruthers, Mary, and Jan M. Ziolkowski. "General Introduction." In *The Medieval Craft of Memory*, edited by Mary Carruthers and Jan M. Ziolkowski, 1–31. Philadelphia: University of Pennsylvania Press, 2002.

Castells, Manuel. *The Rise of the Network Society.* 2nd ed. West Sussex, UK: John Wiley & Sons, 2010.

Chartier, Roger. "Histoire Des Mentalités." In *The Columbia History of Twentieth-Century French Thought*, edited by Lawrence D. Kritzman, Brian J. Reilly, and M. B. DeBevoise, 54–58. New York: Columbia University Press, 2007.

Chilcott, Lesley. "Code: The New Literacy" [Code.org promotional video]. Code.org, August 27, 2013. https://www.youtube.com/watch?v=MwLXrN0Yguk/.

Chilcott, Lesley. "Code Stars" [Code.org promotional video]. Code.org, February 26, 2013. https://www.youtube.com/watch?v=dU1xS07N-FA/.

Chilcott, Lesley. "What Most Schools Don't Teach" [Code.org promotional video]. Code.org, February 26, 2013. https://www.youtube.com/watch?v=nKIu9yen5nc/.

Christoph, Julie Nelson. "Each One Teach One: The Legacy of Evangelism in Adult Literacy Education." *Written Communication* 26 (1) (2009): 89.

Chun, Wendy Hui Kyong. *Control and Freedom: Power and Paranoia in the Age of Fiber Optics.* Cambridge, MA: MIT Press, 2006.

Chun, Wendy Hui Kyong. "Programmability." In *Software Studies: A Lexicon*, edited by Matthew Fuller, 224–229. Cambridge, MA: MIT Press, 2008.

Chun, Wendy Hui Kyong. *Programmed Visions: Software and Memory. Software Studies.* Cambridge, MA: MIT Press, 2011.

"City Announces Open Data Platform Launch." Office of [Pittsburgh] Mayor William Peduto, July 2, 2014. http://pittsburghpa.gov/mayor/release?id=3255/.

Clanchy, Michael T. *From Memory to Written Record: England 1066–1307.* 2nd ed. Malden, MA: Blackwell Publishing, 1993.

Clanchy, Michael T. *From Memory to Written Record: England 1066–1307.* 3rd ed. Somerset, NJ: John Wiley & Sons, 2012.

Clanchy, Michael T. "The Implications of Literacy: Written Language and Models of Interpretation in the Eleventh and Twelfth Centuries, by Brian Stock [Review]." *Canadian Journal of History* 18, no. 3 (1983): 403–404.

Cobb, Matthew. "What Is Life? The Physicist Who Sparked a Revolution in Biology." *Guardian*, February 7, 2013. https://www.theguardian.com/science/blog/2013/feb/07/wonders-life-physicist-revolution-biology/.

"CodeCombat - Learn How to Code by Playing a Game." CodeCombat, accessed September 29, 2015. http://codecombat.com/.

"Code.org Stats: What's Wrong with This Picture?" Code.org, n.d., accessed June 23, 2015. https://code.org/stats/.

"Code Review FAQ." MDN [Mozilla Developer Network], March 14, 2013. https://developer.mozilla.org/en-US/docs/Code_Review_FAQ/.

"CodeSpark Academy with The Foos," codeSpark, accessed October 21, 2016, http://thefoos.com/.

Colegrove, Albert M. "U.S. Unveils Push-Button Defense." *Pittsburgh Press*, January 18, 1956. https://news.google.com/newspapers?nid=1144&dat=19560118&id=hUEq AAAAIBAJ&sjid=5k0EAAAAIBAJ&pg=6449,383706/.

Coleman, E. Gabriella. *Coding Freedom: The Ethics and Aesthetics of Hacking.* Princeton, NJ: Princeton University Press, 2012.

Coleman, E. Gabriella. "Three Ethical Moments in Debian." Working Paper Series. Center for Critical Analysis, Rutgers University, 2005. Social Science Research Network. http://dx.doi.org/ 10.2139/ssrn.805287.

"Computers Are The Future, But Does Everyone Need to Code?" *All Tech Considered* (NPR), January 25, 2014. www.npr.org/blogs/alltechconsidered/2014/01/25/266162832/computers-are-the-future-but-does-everyone-need-to-code/.

"Connections: Global Networks." Computer History Museum, 2006. www.computerhistory.org/revolution/networking/19/374/.

Conyers, Grace. "The ProgeTiiger Initiative." AAAS MemberCentral, March 13, 2013. http://membercentral.aaas.org/blogs/aaas-serves/progetiiger-initiative/.

Cooke, Andrew. "Malbolge: Hello World." Andrew Cooke, accessed May 18, 2015. http://acooke.org/malbolge.html.

Cook-Gumperz, Jenny. "Literacy and Schooling: An Unchanging Equation?" In *The Social Construction of Literacy*. 2nd ed., 19–49. Cambridge, UK: Cambridge University Press, 2006.

Cook-Gumperz, Jenny. "The Social Construction of Literacy." In *The Social Construction of Literacy*. 2nd ed., 1–18. Cambridge, UK: Cambridge University Press, 2006.

Covino, William. "The Eternal Return of Magic-Rhetoric: Carnak Counts Ballots." In *Rhetoric and Composition as Intellectual Work*, edited by Gary Olson. Carbondale: Southern Illinois University Press, 2002.

Cowan, Ruth Schwartz. *Social History of American Technology.* Oxford, UK: Oxford University Press, 1986.

Cox, Geoff, and Alex McLean. *Speaking/Code: Coding as Aesthetic and Political Expression*. Cambridge, MA: MIT Press, 2012.

Cremin, Lawrence. *American Education: The National Experience 1783–1876*. New York: Harper and Row, 1982.

Croarken, Mary. "Eighteenth Century Computers." *Computer Resurrection: Bulletin of the Computer Conservation Society* 39 (2007). http://www.cs.man.ac.uk/CCS/res/res39 .htm#h.

"Dash and Dot, Robots That Help Kids Learn to Code." Wonder Workshop, accessed September 28, 2015. https://www.makewonder.com.

Deloura, Mark, and Randy Paris. "Don't Just Play on Your Phone, Program It." Whitehouse.gov, December 9, 2013. https://www.whitehouse.gov/blog/2013/12/09/ don-t-just-play-your-phone-program-it/.

Del Signore, John. "Police Seek 3 Men For Beating L Train Rider Who Scolded Them for Spitting." *Gothamist*, November 16, 2011. http://gothamist.com/2011/11/16/ police_search_for_men_in_beating_of.php.

Denning, Peter. "The Profession of IT: Voices of Computing." *Communications of the ACM* 51, no. 8 (2008): 19–21.

Derrida, Jacques. *Of Grammatology*. Trans. G. C. Spivak. Baltimore, MD: Johns Hopkins University Press, 1998.

Dijkstra, Edsger. "How Do We Tell Truths That Might Hurt?" In *Selected Writings on Computing: A Personal Perspective*, 129–131. New York: Springer-Verlag, 1982.

diSessa, Andrea. *Changing Minds: Computers, Learning and Literacy*. Cambridge, MA: MIT Press, 2000.

Duggan, Maeve, Nicole B. Ellison, Cliff Lampe, Amanda Lenhart, and Mary Madden. "Social Media Update 2014." Pew Research Center, January 2014. www.pewinternet .org/2015/01/09/social-media-update-2014/.

Edelson, Ed. "Fast-Growing New Hobby, Real Computers You Assemble Yourself." 82–83; 146–147, *Popular Science*, December 1976.

Eisenstein, Elizabeth. *The Printing Press as an Agent of Change*. Vols. 1 & 2. New York: Cambridge University Press, 1980.

Emerson, Lori. *Reading Writing Interfaces: From the Digital to the Bookbound*. Minneapolis: University of Minnesota Press, 2014.

Emig, Janet. *The Composing Processes of Twelfth Graders*. Urbana, IL: National Council of Teachers, 1971.

Ensmenger, Nathan. "Software as History Embodied." *IEEE Annals of the History of Computing* 31, no. 1 (2010): 86–88.

Ensmenger, Nathan. *The Computer Boys Take Over : Computers, Programmers, and the Politics of Technical Expertise*. Cambridge, MA: MIT Press, 2010.

Farr, Marcia. "Los Dos Idiomas: Literacy Practices Among Chicago Mexicanos." In *Literacy Across Communities*, edited by Beverly J. Moss, 9–47. Cresskill, NJ: Hampton Press, 1994.

Felton, Ed. "Source Code and Object Code." Freedom to Tinker, September 4, 2002. https://freedom-to-tinker.com/blog/felten/source-code-and-object-code/.

Ferguson, Jim. "Computing across the Curriculum." *Social Studies* 80, no. 2 (1989): 69–72. doi: 10.1080/00220973.1945.11019944.

Field, Kelly. "New Players Could Be in Line to Receive Federal Student Aid." *Chronicle of Higher Education*, July 2, 2015. http://chronicle.com/article/New-Players -Could-Be-in-Line/231333/.

Fish, Stanley. *Is There a Text in This Class? The Authority of Interpretive Communities*. Cambridge, MA: Harvard University Press, 1980.

Flamm, Kenneth. *Targeting the Computer: Government Support and International Competition*. Washington, DC: The Brookings Institution, 1987.

Flower, Linda, and John R. Hayes. "A Cognitive Process Theory of Writing." *College Composition and Communication* 32, no. 4 (1981): 365–387.

Flower, Linda, and John R. Hayes. "Images, Plans, and Prose: The Representation of Meaning in Writing." *Written Communication* 1, no. 1 (1984): 120–160.

Flusser, Vilem. *Does Writing Have a Future?* Trans. N. A. Roth. Minneapolis: University of Minnesota Press, 2011.

Folkenflik, David. "House Democrats Deliver Gun Control Sit-In Via Periscope, Facebook Live." *All Tech Considered* (NPR), June 23, 2016. www.npr.org/sections/alltechc onsidered/2016/06/23/483205687/house-democrats-deliver-sit-in-via-digital -platforms/.

Ford, Paul. "What Is Code?" *Bloomberg Business*, June 11, 2015. www.bloomberg .com/graphics/2015-paul-ford-what-is-code/.

Fortune, Stephen. "What on Earth Is Livecoding?" DazedDigital, May 2013. www .dazeddigital.com/artsandculture/article/16150/1/what-on-earth-is-livecoding/.

FreeBSD. "FAQ: Chapter 1. Introduction." FreeBSD, n.d., accessed January 3, 2017. https://www.freebsd.org/doc/faq/introduction.html.

Fresco, Nir. "The Explanatory Role of Computation in Cognitive Science." *Minds and Machines* 22, no. 4 (2012): 353–380. doi: 10.1007/s11023-012-9286-y.

Fuller, Matthew. "Introduction, the Stuff of Software." In *Software Studies: A Lexicon*, edited by Matthew Fuller, 1–13. Cambridge, MA: MIT Press, 2008.

"Funding a Revolution: Government Support for Computing Research." National Academies Press, 1999. https://www.nap.edu/read/6323/chapter/1.

Furet, François, and Jacques Ozouf. *Reading and Writing: Literacy in France from Calvin to Jules Ferry*. Trans. Maison des Sciences de l'Homme and Cambridge University Press. Cambridge, UK: Cambridge University Press, 1982.

Gabriel, Richard. "The Art of Lisp and Writing [Foreword to Successful Lisp: How to Understand and Use Common Lisp by David B. Lamkins]." Dreamsongs, 2004. www.dreamsongs.com/ArtOfLisp.html.

Galloway, Alexander. *Gaming: Essays on Algorithmic Culture*. Minneapolis: University of Minnesota Press, 2006.

Galloway, Alexander. *Protocol: How Control Exists after Decentralization*. Leonardo Book Series. Cambridge, MA: MIT Press, 2004.

Gardiner, Beth. "Adding Coding to the Curriculum." *New York Times*, March 23, 2014. http://www.nytimes.com/2014/03/24/world/europe/adding-coding-to-the-curriculum.html?_r=0/.

Gee, James Paul. *Social Linguistics and Literacies*. 2nd ed. Critical Perspectives on Literacy and Education. New York: Routledge Falmer, 1996.

Gee, James Paul. "The New Literacy Studies: From 'Socially Situated' to the Work of the Social." In *Situated Literacies: Reading and Writing in Context*, edited by David Barton, Mary Hamilton, and Roz Ivanič, 180–196. New York: Routledge, 2000.

Gee, James Paul. *What Video Games Have to Teach Us about Learning and Literacy*. New York: Palgrave Macmillan, 2003.

Gibbs, W. Wayt. "Software's Chronic Crisis." *Scientific American*, September 1994: 86–95.

Gillespie, Tarleton. "The Relevance of Algorithms." In *Media Technologies*, edited by Tarleton Gillespie, Pablo Boczkowski, and Kristen Foot, 167–194. Cambridge, MA: MIT Press, 2014.

Gilmore, William. *Reading Becomes a Necessity of Life: Material and Cultural Life in Rural New England, 1780–1835*. Knoxville: University of Tennessee Press, 1989.

Gitelman, Lisa. *Paper Knowledge: Toward a Media History of Documents*. Durham, NC: Duke University Press, 2014.

Glascott, Brenda. "Constricting Keywords: Rhetoric and Literacy in Our History Writing." *Literacy in Composition Studies* 1, no. 1 (2013): 18–25.

Golumbia, David. *The Cultural Logic of Computation*. Cambridge, MA: Harvard University Press, 2009.

Goody, Jack, Ed. *Literacy in Traditional Societies*. Cambridge, UK: Cambridge University Press, 1968.

Goody, Jack. *The Domestication of the Savage Mind*. Cambridge, UK: Cambridge University Press, 1977.

Goody, Jack, Ed. *The Logic of Writing and the Organization of Society*. Cambridge, UK: Cambridge University Press, 1986.

Goody, Jack, and Ian Watt. "The Consequences of Literacy." *Comparative Studies in Society and History* 5, no. 3 (1963): 304–345.

Google. "Women Who Choose Computer Science—What Really Matters." Google, May 26, 2014. https://static.googleusercontent.com/media/www.wenca.cn/en/us/edu/pdf/women-who-choose-what-really.pdf.

Graff, Harvey. *Labyrinths of Literacy: Reflections on Literacy Past and Present*, Revised Edition. Pittsburgh, PA: University of Pittsburgh Press, 1995.

Graff, Harvey. "The Literacy Myth at 30." *Journal of Social History* 43, no. 3 (2010): 635–661.

Graff, Harvey. *The Literacy Myth: Cultural Integration and Social Structure in the Nineteenth Century*. New Brunswick, NJ: Transaction Publishers, 1991.

Graham, Paul. *Hackers & Painters: Big Ideas from the Computer Age*. Sebastopol, CA: O'Reilly Media, 2004.

Greenberger, Martin, Ed. *Computers and the World of the Future*. Cambridge, MA: MIT Press, 1962.

Greenberger, Martin. "The Computers of Tomorrow." *Atlantic*, May 1964. www.theatlantic.com/past/docs/unbound/flashbks/computer/greenbf.htm.

Grier, David Alan. "The ENIAC, the Verb 'to Program' and the Emergence of Digital Computers." *IEEE Annals of the History of Computing* 18, no. 1 (1996): 51–55.

Griswold, Alison. "When It Comes to Diversity in Tech, Companies Find Safety in Numbers." *Slate*, June 27, 2014. www.slate.com/blogs/moneybox/2014/06/27/tech_diversity_data_facebook_follows_google_yahoo_in_releasing_the_stats.html.

Guzdial, Mark. "Anyone Can Learn Programming: Teaching > Genetics." Blog@ CACM, October 14, 2014. http://cacm.acm.org/blogs/blog-cacm/179347-anyone-can-learn-programming-teaching-genetics/fulltext/.

Guzdial, Mark. "Definitions of 'Code' and 'Programmer': Response to 'Please Don't Learn to Code.'" Computing Education Blog, December 20, 2012. https://computinged.wordpress.com/2012/12/20/definitions-of-code-and-programmer-response-to-please-dont-learn-to-code/.

Guzdial, Mark. "How to Teach Computing across the Curriculum: Why Not Logo?" Computing Education Blog, April 13, 2012. https://computinged.wordpress.com/2012/04/13/how-to-teach-computing-across-the-curriculum-why-not-logo/.

Guzdial, Mark. *Learner-Centered Design of Computing Education: Research on Computing for Everyone*. Synthesis Lectures on Human-Centered Informatics. San Rafael, CA: Morgan & Claypool Publishers, 2015.

Guzdial, Mark. "Teaching Computing to Everyone." *Communications of the ACM* 52, no. 5 (2009): 31. doi: 10.1145/1506409.1506420.

Guzdial, Mark, and Eliot Soloway. "Computer Science Is More Important Than Calculus: The Challenge of Living Up to Our Potential." *SIGCSE Bulletin* 35, no. 2 (2003): 5–8.

Haas, Christina. *Writing Technology: Studies on the Materiality of Literacy*. Mahwah, NJ: Lawrence Erlbaum, 1996.

Haefner, Joel. "The Politics of the Code." *Computers and Composition* 16, no. 3 (1999): 325–339.

Hafner, Katie. "Giving Women the Access Code." *New York Times*, April 2, 2012. www.nytimes.com/2012/04/03/science/giving-women-the-access-code.html.

Hafner, Katie, and Matthew Lyon. *Where Wizards Stay Up Late: The Origins of the Internet*. New York: Simon and Schuster, 1996.

Halfhill, Tom R. "The New Wave of Home Computers." 24–40. *Compute*, August 1982. Archive.org.

Hallinan, Blake, and Ted Striphas. "Recommended for You: The Netflix Prize and the Production of Algorithmic Culture." *New Media & Society*, June 23, 2014. doi: 10.1177/1461444814538646.

Harlan, Josh. "Hilary Putnam: On Mind, Meaning and Reality, Interview with Josh Harlan." *Harvard Review of Philosophy* , Spring (1992): 20–24.

Harrell, D. Fox. *Phantasmal Media: An Approach to Imagination, Computation, and Expression*. Cambridge, MA: MIT Press, 2013.

"Harvard Mark I/IBM ASCC." Computer History Museum, accessed September 30, 2015. www.computerhistory.org/revolution/birth-of-the-computer/4/86/350/.

Hasselström, Karl, and Jon Åslund. "Shakespeare Programming Language." Source-Forge, August 21, 2001. http://shakespearelang.sourceforge.net/report/shakespeare/ shakespeare.html#sec:hello/.

Havelock, Eric. *Preface to Plato*. Cambridge, MA: Harvard University Press, 1963.

Hawisher, G., and C. Selfe, Eds. *Critical Perspectives on Computers and Composition Instruction*. New York: Teachers College Press, 1989.

Hayles, N. Katherine. *Electronic Literature: New Horizons for the Literary*. South Bend, IN: University of Notre Dame Press, 2008.

Hayles, N. Katherine. *My Mother Was a Computer: Digital Subjects and Literary Texts.* Chicago: University of Chicago Press, 2005.

Hayles, N. Katherine. "Print Is Flat, Code Is Deep: The Importance of Media-Specific Analysis." *Poetics Today* 25, no. 1 (2004): 67–90. doi: 10.1215/03335372-25-1-67.

Heath, Shirley Brice. *Ways with Words: Language, Life and Work in Communities and Classroom.* New York: Cambridge University Press, 1983.

Heidegger, Martin. "The Question Concerning Technology." In *Basic Writings from Being and Time (1927) and the Task of Thinking (1964)*, edited by David Farrell Krell, 283–317. New York: Harper and Row, 1977.

Helmond, Anne. "The Algorithmization of the Hyperlink." *Computational Culture*, no. 3 (November 2013). http://computationalculture.net/article/the-algorithmization-of-the-hyperlink/.

Henn, Steve. "When Women Stopped Coding." *Planet Money* (NPR), October 21, 2014. www.npr.org/sections/money/2014/10/21/357629765/when-women-stopped-coding/.

Hiltzik, Michael. *Dealers of Lighting: Xerox PARC and the Dawn of the Computer Age.* New York: HarperBusiness, 2000.

Hipwell, Chris. "The Mainframe Years in the Computer Press." *Computer Resurrection: Bulletin of the Computer Conservation Society* 39 (2007). www.cs.man.ac.uk/CCS/res/res39.htm#e.

Hopper, Grace Murray. "The Education of a Computer." In *Proceedings of the 1952 ACM National Meeting*, 243. Pittsburgh, PA: ACM, 1952.

Horrigan, John B., and Sydney Jones. "When Technology Fails." Pew Research Center, November 2008. www.pewinternet.org/2005/07/06/computer-problems-vex-millions/.

Houston, Rab. "The Literacy Campaigns in Scotland, 1560-1803." In *National Literacy Campaigns*, edited by Robert F. Arnove and Harvey J. Graff, 49–64. New York: Plenum Press, 1987.

Hsu, Jeremy, and the Innovation News Daily. "Secret Computer Code Threatens Science." *Scientific American*, April 13, 2012. www.scientificamerican.com/article/secret-computer-code-threatens-science/.

IBM Military Products Division. "On Guard," accessed December 8, 2014. www.ll.mit.edu/about/History/SAGEairdefensesystem.html.

Ingham, Richard, Ed. *The Anglo-Norman Language and Its Contexts.* York, UK: York Medieval Press, 2010.

Innis, Harold A. *Empire and Communications.* Toronto: University of Toronto Press, 1972.

Instagram. "See the Moments You Care About First." Instagram Blog, June 2, 2016. http://blog.instagram.com/post/145322772067/160602-news/.

Ito, Mizuko, Kris Gutierrez, Sonia Livingstone, Bill Penuel, Jean Rhodes, Katie Salen, Juliet Schor, Julian Sefton-Green, and S. Craig Watkins. *Connected Learning: An Agenda for Research and Design*. Irvine, CA: Digital Media and Learning Research Hub, 2013.

Jackson, Herb. "'From Estonia to Leonia', The Record, 23 April 2008." President Ilves Media, Interviews, April 23, 2008. https://web.archive.org/web/20151231223413/ https://www.president.ee/en/media/interviews/3304-qfrom-estonia-to-leoniaq-the -record-23-april-2008/index.html.

Johansson, Egil. "Literacy Campaigns in Sweden." *Interchange* 19, no. 3/4 (1988): 135–162.

Johns, Adrian. *The Nature of the Book: Print and Knowledge in the Making*. Chicago: University of Chicago Press, 2000.

jordanb. "Secret Computer Code Threatens Science (scientificamerican)" [comment]. Hacker News, April 13, 2012. https://news.ycombinator.com/item?id =3844910/.

"Journalism and Computer Science." Columbia University, n.d., accessed January 3, 2017. https://journalism.columbia.edu/journalism-computer-science/.

Jurgenson, Nathan. "The Facebook Eye." *Atlantic*, January 13, 2012. www.theatlantic .com/technology/archive/2012/01/the-facebook-eye/251377/.

Kafai, Yasmin, and Quinn Burke. *Connected Code: Why Children Need to Learn Programming*. MacArthur Foundation Series on Digital Media and Learning. Cambridge, MA: MIT Press, 2014.

Kafka, Ben. *The Demon of Writing: Powers and Failures of Paperwork*. Cambridge, MA: MIT Press / Zone Books, 2012.

Kamenetz, Anya. "Coding Class, Then Naptime: Computer Science For The Kindergarten Set." NPR.org, accessed September 18, 2015. www.npr.org/sections/ ed/2015/09/18/441122285/learning-to-code-in-preschool/.

Kang, Cecilia, and Todd C. Frankel. "Silicon Valley Struggles to Hack Its Diversity Problem." *Washington Post*, July 16, 2015. https://www.washingtonpost.com/ business/economy/silicon-valley-struggles-to-hack-its-diversity-problem/2015/07/ 16/0b0144be-2053-11e5-84d5-eb37ee8eaa61_story.html.

Katsen, Paul. "Programming! = Writing Code," accessed July 14, 2015. http:// katsenblog.com/post/119256226994/programming-writing-code/.

Kay, Alan. "A Personal Computer for Children of All Ages." Xerox Palo Alto Research Center, August 1972. www.mprove.de/diplom/gui/Kay72a.pdf.

Kay, Alan. "User Interface: A Personal View." In *The Art of Human-Computer Interface Design*, edited by Brenda Laurel, 191–207. Reading, MA: Addison-Wesley, 1990.

Kay, Alan, and Adele Goldberg. "Personal Dynamic Media." *Computer* 10, no. 3 (1977): 31–41.

Kelleher, Caitlin, and Randy Pausch. "Lowering the Barriers to Programming: A Taxonomy of Programming Environments and Languages for Novice Programmers." *ACM Computing Surveys* 37, no. 2 (2005): 83–137.

Kemeny, John. *Man and the Computer*. New York: Scribner, 1972.

Kemeny, John. "The Case for Computer Literacy." *Daedalus* 112, no. 2 (1983): 211–230.

Kemeny, John, and Thomas Kurtz. "Dartmouth Time-Sharing." *Science* 162 (1968): 223–228.

Kemeny, John, and Thomas Kurtz. *The Dartmouth Time-Sharing Computing System Final Report*. Course Content Improvement Program. Dartmouth, NH: Dartmouth College, 1967.

Khan, Yasmeen. "City Wants to Spend Millions to Make School Kids Tech Savvy." WNYC, accessed September 18, 2015. www.wnyc.org/story/mayors-plan-will-require -all-nyc-schools-offer-computer-science/.

Khan, Yasmeen. "De Blasio Says to Tackle Inequities, School Kids Must Go Back to the Basics." WNYC, accessed September 18, 2015. www.wnyc.org/story/de-blasio -tackles-inequity-nyc-schools-computer-science/.

Kidder, Tracy. *The Soul of a New Machine*. New York: Back Bay Books / Little, Brown, 2000.

Kirschenbaum, Matthew. *Mechanisms: New Media and the Forensic Imagination*. Cambridge, MA: MIT Press, 2008.

Kirsch, Irwin S., Ann Jungeblut, Lynn Jenkins, and Andrew Kolstad. "Adult Literacy in America: A First Look at the Findings of the National Adult Literacy Survey." U.S. Department of Education Office of Educational Research and Improvement, April 2002. https://nces.ed.gov/pubs93/93275.pdf.

Kitchin, Rob, and Martin Dodge. *Code/Space: Software and Everyday Life*. Cambridge, MA: MIT Press, 2014.

Kittler, Friedrich A. *Gramophone, Film, Typewriter*. Stanford, CA: Stanford University Press, 1999.

Knuth, Donald. *Literate Programming. CSLI Lecture Notes*. Stanford, CA: Center for the Study of Language and Information, 1992.

Ko, Andrew J., Brad Myers, Mary Beth Rosson, Gregg Rothermel, Mary Shaw, Susan Wiedenbeck, Robin Abraham, et al. "The State of the Art in End-User Software Engineering." *ACM Computing Surveys* 43 (2011): 1–44.

Kohanski, Daniel. *The Philosophical Programmer: Reflections on the Moth in the Machine*. New York: St. Martin's Press, 1998.

"Labor Force Statistics from the Current Population Survey." Bureau of Labor Statistics, U.S. Department of Labor, February 26, 2014. www.bls.gov/cps/cpsaat11.htm.

Lakhani, Karim R., and Robert Wolf. "Why Hackers Do What They Do: Understanding Motivation and Effort in Free/Open Source Software Projects." In *Perspectives on Free and Open Source Software*, edited by Joseph Feller, Brian Fitzgerald, Scott A. Hissam, and Karim R. Lakhani, 3–21. Cambridge, MA: MIT Press, 2005.

Lakoff, George, and Mark Johnson. *Metaphors We Live By*. Chicago: University of Chicago Press, 2008.

Langmead, Alison, and David Birnbaum. "Task-Driven Programming Pedagogy in the Digital Humanities." In *New Directions for Computing Education: Embedding Computing across Disciplines*, edited by Samuel B. Fee, Amanda M. Holland-Minkley, and Thomas Lombardi. New York: Springer, forthcoming.

Lapowsky, Issie. "The Startup That's Bringing Coding to the World's Classrooms." *Wired*, May 22, 2014. www.wired.com/2014/05/codecademy/.

Laqueur, Thomas. "The Cultural Origins of Popular Literacy in England: 1500-1850." *Oxford Review of Education* 2, no. 3 (1976): 255–275.

Laquintano, Tim. "Sustained Authorship: Digital Writing, Self-Publishing, and the Ebook." *Written Communication* 27, no. 4 (2010): 469–493.

Laquintano, Timothy. *Mass Authorship and the Rise of Self-Publishing*. Iowa City: University of Iowa, 2016.

Lastowka, Greg. "Copyright Law and Video Games: A Brief History of an Interactive Medium." In *The SAGE Handbook of Intellectual Property*, edited by Matthew David and Debora Halbert. Thousand Oaks, CA: Sage Publications, 2015. http://sk.sagepub .com/reference/the-sage-handbook-of-intellectual-property/i3554.xml.

Latour, Bruno. *Reassembling the Social: An Introduction to Actor-Network Theory*. Oxford, UK: Oxford University Press, 2005.

Lauricella, Tom, Kara Scannell, and Jenny Strasburg. "How a Trading Algorithm Went Awry." *Wall Street Journal*, October 2, 2010. www.wsj.com/articles/SB1000142 4052748704029304575526390131916792/.

Lave, Jean, and Etienne Wenger. *Situated Learning: Legitimate Peripheral Participation*. Cambridge, UK: Cambridge University Press, 1991.

Layton, Lyndsey. "Bill Gates Calls on Teachers to Defend Common Core." *Washington Post*, March 14, 2014. https://www.washingtonpost.com/local/education/bill-gates-calls-on-teachers-to-defend-common-core/2014/03/14/395b130a-aafa-11e3-98f6-8e3c562f9996_story.html.

Lazowska, Ed, Eric Roberts, and Jim Kurose. "Tsunami or Sea Change? Responding to the Explosion of Student Interest in Computer Science." Presented at the National Center for Women & Information 10th Anniversary Summit / Computing Research Association Conference at Snowbird, Utah, May 2014. http://lazowska.cs.washington.edu/NCWIT.pdf.

Lazowska, Ed, and David Patterson. "Students of All Majors Should Study Computer Science." *Chronicle of Higher Education*, November 26, 2013. http://chronicle.com/blogs/letters/students-of-all-majors-should-study-computer-science/.

Le Goff, Jacques. "Mentalities: A New Field for Historians." Trans. Michael Fineberg. *Social Sciences Information. Information Sur les Sciences Sociales* 13, no. 1 (1974): 81–97.

Lenhart, Amanda. "Teens, Social Media & Technology Overview 2015." Pew Research Center, April 2015. www.pewinternet.org/2015/04/09/mobile-access-shifts-social-media-use-and-other-online-activities/.

Lessig, Lawrence. *Code: And Other Laws of Cyberspace*. New York: Basic Books, 2000.

Lessig, Lawrence. *Free Culture: The Nature and Future of Creativity*. New York: Penguin Books, 2004.

Levy, David. *Scrolling Forward*. New York: Arcade Publishing, 2001.

Levy, Steven. *Hackers: Heroes of the Computer Revolution*. New York: Dell Publishing, 1984.

Licklider, J. C. R. "Man-Computer Symbiosis." *IRE Transactions on Human Factors in Electronics*, no. 1 (1960): 4–11. doi: 10.1109/THFE2.1960.4503259.

Licklider, J. C. R., and W. Robert Taylor. "The Computer as a Communication Device." *Science and Technology* 76, no. 2 (1968): 21–41.

Liu, Alan. "Comment on 'On Building,'" Stephen Ramsay [blog], January 11, 2011, http://stephenramsay.us/text/2011/01/11/on-building/#comment-223113606.

Lockett, Alexandria. "I Am Not a Computer Programmer." *Enculturation*, October 12, 2012. www.enculturation.net/node/5270/.

Lockheed, Marlaine E., and Ellen B. Mandinach. "Trends in Educational Computing: Decreasing Interest and the Changing Focus of Instruction." *Educational Researcher* 15, no. 5 (1986): 21–26.

Lockridge, Kenneth. *Literacy in Colonial New England: An Enquiry into the Social Context of Literacy in the Early Modern West*. New York: W.W. Norton, 1975.

"Logo History." Logo Foundation, n.d., accessed January 3, 2017. http://el.media. mit.edu/logo-foundation/what_is_logo/history.html.

Longo, Bernadette. "Edmund Berkeley, Computers, and Modern Methods of Thinking." *IEEE Annals of the History of Computing* 26, no. 4 (2004): 4–18. doi: 10.1109/ MAHC.2004.28.

Longo, Bernadette. "Metaphors, Robots, and the Transfer of Computers to Civilian Life." *Comparative Technology Transfer and Society* 3, no. 5 (2007): 253–273.

Lopes, Cristina Videira. *Exercises in Programming Style*. Boca Raton, FL: Chapman and Hall/CRC, 2014.

Losh, Elizabeth. *The War on Learning*. Cambridge, MA: MIT Press, 2014.

Lovelace (Countess of), Augusta Ada. "Notes on the Sketch of The Analytical Engine Invented by Charles Babbage," 1842. https://www.fourmilab.ch/babbage/sketch. html.

Luckerson, Victor. "How Twitter Slayed the Fail Whale." *Time*, accessed September 30, 2015. http://business.time.com/2013/11/06/how-twitter-slayed-the-fail-whale/.

MacBird, Bonnie. "Seminal Work and Instrumental in the Creation of TRON." Amazon user review, August 21, 2011. www.amazon.com/review/R36QFVARF6SW A1/ref=cm_cr_dp_title?ie=UTF8&ASIN=B003LOB14Q&channel=detail-glance &nodeID=283155&store=books/.

Mackenzie, Adrian. *Cutting Code: Software and Sociality. Digital Formations*. Bern, Switzerland: Peter Lang International Academic Publishers, 2006.

"Made with Code_Google." Made W/ Code, accessed June 23, 2015. https://www .madewithcode.com.

Mahoney, Michael. "The Histories of Computing(s)." *Interdisciplinary Science Reviews* 30, no. 2 (2005): 119–135.

Mahoney, Michael. "Finding a History for Software Engineering." *IEEE Annals of the History of Computing* 26, no. 1 (2004): 8–19.

"Malbolge." Esolang, the Esoteric Programming Languages Wiki, accessed November 12, 2013. http://esolangs.org/wiki/Malbolge/.

Mankoff, Robert. "Computer Games." *From the Desk of Bob Mankoff* [blog], *The New Yorker*, February 23, 2011. http://www.newyorker.com/from-the-desk-of-bob -mankoff/computer-games/.

Manovich, Lev. *Software Takes Command*. Software Studies Initiative. November 20, 2008. http://softwarestudies.com/softbook/manovich_softbook_11_20_2008.pdf.

Mansel, Tim. "How Estonia Became E-Stonia." *BBC News*, May 16, 2013. www.bbc .com/news/business-22317297/.

Margolis, Jane, and Allan Fisher. *Unlocking the Clubhouse: Women in Computing.* Cambridge, MA: MIT Press, 2003.

Marwick, Alice E., and danah boyd. "I Tweet Honestly, I Tweet Passionately: Twitter Users, Context Collapse, and the Imagined Audience." *New Media & Society* 20, no. 10 (2010): 1–20. doi: 10.1177/1461444810365313.

Mateas, Michael. "Procedural Literacy: Educating the New Media Practitioner." *On the Horizon* (Special Issue on Future of Games, Simulations and Interactive Media in Learning Contexts) 13, no. 1 (2005): 1–15.

Mateas, Michael, and Nick Montfort. "A Box, Darkly: Obfuscation, Weird Languages, and Code Aesthetics." *Proceedings of the 6th Digital Arts and Culture Conference, IT University of Copenhagen,* 2005, 144–153. NickM.com, http://nickm.com/cis/a_box_darkly.pdf.

McAllister, Neil. "Meet بلق, the Programming Language That Uses Arabic Script." *Register,* January 25, 2013. www.theregister.co.uk/2013/01/25/arabic_programming_language/.

McCarthy, John. "LISP—Notes on Its Past and Future—1980." John McCarthy's Home Page (Stanford University), March 22, 1999. www-formal.stanford.edu/jmc/lisp20th.pdf.

McElroy, Damien. "Twitter Maintained Service during Iranian Elections after US State Dept Request." *Telegraph,* June 16, 2009. www.telegraph.co.uk/technology/twitter/5552733/Twitter-maintained-service-during-Iranian-elections-after-US-State-Dept-request.html.

McKinley, William. "First Inaugural Address of William McKinley." Yale Law School Lillian Goldman Law Library, accessed October 12, 2016, http://avalon.law.yale.edu/19th_century/mckin1.asp.

McLuhan, Marshall. *The Gutenberg Galaxy.* Toronto: University of Toronto Press, 1962.

McLuhan, Marshall. *Understanding Media: The Extensions of Man.* First MIT Press ed. Cambridge, MA: MIT Press, 1994.

McMillan, Robert. "Oracle Makes Java More Relevant Than Ever—For Free." *Wired,* September 25, 2013. www.wired.com/2013/09/oracle_java/.

Miller, Jennifer. "Teacher's Vision, but Done New York City's Way." *New York Times,* March 29, 2013. http://www.nytimes.com/2013/03/31/nyregion/software-engineering-school-was-teachers-idea-but-its-been-done-citys-way.html.

Minsky, Marvin, and Seymour Papert. *Perceptrons: An Introduction to Computational Geometry.* Expanded ed. Cambridge, MA: MIT Press, 1987.

Misa, Thomas, Ed. *Gender Codes: Why Women Are Leaving Computing*. Hoboken, NJ: Wiley-IEEE Computer Society, 2010.

Misa, Thomas. "How Machines Make History, and How Historians (and Others) Help Them to Do So." *Science, Technology & Human Values* 13, no. 3/4 (1988): 308–331.

Moll, Luis, and Norma González. "Lessons from Research with Language Minority Children." In *Literacy: A Critical Sourcebook*, edited by Ellen Cushman, Eugene Kintgen, Barry Kroll, and Mike Rose, 156–171. Boston: Bedford/St. Martins Press, 2001.

Montfort, Nick. *Exploratory Programming for the Arts and Humanities*. Cambridge, MA: MIT Press, 2016.

Montfort, Nick, Patsy Baudoin, John Bell, Ian Bogost, Jeremy Douglass, Mark C. Marino, Michael Mateas, Casey Reas, Mark Sample, and Noah Vawter. *10 PRINT CHR$(205.5+RND(1)); GOTO 10*. Cambridge, MA: MIT Press, 2014.

Mumford, Lewis. *Technics and Civilization*. With a New Foreword by Langdon Winner. Chicago: University of Chicago Press, 2010.

Munroe, Randall. "Research Ethics" [comic]. xkcd.com, July 4, 2014. http://xkcd.com/1390/.

Nardi, Bonnie. *A Small Matter of Programming: Perspectives on End User Computing*. Cambridge, MA: MIT Press, 1993.

"National Institute for Literacy." *Federal Register*, accessed June 19, 2015. https://www.federalregister.gov/agencies/national-institute-for-literacy/.

Naughton, John. "Why All Our Kids Should Be Taught How to Code." *Guardian*, March 31, 2012. https://www.theguardian.com/education/2012/mar/31/why-kids-should-be-taught-code/.

NeCamp, Samantha. *Adult Literacy and American Identity: The Moonlight Schools and Americanization Programs*. Carbondale: Southern Illinois University Press, 2014.

Neely, Brett. "Devising Aid Programs on Their Laptops." Marketplace, American Public Media, January 18, 2010. http://www.marketplace.org/2010/01/18/your-money/devising-aid-programs-their-laptops/.

Nelson, Katie. "Google Is Putting $50 Million Toward Getting Girls to Code." Mashable, June 20, 2014. http://mashable.com/2014/06/20/google-made-with-code/#6WOwloNGyPqn/.

Nelson, Theodore Holm. *Computer Lib/Dream Machines*. Redmond, CA: Microsoft Press, 1987.

Noble, Safiya Umoja. "Google Search: Hyper-Visibility as a Means of Rendering Black Women and Girls Invisible." *Invisible Culture* 19 (2013). http://ivc.lib.rochester.

edu/google-search-hyper-visibility-as-a-means-of-rendering-black-women-and
-girls-invisible/.

Nofre, David, Mark Priestley, and Gerard Alberts. "When Technology Became Language: The Origins of the Linguistic Conception of Computer Programming, 1950–1960." *Technology and Culture* 55, no. 1 (2014): 40–75.

Nunez, Michael. "Former Facebook Workers: We Routinely Suppressed Conservative News." Gizmodo, May 9, 2016. http://gizmodo.com/former-facebook-workers-we
-routinely-suppressed-conser-1775461006/.

Obama, Barack. "Text of Obama's Speech to the AMA." WSJ Blogs—Health Blog, June 15, 2009. http://blogs.wsj.com/health/2009/06/15/text-of-obamas-speech
-before-the-ama/.

Office of the Mayor [Bill de Blasio]. "Computer Science for All: Fundamentals for Our Future." The Official Website of the City of New York, accessed September 18, 2015. www1.nyc.gov/office-of-the-mayor/education-vision-2015-computer-science
.page.

Ohmann, Richard. "Literacy, Technology, and Monopoly Capital." *College English* 47, no. 7 (1985): 675–689. doi: 10.2307/376973.

Olson, David. *The World on Paper: The Conceptual and Cognitive Implications of Writing and Reading.* Cambridge, UK: Cambridge University Press, 1994.

Ong, Walter. *Orality and Literacy: The Technologizing of the Word.* London: Routledge, 1982.

Ong, Walter. "[Review Of] The Implications of Literacy." *Manuscripta* 28, no. 2 (1984): 108–109.

Ong, Walter. "Writing Is a Technology That Restructures Thought." In *Literacy: A Critical Sourcebook,* edited by Ellen Cushman, Eugene Kintgen, Barry Kroll, and Mike Rose, 19–31. Boston: Bedford/St. Martins Press, 2001.

"Our Mission." *Sunlight Foundation,* n.d., accessed July 1, 2015. http://sunlight foundation.com/about/.

Papert, Seymour. "Educational Computing: How Are We Doing?" [Technological Horizons in Education] *T.H.E. Journal* 24, no. 11 (1997): 78–80.

Papert, Seymour. *Mindstorms: Children, Computers, and Powerful Ideas.* New York: Basic Books, 1980.

Papert, Seymour, and Cynthia Solomon. "Twenty Things to Do with the Computer." Artificial Intelligence Laboratory, MIT, June 1971. www.stager.org/articles/
twentythings.pdf.

Parberry, Ian. "Computer Science Education," 2010. https://larc.unt.edu/ian/
research/cseducation/.

Partovi, Hadi. "The 'Secret Agenda' of Code.org." Anybody Can Learn [blog], January 20, 2014. http://blog.code.org/post/73963049605/the-secret-agenda-of-codeorg/.

Partovi, Hadi. "With Support from Obama to Shakira, Apple to Zuckerberg, the Hour of Code Is Here." Anybody Can Learn [blog], December 8, 2013. http://blog.code .org/post/69469632752/hourofcodeishere/.

Partovi, Hadi, and Ali Partovi. "Iam Hadi Partovi, Co-Founder of Code.org, Here with My Identical Twin Brother Ali Partovi. Ask Us Anything. • /r/IAmA." Reddit, February 28, 2013. https://www.reddit.com/r/IAmA/comments/19eqzm/iam_hadi _partovi_cofounder_of_codeorg_here_with/.

Pea, Roy, and D. Midian Kurland. "On the Cognitive Effects of Learning Computer Programming." *New Ideas in Psychology* 2 (2) (1984): 138.

Perlin, Ken. "Does Universal Programming Even Make Sense?" Ken's Blog, February 24, 2008. http://blog.kenperlin.com/?p=97/.

Perlis, Alan. "The Computer in the University." In *Computers and the World of the Future*, edited by Martin Greenberger, 180–217. Cambridge, MA: MIT Press, 1962.

Poster, Mark. "Introduction." In *Does Writing Have a Future?* by Vilem Flusser, trans. N. A. Roth. Minneapolis: University of Minnesota Press, 2011.

Punday, Daniel. *Computing as Writing*. Minneapolis: University of Minnesota Press, 2015.

Prensky, Marc. "Digital Natives, Digital Immigrants." *On the Horizon* 9, no. 5 (2001): 1–6. doi: 10.1108/10748120110424816.

Protalinski, Emil. "Facebook Passes 1.44B Monthly Active Users and 1.25B Mobile Users; 65% Are Now Daily Users." VentureBeat, April 22, 2015. http://venturebeat .com/2015/04/22/facebook-passes-1-44b-monthly-active-users-1-25b-mobile-users -and-936-million-daily-users/.

Purcell-Gates, Victoria. *Other People's Words: The Cycle of Low Literacy*. Cambridge, MA: Harvard University Press, 1997.

Raja, Tasneem. "'Gangbang Interviews' and 'Bikini Shots': Silicon Valley's Brogram-mer Problem." *Mother Jones*, April 26, (2012). www.motherjones.com/media/2012/ 04/silicon-valley-brogrammer-culture-sexist-sxsw/.

Raja, Tasneem. "Is Coding the New Literacy?" *Mother Jones*, June 2014. www .motherjones.com/media/2014/06/computer-science-programming-code-diversity -sexism-education/.

Ramdas, Lalita. "Women and Literacy: A Quest for Justice." In *Literacy: A Critical Sourcebook*, edited by Ellen Cushman, Eugene Kintgen, Barry Kroll, and Mike Rose, 629–643. Boston: Bedford/St. Martins Press, 2001.

Ramsay, Stephen. "On Building." Stephen Ramsay [blog], January 11, 2011. http:// stephenramsay.us/text/2011/01/11/on-building/.

Ramsay, Stephen. *Reading Machines: Toward an Algorithmic Criticism*. Urbana: University of Illinois Press, 2011.

Rangel, Jasmine. "Class Pairs Journalism, Computer Science Students to Develop Projects." Medill School of Journalism, Northwestern University, December 9, 2013. www.medill.northwestern.edu/experience/news/2013/fall/news-class-pairs-journalism-computer-science-students-to-develop-projects.html.

Reimer, Jeremy. "Total Share: 30 Years of Personal Computer Market Share Figures." *Ars Technica*, December 15, 2005. http://arstechnica.com/features/2005/12/total -share/.

Resnick, Daniel P., and Lauren B. Resnick. "The Nature of Literacy: An Historical Explanation." *Harvard Educational Review* 47, no. 3 (1977): 370–385.

Resnick, Mitchel, and David Siegel. "A Different Approach to Coding: How Kids Are Making and Remaking Themselves from Scratch." Medium.com, November 10, 2015. https://medium.com/bright/a-different-approach-to-coding-d679b06d83a/.

Resnick, Mitchel, John Maloney, Andrés Monroy-Hernández, Natalie Rusk, Evelyn Eastmond, Karen Brennan, Amon Millner, et al. "Scratch: Programming for All." *Communications of the ACM* 52, no. 11 (2009): 60–67.

Resnick, Mitchel, Brad Myers, Kumiyo Nakakoji, Randy Pausch, Ben Shneiderman, Ted Selker, and Mike Eisenberg. "Design Principles for Tools to Support Creative Thinking." Working Paper, Research Showcase @ CMU, Carnegie Mellon Institute for Software Research and School of Computer Science, Pittsburgh, PA, October 30, 2005. http://repository.cmu.edu/cgi/viewcontent.cgi?article=1822&context=isr/.

Richards, Martin. "EDSAC Initial Orders and Squares Program." University of Cambridge Computer Laboratory, n.d. www.cl.cam.ac.uk/~mr10/edsacposter.pdf.

Rieder, David M. "Scripted Writing() Exploring Generative Dimensions of Writing in Flash Actionscript." In *Small Tech: The Culture of Digital Tools*, edited by Byron Hawk, David M. Rieder, and Ollie O. Oviedo, 86. Minneapolis: University of Minnesota Press, 2008.

Robbins, Sarah. *Managing Literacy, Mothering America*. Pittsburgh, PA: University of Pittsburgh Press, 2004.

Roberts, H. Edward, and William Yates. "ALTAIR 8800 The Most Powerful Minicomputer Project Ever Presented—Can Be Built for under $400." cover, 33–38, 73, *Scientific American*, January 1975.

Rushkoff, Douglas. *Program or Be Programmed*. Kindle ed. New York: OR Books, 2010.

Russell, Jon. "Mt. Gox Customers Can Now File Claims For Their Lost Bitcoins." TechCrunch, April 22, 2015. https://techcrunch.com/2015/04/22/mt-gox-claims/.

"SAGE: Semi-Automatic Ground Environment Air Defense System." Lincoln Laboratory, MIT, 2015. www.ll.mit.edu/about/History/SAGE_TOCpage.html.

Salsberg, Art. "THE HOME COMPUTER IS HERE!" [editorial] *Popular Electronics*, January 1975, 4.

Salter, Anastasia. "Code Before Content? Brogrammer Culture in Games and Electronic Literature." Presented at the Electronic Literature Organization, Vancouver, BC, Canada, June 10, 2016. www.slideshare.net/anastasiasalter/code-before-content-elo-slides.

Salvatori, Mariolina. "New Literacy Studies: Some Matters of Concern." *Literacy in Composition Studies* 1, no. 1 (2013): 66–69.

Scaffidi, Christopher, Mary Shaw, and Brad Myers. "An Approach for Categorizing End User Programmers to Guide Software Engineering Research." *Software Engineering Notes* 30, no. 4 (2005): 1–5.

Schmandt-Besserat, Denise. *Before Writing: From Counting to Cuneiform*. Vol. 1. Austin: University of Texas Press, 1992.

Schmidhuber, Jürgen. "Zuse's Thesis: The Universe Is a Computer." Jürgen Schmidhuber's Home Page, n.d. http://people.idsia.ch/~juergen/digitalphysics.html.

Scientific American, Volume 237, Issue 3. *Scientific American*, September 1977. www.scientificamerican.com/magazine/sa/1977/09-01/.

"Scratch." Massachusetts Institute of Technology, accessed September 29, 2015. https://scratch.mit.edu.

Scribner, Sylvia. "Literacy in Three Metaphors." *American Journal of Education* 93, no. 1 (1984): 6–21.

Scribner, Sylvia, and Michael Cole. *The Psychology of Literacy*. Cambridge, MA: Harvard University Press, 1981.

Searle, John R. *Speech Acts: An Essay in the Philosophy of Language*. Cambridge, UK: Cambridge University Press, 1969.

Shaw, Mary. "Progress toward an Engineering Discipline for Software." Presented at the SPLASH/PLoP [Pattern Languages of Programs], Pittsburgh, PA, October 26, 2015. http://2015.splashcon.org/event/plop2015-plop-keynote-mary-shaw/.

Shaw, Mary. "Prospects for an Engineering Discipline of Software." *IEEE Software* 7, no. 6 (1990): 15–24.

Sheils, Merrill. "Why Johnny Can't Write." *Newsweek*, December 8, 1975: 58–65.

Shirky, Clay. "Situated Software." Clay Shirky's Writings about the Internet [blog], March 30, 2004. http://shirky.com/writings/herecomeseverybody/situated_software .html.

"Showcase," Western Pennsylvania Regional Data Center, October 9, 2016, http://www.wprdc.org/category/showcase/.

Simmons, W. Michele, and Jeffrey Grabill. "Toward a Civic Rhetoric for Technologically and Scientifically Complex Places: Invention, Performance, and Participation." *College Composition and Communication* 58, no. 3 (2007): 419–448.

Simon, Stephanie. "Seeking Coders, Tech Titans Turn to Schools." *Politico*, December 9, 2014. www.politico.com/story/2014/12/hour-of-code-schools-obama-113408.

"Software Becomes a Product." Computer History Museum, accessed September 27, 2015. www.computerhistory.org/revolution/mainframe-computers/7/172/.

Solomon, Cynthia. *Computer Environments for Children: A Reflection on Theories of Learning and Education.* Cambridge, MA: MIT Press, 1986.

Soloway, Eliot, and James C. Spohrer. *Studying the Novice Programmer.* Hillsdale, NJ: Lawrence Erlbaum, 1988.

Soper, Taylor. "Analysis: The Exploding Demand for Computer Science Education, and Why America Needs to Keep up." GeekWire, June 6, 2014. www.geekwire .com/2014/analysis-examining-computer-science-education-explosion/.

Soltow, Lee, and Edward Stevens. *The Rise of Literacy and the Common School in the United States: A Socioeconomic Analysis to 1870.* Chicago: University of Chicago Press, 1982.

Stallman, Richard. "The GNU Project." GNU Operating System, 1998. www.gnu.org/gnu/thegnuproject.html.

Star, Susan Leigh. "The Ethnography of Infrastructure." *American Behavioral Scientist* 43, no. 3 (1999): 377–391.

Starosielski, Nicole. *The Undersea Network.* Durham, NC: Duke University Press, 2015.

Steinkuehler, Constance, and Barbara Z. Johnson. "Computational Literacy in Online Games: The Social Life of Mods." *International Journal of Gaming and Computer-Mediated Simulations* 1, 1 (2009): 53–65.

Stelter, Brian. "Philando Castile and the Power of Facebook Live." *CNN Money*, July 7, 2016. http://money.cnn.com/2016/07/07/media/facebook-live-streaming-police -shooting/.

Stephenson, Neal. *In the Beginning Was the Command Line.* New York: Avon Books, 1999.

Stevens, Edward. *Literacy, Law, and Social Order.* DeKalb: Northern Illinois University Press, 1988.

Stevenson, Jill. *Performance, Cognitive Theory, and Devotional Culture.* New York: Palgrave Macmillan, 2010.

Stewart, Bruce. "An Interview with the Creator of Ruby [Yukihiro Matsumoto]." O'Reilly Linux Devcenter, November 29, 2001. www.linuxdevcenter.com/pub/a/linux/2001/11/29/ruby.html.

Stiegler, Bernard. "Die Aufklärung in the Age of Philosophical Engineering." Trans. Daniel Ross. *Computational Culture* 2 (2012). http://computationalculture.net/comment/die-aufklarung-in-the-age-of-philosophical-engineering/.

Stiegler, Bernard. "Interobjectivity and Transindividuation." *Open! Platform for Art, Culture & the Public Domain*, September 28, 2012. http://www.onlineopen.org/interobjectivity-and-transindividuation/.

Stiegler, Bernard. *Technics and Time, 1: The Fault of Epimetheus.* Trans. R. Beardsworth and G. Collins. Stanford, CA: Stanford University Press, 1998.

Stock, Brian. *Listening for the Text: On the Uses of the Past.* Baltimore, MD: Johns Hopkins University Press, 1990.

Stock, Brian. *The Implications of Literacy: Written Language and Models of Interpretation in the Eleventh and Twelfth Centuries.* Princeton, NJ: Princeton University Press, 1983.

Street, Brian V. *Literacy in Theory and Practice.* Cambridge, UK: Cambridge University Press, 1985.

Stuckey, J. Elspeth. *The Violence of Literacy.* Portsmouth, NH: Boynton/Cook, 1991.

Tate, Ryan. "Hack to Hacker: Rise of the Journalist-Programmer." Gawker, January 14, 2010. http://gawker.com/5448635/hack-to-hacker-rise-of-the-journalist-programmer/.

Tathagata. "Good Ways to Join an Open Source Project?" Slashdot, June 22, 2007. https://ask.slashdot.org/story/07/06/22/1526234/good-ways-to-join-an-open-source-project/.

"Teaching Code in the Classroom." Room for Debate, May 12, 2014. www.nytimes.com/roomfordebate/2014/05/12/teaching-code-in-the-classroom/.

Tedre, Matti. *The Science of Computing: Shaping a Discipline.* Boca Raton, FL: CRC Press, Taylor & Francis Group, 2015.

Tedre, Matti, and Peter Denning. "The Long Quest for Computational Thinking," Proceedings of the 16th Koli Calling Conference on Computing Education Research, November 24–27, 2016, Koli, Finland.

The New London Group. "A Pedagogy of Multiliteracies: Designing Social Futures." In *Multiliteracies: Literacy Learning and the Design of Social Futures*, edited by Bill Cope and Mary Kalantzis, 9–38. London: Routledge, 2000.

"The People's Computer Company Newspaper." *Dymax*, October 1972. Stanford University. https://stacks.stanford.edu/file/druid:ht121fv8052/ht121fv8052_31_0000.pdf.

Thomas, Kaya. "Invisible Talent." NewCo Shift, July 14, 2016. https://shift.newco.co/invisible-talent-409a085bee9c.

Thornburg, David. "A Monthly Column: Computers and Society." *Compute 27*, August 1982, 14–16. Archive.org.

Tierney, Brian. *The Crisis of Church and State, 1050–1300*. Englewood Cliffs, NJ: Prentice Hall, 1964.

Tiku, Nitasha. "How to Get Girls into Coding." *New York Times*, May 31, 2014. www.nytimes.com/2014/06/01/opinion/sunday/how-to-get-girls-into-coding.html.

"Timeline of Computer History." Computer History Museum, n.d., accessed January 3, 2017. www.computerhistory.org/timeline/.

Tomczyk, Michael. "Atari's Marketing Vice President Profiles the Personal Computer Market (Interview with Conrad Jutson)." *Compute 5*, August 1980, 16–17. Archive.org.

"Training 100,000 Low-Income Youth to Code: A Q&A with Van Jones [and Angela Glover Blackwell]." PolicyLink, August 6, 2014. www.policylink.org/focus-areas/equitable-economy/at/van-jones-on-yes-we-code/.

Trapani, Gina. "Geek to Live: How to Fix Mom and Dad's Computer." LifeHacker, November 18, 2005. http://lifehacker.com/138113/geek-to-live--how-to-fix-mom-and-dads-computer/.

Trimbur, John. "Literacy and the Discourse of Crisis." In *The Politics of Writing Instruction: Postsecondary*, edited by Richard Bullock and John Trimbur, 277–295. Portsmouth, NH: Heinemann, 1991.

Tufekci, Zeynep. "How the Internet Saved Turkey's Internet-Hating President." *New York Times*, July 18, 2016. www.nytimes.com/2016/07/20/opinion/how-the-internet-saved-turkeys-internet-hating-president.html.

Turing, Alan. "Computing Machinery and Intelligence." *Mind* 59, no. 236 (1950): 433–460.

Turkle, Sherry. *Alone Together: Why We Expect More from Technology and Less from Each Other*. [paperback] New York: Basic Books, 2012.

Turkle, Sherry. *Life on the Screen*. Cambridge, MA: MIT Press, 1995.

Turkle, Sherry. *The Second Self: Computers and the Human Spirit.* 20th anniversary ed. Cambridge, MA: MIT Press, 2005.

Turkle, Sherry, and Seymour Papert. "Epistemological Pluralism: Styles and Voices within the Computer Culture." *Signs* 16, no. 1 (1990): 128–157.

"Uganda—Empowerment of Rural Women Through Functional Adult Literacy." IFAD [The International Fund for Agricultural Development, a Specialized Agency of the United Nations], n.d., accessed January 3, 2017. https://www.ifad.org/topic/ tools/tags/gender/gender/knowledge_note/2594004/.

U.K. Department for Education. "National Curriculum in England: Computing Programmes of Study." Statutory Guidance. U.K. Department for Education, September 11, 2013. https://www.gov.uk/government/publications/national-curriculum-in -england-computing-programmes-of-study/national-curriculum-in-england -computing-programmes-of-study [sic].

United States National Commission on New Technological Uses of Copyrighted Works (CONTU). "Final Report of the National Commission on New Technological Uses of Copyrighted Works." *Computer/Law Journal* 3 (1) (1981): 53–104.

U.S. Department of Education. *A Nation at Risk,* 1983. www2.ed.gov/pubs/NatAtRisk/ risk.html.

U.S. Department of Education, Office of Vocational and Adult Education. *An American Heritage—Federal Adult Education: A Legislative History 1964-2013.* Washington, DC: U.S. Department of Education, 2013. http://lincs.ed.gov/publications/pdf/ Adult_Ed_History_Report.pdf.

U.S. Census Bureau. "History: Overview." U.S. Census Bureau, accessed January 5, 2010. www.census.gov/history/www/through_the_decades/overview/index.html.

U.S. Census Bureau. "UNIVAC I." U.S. Census Bureau, accessed April 23, 2010. www .census.gov/history/www/innovations/technology/univac_i.html.

Vam, Pedro. "Conway's Game of Life." Accessed July 1, 2015. http://pmav.eu/stuff/ javascript-game-of-life-v3.1.1/.

Van Rossum, Guido. *Computer Programming for Everybody (Revised Proposal).* Reston, VA: Corporation for National Research Initiatives, 1999. http://legacy.python.org/ doc/essays/cp4e.html.

Varela, Francisco J., Evan Thompson, and Eleanor Rosch. *The Embodied Mind: Cognitive Science and Human Experience.* [first MIT Press paperback] Cambridge, MA: MIT Press, 1993.

Vee, Annette. "Carving up the Commons: How Software Patent Law Impacts Our Digital Composition Environments." *Computers and Composition* 27, no. 3 (2010): 179–192.

Vee, Annette. "Is Coding the New Literacy? Moving Beyond Yes or No." *Nettework*, December 11, 2013. www.annettevee.com/blog/2013/12/11/is-coding-the-new-literacy-everyone-should-learn-moving-beyond-yes-or-no/.

Vee, Annette. "Proceduracy: Writing to and for Computers." Presented at the Watson Conference, Louisville, KY, October 2008.

Vee, Annette. "Software Patent Law in Global Contexts: A Primer for Technical Writing Specialists." In *Legal Issues in Global Contexts: Perspectives on Technical Communication in an International Age*, edited by Martine Courant Rife and Kirk St. Amant, 169–190. Amityville, NY: Baywood Publishing, 2014.

Vee, Annette. "Text, Speech, Machine: Metaphors for Computer Code in the Law." *Computational Culture* 2 (2012). http://computationalculture.net/article/text-speech-machine-metaphors-for-computer-code-in-the-law/.

Victor, Bret. "Learnable Programming: Designing a Programming System for Understanding Programming." Worry Dream [blog], September 2012. http://worrydream.com/#!/LearnableProgramming/.

Vieira, Kate. *American by Paper: How Documents Matter in Immigrant Literacy*. Minneapolis: University of Minnesota Press, 2016.

Vieira, Kate. "On the Social Consequences of Literacy." *Literacy in Composition Studies* 1, no. 1 (2013): 26–32.

Vincent, David. *The Rise of Mass Literacy: Reading and Writing in Modern Europe*. Themes in History. Cambridge, UK: Polity, 2000.

Von Neumann, John. "First Draft of a Report on the EDVAC," edited by Michael D. Godfrey. *IEEE Annals of the History of Computing* 15, no. 4 (1993): 27–75.

Wardrip-Fruin, Noah. *Expressive Processing: Digital Fictions, Computer Games, and Software Studies*. Cambridge, MA: MIT Press, 2009.

Weber, Steve. *The Success of Open Source*. Cambridge, MA: Harvard University Press, 2004.

"When Patents Attack!" This American Life, July 22, 2011. www.thisamericanlife.org/radio-archives/episode/441/when-patents-attack.

whytheluckystiff. "The Little Coder's Predicament." *Advogato*, June 11, 2003. www.advogato.org/article/671.html.

Williams, Kathleen Broome. *Grace Hopper: Admiral of the Cyber Sea*. Annapolis, MD: Naval Institute Press, 2004.

Wing, Jeannette. "Computational Thinking." *Communications of the ACM* 49, no. 3 (2006): 33–35.

Winograd, Terry, and Fernando Flores. *Understanding Computers and Cognition.* Norwood, NJ: Ablex Publishing Corporation, 1986.

Wolf, Gary. "Know Thyself: Tracking Every Facet of Life, from Sleep to Mood to Pain, 24/7/365." *Wired,* June 22, 2009. https://www.wired.com/2009/06/lbnp -knowthyself/.

Wysocki, Anne, and Johndan Johnson-Eilola. "Blinded by the Letter: Why Are We Using Literacy as a Metaphor for Everything Else?" In *Passions, Pedagogies, and 21st Century Technologies,* edited by Gail Hawisher and Cynthia Selfe, 349–368. Logan: Utah State University Press, 1999.

Zuckerman, Daniel M. "All Pittsburgh Students Should Learn Computer Programming [op-ed]." *Pittsburgh Post-Gazette,* September 8, 2013. www.post-gazette.com/ opinion/Op-Ed/2013/09/08/All-Pittsburgh-students-should-learn-computer -programming/stories/201309080158/.

Zuse, Konrad. *Calculating Space, Translation of Rechnender Raum.* Trans. Aztec School of Languages. Cambridge, MA: MIT Project MAC, 1970. ftp://ftp.idsia.ch/pub/ juergen/zuserechnenderraum.pdf.

Index

Note: locators containing an "n" indicate end notes

McCarthy, John (cont.)
  on procedural knowledge in
    programming, 100
McGovern, George, 228n9
McKinley, William, 53, 57
McLuhan, Marshall
  bias in communication, 102–103
  "electronic man," 104, 192
  eras in the development of literacy,
    30
  great divide between oral and literate
    cultures, 192
  Harvey Graff on, 33
  literacy as progress, 31
  "literate man," 192
  "oral man," 192
  sociomaterial approach to writing
    technologies, 102–104
  "the medium is the message," 103
  writing as an extension of man, 95
Means-and-metaphor model of the
  world, 202
Measuring literacy. See also Literacy
  campaigns; Literacy rates
  American National Adult Literacy
    Surveys, 57, 247n72
  low literacy levels, 57
  overview, 56–58
  takeoff theory of literacy, 57,
    247n71
  U.S. Department of Education, 57
"Mechanizers," in government, 187
Media archaeology, 104
Memex, 99, 197
Memorization, medieval England,
  146–147
Memory palace, 146
Mentalities. See also Literate mentality
  definition, 181
  history of, 281n14
Mesopotamia
  ancient censuses, 272n57
  early writing, 269n10

Metaphors for literacy. See also
  Keywords metaphor
  as adaptation, 48
  definition, 27, 238n120
  driving literacy promotion, 48
  functional literacy, 48
  lessons for society, 45
  as power, 48
  promoting programming in K-12
    schools, 252n145
  as a state of grace, 48
Microsoft
  diversity, 17
  launching of, 169
Military, literacy in, 54–55
Mill, James, 188
Mind and self, models of. See
  Computational models of the mind
  and self
Mindstorms, 79, 171, 254n162
Minorities in technical positions, 17
Minority Report, 177
Minsky, Marvin, 203
Mission statements
  Code.org, 13, 232n56
  National Institute for Literacy, 61
MIT
  artificial intelligence and human
    psychology, 203
  BASIC on the Altair 8800, 70
  Free Software Movement, 71
  history of the SAGE project, 276n111
  Lifelong Kindergarten Team, 80
  mass programming campaigns, history
    of, 65
  Project Whirlwind, 159
  promoting computational literacy, 218
  Scratch language, 1, 44, 80–81, 110
Modernism vs. post modernism, 284n80
Modkit language, 111
Modularity of computers, 109
Moldovan elections, 213
Moll, Luis, 182, 186

Programming *vs.* writing (cont.)
illocutionary force, 115–116
locutionary force, 115–116
performative statements *vs.*
descriptive, 114–116
perlocutionary force, 115–116
programming as a sociolinguistic
system, 115
social context for computers, 115
speech act theory, 97, 106, 114
speech rules, 115
Programs, debugging. *See* Debugging
code
Project Whirlwind, 159
ProLiteracy, 60
Property boundaries, medieval England,
147, 148
Pseudocode, 122
Publications. *See* Books and publications
Public information. *See also*
Government, information
transparency
democratized data, 25
Pittsburgh area, 25
tracking, 25
Python language
creator of, 43
definition, 243n3
*Exploratory Programming for the Arts
and Humanities*, 16–17
introduction to programming with,
16–17
in the One Laptop Per Child (OLPC)
project, 74
promoting computational literacy,
218
role of literacy in creation of, 43–44

Quantified self movement, 204
Quasi-literacy, 185–186
Queneau, Raymond, 123
"The Question Concerning
Technology," 96–97

Race, Rhetoric, and Technology, 74
Ramsay, Stephen
algorithmic criticism, 16
on digital humanists, 234n68
on learning new ways to think, 80
Raspberry Pi, in wearable technologies,
1, 227n6
Rationalization of
bureaucratic control, 144
information through digital
technology, 120
the world, 119
Reading. *See also* Writing
comparative contexts for
programming, 4–5
heritage of moral goodness, 1–3
history of, 5
as literacy, 47
shifts in methods, 191–193
software for, 33
technology of, 228n9
vs. writing, focus of literacy
campaigns, 62
Rechnender Raum (Calculating Space),
201, 287n126
"The Regime of Computation," 121,
177
Religion, ideological driver of literacy
campaign, 59, 60
Religious representations, medieval
England, 153
Resnick, Mitchel
on learning new ways to think, 80–81
mercenary focus of learning
programming, 64
promoting computational literacy, 218
support for learning programming, 75
trends in education and work, 87–88
Resources. *See* Books and publications;
Online resources; Video, TV, and
movies
Restricted code, 123, 265n103
Restricted literacy, 150, 209